Comic Gothic

Edinburgh Companions to the Gothic

Series Editors
Andrew Smith, University of Sheffield
William Hughes, Bath Spa University

This series provides a comprehensive overview of the Gothic from the eighteenth century to the present day. Each volume takes either a period, place, or theme and explores their diverse attributes, contexts and texts via completely original essays. The volumes provide an authoritative critical tool for both scholars and students of the Gothic.

Volumes in the series are edited by leading scholars in their field and make a cutting-edge contribution to the field of Gothic studies.

Each volume:
- Presents an innovative and critically challenging exploration of the historical, thematic and theoretical understandings of the Gothic from the eighteenth century to the present day
- Provides a critical forum in which ideas about Gothic history and established Gothic themes are challenged
- Supports the teaching of the Gothic at an advanced undergraduate level and at masters level
- Helps readers to rethink ideas concerning periodisation and to question the critical approaches which have been taken to the Gothic

Published Titles
The Victorian Gothic: An Edinburgh Companion
　　Andrew Smith and William Hughes
Romantic Gothic: An Edinburgh Companion
　　Angela Wright and Dale Townshend
American Gothic Culture: An Edinburgh Companion
　　Joel Faflak and Jason Haslam
Women and the Gothic: An Edinburgh Companion
　　Avril Horner and Sue Zlosnik
Scottish Gothic: An Edinburgh Companion
　　Carol Margaret Davison and Monica Germanà
The Gothic and Theory: An Edinburgh Companion
　　Jerrold E. Hogle and Robert Miles
Twenty-First-Century Gothic: An Edinburgh Companion
　　Maisha Wester and Xavier Aldana Reyes
Gothic Film: An Edinburgh Companion
　　Richard J. Hand and Jay McRoy
Twentieth-Century Gothic: An Edinburgh Companion
　　Sorcha Ní Fhlainn and Bernice M. Murphy
Italian Gothic: An Edinburgh Companion
　　Marco Malvestio and Stefano Serafini
Irish Gothic: An Edinburgh Companion
　　Jarlath Killeen and Christina Morin
Queer Gothic: An Edinburgh Companion
　　Ardel Haefele-Thomas
Comic Gothic: An Edinburgh Companion
　　Avril Horner and Sue Zlosnik

Visit the Edinburgh Companions to the Gothic website at:
www.edinburghuniversitypress.com/series/EDCG

Comic Gothic

An Edinburgh Companion

Edited by
Avril Horner and Sue Zlosnik

EDINBURGH
University Press

Edinburgh University Press is one of the leading university presses in the UK. We publish academic books and journals in our selected subject areas across the humanities and social sciences, combining cutting-edge scholarship with high editorial and production values to produce academic works of lasting importance. For more information visit our website: edinburghuniversitypress.com

© editorial matter and organisation © editorial matter and organization, Avril Horner and Sue Zlosnik 2024
© the chapters their several authors 2024

Edinburgh University Press Ltd
13 Infirmary Street
Edinburgh EH1 1LT

Typeset in 10.5/13 Sabon by
by Cheshire Typesetting Ltd, Cuddington, Cheshire, and
printed and bound in Great Britain

A CIP record for this book is available from the British Library

ISBN 978 1 3995 0575 8 (hardback)
ISBN 978 1 3995 0576 5 (webready PDF)
ISBN 978 1 3995 0577 2 (epub)

The right of Avril Horner and Sue Zlosnik to be identified as the editor of this work has been asserted in accordance with the Copyright, Designs and Patents Act 1988, and the Copyright and Related Rights Regulations 2003 (SI No. 2498).

Contents

List of Illustrations vii
Acknowledgements ix

    Introduction: Dread and Dark Laughter 1
    Avril Horner and Sue Zlosnik

PART I FROM 1740 TO THE MID-NINETEENTH CENTURY

1. The Satirical Gothic Vampire in England, 1740–1850 13
Jerrold E. Hogle

2. Cartoons and Comic Gothic in Early Nineteenth-Century Chapbooks 27
Franz Potter

3. The Horror and Humour of Women's Rights: Early Gothic Parody and Anti-Feminism 49
Natalie Neill

4. Poe's Comedy: Carnival and Gothic Laughter 64
Timothy Jones

5. Dickens and the Comic Gothic 77
Michael Hollington

PART II FROM THE 1890S TO THE TWENTY-FIRST CENTURY

6. Oscar Wilde: Performing the Gothic 93
Neil Sammells

7. The Comic Gothic of Edith Wharton's Witches 108
Sarah Whitehead

8. Rational Rickets and Reluctant Canadians: Gothic Colonial Cringe in Robertson Davies's *High Spirits* 122
Cynthia Sugars

9. Laughter through Tears: A Jewish Perspective on the Comic Gothic 136
Faye Ringel

10. The Comic Gothic in Youth Literature: From the Explained Supernatural to the 'Whimsical Macabre' 150
Karen Coats

PART III COMIC GOTHIC AND THE NEW MILLENNIUM

11. Post-Apocalyptic Film and TV Capers: The Comedy Zombie, Capitalist Realism and the (End of the) Neoliberal World 167
Linnie Blake

12. Haunting Me, Haunting You: Gothic Parody and Melodrama in Thai Popular Horror 181
Katarzyna Ancuta

13. The 'Inverse Uncanny': Humour and Tim Burton's Gothic Parodies 195
Monica Germanà

14. 'Your Girlfriend is a Bloody Ghost!': Indian Horror / Gothic Comedy Cinema 211
Deimantas Valančiūnas

15. Rural Hauntings and Black Sheep: Comic Turns, Violence and Supernatural Echoes in New Zealand's Gothic Comedy Films 225
Lorna Piatti-Farnell and Angelique Nairn

16. 'Girls Just Wanna Have Fun': Feminist Camp Gothic 239
Thomas Brassington

17. Haunted TikTok: Comedy in Gothic Times 255
Megen de Bruin-Molé

Notes on Contributors 272
Index 277

Illustrations

Figures

2.1	Frontispiece from *The Skeleton; or, Mysterious Discovery. A Gothic Romance*. Published by A. Neil. Sadleir-Black Collection of Gothic Fiction, Albert and Shirley Small Special Collections Library, University of Virginia via Project Gothic.	28
2.2	Frontispiece from *The Castles of Montreuil and Barre; Or the Histories of the Marquis La Brun and the Baron La Marche, the Late Inhabitants and Proprietors of the Two Castles. A Gothic Story*. Published by Simon Fisher.	32
2.3	Frontispiece from *Gothic Stories. Sir Bertrand's Adventures in a Ruinous Castle, The Story of Fitzalan: The Adventure James III of Scotland had with the Weird Sisters . . . The Story of Raymond Castle: Vildac, or the Horrid discovery, etc*. Published by Simon Fisher.	33
2.4	Frontispiece from *The Black Forest; or, the Cavern of Horrors*. Published by Ann Lemoine. Author's image from copy at UCLA Library.	34
2.5	Frontispiece from *Father Innocent, Abbot of the Capuchins; or, The Crimes of Cloisters*. Published by Thomas Tegg. Author's image from copy at UCLA Library.	36
2.6	Title page and Frontispiece from *The Castle of the Appennines: a Romance*. Published by Thomas Tegg. Archives & Special Collections, The University of Melbourne.	38
2.7	Frontispiece from *The Castle of Lindenberg; or, the History of Raymond and Agnes; including Raymond's Adventures with the Banditti, in the Forest of Rosenwald, and His Being	

	Hunted by the Spectre of the Bleeding Nun. Published by John Bailey.	41
2.8	Frontispiece from *Raymond and Agnes; or, The Bleeding Nun of the Castle Lindenberg*. Raymond and Agnes, Public domain, via Wikimedia Commons.	44
2.9	Frontispiece from *The Bleeding Nun of the Castle of Lindenberg; or, The History of Raymond & Agnes*. Published by Hodgson and Co. Rare Books and Special Collections, McGill University Library. Permission from McGill University.	45
2.10	Frontispiece from *Wolfstein; or, the Mysterious Bandit. A Terrific Romance. To Which Is Added, The Bronze Statue. A Pathetic Tale*. Published by John Bailey. Sadleir-Black Collection of Gothic Fiction, Albert and Shirley Small Special Collections Library, University of Virginia via Project Gothic.	46
13.1	In-Between: Gothic Humour. Created by Monica Germanà.	200
17.1	[Left] A #ghostphotoshoot TikTok video (@hanydavalos 2022). Screenshot by the author. [Right] A group of Klansmen at a christening. Triangle Studio Of Photography 1924.	267

Table

13.1	'Gothic' and 'Humour' Correspondences. Created by Monica Germanà.	198

Acknowledgements

We should like to thank all those in the international community of Gothic scholars who have offered intellectual stimulation and support as the field of Gothic studies has developed and flourished over the years.

It has been a pleasure to work again with the series editors, William Hughes and Andrew Smith, with Jackie Jones and, for the first time, with Susannah Butler at Edinburgh University Press. Thanks are due to all of them.

Introduction: Dread and Dark Laughter
Avril Horner and Sue Zlosnik

In this collection we examine closely and celebrate the place of comedy in the Gothic. Research in this area has burgeoned and now academics are investigating the role of Comic Gothic not only in the work of established authors and celebrated films, but also in children's literature, cartoon mash-ups, performance art and modern media. Gothic scholars no longer easily dismiss humour in dark texts as 'comic relief' and their work is altogether more nuanced and sophisticated in its understanding of how, and to what end, comedy informs Gothic texts.

When our book *Gothic and the Comic Turn* was published in 2005, we hoped that it would open a new line of enquiry into Gothic literature and film. We argued then that the contemporary understanding of Gothic did not capture the hybridity of most Gothic works; significantly, their juxtaposition of incongruous textual effects – in particular comedy and horror – tended to be overlooked. We suggested this aspect of the Gothic mode, combined with its inherent instability and hybridity, enabled it simultaneously to appal and amuse. The 'comic turn' in Gothic is not, we claimed, an aberration or a corruption of a 'serious' genre; rather, it is intrinsic to a mode of writing that has been hybrid since its very inception.

It is perhaps no coincidence that the rise of Gothic was contemporary with the rise of opera and melodrama. Creators of all three were castigated for ignoring generic conventions; for embracing surface rather than depth; for delighting in excess: the result is 'absurd' and 'monstrous' works that evoke laughter as well as horror. Building on Peter Brooks's argument in *The Melodramatic Imagination* (1995), that 'the melodramatic mode is an inescapable dimension of modern consciousness', we suggested that the comic within the Gothic foregrounds a self-reflexivity and dialectical impulse intrinsic to the modern subject. Aspects of comedy, such as irony, satire, parody, pastiche and the absurd, play important roles within this dialectic. It is also clear that theatricality, comedy and melodrama are essential aspects of the Gothic's rejection of naturalism and realism as dominant modes for representing modern subjectivity.

If the Gothic text demonstrates the horror attaching to a shifting and unstable world, it also, in its comic dimension, celebrates the possibilities thereby released. This is perhaps most evident in Gothic's ludic qualities, particularly its interest in intertextuality and its playful concern with fakery. The Gothic's emphasis on fakery in the representation of extremes of feeling and experience inevitably invites the ludicrous excess of further layers of fakery in the form of parody. Thus parody can function as a key aspect of Comic Gothic, not in the traditional sense of being parasitic upon an 'original' text, but because, through 'repetition with critical difference', to use Linda Hutcheon's words, it foregrounds the production of the modern subject through discourse. The parody of Comic Gothic involves an exploitation of the stylised theatricality of the Gothic device, producing at its extreme a phenomenon such as *The Rocky Horror Picture Show*, the film adaptation of which (1975) endures as a cult classic. The result is not so much an abdication of the powers of horror as a process of turning them to creative purpose. Comic Gothic, then, invites a conscious, self-reflexive engagement with the Gothic mode that sets up a different kind of contract between the reader or viewer and the text, offering a measure of detachment from scenes of pain and suffering that would be disturbing in a different Gothic context.

Diane Hoeveler, in her book *Gothic Riffs* (2010), explored an iterative process at work as modernity increasingly turned from the sacred to the secular in the late eighteenth and early nineteenth centuries and the modern subject was formed in the Western world. The emergence of Comic Gothic, she argued, was an intrinsic part of this process and has continued to be so. As classic Gothic tropes have become familiar, they have become more susceptible to parody, producing the distancing effect of the spoof in which the monsters are metaphorically defanged. Monstrosity and terror have needed to adopt different forms. Rather than setting up a binary between 'serious' and 'comic' Gothic texts, then, it is best to think of Gothic writing as a spectrum that, at one end, produces horror writing containing moments of comic hysteria (as in Bram Stoker's *Dracula*) and, at the other, works in which there are clear signals that nothing is to be taken seriously (as in the BBC One television series *Ghosts* or the highly successful *What We Do in the Shadows*).

This collection reflects the innovative work being done to explore the affective paradox of Comic Gothic: that is, simultaneously to appal and amuse. Contributors also examine the social, cultural and political implications of Comic Gothic which often gesture towards the possibility of escape from ideological frameworks. Distinguished critics are joined by influential mid-career scholars and younger scholars, including a postgraduate researcher. While they offer different perspectives and use various methodologies, each of our contributors makes a valuable addition to the study of Comic Gothic. The seventeen chapters in this volume illustrate a wealth of subject matter. Readers might, however, wonder why we have excluded work on Black Horror films that could be described as Comic Gothic, such as *Scary Movie* and *Boo! A Madea Halloween*. Apart from our reservations about the quality of such films, which tend to the formulaic, we decided that anti-Black violence is – sadly – still too frequent a reality to laugh at in the form of a Comic Gothic Horror film. We also came to the conclusion that, as Comic Gothic requires a certain distancing, the open wound of racial injustice is not susceptible to being treated in this way. Indeed, such a treatment – including even academic analysis of past texts – might attract charges of insensitivity, particularly in the current climate of 'Black Lives Matter'.

Part I, which covers the historical period 1740 to the mid-nineteenth century, comprises five chapters. In the opening chapter, Jerrold E. Hogle examines the satiric use of the vampire during the eighteenth century and beyond. A thoroughly Gothic symbol by 1850, the vampire also harks back to ancient-romance assumptions of supernatural agency, still attractive to readers, even as those were put into question by more modern-romance beliefs and practices. But that very contest, the deliberately conflicted core of the Gothic mode, also frees *and* captures the vampire into being a metaphor for more and more kinds of behaviour, including the dominance of the aristocracy and the power wielded by men over women as well as financial exploitation, a bloodsucking mode endemic to capitalism.

Hogle's chapter is followed by Franz Potter's examination of how illustrations in Gothic chapbooks and pamphlets of the early nineteenth century evolved in relation to the rise and fall of the Gothic novel. He carefully explores how illustrations moved from the horrific and the chilling to the melodramatic, leading him to reflect on how the artists' repurposing and recycling of Gothic iconography initially expanded Gothic's visuality but eventually mutated into self-parody and the comic.

In the next chapter, Natalie Neill ranges widely across Comic Gothic novels of the late eighteenth and early nineteenth century and argues that these works – especially those written by female authors – are necessarily ambivalent about the texts, authors and readers they ostensibly critique. Although they frequently reaffirm stereotypes of female writers and give voice to anti-feminist sentiments, they also hold the potential for feminism and subversion. Ultimately, these parodies provide an important window onto Romantic-era thought, reflecting the tensions in the period's complex debates about the rights of women.

The two chapters that follow focus on individual authors. Timothy Jones draws on theories of carnival in order to claim that the laughter evoked by Poe's work is often associated with the realisation of one's own undoing, or the destruction of another figure. He suggests that Poe's tales – and the various films and texts that descend from them – inflect American Gothic so as to introduce laughter into a world of terror, awe, wonder, nastiness and sardonic campness. Seeing this laughter as akin to the carnival laugh, Jones argues that Poe's carnivalesque approach to the Gothic allows him to present catastrophe with a kind of zany energy so as to complicate our response to horror.

For Michael Hollington, Dickens's use of grotesque effects that mutate into Comic Gothic is indicative of what he calls the 'inward turn of the Gothic', a decisive move away from exotic locations in time and space in order to focus on the marvellous and terrifying to be found in the everyday reality of England. Closely examining the violence and cruelty in *The Pickwick Papers* (1836–7), he claims nevertheless that it is a book of life, and that the violence within it is a force of energy that can enable the making of a vigorous and purposeful existence, especially when that violence is steered into a powerful hatred of injustice.

The first three chapters of Part II, which covers the period from the *fin de siècle* to the early twenty-first century, also focus on individual authors. Neil Sammells, in 'Oscar Wilde: Performing the Gothic', examines *The Picture of Dorian Gray* (1891) in relation to the comic strategies Wilde employed in *The Canterville Ghost* (1887) and *Lord Arthur Savile's Crime* (1887). Drawing on the work of Susan Sontag and Allan Pero, he argues that *Dorian Gray* is a camp novel; a work in which identity is shown to be performative and in which moral content is highly stylised. Noting Wilde's interest in the Irish Gothic fiction of Maturin, Le Fanu and Bram Stoker and his use of motifs from popular Gothic novels of the 1880s and 1890s, Sammells suggests that Wilde exploits the liminality of the Gothic in order to express a particular set of attitudes while self-consciously *performing* the Gothic. The resulting satiric tone of *Dorian Gray* is inflected by the playfulness we associate with Camp: a playfulness which Wilde would have recognised as part of a classical tradition encompassing Menippean and Lucianic satire. Sammells concludes that in writing his doppelgänger novel, Wilde moved from the campiness of his earlier short stories to the distinctive camp Gothic of *Dorian Gray*, thereby recalibrating the genre's balance of laughter and terror.

In 'The Comic Gothic of Edith Wharton's Witches', Sarah Whitehead examines the older women in Wharton's Gothic short stories, often vilified by readers and critics. Whitehead argues, on the contrary, that characters such as Zeena Frome in *Ethan Frome* (1911), Prudence Rutledge in 'Bewitched' (1926), Sarah Clayburn in 'All Souls" (1937) and the eponymous Mary Pask (1925) should be seen as indicative of Wharton's ludic dialogue with witchlore and its literary heritage found in her fictional portraits of lonely, ageing women. It is, she suggests, precisely the grotesque comedy of these figures that challenges the cultural frames of the texts in which they appear and which serves to parody the misogyny of witchcraft narratives in a comic riposte to a tradition of fear of female agency and ageing. Drawing on the work of Kristeva, Russo and Bakhtin, and noting that three of these short stories are focalised through a young male narrator who unconsciously links the grotesque to female ageing, Whitehead suggests that Wharton uses the Comic Gothic to invalidate their perspectives which have been shaped by a patriarchal culture. In her 'witch' stories, Whitehead concludes, Wharton uses Comic Gothic in order to interweave competing narrative legacies so as to entertain but also to challenge and subvert conventional attitudes to the older woman.

Cynthia Sugars, in 'Rational Rickets and Reluctant Canadians: Gothic Colonial Cringe in Robertson Davies's *High Spirits*', uses the work of Robertson Davies to explore the ambiguous position of the ghost in Canadian culture. In Davies's short stories, Massey College in Toronto, built in 1962, becomes the site of ghostly hauntings. Sugars sees the college as emblematic of Canada itself: on the one hand, she suggests, the ghost offers an implied sense of cultural ancestry and history which Canada as a nation lacks; on the other, it signifies a cultural nostalgia for the traditions and superstitions of a colonial power, deeply inappropriate for a country still establishing its own identity. This cultural conflict, she argues, makes the Comic Gothic a perfect lens for Canadian self-perception. Focusing on *High Spirits* (1982), she examines how the stories offer ways for Canadians to laugh at their Anglophilic pretensions and colonial inheritance while simultaneously accommodating their embarrassed predilection for Gothic cultural affirmation. Sugars concludes that, in relation to the 'Southern Ontario Gothic' school, Robertson Davies stands out for his ability to simultaneously Gothicise and ironise colonial belatedness so as to offer a relentless postcolonial Comic Gothic take on the process of Canadian self-Gothicisation.

Faye Ringel opens her chapter, 'Laughter through Tears: A Jewish Perspective on the Comic Gothic', with the observation that Jews have not been treated well in Gothic texts. Feared, ridiculed and often linked to the figure of the vampire, they have invariably been used to represent the Other and the Outsider. However, she goes on to argue that many Jewish authors have invited readers and viewers to laugh at such outmoded superstitions while acknowledging their power to arouse fear. Thus dybbuks, demons and golems are often satirised and deconstructed in twentieth-century and contemporary Jewish Gothic fiction. Ranging across a number of Jewish authors, she suggests that many of them have used the rhetorical devices of comic irony, deflation and exaggeration in order to reflect the maxim of the Yiddish theatre – 'laughter through tears' – that is, dealing with the most tragic subjects through comedy. From the Middle Ages to the nineteenth-century Golden Age of Yiddish, to present-day America and many other countries, she concludes, Jewish writers of the Comic Gothic have turned tears into laughter, and through that laughter conquered fears.

In the last chapter in Part II, 'The Comic Gothic in Youth Literature: From the Explained Supernatural to the "Whimsical Macabre"', Karen Coats begins by offering an overview of how children's literature from the seventeenth and eighteenth centuries was written to be morally instructive and was protected from infiltration by Gothic fiction, which was becoming popular with adult readers. However, she argues that the Romantics' celebration of the supernatural began to influence literature written for children, with the result that a tension between Enlightenment values and a belief in the supernatural became evident in books written for young readers at this time. From then on, the use of Comic Gothic, as it appears in texts such as Hoffmann's *Der Struwwelpeter* (1845) through to Chris Riddell's Goth Girl whimsical macabre series (2013–17), reflects that tension. While they parody previous Gothic texts in order to entertain the reader, such works represent an assertion of superiority over previous ways of thinking about the education of children. This includes an understanding of how reading about and imagining the ghostly, the uncanny and the frightening can help children develop psychologically. As she concludes, the popularity of the Comic Gothic in children's literature may have waxed and waned over time, 'but like any good monster, it always returns'.

Part III, comprising seven chapters, reflects our belief that the Comic Gothic burgeoned in the twentieth century and continues to evolve in the current century, informing film, television and modern media, including TikTok. The first chapter in this section, 'Post-Apocalyptic Film and TV Capers: The Comedy Zombie, Capitalist Realism and the (End of the) Neoliberal World', by Linnie Blake, focuses on the figure of the zombie. Arguing that the zombie typifies what she terms 'Neoliberal Gothic', she suggests that it represents 'both the dehumanised incarnation of the 99% of us who have been failed by free market economics, and an abject embodiment of the avaricious appetites that neoliberalism embodies and enacts'. She goes on to argue, however, that the bleakness of the apocalyptic landscape in which zombies roamed in earlier films and programmes has been replaced by a scenario altogether more comic, in which the zombie becomes a focus for laughter. Ranging over a number of films from this century, she analyses their satirical content and suggests that laughter is the only available response to the neoliberal condition – a profoundly reactionary vision. Nevertheless, she concludes that certain Comic Gothic films, such as *American Zombie* (2007), offer a radical and subversive message. It would seem, then, that zombie films 'proffer revolution and reaction' in equal measure, reflecting perhaps our own ambivalence to late capitalism.

Katarzyna Ancuta, in 'Haunting Me, Haunting You: Gothic Parody and Melodrama in Thai Popular Horror', argues that Thai horror films – while related to Gothic mainstream conventions - are *sui generis* in their hybridity, often combining comedy, horror and the characteristics of an action film. Ancuta focuses on two film series: *Buppah Rahtree* (2007), directed by Yuthlert Sippapak and *Hor Taew Tak* (2015), directed by Poi Armon. *Buppah Rahtree* concerns a very stubborn female ghost, Buppah, who refuses to leave her apartment and who clearly resembles other Asian female ghosts, women who lacked agency and were abused in life but became angry and powerful in death. *Hor Taew Tak* introduces a group of ghost-fighting drag queens in loosely structured plots that involve confrontation with various supernatural phenomena. Ancuta notes that while *Hor Taew Tak* films are clearly horror comedies targeting LGBTQ+ audiences, the *Buppah Rahtree* series stays closer to conventional horror using humour to offset its Gothic content. She concludes that, despite their differences, the comic elements of these films are 'an indispensable part of their Gothic framework and intrinsic to Thai popular horror film in general'.

In 'The "Inverse Uncanny" of Gothic Humour and Tim Burton's Gothic Parodies', Monica Germanà examines those films by Burton that are clearly rewritings of earlier Gothic tales and suggests that his self-conscious strategies – particularly his use of humour – take his work into the realm of the 'meta-Gothic', that is, a Gothic that reflects upon its own conventions, themes and preoccupations. She goes on to argue that viewers simultaneously experience familiarity while watching the reworking of well-known themes and characters (for example, Frankenstein) and disorientation 'in the subversive twists the parodies deliver'. Her analysis of Burton's films *Corpse Bride* (2005), *Alice in Wonderland* and (2010) and *Frankenweenie* (2012) leads Germanà to conclude that while they entertain, they also prompt reflection on serious issues, such as forced marriage, sexual violence, female sacrifice, and the corrupting and destructive aspects of power and authority.

In '"Your Girlfriend is a Bloody Ghost!": Indian Horror / Gothic Comedy Cinema', Deimantas Valančiūnas notes that Indian 'horror comedies' are a relatively recent phenomenon, dating from the mid-2000s. He argues that the emergence of such hybrid works meets the need for a new kind of narrative about sociocultural transformations and national tensions within India, thereby creating a potential space for political critique. Analysing the films *Bhoothnath* (*Lord of Ghosts*) (2008) and *Bhooter Bhabishyat* (2012), for example, he suggests that their directors have used a combination of Gothic features and elements of comedy in order to draw attention to the serious issues of displacement and migration, heritage and familial memory. Valančiūnas's analysis of other recent Indian films, including *Stree* and *Roohi*, suggests that the figure of the chudail, a female ghost, has been reinvented in Indian contemporary horror-comedy genre in order to address contemporary national sociocultural anxieties concerning women's safety, assault on the body, personal freedom and marriage, and gender fluidity. Indian 'horror comedies', he concludes, cross generic boundaries in order to articulate pressing questions concerning gender, identity and nationhood.

In their chapter, 'Rural Hauntings and Black Sheep: Comic Turns, Violence and Supernatural Echoes in New Zealand's Gothic Comedy Films', Lorna Piatti-Farnell and Angelique Nairn examine how Gothic narratives offer an exploration of the insecurities of the nation and the anxieties that plague the country's cultural identity, including concerns about genetic engineering, organic farming and family dysfunction. Certain films, they suggest, reveal much about a country that has a short, but often violent and oppressive, history and a landscape that can be threatening as well as idyllic. Exploring how the Gothic comic turn manifests itself in horror-comedy films such as *Housebound* (2014) and *Black Sheep* (2006), they argue that both films rely on what is often commonly referred to as 'Kiwi humour': a deadpan, laconic and parodic type of comedy that is attuned to local ways of life but which also draws attention to the geographically isolated and often culturally secluded nature of New Zealand. They suggest that, through the construction of multiple comic turns, both films exploit and subvert Gothic horror narratives and iconographies, while also crafting an uncanny yet funny representation of twenty-first-century everyday life. They conclude that, ultimately, the result of this mixture is the creation of an Antipodean Comic Gothic mystique, in which metaphorical horrors and fears become paradoxically tangible, yet hidden within the layers of the seemingly 'normal' New Zealand cultural context.

Tom Brassington, in '"Girls just wanna have fun": Feminist Camp Gothic', sets out to define Gothic camp and to examine its feminist potential and its relation to Comic Gothic. He concludes that Camp provides a means of understanding moments of humour in the Gothic characterised by a queer form of self-reflexivity. This, in its turn, modulates the affective responses to pleasurable fear and interrogates Comic Gothic with a fresh critical eye. The feminist possibilities of such a formulation of Comic Gothic as feminist camp Gothic are therefore a continuation of those additive and accretive qualities which characterise camp as a loving reclamation of the detritus left on the Gothic cusp.

In the final chapter, Megen de Bruin-Molé claims that the kinds of Gothic comedy discussed elsewhere in this book are present on mobile media. Today's internet, mediated through the mobile phone, is repetitive yet forgetful, is full of paranoia all along the political spectrum, and offers a potentially endless source of the taboo and barbaric. Bruin-Molé focuses on one particular corner of the social internet where Gothic modes and forms converge through the use of melodrama, irony and the absurd: a 'core aesthetic' called #HauntedTikTok. Having discussed both the political implications of TikTok usage and its Gothic horror content, she argues that the 'urban legends' circulating on TikTok offer especially fruitful ground for looking at the intersections of the Gothic, the comic, and mobile horror, since it is here where the lines between fiction and reality blur, where interpretations become layered on interpretations, and where user replies range all the way from frightened to angry to amused. It is at such moments that we see a shift from clear-cut horror to a more complex Gothic ambiguity, and potentially to a comic turn.

This volume confirms that comedy has been intrinsic to the Gothic mode, whether as satire, irony, camp or farce, since the eighteenth century. However, it is only relatively recently that scholars of the Gothic have begun to analyse the complex nature of that interaction and its dynamic as social and political critique. Over the last thirty years, during a period which has seen disturbing developments in politics, increasing inequality and alarming signs of climate change, Comic Gothic has come more to the fore in books, film, television and social media. In today's precarious world in which, increasingly, extreme people and events seem sometimes to have moved beyond parody and satire, it has become important to understand the evolving nature and social function of Comic Gothic. We hope this book will contribute to a better understanding of this shift in cultural representation.

References

Brooks, Peter. [1976] 1995. *The Melodramatic Imagination: Balzac, Henry James, Melodrama and the Mode of Excess*. New Haven, CT and London: Yale University Press.
Hoeveler, Diane Long. 2010. *Gothic Riffs: Secularizing the Uncanny in the European Imaginary, 1780–1820*. Columbus: The Ohio State University Press.
Horner, Avril and Sue Zlosnik. 2005. *Gothic and the Comic Turn*. Basingstoke: Palgrave Macmillan.
Hutcheon, Linda. 1985. *A Theory of Parody: The Teachings of Twentieth-Century Art Forms*. London: Methuen.
Riddell, Chris. 2017. *Goth Girl Collection 5 Book Set: Goth Girl and the Ghost of a Mouse; Goth Girl and the Fete Worse than Death; Goth Girl and the Wuthering Fright; Goth Girl and the Sinister Symphony; Goth Girl and the Pirate Queen*. London: Macmillan.

Part I

From 1740 to the Mid-Nineteenth Century

Chapter 1

The Satirical Gothic Vampire in England, 1740–1850

Jerrold E. Hogle

As we all know, the vampire figure has often been parodied comically and satirically over the last century and a half. We have Gilbert and Sullivan's operetta *Ruddigore* (1887) and the comic moments in Bram Stoker's original *Dracula* (1897; see Nadel 2017); 'happy Gothic' films from *Love at First Bite* (1979) to *What We Do in the Shadows* (2014; see Spooner 2017, 121–43); and the satires targeted at major social ills via transmogrified vampires in novels such as Scott Westerfield's *Peeps* (2006) and Michael Logan's *Apocalypse Cow* (2012; see Keane 2014). Few of us are aware, though, that all of these were anticipated by the way in which the vampire legend came into British writing by the 1740s alongside the humorous use of it as a satiric metaphor. The anonymous *Travels of 3 English Gentlemen . . . in the Year 1734* (circulated in the 1740s, though not published until 1810) reflected on the Slavic origin of the word 'vampire', linked it to reports about folk beliefs in Eastern Europe and then provided one of the first full English definitions: 'Vampyres are supposed to be the bodies of deceased persons, animated by evil spirits, which come out of the graves in the night time, suck the blood of many of the living and thereby destroy them' to the point where 'those who are destroyed . . . become Vampyres' themselves (Wilson 1985, 581). At nearly the same time, there was also Charles Forman's *Observations on the Revolution in 1688* (1741), in which government officials who have appropriated money brought into England by its merchants and channelled it 'out again to foreign countries' are dubbed 'Vampires of the Publick' much like tax collectors (581). While it was becoming anchored to a folkloric reference-point, 'vampire' was already a signifier floating away from that signified (to use the terms of Ferdinand de Saussure) and thereby available to refer to sinister cultural phenomena and the socio-economic debates underlying them. This 1740s anomaly set the stage for the vampire figure to become what it has often been since: a symbol, though always alluding to fantastic bloodsuckers, that can be shifted, often satirically, to intimate half-hidden but pervasive social and psychological conflicts.

As I want to argue in what follows, the vampire's absorption by the Gothic has greatly expanded this symbolic potential, its satiric/comic capacity and its exposure of cultural undercurrents from the 1740s through to the 1840s, even though the fully *Gothic* vampire took time to develop and underwent several transformations. That process was enabled by Horace Walpole's *The Castle of Otranto* (1764–5), the first text to be called 'a Gothic Story' from its second edition on, despite none of its spectres being exactly vampiric. Its second Preface takes 'Gothic', already a floating signifier torn between excoriating a 'monstrous' and reviving an 'imaginative' medieval past (see Townshend 2019, 33–44) and makes it designate a 'blend of the two kinds of romance, the ancient and the modern' (Walpole 1996, 9). 'Ancient' refers to the supernatural, Catholic and aristocratic quest-romances of the 1100–1600s, while 'modern' points to the more empirically based, Protestant and middle-class novels of Walpole's own time. Together these root the 'Gothic Story' in a deliberate tug of war between opposed systems of belief and that very mixture opens it to satire, not just of it but within it. Much of older romance, while still nostalgically attractive, is now 'improbable' according to modern thinking in Walpole's second Preface (10) and that admission echoes the first Preface, which urges readers not to believe in the 'preternatural' apparitions as this tale's twelfth-century characters do because the metaphysical groundings of them have been 'exploded even from romances' (6). Readers thus enter the story with a sense that its ghosts have been hollowed out, uprooted from their foundations in the 'dark ages' (6). Such *Otranto* 'miracles' as the huge ghost-fragments recalling the statue on the tomb of the Castle's founder (21) or the shade of the current Prince's murderous grandfather walking out of its 'portrait' (26) – figures of what are already just figures – are consequently satirised both in the first Preface, where they are products of 'ancient errors and superstitions' (5), and in the main text when a Castle servant provokes laughter as he recalls how 'his hair stood on end' when he encountered 'part of [the] leg' of the 'giant' (35). Readers must hover, then, between half-sympathising with the 'actors' as 'believing' in 'the empire of superstition' (5–6) and questioning, within the assumptions of modern empiricism, 'what mere men and women would do' when reacting to 'extraordinary' events with minds controlled by the beliefs of their era (10). This conundrum can make the characters objects of satire too and turn what they see into projections from their education and psychology rather than evidence of the supernatural. Though the helmet of the giant ghost has 'dashed out the brains' of the current

Prince's son rather than sucked his blood (21), such a 'Gothic' image of the 1760s parallels the status of 'vampire' in the 1740s. Both haunt the Western world with 'supposed' spectral threats, not necessarily commanding belief outside village folklore or old Catholicism, *and* as mobile metaphors calling out targets of modern derision while also revealing deep-seated tugs of war in Western culture between older and newer ideologies.

These figurations, while both look backwards and forwards, never really came together in literature until the turn of the eighteenth into the nineteenth century. When they did, the result was at least doubly symbolic – and quite often satiric and at least momentarily comic. The growth of the vampire figure after the 1740s was greatest in German poetry, which frequently employed it for satire as well as terror, as Erik Butler has shown (2010, 61–6). This combination, embodied by a female vampire in J. W. von Goethe's 'The Bride of Corinth' (1797; Butler, 64–5), was brought most prominently into English literature in Robert Southey's *Thalaba the Destroyer* (1797–1801). There the Muslim hero faces 'the vampire corse' of his dead wife, created by false-Muslim sorcerers, that leaves him 'palsied of all power' until his companion can 'thrust his lance' into her 'dreadful form', whereupon 'its fiendish tenant' gives way to the wife's shining 'spirit' (Southey 1853, 277–8 [*Thalaba* VIII, 9–10]). This scene recalls how 'Una' in Edmund Spenser's *The Faerie Queene* (1591–5) emerges as the True Anglican Church, compared to which the 'Duessa' who resembles her becomes satirised as a deceptive religion that has mixed Catholicism with Islam when she is 'despoiled' to reveal her 'misshaped parts' (Spenser 1968, 97 [*FQ* I.viii.46]). This layering of figures is transmuted by Samuel Taylor Coleridge into the first Walpolean Gothic vampire, though he does not use the word, when he fashions in his 'Christabel' (circulated from 1799 and published in 1816) the alluring, tall, statuesque 'Geraldine', reminiscent of the enlarged ghost of a statue in *Otranto* as well as the female vampires of Goethe and Southey, and has the princess Christabel sneak this 'lady' into her bed within her father's Otranto-like castle (Coleridge 1991, ll. 116–31). The next morning the princess awakens feeling enervated and beholds Geraldine's engorged, 'heaving breasts', which show that she has 'drunken deep' all night (ll. 356–62). Christabel then recalls her 'vision' of the evening before (ll. 433–41) as, when undressing, Geraldine revealed on 'her bosom and half her side / A [reptilian] sight to dream of, not to tell!' (ll. 246–7), another allusion to Spenser's Duessa.

This figure unquestionably re-enacts Walpole's Gothic tension between 'ancient' and 'modern' belief systems. On the one hand, Geraldine 'leaps up suddenly' under a tree before Christabel, suggesting a supernatural visitation of old (Coleridge, l. 39), but, on the other, the princess the next morning realises that her bedmate is 'the same whom *she / Raised up* beneath the old oak tree' (ll. 354–5, my italics). We now see that Geraldine's features may be psychologically projected onto a visitor by a young woman longing for a reunion with her dead mother (ll. 191–7), a desire which she believes only 'saints will aid if men will call' (ll. 317–18) – a Catholic sentiment as worthy of satire for the Protestant Coleridge as it was for Walpole. Coleridge's answer to Christabel's hope is no saint, after all, but the opposite: an enactor of counter-Anglican evil as much as the satirised Duessa and the vampire of the 1740s, an un-dead spectre who drains blood from the living for its own survival and hence an inversion of Jesus Christ, who offers disciples his own blood for *their* eternal life.

From such moments on, the satiric suggestions in 'Christabel' increase, ultimately pointing to contests among belief systems around 1800 that were cultural undercurrents just as much as the ideological debates fictionalised by Walpole. One implication is that belief in the supernatural, not yet completely abandoned, may too readily be used to explain human projections of inner desires. This irony makes the vampire a metaphor for a cultural shift in progress: possibly a sign of a preternatural force outside us, now a satirised idea as per Walpole's first *Otranto* Preface, yet more probably a locus of the 'hidden affective investment that Freud, some [ninety] years later, would call the Unconscious' (Butler 2010, 62). At the same time, Geraldine, by suggesting this contradiction in the *cultural* unconscious, serves to satirise, as Walpole does, the vanities of aristocratic male dominance that look back to medieval times. This vampire seduces Christabel's father, Baron Leoline, with laughable ease, in part by claiming, with no evidence but herself, aristocratic descent from 'Lord Roland de Vaux', his best 'friend in youth' (ll. 389–90). The Baron then irrationally 'proclaims' his intention to call out her enemies as 'recreant traitors' and, ironically, 'dislodge their *reptile* souls / From the forms and bodies of men!' (ll. 416, 422, 424–5, my italics), even though he has no idea who they – or Geraldine – are. Even 'visions of fear' dreamt by his daughter and his bard that see her as a reptile coiling around the whole kingdom (ll. 433–41, 526–39) cannot sway 'the Baron's heart and brain' (l. 621), besotted as they are by the iconography of ancient rank joined to surface beauty. He therefore punishes 'his own sweet maid' with 'stern regard' (ll. 633–8), leaving her as submissive and childlike as he has always tried to make her.

The vampire's arousal of this aristocratic fixation thereby shifts to another satiric register: exposing how excessive patriarchal control reduces young women to passive objects drained of independent agency. As I have shown elsewhere (see Hogle 2005), 'Christabel' consequently enters the intensified debates of the 1790s about the status of women that followed the French Revolution and Mary Wollstonecraft's *Vindication of the Rights of Woman* (1792). On this level, too, the satire becomes double-edged by way of a seductive doppelgänger who is also a vampire. Christabel, it can be argued, *had* to have 'rais'd up' Geraldine because such a larger double of herself may be, in 1799, the only way she can gain any power as a downcast daughter, perhaps by joining the company of another woman to strengthen herself in a patriarchal world. Nonetheless, by doing so, Christabel gives her lifeblood to a kind of Amazon, a conniving woman of overweening power who could destroy a whole kingdom by controlling its ruling men. In addition, by bedding and temporarily aligning herself with Geraldine, Christabel raises the spectre of same-sex relations that threaten the accepted natural order of male-female reproduction. All at once, satire-by-vampire excoriates both the age-old male dominance that subjugates women and the potential for women, in the wake of Wollstonecraft, to rise to a level of power that threatens men, heterosexuality and public order. The Gothic-vampiric satire in 'Christabel', it turns out, makes all its suggestions about mistaken beliefs and inequities in ways that half disguise yet also suggest several undercurrents of its moment. Its vampire conflates unresolved debates about the supernatural versus the psychological, old aristocratic versus new Enlightenment assumptions, same-sex versus opposite-sex desire and women as victims of unfair dominance and ravenous seekers of dominance themselves.

In this fashion, I would argue, Coleridge set something of a standard for how the Gothicised vampire gained even more symbolic and satiric resonance over the next fifty years. It was Lord Byron's insistence on his guests reading out 'Christabel', along with some other Gothic tales, during the summer of 1816 at the Villa Diodati near Geneva, after all, that led, once he challenged those guests to write 'ghost stories', to several writings that became quite influential. The most Gothic *and* satirical of these was *The Vampyre* (1819) by Dr John Polidori, Byron's live-in physician, who came to hate his employer after the latter dismissed him (see Hogle 2017). With that novella's creation of Lord Ruthven (pronounced 'rivven'), the first *male* aristocratic vampire in Gothic fiction, Polidori can satirise his version of Byron as a colder-blooded version of Geraldine. Building on Lady Caroline Lamb's naming her Byron-character 'Clarence de Ruthven' in her revenge novel *Glenarvon* (1816) and reworking Byron's own attempted 'ghost story' on the 'Augustus Darvell' of 'ancient family' who turns out to have lived for centuries without ever being clearly a vampire (see again Hogle 2017, 17–23),

Polidori turns Geraldine into a Ruthwen with a 'dead grey eye' whose 'form' and 'winning tongue' may seem 'beautiful' but whose 'deadly hue' (Polidori 1990, 27–9) shows him to be long dead and emptied of former meanings like a Walpolean Gothic spectre. Aristocracy, albeit superficially alluring, is now exposed *first* as a deception like Geraldine's, *then* as a ghost of its age-old stature, hollowed out of its past powers and cultural centrality, and *then* as gaining its ongoing viability only from the lifeblood and funds that it sucks out of impressionable sycophants, making it just as vampiric as tax collectors.

The most impressionable devotee in The Vampyre is young Aubrey, a version of Polidori when under Byron's spell, and this character's satirised worship of Ruthwen, especially as repeated by women and other young men, opens up other targets of satire. Aubrey becomes fascinated with Ruthwen because he sees the un-dead Lord as 'the hero of a romance', and that is because Aubrey has limited himself to readings for which 'there was no foundation in real life' (Polidori, 30–1). Such texts are ridiculed here for being just as empty of solid meaning as 'ancient romances' are for Walpole yet as so concerned, like those, with the power of the aristocracy that, in Aubrey's eyes, they fill the empty Ruthwen with heroic signifieds that are really outdated signifiers, even though Ruthwen/Byron in The Vampyre is as financially bankrupt – euphemistically, 'embarrassed' – as he is increasingly empty of life and meaningful rank (32). This overvaluation of romance alongside aristocracy leads to another target of ridicule when Aubrey joins Ruthwen for the Grand Tour of Europe, which has long 'enabled the young' travelling with older men to 'take some rapid steps' toward 'vice' (32), including male versions of the same-sex relations in 'Christabel'. This journey has become even more questionable in 1819 after the Napoleonic Wars have further ruined the old world; the Tour is now just as much a drainer of money from travellers as those 1740s 'Vampires of the Publick' and with considerably less gain in *cultural* capital for the younger tourist (see Giddey 1991). Moreover, Ruthwen on the Tour, while playing the 'generous' aristocrat without truly deep pockets, turns young men, via support for their gambling, into 'formerly affluent youth', leaving even their wealthy parents 'without a single farthing'; he also hurls women 'from the pinnacle of unsullied virtue' into complete 'degradation', though in doing so he also leaves them exposed as 'having thrown even the mask aside' (Polidori 1990, 34–7).

This 'vampyre' thus provides a staging ground for self-destructive tendencies already there in his victims. They become almost laughable if they blame anyone other than themselves for what has been sucked out of them and exposed in them. Indeed, what they lose, as in Ruthwen's own gambling losses, may be more surface signifiers than their more underlying and complex realities, which turn out to be more satirically revealed than vampirically drained. Aubrey's growing suspicion that 'something supernatural' may be behind all this (Polidori, 42–3) shows only more complexity in the conflicts of belief that Polidori's vampire embodies. True, we see again the hesitation, now in the 1810s, between marvellous and psychological explanations for human behaviour, with the latter satirising the former. But we also see hints of a parallel conflict between regarding motivation as entirely internal, with the vampire only bringing that level out, and motivation as generated, even outside theatres, by a theatrical process of people imitating or countering a force external to them: the vampire as their interlocutor and prompter. In this ideological tug of war around 1819–20, where each position can be satirised by the other, people do not fully act out before they are acted upon, before a commanding figure, their source of capital (albeit fraudulently) in this case, provides them with a scenario that vampirically promises supernatural self-expansion only to deliver an all-too-natural self-depletion. Polidori's vampire, building on the theatricality that is an admitted part of Gothic fiction since *The Castle of Otranto* (see Walpole 1996, 10–14), therefore satirises a world that has become so performative that everyone wears a mask and too readily responds to the mask of the alluring other, especially if that allure has been projected there from romances. Ultimately, Aubrey, his social circle and even British officials are satirised as helplessly enthralled by Ruthwen's series of masks, especially when Aubrey swears an oath, as Ruthwen is apparently dying, to keep all the Lord's secrets so that his aristocratic 'honour' remains 'free from stain' (Polidori 1990, 55). They take no effective steps, with Aubrey's protests suppressed under the mask of 'maniac' imposed on him (70), to prevent the vampire now redisguised as 'the Earl of Marsden' (66) from marrying Aubrey's sister and 'glutt[ing his] thirst' upon her (72). As with the Gothic vampire from 'Christabel' on, satire finally gives way to tragedy, leaving Ruthwen a symbolic locus of unresolved, interwoven conundrums from contrasting beliefs about the basis of human motives to the blurring of the boundaries between the psychological and the supernatural and between theatricality and narrative romance that is part ancient / part modern.

Theatricality, as it happens, is what then allowed the Gothic vampire in the 1820s to acquire even more satirical power and to become at least half-comical again. Polidori's *Vampyre* was so rapidly embraced in France, with Byron often seen as the author of, as well as the model for, Lord Ruthwen, that there were at least eight *un*faithful stage adaptations of it in 1820, nearly all in Paris. Most of these took the form, in semi-respectable theatres, of melodrama, which had evolved from being 'pantomime accompanied by music' to a 'theatre of emotion' targeting 'the common people'; it presented a 'Manichean' world 'divided into good and evil' that reeled from 'comedy' – with some leanings toward satire – to 'pathos', still with music, and so eschewed 'purity of genre', often incorporating features of the already theatrical and equally impure Walpolean Gothic (Stuart 1994, 41–4). The most influential and imitated of these, after its Paris opening in June 1820, was *Le Vampire*, co-authored by Pierre Carmouche, Achille de Jouffrey and the very prominent Charles Nodier, a Byron aficionado and by 1819 a defender, as he put it, of the 'myth of the vampire' as 'perhaps the most universal of our superstitions' (Stuart, 46). This *mélodrame* pointedly echoed Polidori's novella in some characters and scenes but changed the locale to Scotland, Byron's ancestral home; highlighted a 'Rutwen' (spelled this way and pronounced 'root-wain') who could die and be Gothically revived by moonlight; made him driven to pursue only young women whom he must legally marry before he can suck their blood, lest he die for good at the next setting of the moon (a dark satire on marriages of convenience); and combined him with some features of the Don Giovanni of Mozart's quite satirical opera of 1787, playing up Byron's known association with Don Juan by 1820 and the affinity of both melodrama and Gothic with such heightened and sardonic theatricality (Stuart, 47–9). So immediately popular was this reincarnation that it was imitated *and* parodied just as prominently on stage in London as soon as August 1820 in James Robinson Planché's *The Vampire or, The Bride of the Isles*, itself the instigator for decades of British imitations, satires and downright burlesques (Stuart, 65–6, 91–106).

All these dimensions are very much present in Planché's *Vampire*, especially in its differences from its French original. Planché starts with an 'Introductory Vision' that recalls the Carmouche/Jouffrey/Nodier 'Prologue' set in a vast Gothic cave full of quasi-Scottish spirits. Their conversation in the French play establishes vampires as 'malefic dead souls' that have re-'animated' the 'forms they have lost in the tomb' (Stuart, 269). For the spirits in Planché's version, however, such 'wicked souls' are 'permitted oft / To enter the dead forms of *other* men, / Assume their speech, their habits and their knowledge' (my italics); only after this transference are vampires 'subject' to the 'dreadful tribute' of having to 'wed', then 'Drain', a 'virtuous maiden', observing convention before flouting it, to avoid dissolution into an absolute 'nothingness' (Planché 1826, 'Introductory', ll. 47–59), a translation of 'Le néant', the pre-existentialist void feared by the French 'Rutwen' far more than Hell in the French *Vampire* (Stuart 1994, 270). This revision provides a clearer rationale for the vampire's half-comic shift, à la Don Giovanni, from one love-object to another, from the high-class 'Lady Margaret' to the servant-girl 'Effie' (Planché, Act I, scene iii). As the spirits put it, it is the transmission of some already spectral 'souls' into different 'dead forms', the very basis of vampires, that explains how incessantly 'from form to form they fleet', maiden after maiden, *and* that lends the seducer the 'wond'rous art', an aura from another world, to make 'the hapless victim . . . / Blindly adore' him the moment she beholds his visage, the spectral re-embodiment of an older spectre (Planché, 'Introductory', ll. 63–6). This scheme consigns the vampire to the hollowed-out condition of Walpole's Gothic ghosts, all signs of signs of the dead, though it apparently refills its motivating spectre with old beliefs about transmigrating spirits. Such an infusion of a dead figure (the new vampire) with a longing from some previous 'soul' means that this drive, as well as his love-object's enthralment by him, really comes from outside him, now less from a theatrical prompter and more from a vague earlier trace of a spirit that is more the motivator than he is and a figure once motivated by the same prior impulse. It is no wonder that Planché's Ruthwen (restoring Polidori's spelling), already disguised as 'Marsden's Earl' *and* a kind of Don Giovanni, 'shrinks', in his own words, 'from the appalling act' that he keeps repeating but still, to escape total 'annihilation', lets himself be a puppet controlled by a much older force, half-dead / half-alive, that is now resuscitating the 'little that remains of [his] heart' (Planché, I.ii). We here behold one of the first quasi-sympathetic, as well as self-satirising, vampires in English writing because this play exposes his kind of desire as always already mimetic, as the late René Girard might say, always the desire of some other's desire and the re-enactment of a desiring role that has already been played out over and over, even though we all, even vampires, keep hoping that our desires are our own.

In trying to ground the hollowed-out vampire in a supernatural pre-soul, it turns out, Planché has imbued that figure with a post-Enlightenment sense of desire as well. He thereby reveals another tension of his time between 'ancient' and 'modern' beliefs in exposing his culture's hesitation between believing in desire as supernaturally infused, regarding desire as determined by its individual agents and fearing desire as naturally an interpersonal – and almost *im*-personal – contagion, especially visible in theatre where characters are infused with the feelings of those who play them in the hope of transferring those feelings to the audience. That tension, in fact, is echoed in several other satirical elements and their consequences in this English *Vampire*. In a nod back to Walpole, the lower-class '*Retainers*' in the initial '*Castle*' have their hyperboles about vampires laughed at as 'Mother Bunch's fairytales'

(Planché 1826, I.i) while they also prove to be ignorant of the transmigration of souls revealed in the 'Introductory Vision'. Meanwhile, most of the songs in this play, usually performed by the non-vampiric lovers, uphold the faithfulness to one object that 'light[s] the heart to love' (I.i), condemning the vampire's switching of love-objects as sinful. Yet, as this drama progresses, that age-old standard is satirised as dangerously sentimental given the primordial transmigration of souls and insatiability of desire. When Planché's Ruthwen finally steps between all the couples to claim his 'tributary victim' and is stopped only when the '*Moon is seen going down*' before he can marry anyone and '*a thunder-bolt*' casts him '*through the ground*' (II.iv), he disappears into a trap invented by Planché for this production (Stuart 1994, 79). For the audience, this trap is the same stage location from which a generalised vampiric 'Phantom' has '*rises[n] from the tomb*' in the opening grotto to migrate into the form of Ruthwen (Planché 1826, 'Introductory', ll. 90–102). The vampire can rise again from the same trap the following night, as the audience well knows, satirically undermining the constancy of 'form' in the lovers' songs and intimating that vampirism, as a stage figure or a metaphor, embodies a transferable drive of desire that can keep reappearing in one enactment after another.

Consequently, it turns out, a London *Examiner* critic in 1820 who viewed this Planché 'Melo-Drama' saw its transfer-based vampire as transferable off the stage. In his view, Planché's kind of theatre makes us recognise 'Vampires who waste the heart and happiness of those they are connected with, Vampires of avarice, Vampires of spleen, Vampires of debauchery, Vampires in all the shapes of selfishness and domestic tyranny' (quoted in Stuart 1994, 97). From being a vague 'soul' of longing and predation entering an 'other' form, the vampire has been turned into a metaphor even more mobile than it was in the 1740s. It now openly satirises numerous forms of everyday (not fictional) and all-too-natural (not supernatural) behaviour, extending the transferability of the vampire figure into many objects of critique that reveal ongoing conflicts throughout human society along with the conflicting systems of belief that have generated metaphors for those conflicts.

One consequence of this phenomenon in England, apart from imitations of Planché and his French source, was comic theatre where prominent characters were thought to be vampires and laughingly turned out not to be, although they could be satirised as having vampiric qualities (Stuart, 271–5). But another trend in the 1840s returned to an aspect of the vampire in *1740s* definitions that had been forgotten by Coleridge, Polidori, the French dramatists and Planché: the belief that vampires can turn their victims into bloodsuckers like themselves, proliferating their kind in a perverse form of sexual-yet-non-sexual reproduction. This recovered element becomes crucial to the fulsomely Gothic – and often satirical – effulgence of the aristocratic vampire in the anonymous English serial *Varney the Vampire*, most likely by James Malcolm Rymer, that unfolded from 1845 to 1847 in 109 short 'penny dreadful' circulars (Rymer 2008, 14–16). Though Rymer's title character does help solidify, pre-Dracula, what has become the archetypal image of the vampire cloaked in black – 'tall and gaunt' with a 'perfectly white' face, 'long nails' and 'fang-like' teeth (Rymer, 36–7) – when he first preys on Flora Bannerworth in the dead of night (though not enough to kill her), her family's reaction and Varney's own later statements of motive swerve away from desire as mainly sexual predation, though that is fleetingly suggested. Her relatives are more fearful that she may, once married, turn into a 'mother of . . . babes coming at . . . midnight to drain from their veins the very life blood she gave to them' (83) because all 'those in life who have been bled by a vampyre, become themselves vampyres' (49). Indeed, anyone can be so bled and *every*one who has been can thus become vampiric, like the 'mutable' shape-shifting Varney (Auerbach 1995, 29), without their usual visage showing that fact until midnight.

Hence 'the vampire and the socialised characters' in this serial, as Nina Auerbach puts it, 'become increasingly difficult to distinguish' (Auerbach, 29) to the point where the main characters, often hilariously, cannot tell if anyone approaching them, or one of *them*, is or is not a vampire. The metaphoricity of the bloodsucker noted by that 1820s reviewer has now become ubiquitous *within* the fiction about the vampire, making any person potentially subject to being seen and satirised as vampire-like, on the one hand, and Varney able to be feared, mocked or sympathised with as all too human, on the other. After all, Rymer's narrator tells us, 'Everywhere . . . public as well as private, something was being continuously said of the vampyre' as a folkloric horror imported to England from Eastern Europe (Rymer 2008, 91), even though there is only a 'dim and uncertain condition' far in the past at the root of all this gossip (196). The potential transferability of the vampire from character to character is made satirically parallel to the transferability of the amorphous vampire legend. The sheer circulation of 'vampire' as a spoken signifier, like an emptied-out spectre in the Gothic of Walpole, becomes hard to distinguish from every person's appearance as possibly that of a vampire or possibly not. That signifier can be attached to any person or to some wider social activity whether or not he, she or it can show that label to be a literal descriptor. A 'landlord' who helps channel such gossip in this tale even regards 'a vampyre as very nearly equal to a contested election' (91). By 1847, vampire as bogey and vampire as metaphor have become more interchangeable – and are, as a result, more widely floating signifiers – than ever they were in the 1740s. Now they are carriers of satire by exposing that very transferability, as well as many other undercurrents of Western culture.

And, of course, there *are* further undercurrents in *Varney the Vampire*, all enabled by this wide circulation manifested, in part, by the proliferation of penny dreadfuls in the nineteenth-century explosion of print culture. When Varney, well after his opening attack on Flora, 'eloquen[tly]' plays out the cliché of declaring 'surpassing' love for her, he drops that pretence and pleads his real reason for wanting an attachment to her: 'I covet Bannerworth Hall' (Rymer 2008, 117), despite its ageing and indebted state. We later discover that 'a large sum of money' has long been 'concealed' there by Varney himself, the one-time owner whose portrait still hangs on a wall (359), like that picture of an *Otranto* ghost who was secretly a murderer. Now, as Carol Senf declares, the 'bloodsucker' becomes clearly, and I would say satirically, linked 'to economic parasitism' (Senf 1988, 46). He extends the 1740s metaphor of vampire as money-grubber into a ravenous drive for acquisitiveness, in which his own shape-shifting and potential breeding of others like him becomes a symbol of Victorian-era capitalism run rampant under the guise of the retrograde aristocrat and romantic lover. Just in the way Auerbach says, he becomes 'the paradigmatic citizen of a decade that named itself the "Hungry [18]40s"' during which, as Marx would write in *Das Kapital* (1867), 'Capital' became 'dead labor, which, vampire-like, lives only by sucking living labor' while pretending only to be recirculating the currency left over from the profits that labour generates, all at another time of profound cultural conflict (Auerbach 1995, 31–2). Varney's attempt to suck up sequestered funds now out of circulation deep in a Gothic mansion is but a decoy hiding his similarity to the money-seekers around him while they feel pulled, consciously or not, towards being a vampire like him. All this makes him 'the confederate', not the 'other', of 'commercial society' (Auerbach, 33), the ultimate expanded embodiment of the satiric vampire metaphor that has long connected bloodsucking with the intake and flow of money.

To be sure, as he is about to engage in an old-style duel, Varney tries to position himself on an ancient supernatural plane, hearkening back to Polidori's Lord Ruthven on the page and stage. He asks that, if he is 'killed', he be 'laid' with his 'face upwards . . . before the moon rises' so that he can be brought back to life by its beams (Rymer 2008, 191). This is a resurrection that has occurred many times if we believe his own account of his past vampiric life, which includes incessant quests for 'considerable sums of money', in the flashback narrative (Rymer, 748–58) with which he concludes 109 printed issues. Nonetheless, Varney's pre-duel request is followed, after he fires in the air, with 'people of all kinds coming out of the village' nearby, as 'armed' as he is and trying to kill him; they form a mob of wild-eyed avengers just as bloodthirsty as he is reputed to be in all the gossip that has been circulating among them (193–9), furiously blurring clear distinctions between the vampire and themselves in one of this serial's most comic and satiric sequences. There are clearly unresolved, subliminal quandaries, as both the English population and capitalism expand in the 1840s, about where the line can be drawn between average human behaviour and bloodsucking evil, since the vampire-figure as a site of transferable qualities drifts across almost everyone even as almost everyone tries to localise its threats in one scapegoat figure. Granted, as a thoroughly Gothic symbol by 1850, the vampire does try to harken back to ancient-romance assumptions of supernatural agency, still attractive to readers, even as those efforts are put into question by the more modern-romance beliefs and practices that effectively break the old ones up, just as Walpole advocated. But that very contest, the deliberately conflicted core of the Gothic mode, also frees *and* captures the vampire into being a metaphor for more and more kinds of behaviour. As a result, its equally contradictory make-up evolves to satirise wider and wider ranges of humanity – and several different conflicts among competing beliefs at different times – from the middle of the eighteenth to the middle of the nineteenth century and beyond.

References

Auerbach, Nina. 1995. *Our Vampires, Ourselves*. Chicago: University of Chicago Press.
Butler, Erik. 2010. *Metamorphoses of the Vampire in Literature and Film: Cultural Transformations in Europe, 1732–1933*. Rochester, NY: Camden House.
Coleridge, Samuel Taylor. 1991. *Christabel 1816*, intro. Jonathan Wordsworth. Oxford: Woodstock Books.
Giddey, Ernest. 1991. '1816: Switzerland and the Revival of the Grand Tour'. *The Byron Journal* 19: 17–25.
Hogle, Jerrold E. 2005. '"Christabel" as Gothic: The Abjection of Instability'. *Gothic Studies* 7, no. 1: 18–28.
Hogle, Jerrold E. 2017. 'The Gothic Image at the Villa Diodati'. *The Wordsworth Circle* 48, no. 1: 16–26.
Hogle, Jerrold E. 2020. 'The Mutation of the Vampire in Nineteenth-Century Gothic'. In *The Cambridge History of the Gothic, Volume II: The Nineteenth*

Century, edited by Dale Townshend and Angela Wright, 65–84. Cambridge: Cambridge University Press.

Keane, Beppie. 2014. '"Meat, Masculinity, and Pathologised Adolescence" in Michael Logan's *Apocalypse Cow* and Scott Westerfield's *Peeps*'. *Jeunesse* 6, no. 1: 13–35.

Nadel, Ira B. 2017. '"Count Me In": Comedy in *Dracula*'. In *Victorian Literary Cultures: Studies in Textual Subversion*, edited by Kenneth Womack and James M. Decker, 129–52. Madison, NJ: Fairleigh Dickinson University Press.

Planché, J[ames] R[obinson] [1820] 1826. *The Vampire or, The Bride of the Isles: A Romantic Melo-drama*. London: John Cumberland.

Polidori, John William. [1819] 1990. *The Vampyre*, intro. Jonathan Wordsworth. Oxford: Woodstock Books.

Rymer, James Malcolm. [1845–7] 2008. *Varney the Vampire: or, The Feast of Blood*, edited by Curt Herr. Crestline, CA: Zitow Press.

Senf, Carol 1988. *The Vampire in Nineteenth Century English Literature*. Madison: University of Wisconsin Press.

Southey, Robert. [1794–1837] 1853. *The Poetical Works*. London: Longman.

Spenser, Edmund. 1968. *Edmund Spenser's Poetry: A Norton Critical Edition*, edited by Hugh Maclean. New York: W. W. Norton.

Spooner, Catherine. 2017. *Post-Millennial Gothic: Comedy, Romance and the Rise of the Happy Gothic*. London: Bloomsbury.

Stuart, Roxana. 1994. *Stage Blood: Vampires of the Nineteenth-Century Stage*. Bowling Green, OH: Bowling Green State University Popular Press.

Townshend, Dale. 2019. *Gothic Antiquity: History, Romance and the Architectural Imagination, 1760–1840*. Oxford: Oxford University Press.

Walpole, Horace. [1764–5] 1996. *The Castle of Otranto: A Gothic Story*, edited by W. S. Lewis and E. J. Clery. Oxford: Oxford University Press.

Wilson, Katharina M. 1985 'The History of the Word "Vampire"'. *Journal of the History of Ideas* 46, no. 4: 577–83.

Chapter 2

Cartoons and Comic Gothic in Early Nineteenth-Century Chapbooks
Franz Potter

The Gothic chapbook is a well-known progeny of the popular Gothic novel. These short tales of terror and horror were largely original and innovative, although some were redacted, abridged or extracted from the lengthier Gothic novels and dramas. Their most distinctive and perhaps provocative feature is a unique frontispiece. Each pamphlet was illustrated, originally with woodcuts and eventually with an exquisite copper engraving, with a dramatic scene from the tale. Perhaps one of the most recognisable of these frontispieces appears in Isaac Crookenden's *The Skeleton; or, Mysterious Discovery. A Gothic Romance* from 1805. The black-and-white etching issued by the publisher Arthur Neil shows a frightened Adolphus discovering the skeleton of Baron de Morfield set into a recess in the wall above him. The figure of Adolphus is reeling back in horror with a lantern in his right hand extended in front of him; his left arm dangles at his side, clasping an impotent dagger. His face bears all the hallmarks of shock and horror with his hair standing on end. The illustration is replete with the visuality of the Gothic, a dark and claustrophobic corridor with Gothic arches, chains and manacles, and a skeleton with vacant eyes. The frontispiece reveals a publisher's and illustrator's predilection for sensational episodes and occurrences which would induce a reader to spend sixpence or a shilling to experience the horrors themselves.

The joint venture between the publisher and an illustrator of chapbooks was predicated on a mutual understanding of what would appeal to the consumer. For publishers, chapbooks were seen as cheap fiction and a collectable and profitable commodity. Significantly, the publisher made a substantial financial commitment by paying the author, the illustrator and the printer before the pamphlet entered the marketplace. For illustrators, their primary task, as Frederick S. Frank observed, was:

Figure 2.1 Frontispiece from *The Skeleton; or, Mysterious Discovery. A Gothic Romance*. Published by A. Neil. Sadleir-Black Collection of Gothic Fiction, Albert and Shirley Small Special Collections Library, University of Virginia via Project Gothic.

to select the most emetic, erotic, or sensationally supernatural episode in the chapbook, then pictorialize it to lure the Gothic consumer. If no such satisfactory horrific event could be located by the illustrator, the artist then fabricated his own. Thus, the connection between an illustration and a corresponding textual event is sometimes mysterious or nonexistent. In a few cases, the illustrations approach the nightmare brilliance of Fuseli, Goya, or Dore, but mainly they reflect a crassly promotional group style. (Frank 1987, 312)

Frank's recognition of a distinctive 'Gothic consumer' and what he views as a 'crassly promotional group style' is significant as it points to the use (or abuse) of specific Gothic iconography as a means to appeal to readers' aesthetic sensibilities. The illustrator's role is to connect the text to the reader via Gothic's visuality; the frontispiece is an embodiment of those expectations. However, as Elizabeth McCarthy notes, the Gothic has a complex 'relationship with visuality, in which text and image continually mutate. [. . .] Mutation is, after all, a form of adaptation, and it is this mutative ability of the form and content of Gothic horror, as a whole, which holds our attention and fixes our gaze' (McCarthy 2014, 341–2). We must consider how the artists' repurposing and recycling of Gothic iconography initially expanded Gothic's visuality and then how it eventually mutated into self-parody and the comic.

It is not surprising then that the Gothic and comic converge visually, offering a glimpse of how the monstrous distorts the line between the humorous and horrific. It is clear that the comic has manifested itself visually since the rise of Gothic chapbooks in the early nineteenth century. For example, the frontispiece of Crookenden's *The Skeleton; or, Mysterious Discovery. A Gothic Romance*, while abounding in sensational images, shows Adolphus with his hair standing on end, which, in part, reduces the scene of abject horror to one of caricature. His exaggerated reaction undermines the terror of the scene, reducing the horrific discovery to the comic. That boundary between the sensational and the comic was regularly blurred, if not exploited, in Gothic chapbooks.

This chapter explores the comic in the illustrations and cartoons of Gothic chapbooks and pamphlets in the early nineteenth century. My intent here is twofold: first, to examine the utilisation of Gothic iconography and aesthetics in early frontispieces; and second, to consider the cartoons and illustrations of George and Robert Cruikshank and their repurposing of that Gothic iconography by recycling the same images that had originally expanded Gothic's visuality, but with a tendency towards self-parody. In this context, the cartoon is an illustrative parody that employs caricature to characterise the Gothic's collective visuality and aesthetic.

Gothic Iconography and the Frontispiece

By the end of the eighteenth century, traditional chapbooks were disappearing, and better higher-quality chapbooks, often referred to colloquially as bluebooks, were emerging. These improved chapbooks contained superior materials and were redesigned to appeal to the middle-class reader. Significantly, these new chapbooks included elaborately detailed frontispieces and illustrations. The frontispiece began to be a marketing tool with publishers advertising that their pamphlets were '[e]legantly printed on fine wove Paper, embellished with ... Highly-finished Engravings... from a Painting... [and] ... An Elegant Vignette Title ... engraved' (*The Ipswich Journal*, 24 April 1802). Printers began employing the aquatint process by combining tonal gradations using acid for etching copper plates for illustrations. Publishers also began to employ professional artists and engravers to illustrate, etch the image and hand-colour it with a yellow, red and blue tint. These higher-quality features, discernibly distinct from the usual street ephemera, were intended to present readers with a unique experience usually reserved for upper-class readers but at a significantly lower price. For readers of Gothic chapbooks and pamphlets, the frontispiece is a distinguishing feature which serves a dual purpose. Primarily, it provides a visual representation of the contents, allowing the reader to select a work that indicates the level of sensationalism in the text. The frontispiece is similar to the Gothic double-barrelled title offering the reader a visual narrative and suggesting the intended audience. Additionally, it denotes the quality and value of the pamphlet. After all, the Gothic chapbook was a valuable commodity, and publishers quickly reacted to the shift in readers' interests within this specialised marketplace.

While Gothic's visuality is considered lurid and sensational, the early Gothic frontispieces are remarkably restrained. They predominately described critical moments from the tales with dramatic yet elegant etchings to denote the tone of the tale. A majority of early Gothic chapbooks, 1798–1800, were reprints of short tales from popular magazines including *Lady's Magazine* (1770–1818), *Belle Assemblée, or Bell's Court and Fashionable Magazine* (1806–32) and *Lady's Monthly Museum, or Polite Repository of Amusement and Instruction* (1798–1832). These tales focused more on terror and mystery than the supernatural and horror. These frontispieces tend to reflect their intended audience. For example, the publisher Simon Fisher issued *The Castles of Montreuil and Barre; Or the Histories of the Marquis La Brun and the Baron La Marche, the Late Inhabitants and Proprietors of the Two Castles. A Gothic Story* with a frontispiece drawn by Tomkins and engraved by Harley in 1799. The etching illustrates the moment that Pierre Le Motte discovers a young woman, Ella, bent over the form of the injured Edgar, stanching his wound, thus preserving his life. The scene is beautifully rendered, with details of a small stream in the foreground and a large tree and receding hills in the background. The unassuming illustration is derived from the first two pages of the dramatic tale, which follows in the footsteps of Ann Radcliffe rather than Matthew Lewis. The elegant frontispiece reflects its more refined tale, first printed in *The Lady's Magazine* in 1798, and would have appealed to readers who would have initially enjoyed the tale in that form.

Likewise, the depictions of the supernatural in early frontispieces were remarkably restrained. Simon Fisher's *Gothic Stories* (1799), a collection of six Gothic tales from popular magazines, including 'Sir Bertrand's Adventures in a Ruinous Castle' and 'The Story of Fitzalan', contains a full-page frontispiece, an etching by J. Wyatt, and features a scene from 'The Story of Fitzalan'. It depicts Sir Fitzalan confined in a dungeon as the spectre of his murdered father appears before him. At the spectre's feet lies a human skull, and Fitzalan is bent forward, recovering a dagger, the caption reading, 'Fitzalan shudder'd at the sight; and involuntarily stooping took up the Dagger.' Perhaps the most well-known frontispiece to contain supernatural Gothic iconography is *The Black Forest; or, the Cavern of Horrors*, published by Ann Lemoine and John Roe in 1802. The illustration shows Henry encountering a skeleton holding a bloodied sword above its head. The pair is in a well-lit passage with a bright lantern, weapons of war, and military banners mounted on the wall. Initially, Henry appears frightened, recoiling slightly at the sight, remarkably composed for someone encountering the supernatural. However, a closer examination of Henry's features reveals a hesitant expression of doubt and incredulity. His side glance at the skeleton encourages viewers to suspend their willingness to embrace the supernatural. While the caption reads 'The terror of Henry at the appearance of a Skeleton waving a Bloody Sword', the unknown artist's scepticism is evident in the rendering of Henry's 'terror'. Here terror becomes burlesque despite the plethora of Gothic paraphernalia in the image. The frequent utilisation of Gothic iconography in these frontispieces underscores the publishers' interest in capturing readers' attention.

The most representational Gothic frontispieces are in the *Marvellous Magazine or Compendium of Prodigies*. This series of pamphlets consisting of abridgements of popular Gothic titles printed in duodecimo, each with a copperplate frontispiece, was published between May 1802 and April 1804. Each pamphlet was to be sold individually or collected into a bound volume. The plan for the 'magazine' was to issue one

32 Franz Potter

London Published Nov.r 10.th 1803 by S. Fisher.

Drawn by Tomkins. Engd by Hartley.

Pierre la Motte approached, and beheld Youth staunching the blood of his wounded companion.
Page. 4.

Figure 2.2 Frontispiece from *The Castles of Montreuil and Barre; Or the Histories of the Marquis La Brun and the Baron La Marche, the Late Inhabitants and Proprietors of the Two Castles. A Gothic Story*. Published by Simon Fisher.

Figure 2.3 Frontispiece from *Gothic Stories. Sir Bertrand's Adventures in a Ruinous Castle, The Story of Fitzalan: The Adventure James III of Scotland had with the Weird Sisters . . . The Story of Raymond Castle: Vildac, or the Horrid discovery, etc.* Published by Simon Fisher.

monthly pamphlet averaging seventy-two pages. After six issues, the titles could be compiled into a single volume. The original plan called for this to be a series of tales, adventures, travels, biographies and romances designed to appeal to a general readership. Notwithstanding the wide-ranging subject mandate, the series would feature no biographies, tales of courage, or shipwrecks; it did, however, contain a profusion of haunted castles, spectres, dangerous monks and tales of terror and horror. The benchmark was set with the release of the first issue of *The Midnight Assassin; or, Confession of the Monk Rinaldi*. The full-page frontispiece, dated 1 May 1802, depicts the Monk Rinaldi stooped over and gazing on the sleeping form of Amanda Lusigni. The monk holds a lamp in his left hand and a dagger in the right, poised to strike her bosom. A small window allows the moonlight into the room, but the viewer is drawn by the lamp's light to the sleeping heroine revealing a locket. The room's shadows distort Rinaldi making him appear grotesque and threatening.

Figure 2.4 Frontispiece from *The Black Forest; or, the Cavern of Horrors*. Published by Ann Lemoine. Author's image from copy at UCLA Library.

There is no caption, but the page number provides the reader with direct access to the terrifying scene. The image, engraved by Rhodes from a painting by Craig, presents an iconic scene that readers could quickly identify from Ann Radcliffe's *The Italian; or, The Confessional of the Black Penitents* (1797).

Similarly, *Father Innocent, Abbot of the Capuchins; or, The Crimes of Cloisters*, an adaptation of Matthew Lewis's *The Monk* (1796), appeared in the *Marvellous Magazine* on 1 April 1803. The frontispiece, engraved by J. Walker from a drawing by J. Hamilton, is a strikingly dark and mysterious illustration with three figures in a gloomy cavern. In the bottom left corner, Father Innocent, clothed in his monastic apparel, is kneeling and staring rapturously at Sabina. She stands upright, clad in a black dress adorned with astrological symbols. She raises a long staff above her head in her right hand, and her left hand, which holds a bouquet of poppies, is outstretched to a kneeling Lucifer. The Devil is angelic and nude (though modestly) and has two large dark wings on his back. His right hand is reaching out and grasping the proffered poppies. An empty basket lies at their feet, as does a small lamp providing the only light. The blackness behind the figures seems to hold shifting shadows that underscore the perils of the unholy pact. Again, the image contains conventional iconography of the Gothic that is immediately familiar to readers, not just those familiar with *The Monk*. The frontispieces in the *Marvellous Magazine* are important because they not only expanded the Gothic's visuality to a more extensive and diverse readership, but they reinforced the importance of Gothic iconography in marketing these tales of terror.

As the Gothic marketplace expanded in the first decade of the nineteenth century, by 1810, there were indications that the readers' interest had peaked and was beginning to wane. Noting this, the publisher Thomas Tegg issued his last series of six Gothic chapbooks, including James Vincent's *The Castle of the Appennines. A Romance* and the anonymous *Female Intrepidity; or, The Heroic Matron. A Tale*. Tegg hired the caricaturist Thomas Rowlandson to draw the frontispieces for these pamphlets. Rowlandson had worked closely with Tegg since 1807 on several projects, including *Tegg's Caricature Magazine or Hudibrastic Mirror* and *Rowlandson's Caricature Magazine*. The decision to allow a caricaturist to illustrate the frontispieces reflects, perhaps, Tegg's weariness with the sensational Gothic iconography that still flooded the marketplace. After all, the frontispieces in Tegg's editions of *Marvellous Magazine* exemplify the Gothic aesthetic and utilise that iconography to define the entire series as 'Gothic'. However, Rowlandson's illustrations for Tegg's chapbooks are cartoons that employ caricature to exploit the familiar Gothic iconography and aesthetic.

36 Franz Potter

FATHER INNOCENT.
London Pub.d by Tegg, and Co April 1st 1803

Figure 2.5 Frontispiece from *Father Innocent, Abbot of the Capuchins; or, The Crimes of Cloisters*. Published by Thomas Tegg. Author's image from copy at UCLA Library.

In *The Castle of the Appennines*, Rowlandson sketched both the frontispiece and the illustration on the title page. The frontispiece shows a dungeon with a low vaulted ceiling where Alberto di Capella encounters the spectre of his father. Alberto recoils with both hands in the air, with a look of bemused horror on his face. The spectre, clothed only in a loose white sheet (though in the text, it is depicted as a travel cloak), stands in front of Alberto with his left hand extended upwards, grasping the sheet. There is a gash on his right chest, and fresh blood pours from the wound. The spectre appears startled rather than sorrowful. Alberto and the spectre are caricatures with exaggerated expressions of fear, as if the two had just unexpectedly encountered each other. While the frontispiece captures the supernatural occurrence saturated in Gothic iconography, it is devoid of absolute terror or horror. Rowlandson's vignette on the title page is smaller but filled with more conflict and actual terror. It captures a moment of violence when Marchese di Capella is dragged from his carriage and brutally stabbed repeatedly by two banditti. The Marchese faces the viewer with his right hand extended to heaven, a look of agony on his face while only the backs of the banditti are visible. His body is in the same position as Alberto's in the frontispiece. This scene of violence plays out on the right-hand side of the illustration, while a stopped cabriolet occupies the centre. A young woman screams in distress as banditti open her door. The figure is a caricature of a distressed woman with long extended arms waving above her head and a look of terrified shock registering on her face. By utilising the familiar Gothic imagery of the ruthless banditti and the obligatory attempted kidnapping, Rowlandson renders the scene sufficiently terrifying to balance the caricature of the frontispiece.

In 1818, publisher William Mason issued an adaptation of *The Monk* whose title revealed the entire plot: *The Monk, A Romance in which Is depicted the Wonderful Adventures of Ambrosio, Friar of the order of capuchins, who was diverted from The track of virtue, by the Artifices of a Female Demon, That entered his Monastery disguised as a Novice, and after seducing him from his vow of celibacy, presented him with a branch of Enchanted Myrtle, to obtain the person of the beautiful Antonia of Madrid; how he was discovered in her chamber by her mother, whom he murdered, to keep his crime a secret; and the particulars of the means by which he caused the body of Antonia to be conveyed in a sleep to the dreary vaults of his own convent, where he accomplished his wicked machinations on the innocent virgin, whom he then assassinates with a dagger, presented him by his attendant fiend, who afterwards betrays him to the judges of the inquisition, in the dungeons of which he is confined, and suffer torture; and how, to escape from thence, he assigns over his soul and body to the Devil, who deceives him, and inflicts a most ignominious death*. Mason's frontispiece image contains a gigantic devil covered with scales with black wings, a large tail, hooved feet and claws. His left claw, which is raised, grasps thunderbolts. In his right claw, a scroll is unwound with the words 'SOUL & BODY forever' printed in surprisingly large print. A fallen cross lies beneath him on the ground, and the wall of inquisition is seen on the right side. The kneeling figure, Ambrosio, occupies the bottom right corner, and his left hand is chained to the wall. He is clothed in red robes, and with his right hand, he signs the scroll with his name. The scene is a caricature of Gothic iconography with the Devil mutating into a grotesque fiend, occupying most of the image as he triumphantly hovers over the dejected monk. The image creates a visual narrative that, while similar to the actual text, is nevertheless a monstrous distortion of salvation and redemption.

The number of Gothic chapbooks published had been steadily declining as early as 1815. The publishers still involved in the Gothic

Figure 2.6 Title page and Frontispiece from *The Castle of the Appennines: a Romance*. Published by Thomas Tegg. Archives & Special Collections, The University of Melbourne.

chapbook marketplace scrambled to respond to the readers' shifting interest. Gothic frontispieces began to move away from the elegant and visually refined images and etchings popular in more extensive series such as the *Marvellous Magazine* towards cartoons where a collection of Gothic iconographies was arranged and presented in a similar dispassionate four-panel sequence. The same stock images that had once expanded the Gothic's visuality began to appear excessive. Rather than being characteristic of the entire genre, they became trite and pastiched, positioning them in the direction of self-parody. A good case in point is the chapbook *The Castle of Lindenberg*. As W. B. Gerard notes:

> [b]etween 1798 and 1823, a particularly popular abridgement variously titled *The Castle of Lindenberg or Raymond and Agnes* appeared in nine distinct illustrated editions; adapted from the controversial best-selling novel *The Monk* by Matthew Lewis, these volumes, primarily appearing in the form of bluebooks, flourished in a culture apparently fascinated by its multifaceted story. (Gerard 2016, 393)

In 1820, John Bailey published *The Castle of Lindenberg; or, the History of Raymond and Agnes; including Raymond's Adventures with the Banditti, in the Forest of Rosenwald, and His Being Hunted by the Spectre of the Bleeding Nun*, which was abridged by Sarah Wilkinson (Fig. 2.7). John Bailey of 116 Chancery Lane was an experienced printer/publisher who had been actively involved in the Gothic chapbook trade since 1805. His primary stock consisted of a wide variety of pamphlets, including historical romances, sentimental tales, voyages, adventures, popular dramas and reprints of standard popular works. He published a number of six-penny chapbooks that included current affairs, political and social scandals, trials, religious material, and popular activities from angling to consumption to cookery and valentine writers.

As a female author, Sarah Wilkinson (1779–1831) provides an interesting perspective on the Gothic chapbook trade. Her broad range of Gothic narratives underscores the changes in the Gothic marketplace for authors and publishers. As the author of at least sixty-three Gothic chapbooks, she had the uncanny ability to respond rapidly to the shifting interests of readers. Her abridgement of Lewis's *The Monk*, in particular, reflects a shift in '[t]he visual and textual development of the Gothic chapbook' (Thomson and Fall 2019, 263). In the tale of the bleeding nun, we can see the evolution (or mutation) of the Gothic's visuality. The frontispiece depicts Raymond, Baptiste and Margaretta in the middle of a room with Baroness Lindenberg asleep in a chair, unaware of the imminent danger. Raymond, on the left, struggles with a surprised Baptiste (replete with a hat and moustache) as Margaretta, on the right, readies the dagger, ready to act. Raymond's face conveys his unbridled anger, and Baptiste's is full of fear. Margaretta, equipped with a dagger, is oddly passive, devoid of emotion. The caption reads:

> Raymond was unarmed but desperation gave him Herculean strength; he sprang upon the treacherous wretch, and with both hands firmly grasped him. The surprise of the action caused Baptiste to drop the dagger which was seised [sic] by Margaretta, who immediately plunged it into the Villains heart. (Wilkinson 1820)

Despite the caption's description of Margaretta's violence, the scene is entirely sanitised and lacks the closeness of the actual violent encounter. As Doug Thomson and Wendy Fall observe:

> this chapbook demonstrates that Wilkinson and publishers were able to use text and graphic content together to create a product that reflected their buyers' aesthetic sensibilities, which in 1820 were moving away from the hyperbolic Lewisite Gothic and towards more reserved and hybridised styles. (Thomson and Wall 2019, 264)

These changes reflect a more significant shift in readers' predilection for violence and sensationalism. The illustration appears theatrical and staged rather than sensational and shocking. Indeed, it lacks the usual Gothic images and indicates a reassessment of those visual markers.

The Bailey/Wilkinson frontispiece differs sharply from the first chapbook adaption of *The Monk*, titled *Castle of Lindenberg; or the History of Raymond & Agnes; with the Story of the Bleeding Nun: and the Method by which the Wandering Jew Quieted the Nun's Troubled Spirit* and published by Simon Fisher in 1798. Fisher's first edition contains two black-and-white illustrations and runs to some 148 pages. The first image illustrates the same murder of the bandit Baptiste at the hands of Marguerite and Raymond. Unlike Bailey/Wilkinson's illustration, this image depicts a violent struggle between Raymond and Marguerite as they subdue the bandit Baptiste. The caption reads, 'I threw him upon the ground; I grasped him still tighter; and while I fixed him without motion upon the floor, Marguerite wresting the dagger from his hand, plunged it repeatedly in his heart till he expired' (Anon: Fisher edition 1798, 31). The brutality of Baptiste's death is partially obscured in shadows in the foreground, while a blazing hearth in the back casts light on the slumbering Baroness Lindenberg in a chair. Even in the shadows, the violence of the spectacle is placed disturbingly in the foreground. Marguerite's face is contorted with anger, and Raymond's hands are wrapped around Baptiste's neck. The illustration highlights the viciousness and excess of

Cartoons in Early Nineteenth-Century Chapbooks 41

Raymond was unarmed, but desperation gave him Herculean strength; he sprang upon the treacherous wretch, and with both hands firmly grasped him. The surprise of the action caused Baptiste to drop the dagger, which was seized by Margaretta, who immediately plunged it into the Villains heart. vide page 14

Figure 2.7 Frontispiece from *The Castle of Lindenberg; or, the History of Raymond and Agnes; including Raymond's Adventures with the Banditti, in the Forest of Rosenwald, and His Being Hunted by the Spectre of the Bleeding Nun*. Published by John Bailey.

Lewis's narrative, providing the reader with a visual narrative that revels in the transgressive nature of the Gothic.

The Fisher edition contains a second illustration which depicts the frantic bedroom scene where the Wandering Jew confronts the bleeding nun as she attacks Raymond. The Wandering Jew is positioned between the spectral nun who advances menacingly with arms outstretched and a cowering Raymond recoiling with palpable horror. The supernatural scene is replete with Catholic iconography and dark Gothic aesthetic, including an empty box, three sets of skull and crossbones lay at the feet of each figure and the rosary on the right hand of the nun as she reaches for Raymond. Interestingly, the bleeding nun stands taller than the other figures, and the expression on her face is not merely frustrated but angry. The illustration seems to revel in the otherworldly and supernatural, daring the viewer to disbelieve.

Dean and Munday's edition of *Raymond and Agnes; or, the Bleeding Nun* (c. 1820), provides yet another view into the evolving Gothic iconography. The four panels capture the key scenes, some of which are rendered in earlier editions. The top left panel reads, 'Baptiste preparing to murder Don Raymond'. In a departure from other iterations of the Baptiste illustration, Marguerite and Baptiste are placed in the foreground while Raymond and Baroness Lindenberg are asleep at the dinner table. Baptiste holds a dagger and is about to turn and dispatch Raymond. Marguerite appears devoid of emotion, yet the movement of her body indicates her fear and anxiety. Again, bloodless and sanitised, the artist removes the violence of Marguerite and her ultimate liberation. The top right panel reads 'Raymond and the Bleeding Nun' and it captures the iconic moment of Raymond reaching for Agnes disguised as the Bleeding Nun as she emerges from the Eastern Tower. The Bleeding Nun carries a lamp in her left hand, a dagger in her right hand drips with blood while bloodstains dapple the nun's vestments, and a veil hides her features. However, the figure lacks supernatural presence, anger or malice and appears impotent. The bottom left panel reads 'Raymond and Agnes in the Garden of the Convent'. Here Raymond kneels before an anxious Agnes with a euphoric and amorous look. A lone shovel at Raymond's feet blandly reminds the viewer of the gardener's help in planning this clandestine rendezvous. The bottom right panel reads, 'Agnes discovered in the Dungeon'. It illustrates the moment when Lorenzo and Virginia discover Agnes chained to the floor, cradling her dead child. Agnes stares blankly at her dead child, unaware that two figures have discovered her. The sorrow is palpable in her figure as she sits up, holding the baby. The focal points of Dean and Munday's illustration are not the principal conflicts in the narrative but rather the moments before those events that would lead the characters to their destruction. Wilkinson's narrative, like the illustration, avoids the sensationalism and excess of Lewis's novel by concealing horrific events such as the murder of Baptiste to appeal to an ever-shifting readership. However, in doing so, the illustration becomes cartoonish in its caricature of Gothic iconography as it attempts to adjust the narrative's focus away from the sensational.

In 1823, the caricaturist Robert Cruikshank (1789–1856) was hired by the publisher William Hodgson to illustrate yet another edition of *The Bleeding Nun of the Castle Lindenberg; or, The History of Raymond & Agnes* (Fig. 2.9). His coloured cartoon contains four panels, each representing significant scenes from the narrative, with a round portrait of the bleeding nun in the centre of the panel. Each panel is replete with sensational imagery and exaggerated features and is drawn theatrically. The top left panel reads 'Death of Baptiste' and is a shockingly violent rendering of the banditti's death. Framed by a fireplace, a brace of pistols mounted on the mantel, Raymond struggles with the prone Baptiste as Margarite plunges the dagger into his chest. A trickle of blood seeps from the fatal wound in a rare exhibit of gore. Cruikshank's dramaturgical rendering removes the viewer from the bandit's house, where the attack takes place and relocates the struggle to a stage. The theatricality continues in the top right panel, which captures the moment Baroness Lindenberg, clad in a green gown indicative of her jealousy, discovers Raymond and Agnes as they examine a drawing of the bleeding nun. The bottom left panel contains the bleeding nun's dreadful appearance, though the moment feels staged again. Raymond is reclined in his bed, recoiling from a languid and disinterested nun, whose exaggerated anatomy, and vacant eyes, render her a comic facsimile of the terrifying and vindictive spirit seen in Fisher's 1798 edition. The nun's vestments are a bright red, and she wears a yellow wimple to remind the viewer of her distinguishing moniker. The final panel in the bottom left reveals 'Agnes with her Child in the Dungeon'. The bottom right panel features Agnes cradling her dead infant while cruelly chained in the dungeon under the abbey. As Gerard notes:

> One of the Prioress's minions, appearing in a dim, distant doorway with provisions, adds to the pathos, as does the compositional gesture of secreting Agnes under the frontispiece's central medallion, which within the layout of the composite plate hints at the disruptive role of the Bleeding Nun. (Gerard 2016, 401)

Cruikshank's entire stagecraft is displayed in this cartoon of the bleeding nun. His illustrations feature representations of familiar Gothic images that are staged and manufactured. The familiar scenes are stripped of their horror through sheer repetition and reduced to cartoons comprised of stock Gothic imagery and iconography that has become a parody of itself. His theatrical composition and use of Gothic aesthetics also reflect the influence of his publisher William Hodgson. Hodgson had entered the Gothic marketplace just as interest was waning, releasing several redactions and abridgements of popular novels (including Sir Walter Scott) and contemporary dramas. Hodgson and his partner William Cole were also publishing toy theatre sheets which consisted of illustrations of scenery and actors to be cut out and mounted on cardboard. Hodgson would employ multiple artists, such as the Cruikshank brothers, to attend popular dramas to draw the actors and capture their theatrical poses.

George Cruikshank (1792–1878), Robert's younger brother, was similarly actively involved in illustrating Gothic chapbooks with Hodgson and several publishers including Dean and Munday and John Bailey. He illustrated at least thirty wide-ranging pamphlets, including valentine readers, criminal accounts, books on consumption, and of course, Gothic tales. Notwithstanding his varied output, George Cruikshank scholars tend to ignore these or reduce them to mere side hustle, as Anthony Burton does when he notes that:

Figure 2.8 Frontispiece from *Raymond and Agnes; or, The Bleeding Nun of the Castle Lindenberg*. Raymond and Agnes, Public domain, via Wikimedia Commons.

Many of his earliest illustrations for fiction – mere bread and butter work – were done in the second and third decades of the nineteenth century for children's books and cheap chapbooks. Often enough he contributed only a crudely etched frontispiece which would later be blotched with color by hand; *there is seldom much to be learned from a frontispiece about an artist's comprehension of a work.* ... If these illustrations really are, as the title-pages claim, by Cruikshank, they are quite uninspired. (Burton 1973, 97) (my italics)

This off-handed dismissal of these chapbook and pamphlet productions highlights the marginalisation of 'down-market' ephemera as 'uninspired' and, therefore, not worth considering. However, Burton's assumption about 'an artist's comprehension of a work' is misguided, considering the fine line between horror and the comic the brothers so often blurred. Like Robert, George understood the publisher's expectations in terms of shifting readers' interest and marketing and recognised which sensational content would engage the reader as a consumer. His familiarity with Gothic iconography is evident in his illustrations, where he normalises the excess associated with it by ridiculing it.

An example of this is observed in George's frontispiece of *Wolfstein; or, The Mysterious Bandit. A Terrific Romance* for the publisher John Bailey. The frontispiece is folded and hand-coloured, featuring a staple of Gothic iconography, a skeleton emerging from a swirl of clouds amid

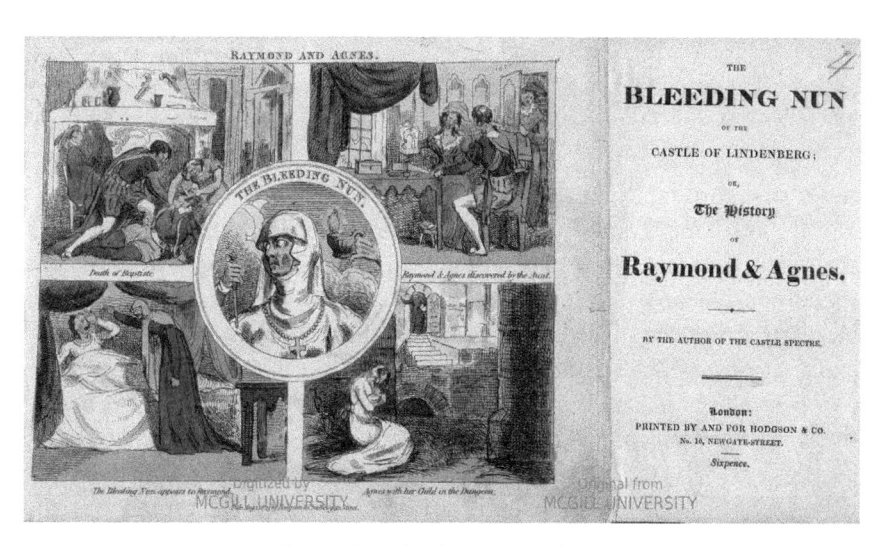

Figure 2.9 Frontispiece from *The Bleeding Nun of the Castle of Lindenberg; or, The History of Raymond & Agnes*. Published by Hodgson and Co. Rare Books and Special Collections, McGill University Library. Permission from McGill University.

46 Franz Potter

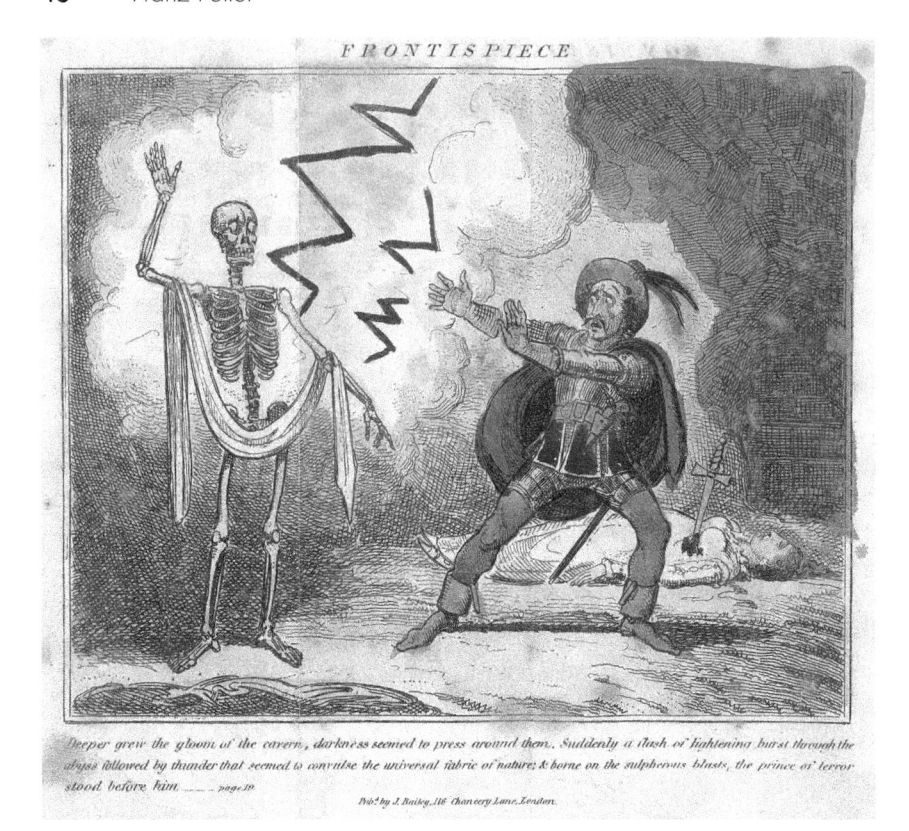

Figure 2.10 Frontispiece from *Wolfstein; or, the Mysterious Bandit. A Terrific Romance. To Which Is Added, The Bronze Statue. A Pathetic Tale*. Published by John Bailey. Sadleir-Black Collection of Gothic Fiction, Albert and Shirley Small Special Collections Library, University of Virginia via Project Gothic.

forks of lightning. The skeleton's right arm is raised above the head, and its left hand points to a dead body on the ground. A long shroud is draped over each arm, surreptitiously covering its pelvis. While the skeleton's curious modesty is comical, the skull provides the clearest indication that the illustration is a cartoon mocking the Gothic readers' expectations. The startled expression of the skull is considerably more expressive than its behaviour. The skeleton is none other than the prince of terror confronting a shocked Wolfstein who recoils in fear with an expression of bemused horror on his exaggerated face, his arms raised in front of himself as if repelling the vision. The only genuinely horrific image of the illustration is of a beautiful, prone and surprisingly stoic woman pierced with a blade with a less than artful dab of red to remind the viewer that she is indeed dead. Beneath the illustration, a caption reads:

> Deeper grew the gloom of the cavern, darkness seemed to press around them. Suddenly a flash of lightning burst through the abyss followed by thunder that seemed to convulse the universal fabric of nature; & borne on the sulphurous blasts, the prince of terror stood before him.

This cartoon underscores Cruikshank's ability to caricature Gothic iconography by blurring the line between horror and the comic. While the textual narrative maintains its horror and suspense, the illustration suggests that the Gothic's visuality has been reduced to caricature.

In the end, it was shifting readers' interest and an evolving literary marketplace driven by an increase in cheap fiction that led to the decline of the Gothic chapbook. Publishers such as John Bailey and William Hodgson, who had once exploited the predilection for short tales of terror, followed the readers to children's books, toy theatres and periodicals where traces of the Gothic remained.

References

Anon. 1802. 'A New and Entertaining Magazine'. *The Ipswich Journal*, 24 April. https://www.newspapers.com/image/390324691

Anon. 1803. *The Black Forest; or, the Cavern of Horrors*. London: Ann Lemoine and John Roe.

Anon. 1823. *The Bleeding Nun of the Castle of Lindenberg; or, The History of Raymond & Agnes*. London: W. Hodgson.

Anon. 1798. *The Castle of Lindenberg; or the History of Raymond and Agnes*. London: S. Fisher.

Anon. 1799. *The Castles of Montreuil and Barre; Or the Histories of the Marquis La Brun and the Baron La Marche, the Late Inhabitants and Proprietors of the Two Castles. A Gothic Story*. London: S. Fisher.

Anon. 1803. *Father Innocent, Abbot of the Capuchins; or, The Crimes of the Cloister*. London: Tegg and Castleman.

Anon. 1799. *Gothic Stories. Contents: Sir Bertrand's Adventures in a Ruinous Castle: – The Story of Fitzalan: – The Adventure James III of Scotland had with the Weird Sisters: – The Story of Raymond Castle: – Vildac; or, The Horrid Discovery: – Henry; or, The Portrait of Mary: – The Ruin of the House of Albert*. London: S. Fisher.

Anon. 1802. *The Midnight Assassin; or, Confession of the Monk Rinaldi, Containing a complete history of his diabolical machinations and unparalleled ferocity. Together with a circumstantial account of that scourge of mankind the Inquisition with the manner of bringing to trial those unfortunate beings who are at its disposal*. London: T. Hurst.

Anon. 1820. *The Monk, A Romance in which Is depicted the Wonderful Adventures of Ambrosio, Friar of the order of capuchins*. London: W. Mason.

Anon. n.d. *Raymond and Agnes; or, the Bleeding Nun*. London: Dean and Munday.

Anon. n.d. *Wolfstein; or, The Mysterious Bandit. A Terrific Romance.* London: J. Bailey.
Burton, Anthony. 1973. 'Cruikshank as an Illustrator of Fiction.' *The Princeton University Library Chronicle* 35, no. 1/2: 93–128. https://doi.org/10.2307/26409887.
Crookenden, Isaac. 1805. *The Skeleton; or, Mysterious Discovery. A Gothic Romance.* London: A. Neil.
Frank, Frederick S. 1987. *The First Gothics: A Critical Guide to the English Gothic Novel.* New York: Garland Publishing, Inc.
Gerard, W. B. 2016. '"Absence has not abated your love": the nostalgia for an idealised aristocracy in The Castle of Lindenberg during the Romantic era'. *Word & Image* 32, no. 4: 393–408. DOI: 10.1080/02666286.2016.1215121
Lewis, Matthew. [1796] 1992. *The Monk*, edited by Howard Anderson. Oxford: Oxford University Press.
McCarthy, Elizabeth. 2014. 'Gothic Visuality in the Nineteenth Century'. In *The Gothic World*, edited by Glennis Byron and Dale Townshend, 341–53. Abingdon: Routledge.
Thomson, Doug and Wendy Fall. 2019. 'Gothic Chapbooks and Ballads: Making a Long Story Short'. In *The Edinburgh Companion to Gothic and the Arts*, edited by David Punter, 259–70. Edinburgh: Edinburgh University Press.
Vincent, James. 1810. *The Castle of the Appennines. A Romance.* London: Thomas Tegg.
Wilkinson, Sarah, 1820. *Castle of Lindenberg, or the History of Raymond and Agnes; Including Raymond's Adventures With the Banditti in the Forest of Rosenwald, and His Being Haunted by the Spectre of the Bleeding Nun.* London: J. Bailey.

Further Reading

Frank, Frederick S. 1998. 'Gothic Gold: The Sadleir-Black Collection of Gothic Fiction'. *Studies in Eighteenth-Century Culture* 26: 287–312. https://doi.org/10.1353/sec.2010.0119
Potter, Franz. 2005. *The History of Gothic Publishing, 1800–1835: Exhuming the Trade.* Basingstoke: Palgrave Macmillan.
Potter, Franz. 2021. *Gothic Chapbooks, Bluebooks and Shilling Shockers*, 1797–1830. Cardiff: University of Wales Press.
Punter, David. 1996. *The Literature of Terror: A History of Gothic Fictions from 1765 to the present day, Volume One.* Harlow: Longman Group Limited.

Chapter 3

The Horror and Humour of Women's Rights: Early Gothic Parody and Anti-Feminism
Natalie Neill

The anonymous author of *The Posthumous Daughter* (1797) was praised in a review for 'avoiding the ghosts, castles, and enchantments lately so much in fashion' and for writing a work whose 'general tendency is friendly to virtue' ('New Publications', 460). In the Romantic period, reviewers disparaged the Gothic for its well-worn tropes and supposed immorality. Parodists likewise criticised the genre, although their works also benefited from its popularity. A significant number of parodies took aim at so-called 'female' or Radcliffean Gothic novels to denigrate female authorship and express fears about the Gothic novel's perceived threat to women's domesticity. Especially after the publication of Mary Wollstonecraft's *Vindication of the Rights of Woman* (1792) and feminist Gothic novel *Maria; or the Wrongs of Woman* (1798), Gothic parody became a crucial site for debates about women's status and education. William Beckford's *Modern Novel Writing* (1796) and *Azemia* (1797), Mary Charlton's *Rosella, or Modern Occurrences* (1799), Maria Edgeworth's 'Angelina; or, L'Amie Inconnue' (1801), Eaton Stannard Barrett's *The Heroine* (1813), and other such texts, satirise female readers and writers in order to express concerns over Gothic's influence and regulate women's entrance into public discourse. Yet these Comic Gothic works – especially those written by female authors – are necessarily ambivalent about the texts, authors and readers they ostensibly critique. Ultimately, the tensions in the parodies reflect the period's complex debates about the rights of women.

General Overview of Gothic Parody, 1790–1820

At least as far back as Horace Walpole's *The Castle of Otranto* (1764), the Gothic has been associated with parody and self-parody. As scholars have long argued, Gothic texts have always vacillated between horror and humour (Weiss 1980; Sage 1994; Horner and Zlosnik 2005). Arguably, the genre is so 'acutely self-reflexive' (Horner and Zlosnik 2005, 32) that parodies simply magnify humorous tendencies that already exist within the targeted texts. It can be difficult to categorise early parodies like the anonymous *Powis Castle* (1788) and James White's *Earl Strongbow* (1789) because they make fun of the Gothic even as the genre was still being established. The number of parodies rose dramatically in the 1790s and first decades of the nineteenth century as Gothic grew in popularity and became more conventional. Today, Jane Austen's *Northanger Abbey* (1818), Thomas Love Peacock's *Nightmare Abbey* (1818) and Barrett's *The Heroine* remain familiar, but other parodies from the period may be less so. In addition to those already mentioned, examples include Bullock's *Susanna; or, Traits of a Modern Miss* (1795), R. S.'s *The New Monk* (1798), F. C. Patrick's *More Ghosts!* (1798), Eliza Parsons's *Anecdotes of Two Well-Known Families* (1798), Bellin de la Liborlière's *The Hero* (1799; English translation 1817), Edward Du Bois's *St. Godwin* (1800) and *Old Nick* (1801), Sarah Green's *Romance Readers and Romance Writers* (1810), Ircastrensis's *Love and Horror* (1812) and the anonymous *Hardenbrass and Haverill; or, The Secret of the Castle* (1817). Gothic parody also appeared in forms other than novels; there were parodic plays, stories, cartoons and poems, including such comical verse 'recipes' as Mary Alcock's 'A Receipt for Writing a Novel' (1799) and the oft-quoted recipe in 'Terrorist Novel Writing' (1797).[1]

As I have argued elsewhere, the parodies target Gothic as 'bad writing' in both senses of the phrase (Neill 2016, 190). Gothic texts were mocked for their aesthetic shortcomings and purported pernicious effects. The main aesthetic criticism had to do with Gothic's formulaic qualities. The unoriginality of mass-market Gothic fiction is highlighted in the recipes and by critics like Samuel Taylor Coleridge, who noted in his review of *The Monk*, 'with how little expense of thought or imagination this species of composition is manufactured' (1797, 296). As Elizabeth Neiman argues, presses like Minerva fostered a 'model of collective authorship' (2019, 27) that involved the recycling and reworking of familiar plots and motifs. In parodies like *Modern Novel Writing* and *Love and Horror*, expected Gothic scenes concerning ghosts and robbers, abductions and reunions, castles and cottages, mysterious manuscripts (and so on) are ludicrous in part because they appear in rapid succession, with little logical connection. In Ircastensis's parody, chapters alternate in focus between the adventures of the hero Thomas Bailey and heroine Annabella Tit, with cliff-hanger chapter endings giving way abruptly to new, shocking predicaments. For example, one chapter ends after Annabella sees a 'form, covered in blood' emerge from a door in a pillar; the next chapter returns us to Thomas in the midst of fending off a surprise attack by a dagger-wielding villain (Ircastrensis 2008, 23). In such parodies, the humour depends on the readers' recognition of typical Gothic scenes, which are crowded together and rewritten in a comical register.

Gothic's lack of realism is a major focus of the parodies. Works like *Love and Horror* exaggerate to a preposterous (and entertaining) degree the kinds of escapades depicted in Gothic novels. For example, Thomas manages to escape his pursuers by floating across the Channel in a tub. The narrator interjects to offer a nonsensical explanation because, as he writes, 'We are anxious lest some readers ... might suppose that we have a little violated probability, to account for the floating of Thomas' (Ircastrensis 2008, 61). The pretence of realism is the butt of humour in many parodies that include mock ghosts of the 'explained supernatural'. In *Nightmare Abbey*, a ghost is revealed to be Glowry's steward Crow 'walking in his sleep, and ... the shroud and bloody turban were a sheet and a red nightcap' (Peacock 2007, 129). In Beckford's *Azemia*, the heroine explores a lumber room and is terrified by an apparition; however, it is '*not a real ghost*, or even a *wax-work figure*' but merely a Chinese statue (2010, 42). In *The New Monk*, a spectre with flashing eyes turns out to be a jack-o'-lantern (R. S. 2007, 176). Such scenes parody the 'rational' explanations for apparently supernatural occurrences that appear in Gothic novels with increasing regularity after Ann Radcliffe popularised the device.

Overworked tropes and improbabilities of plot and character are important targets in parodies like *Rosella*, *The Hero*, 'Angelina', *Northanger Abbey*, *Romance Readers and Romance Writers* and *The Heroine* (and many others) that feature quixotic readers whose expectations are shaped by their Gothic reading. Instead of exaggerating Gothic scenes for laughs, many such texts present the expected plotlines in a more realistic guise. In *Northanger Abbey*, Catherine Morland is not kidnapped by a Gothic villain, but she is forced to endure a carriage ride with the odious John Thorpe. The heroine of Edgeworth's 'Angelina' (1802) visits a cottage but finds that it is not as charming as those she has read about; instead, it is damp, the kitchen smokes, and the furniture is moth-eaten. She decides that cottage life is 'not quite so satisfactory in actual practice, as in poetic theory' (Edgeworth 2003, 268). Authors of Quixote fictions rely on the actual readers' familiarity (indeed over-familiarity) with Gothic to achieve a satiric effect. One example is seen in *Susanna*: contrary to what a reader well-read in Minerva novels might expect, when the titular heroine finally succeeds in escaping from her husband's home, her flight (much like Catherine's miserable ride from Northanger Abbey to Fullerton) is completely uneventful. No obstacles prevent her from arriving safely at her destination. The narrator remarks:

> What mortal, but a brainless author like myself, would miss such an opportunity as this, when I am conducting her over the pathless heath, in a dark winter's night, without introducing an *uninhabited chateau*, a *ghost*, or a *lover*. Forgive me this time, good reader, and my next work shall be as full of hobgoblins as of lines. (Bullock 1795, 3.209)

Charlton's *Rosella* is another example of a parody that highlights Gothic's lack of verisimilitude. The difference between Charlton's text and most other Gothic Quixote tales is that the young female protagonist (Rosella) is not the Quixote figure, but rather her mother is. Rosella does not consider herself to be a heroine; it is her mother who sees her in the role. Like Austen's Catherine, Rosella is a far more ordinary adolescent girl than the Gothic heroines with whom she is compared. Unlike the typical Radcliffean heroine, for example, Rosella is an indifferent artist, whose 'modest opinion of her ability' causes her to decline a request to sketch a picturesque landscape (Charlton 2023, 106). At one point, she wishes to shorten a ramble across the countryside because she is hungry and has 'wet shoes' (108). And in her spare time, she takes up her work, 'a vulgarity a heroine is scarcely ever caught at, her elegant and simple wardrobe being composed of such sublime materials as never to require alteration or repair' (232). Most importantly, Rosella does not share her mother's enthusiasm for Gothic romance. Instead, she tends to look upon her mother's favourite novels with a satiric eye:

> she could with great patience cry through a dozen pages, and tremble through as many more. But then a continuation of crying and trembling, according as the superb pen of the writer varied from pathos to horrors, and from horrors to pathos, throughout several volumes, she found far exceeding any curiosity she could feel, to learn in which of the damp dungeons, all over-run with spiders and black beetles, the most lucky of the heroine's three or four dozen lovers found a clean spot to throw himself at her feet. (121)

There is a strong didactic impulse in parodies like *Rosella*, which set out to correct the distortions of reality found in Gothic texts. In fact, most Gothic parodies are vehicles for moral and ideological criticism. However much the parodists mock Gothic texts for their misrepresentations of reality, and Gothic readers for their gullibility, the parodies betray serious concerns about Gothic's links to, and influence on, the real world.

In the reactionary 1790s, the most controversial Gothic texts naturally attracted the most parody. Matthew Lewis's lurid *The Monk* (1796) is parodied in many works including *Rosella* (122) and *The Hero*, which ends with the novel-reading protagonist making a pact with the Devil in an episode that reworks the conclusion of Lewis's book. Sustained parodies of *The Monk* like R. S.'s *The New Monk* (1798) reflect fears about the work's 'evil ... effect' in England (R. S. [1798] 2007, 1). 'My aim', R. S. explains in his preface, 'is to set in a ridiculous and disgusting light, a style of writing, which only waited for toleration to become general' (2). Criticism of the Gothic became increasingly 'urgent and patriotic' after radical writers like William Godwin took up the genre to disseminate political and philosophical ideas (Wright 2007, 17). In *Caleb Williams* (1794) and *St. Leon* (1799), Godwin uses Gothic conventions to narrativise arguments expressed in *Political Justice* (1791). In turn, anti-Jacobin parodies like Du Bois's *St. Godwin* (1800) and Charles Lucas's *The Infernal Quixote* (1801) ridicule the Gothic in order to counteract the spread of Godwinian ideas.

Although Lewis and Godwin drew significant attention, female writers and their texts were by far the most frequent targets of parodists in this period. Wollstonecraft and other radicals were singled out for censure, but female authors in general were derided for their unoriginal productions and 'unrealistic' depictions of women and their lives. As the next section explores, these criticisms were not merely aesthetic: they reflect a larger, ideologically driven reaction to women's growing participation in the literary market.

Gothic Parody and Anti-Feminist Satire

Alcock concludes her 'receipt' for writing a Gothic novel by identifying women as the producers of unimaginative terrors; after cataloguing Gothic conventions, she writes: 'These stores supply the *female* pen, / Which writes them o'er and o'er again' (1799, 69–70, my italics). By the 1790s, the Gothic had become strongly associated with female writers and readers. The gendering of the genre as 'female' is apparent in most parodies. As Angela Wright observes, parodists 'seemingly insisted upon the formulaic and derivative nature of Gothic writing by women, and the dangerously overheated responses of its female readership' even though 'neither the readership nor the authorship of Gothic romance was straightforwardly female' (2015, 67).

The gendering of the Gothic undoubtedly reflects the prominent position of female writers in Gothic's early history, as well as the prevalence of female-centred Gothic narratives. But there are other reasons why women and the Gothic are linked in critical responses to the genre. There is a long tradition of feminising targets to attack them. Examples include the Roman satirist Juvenal's depictions of feminised men and Alexander Pope's use of Belinda to satirise the vanity and idleness of the British upper classes in 'The Rape of the Lock' (1712). Similarly, parodists and reviewers emphasise Gothic's female associations to characterise the genre as lowly and trivial.

Early assessments of female Gothic also reflect common prejudices against female writers. In her discussion of gender biases in reviews of Minerva novels, Hannah Doherty Hudson notes: 'while *all* authors of popular novels were potentially subject to accusations of being "hackneyed", "improbable", "incomprehensible" and "uninteresting", authors thought to be women were subject to particular scrutiny' (2020, 49). Generally, female novelists were considered less educated and skilled than their male counterparts; moreover, women were held to a different standard by critics who had specific ideas about what forms of writing (including forms of Gothic writing) were suitably feminine. When Charlotte Dacre trespassed onto 'masculine' territory by writing *Zofloya* (1806), a work of sensational and sensual horror, she was met with critical hostility: 'There is a voluptuousness of language and allusion, pervading these volumes', notes the reviewer for *The Annual Review*, 'which we should have hoped, that the delicacy of a female pen would have refused to trace . . . [and] been shocked to imagine' (1806, 542). Female writers were open to charges of overreaching, regardless of the genre in which they worked. Matthew Lewis expresses a familiar view of female authorship when he argues that publication constitutes a threat to femininity because of the exposure it gives to women. '[A] woman has no business to be a public character', he comments, 'and . . . in proportion as she acquires notoriety, she loses delicacy. I always consider a female author as a sort of half-man' (Lewis [1804] 1839, 278). Here, Lewis reproduces a stereotype found in such antifeminist satires as Thomas Mathias's *The Pursuits of Literature* (1797) and Richard Polwhele's *Unsex'd Females* (1798) – that of the unnatural, 'unsexed' female writer. A pictorial example is 'Mrs. Godwin', the 1798 caricature of Wollstonecraft engraved by John Chapman after an unknown artist, in which she is shown wearing a man's hat. Critics trivialised the Gothic by characterising it as 'women's writing', even as they demeaned female writers by presenting them as masculine.

These prejudices find expression in parodies of female-authored Gothic texts, and in the satirical portrayals of female writers that are frequently found in the parodies. Beckford adopts feminine pseudonyms and authorial personae – 'Lady Harriet Marlow' in *Modern Novel Writing* (1796) and 'Jaquetta Agneta Mariana Jenks' in *Azemia* – to satirise female authors. At the end of the latter work, Jaquetta Jenks acknowledges Harriet Marlow and the other writers (all female) whose style she has emulated. Her list, which includes Ann Radcliffe, Mary Robinson, Sophia Lee, Elizabeth Inchbald, Charlotte Smith, Susannah and Elizabeth Gunning, and Helen Maria Williams, identifies Beckford's main targets (2010, 201–2). Both of Beckford's parodies are obviously derivative, and yet Harriet Marlow insists, in the dedication to *Modern Novel Writing*, that her story possesses a 'bold originality' which does her credit as a 'daughter of the Muses' (2008, 36). She refers to her heroine's 'uncommon destiny' at the beginning of the novel (37); however, the irony of the statement is soon apparent from the sheer predictability of the narrative.

Beckford mocks the sameness of women's sentimental and Gothic fictions; he also characterises women's writing as diffuse, rambling and incoherent. In *Modern Novel Writing*, important plot events are de-emphasised while inconsequential details are dwelled upon at length: the deaths of the principal characters Amelia Gonzales and Lucinda Howard are described in a few short sentences (Beckford 2008, 146, 147), but a misdirected letter with no bearing on the story is given two pages (78–9). New characters are introduced and then never mentioned again. Such absurdities are attributed to the lack of inventiveness and talent of the 'authoress', who openly acknowledges her difficulties in managing the story. She expresses, for example, how troublesome it is to bring the work to a close:

> It is one of the easiest things in nature to begin a novel, but as the work proceeds, then comes the difficulty – Characters grow out of characters, fresh persons must be brought forward to heighten the interest, and as it approaches toward a conclusion, the plague is how to get rid of the good folks with decency – Some must be *married*, some must be KILLED OFF and all must be properly disposed of. (Beckford 2008, 171)

Near the end of the novel, she provides a solution to this problem by introducing a tainted celery that poisons a dozen characters at once (including one of the heroines) (147).

Depictions of female authors reveal hostile attitudes towards educated women. Satirical portraits of female 'upstarts' and intellectuals abound in Gothic parodies. In *Old Nick*, Edward Du Bois satirises feminine pretension to learning through Mrs Pawlet, a woman of weak understanding who assumes the character of a great scholar. Beckford includes several comical bluestockings in his parodies. One is Mrs De

Malthe, a caricature of Hester Lynch Piozzi. Mrs De Malthe disguises her ignorance with great shows of erudition. Beckford drops his authorial persona briefly to describe her: 'To be distinguished as a woman of learning', he explains, 'she had ransacked all of the indexes of books of science, and of the classics; her writings and discourse were larded with scraps of Latin and Greek, with far-fetched allusions, and obsolete quotations' (Beckford [1796] 2008, 84). Beckford suggests, in short, that much like the imitative Gothic novelists, Mrs De Malthe's writings are made up of shreds and patches of earlier works.

In *Rosella*, Charlton makes fun of Sophia Beauclerc (Rosella's mother) for being so often at her writing desk where she records their Gothic adventures and 'journalize[s] [*sic*] herself into a violent fit of enthusiastic heroism' (2023, 254); however, Charlton directs more satire at another female writer, Mrs Methwald, with whom Rosella is forced to live when her mother's overactive imagination leads (horrifyingly) to her confinement in an asylum for the insane. Mrs Methwald, like Sophia, is frequently occupied with writing, but her obsessions include systems of female education, science and modern philosophy, rather than Gothic and sentimental romance. When Rosella is finally freed from Mrs Methwald's guardianship, she gladly leaves her 'and her simpering daughter to astronomize, botanize, and philosophize at their leisure' (359). Charlton's mockery of botanising women, in particular, would seem to align her with anti-Jacobin satirists like Polwhele, who, in addition to satirising female writers, dwelled upon botany as an unseemly pastime for women.

In the parodies, women with intellectual interests are mocked for putting on airs. The parodists also ridicule female accomplishments and self-expression, more generally, through comical representations of artistic Gothic heroines. The extemporaneous poetical effusions of Radcliffe's heroines are a conventional target: in *Modern Novel Writing*, for example, one of the heroines 'relieve[s] her anxious mind' by penning a poem 'On a Dead Goldfinch' (Beckford 2008, 94–5); in *Azemia*, a young lady at a party entertains other guests by reciting an 'Elegiac Sonnet to a Mopstick' (Beckford 2010, 127). However, the parodists are less troubled by female creativity per se, than they are by the idea that women who pursue intellectual or creative endeavours do so at the expense of fulfilling more traditional feminine duties. Female Quixote fictions are almost always cautionary tales about the dangers of rejecting prescribed gender roles. The would-be heroines of such works are misled by their reading into overestimating women's importance and field of action. This is an idea that Anna Laetitia Barbauld captures in 'On the Origin and Progress of Novel-Writing' (1810) when she observes that young ladies who read novels excessively will be unprepared 'for the neglect and tedium' that life has in store for them (Barbauld 2002, 412).

Many parodists seem to agree with the anonymous author of 'Terrorist Novel Writing', who suggests that women should occupy themselves with 'needle-books' rather than Gothic books (1797: 224–5). The romance-reading heroines of Gothic parody often neglect domestic tasks, or are ill-equipped to perform them, because such matters are not mentioned in Gothic novels. In *Rosella*, Sophia realises while eating an unsatisfactory dinner that she

> had never read of a heroine being compelled to rise from table to rince her own glasses, call for a napkin to wipe the dust from her plate, or take up her salt with a table spoon; all this discomposed her exceedingly, for such a minutia had not even entered her head, when she had devoured, in delighted admiration [her treasured books]. (Charlton 2023, 222)

Meanwhile, her friend Selina Ellinger (also an enthusiastic reader) keeps a messy house and allows a pile of garbage to fester in her courtyard because her 'elevated notions ... prevented her from observing [it]' (Charlton 2023, 52). Clearly, being engrossed in a world of Gothic fantasy and good household management are not compatible.

Reflecting worries that female readers will be unduly influenced by Gothic novels, the parodies highlight the spurious virtues of comic heroines. In *Modern Novel Writing*, Beckford uses the conduct of the 'virtuous' female characters to satirise the supposed moral hypocrisy of the Gothic. In her 'Humble Address' to reviewers, Harriet Marlow insists that her novel exhibits a 'pure moral tendency' (Beckford [1796] 2008, 183), a claim belied by the infidelities of her heroines. '[W]ho can be wise at all times?' shrugs Amelia, when recounting a secret meeting between herself and a handsome captain (65). Yet, most concern was reserved for radical writers and their influence. Satiric venom was directed at Mary Wollstonecraft, Charlotte Smith, Mary Robinson and other revolutionary women – those *'unsexed* female writers' (to quote Mathias) who 'instruct, or confuse, us and themselves, in the labyrinth of politics, or turn us wild with Gallic frenzy' (Mathias [1797] 1808, 244). In *Unsex'd Females*, Polwhele mentions several Gothic writers including Radcliffe, but he saves most of his criticism for women who use fiction for polemical purposes. He condemns Robinson for her support of the French Revolution, noting: 'Robinson to Gaul her Fancy gave' (Polwhele [1798] 1800: 20). He condemns Wollstonecraft (to whom he devotes most space) primarily for her feminism. His 28-line diatribe against her opens with the couplet 'See Wollstonecraft, whom no decorum checks, / Arise, the intrepid champion of her sex'! (16).

Wollstonecraft's calls for a 'revolution in female manners' ([1792] 2009: 49, 202) and apparent disregard for social convention were threatening to the status quo. After the publication of the *Memoirs of the Author of A Vindication of the Rights of Woman* (1798), in which Godwin revealed his wife's love affairs, her pregnancies out of wedlock, and other details of her private life, Wollstonecraft was branded an immoral woman whose 'vicious writings risked corrupting other women' (Faubert 2012: 30). Wollstonecraft's unfinished novel *Maria* – the harrowing epistolary account of a woman imprisoned in an asylum by her husband – met with critical 'horror', not due to the Gothic plight of the heroine, but due to the work's potential to set a dangerous precedent. The reviewer for the *Monthly Review* criticised the 'moral tendency' of *Maria*, arguing that the cruelties of Maria's husband did not justify her adulterous relationship with Henry Darnford, another inmate (Review of *Posthumous Works* 1798, 326). As one would expect, the review in the *Anti-Jacobin* was even more disapproving. Describing *Maria* as 'a tale intended to illustrate the doctrines in "Rights of Woman"', the reviewer responds to Godwin's prefatory claim about the novel's beneficial social influence with a sarcastic dismissal of the 'purity of [Wollstonecraft's] *conception of female excellence*, and the usefulness to society of the conduct to which she exhorts her sex' (Review of *Maria* 1798, 91).

Wollstonecraftean feminists are satirised directly and indirectly in the parodies. In Edgeworth's 'Angelina', the titular heroine finally overcomes her addiction to romances when she meets the celebrated female author 'Araminta'. Miss Hodges (the writer's real name) has 'a face and figure which seemed to have been intended for a man' and 'a voice more masculine than her looks' (Edgeworth [1802] 2003, 288). Her 'favourite topic' is the rights of women (291). *Rosella*, which appeared one year after the publication of Wollstonecraft's memoirs and posthumous writings, includes *Maria* among its targets. Sophia presents her daughter with a tear-blotted packet of pages, '*Memoirs of the hapless Mother of Rosella*' (Charlton 2023, 255), which is arguably a spoof of Maria's writings to the daughter who has been taken from her. Sophia's unjust consignment to the asylum by a male relation also ties her to Wollstonecraft's heroine. In Charlton's parody, Sophia's cousin uses her book-fuelled eccentricities as a pretext for locking her up so that he can steal her property. Like Wollstonecraft, Charlton presents the imprisonment of the heroine as an appalling abuse of male authority. The capture of Sophia is a truly Gothic moment in an otherwise humorous text. However, Charlton also suggests that Sophia ends up in the asylum because she steps outside her 'proper' sphere. Chasing Gothic adventures, Sophia takes Rosella on a long trip through northern England and Scotland, during the course of which she proves herself to be a flighty and inadequate chaperone to her daughter. Rosella's safety and reputation are jeopardised by the romantic schemes of her mother. Incarceration in the asylum, however awful, is a narrative device used to correct and subdue the independent Sophia. *Rosella* ends with Sophia's reformation: released from the asylum, she 'is settled in her residence, and no longer harasses herself by moving from place to place' (Charlton 2023, 271). As in Barrett's later parody *The Heroine* (1813), women's wandering imaginations are linked to their wanderings away from home. In Barrett's text, the heroine Cherubina runs away because she fears that she is 'doomed to endure the security of a home, and the dullness of an unimpeached reputation' (2011, 9). In the end, both Cherry and Sophia are domesticated back into prescribed feminine roles. Cured of romantic notions about female independence, the Quixotes learn to mistrust the truth of Gothic novels and 'respect the prejudices of the world' (Charlton 2023, 265).

Parodies like *Rosella* and *The Heroine* include mocking portrayals of women who try to free themselves from societal expectations. The parodies also make light of the explicit and implicit feminist critiques found in female Gothic texts. For example, parodists appear to laugh off legitimate concerns about women's lack of freedom and rights when they heap derision on Gothic representations of female persecution and imprisonment. In one especially misogynistic scene in *The Heroine*, Cherry discovers her 'mother' imprisoned in a subterranean cell, but she is dismayed to find that she is rude, overweight and grotesque – 'a living mountain of human horror' (Barrett [1813] 2011, 152). In *Love and Horror*, Annabella is abducted and locked up repeatedly, but she manages to escape each time through preposterous means: at one point, she wins the sympathy of her captors by playing a tune on her Jew's harp (Ircastrensis [1812] 2008, 28–9); later, she is kidnapped again, but she gets away by fashioning a costume from wool and disguising herself as a dog (77–8). Here, Ircastrensis makes fun of resourceful heroines, but such scenes also dismiss as laughable what is arguably one of the central concerns of the female Gothic: the subjection of women.

Conclusion: 'the tendency of this work': Ambivalences in the Parodies

Gothic parodies make fun of feminist aspirations and concerns, but they are far from straightforward in their mockery of female-authored Gothic texts. Many parodists offer their criticisms with self-awareness and even self-parody. When Austen concludes *Northanger Abbey* by raising questions about the 'tendency of this work' ([1818] 2002, 204), she is certainly satirising reviewers' cant, but she is also poking fun at the didacticism inherent in narratives about female quixotism. Parodies like Austen's betray affection for, or at least 'ambivalent dependence' (Rose 1993, 51) on, the texts they would seem to deprecate. In part, this is because of the double-voiced nature of parodies. As Linda Hutcheon has emphasised, parody is as much an imitation as it is a critique; therefore, 'parody always implicitly reinforces even as it ironically debunks' (Hutcheon [1985] 2000, xii). The parodists exploit the success of the Gothic while seeming to reject the genre. By extension, their Comic Gothic works cater to fans and decriers of the genre by providing the double pleasure of Gothic narrative and ironic detachment.

The parodists sometimes draw attention to the conflicts of interest inherent in parody. In her reader's address at the beginning of *Susanna*, for example, Bullock asks: 'Shall she, who points the shafts of ridicule against novel-readers, expect *her* novel to be read?' (Bullock 1795, 1.2). If female parodists are especially ambivalent towards their targets, as argued at the outset, they are strategically so. Writers like Edgeworth and Austen mock certain kinds of fiction by women to define their own style and bolster their professional reputations. Indeed, parody can be seen as a canny publishing strategy for women during a period when female authors were especially scrutinised. By parodying the works of others, authors forestall objections to their own work. As such, the moral and ideological criticisms in the parodies cannot be taken at face value, for they may be conventional postures offered to anticipate the potential concerns of reviewers.

The parodies can be nuanced in their treatment of feminist ideas. Despite their seeming conservatism, stories about uncritical Gothic readers tend to support Wollstonecraft's views regarding the importance of female rationality, as well as her opposition to 'over exercised sensibility' in women (Wollstonecraft [1792] 2009, 65). Although the Quixote tales usually consign women to traditional roles, these texts echo Wollstonecraftean concerns about the lack of female education. In *Susanna*, Bullock is explicit in attributing the protagonist's taste for popular novels to the faulty education she received at boarding school, where 'two hours in every day were spent in practicing how to get in and out of a carriage with dignity, and in entering and quitting a room avec une *air degagée*' (Bullock 1795, 1.12). Mocking portraits of artistic heroines are not always attacks on female creativity; sometimes their purpose is to satirise the superficial accomplishments that passed for female education.

As Mercy Cannon argues, Comic Gothic works often 'take a ... Gothic swerve' – as *Rosella* does when Sophia is imprisoned in the asylum – 'in order to present matters of earnest concern, including inadequate education for women, abusive parental relationships, and women's troubling lack of social and political power' (Cannon 2020, 590–1). Even parodies with the most conservative endings open themselves to feminist readings. Comic heroines like Charlton's Sophia and Barrett's Cherubina can be seen as feminist 'rabble rousers' (Horner and Zlosnik 2000, 11). The Quixotes' joyous defiance of social expectations is what one remembers most about such texts (not the de rigueur domesticating endings). The parodies do not, in the end, succeed in containing the 'excesses' of the Gothic.

To conclude, parodies targeting female Gothic texts reaffirm stereotypes about female writers and give voice to anti-feminist sentiments, but they also hold the potential for feminism and subversion. Ultimately, the parodies provide an important window onto Romantic-era debates about women. Their discursive and ideological ambivalences mirror the complex and contradictory attitudes towards women's changing roles in the period.

Note

1. For recent overviews of Romantic-period Gothic parodies, see Thomson (2014), Neill (2016) and Münderlein (2021).

References

Alcock, Mary. 1799. 'A Receipt for Writing a Novel'. In *Poems, &c. &c. by the Late Mrs Mary Alcock*, 89–93. London: C. Dilly.

Anon. 1797. 'Terrorist Novel Writing'. In *The Spirit of the Public Journals for 1797*, vol. 1, 223–5. London: James Ridgway.

Austen, Jane. [1818] 2002. *Northanger Abbey*, edited by Claire Grogan. Peterborough, ON: Broadview.

Barbauld, Anna Laetitia. [1810] 2002. 'On the Origin and Process of Novel-Writing'. In *Anna Laetitia Barbauld: Selected Poetry and Prose*, edited by William McCarthy and Elizabeth Kraft, 377–417. Peterborough, ON: Broadview.

Barrett, Eaton Stannard. [1813] 2011. *The Heroine*, edited by Avril Horner and Sue Zlosnik, Kansas City: Valancourt Books.

Beckford, William. [1796] 2008. *Modern Novel Writing*, edited by Robert J. Gemmett. Stroud: Nonsuch.

Beckford, William. [1797] 2010. *Azemia*, edited by Robert J. Gemmett, Kansas City: Valancourt Books.

Bellin de la Liborlière. [1817] 2011. *The Hero; or, The Adventures of a Night*, edited by Natalie Neill. Kansas City: Valancourt Books.

Bullock, Mrs. 1795. *Susanna; or, Traits of a Modern Miss*, 3 vols. London: Minerva.

Cannon, Mercy. 2020. 'On the Edges of Gothic Parody: The Neglected Work of Mrs F. C. Patrick and Sarah Green'. *Eighteenth-Century Fiction* 32, no. 4: 579–8.

Charlton, Mary. [1799] 2023. *Rosella, or Modern Occurrences*, edited by Natalie Neill. London and New York: Routledge.

Coleridge, Samuel Taylor. 1797. Review of *The Monk*, *The Critical Review* 19: 194–200.

Edgeworth, Maria. [1802] 2003. 'Angelina'. In *The Novels and Selected Works of Maria Edgeworth*, vol. 10, edited by Elizabeth Eger and Clíona ÓGallchoir, 255–302. London and New York: Routledge.

Faubert, Michelle. 2012. Introduction to *Mary, a Fiction and The Wrongs of Woman, or Maria*, by Mary Wollstonecraft, edited by Michelle Faubert, 11–65. Peterborough, ON: Broadview.

Horner, Avril and Sue Zlosnik. 2000. 'Dead Funny: Eaton Stannard Barrett's *The Heroine* as Comic Gothic'. *Cardiff Corvey: Reading the Romantic Text* 5, no. 2: 2–12.

Horner, Avril and Sue Zlosnik. 2005. *Gothic and the Comic Turn*. Basingstoke: Palgrave Macmillan.

Hudson, Hannah Doherty. 2020. 'Gothic before Gothic: Minerva Press Reviews, Gender and the Evolution of Genre'. In *Women's Authorship and the Early Gothic*, edited by Kathleen Hudson, 43–64. Cardiff: University of Wales Press.

Hutcheon, Linda. [1985] 2000. *A Theory of Parody*. New York: Methuen.

Ircastrensis. [1812] 2008. *Love and Horror*, edited by Natalie Neill. Kansas City: Valancourt Books.

Lewis, Matthew. [1804] 1839. 'To his mother', 18 March. In *The Life and Correspondence of M. G. Lewis*, vol. 1, 278–81. London: Henry Colburn.

Mathias, Thomas James. [1797] 1808. *The Pursuits of Literature*. 14th edn. London: T. Becket.

Münderlein, Kerstin-Anja. 2021. *Genre and Reception in the Gothic Parody*. New York and London: Routledge.

Neill, Natalie. 2016. 'Gothic Parody'. In *Romantic Gothic*, edited by Angela Wright and Dale Townshend, 185–204. Edinburgh: Edinburgh University Press.

Neiman, Elizabeth A. 2019. *Minerva's Gothic's: The Politics and Poetics of Romantic Exchange, 1780–1820*. Cardiff: University of Wales Press.

'New Publications', by Geo. Cawthorn, No. 132, Strand'. 1800. In *The Life of Edmund Burke*, by Robert Bissett, 459–60. London: George Cawthorn.

Peacock, Thomas Love. [1818] 2007. *Nightmare Abbey*, edited by Lisa Vargo. Peterborough, ON: Broadview.

Polwhele, Richard. [1798] 1800. *The Unsex'd Females; A Poem*. New York: Wm. Cobbett.

R. S. Esq. [1798] 2007. *The New Monk*, edited by Elizabeth Andrews. Chicago: Valancourt Books.

Review of *Maria, or the Wrongs of Woman*, by Mary Wollstonecraft. 1798. In *The Anti-Jacobin Review* (July 1798): 91–3.
Review of *Posthumous Works of the Author of A Vindication of the Rights of Woman*. 1798. In *The Monthly Review* 27, 325–7.
Review of *Zofloya: or, The Moor*, by Charlotte Dacre. 1806. In *The Annual Review* 5, 542.
Rose, Margaret A. 1993. *Parody: Ancient, Modern, and Post-Modern*. Cambridge: Cambridge University Press.
Sage, Victor. 1994. 'Gothic Laughter: Farce and Horror in Five Texts'. In *Gothick Origins and Innovations*, edited by Alan Lloyd-Smith and Victor Sage, 190–203. Amsterdam: Rodopi.
Thomson, Douglass H. 2014. 'The Earliest Parodies of Gothic Literature'. In *The Gothic World*, edited by Glennis Byron and Dale Townshend, 284–96. New York: Routledge.
Weiss, Fredric. 1980. *The Antic Spectre: Satire in Early Gothic Novels*. New York: Arno.
Wollstonecraft, Mary. [1792] 2009. *A Vindication of the Rights of Woman*, edited by Deidre Shauna Lynch. New York and London: Norton.
Wright, Angela. 2007. *Gothic Fiction*. Basingstoke: Plagrave Macmillan.
Wright, Angela. 2015. 'The Gothic'. In *Women's Writing in the Romantic Period*, edited by Devoney Looser, 58–72. Cambridge: Cambridge University Press.

Chapter 4

Poe's Comedy: Carnival and Gothic Laughter
Timothy Jones

Vincent Price may well be Poe's greatest reader. Baudelaire might have elevated Poe to the role of philosopher and placed him alongside European giants such as Diderot, Goethe and Balzac; Marie Bonaparte recognised the unhappy depths of the Freudian mind in his work. Price, however, gets the joke, and his performances, particularly in Roger Corman's cycle of Poe films (1960–4) have shared his understanding of Poe with a huge popular audience. Price highlights a weird kind of comedy in Poe, and signals his understanding with the way he laughs, or nearly laughs, when he plays the villain. He watches the blade descend on John Kerr in *The Pit and the Pendulum* (1961) with considerable glee. When he's Prince Prospero in *The Masque of the Red Death* (1964) he lectures Francesca about how the world is governed by war, famine, pestilence, and says that there is 'Very little hope, I assure you.' He eats grapes and smiles, just short of a laugh. The laugh itself is probably most famously rendered at the end of the video for Michael Jackson's 'Thriller' (1982). The laugh does not stop. It is not a joyful laugh, or if there is joy there, it is joy in the misfortune of others or self. It goes on too long; the Gothic is, after all, a tradition of excess. It is too much.

This chapter casts Gothic laughter as a Poevian phenomenon. It discusses Poe's carnivalesque approach to the Gothic across a number of his stories, including 'The Cask of Amontillado' (1846), 'Hop-Frog' (1849), 'King Pest' (1835) and 'The Fall of the House of Usher (1839). Poe uses comic techniques for ends that are, in many ways, more horrifying than humorous, particularly when it comes to his use of pranking and slapstick. The productive confusion between horror and comedy, and the expansion of laughter so that it has a particularly Gothic affective value, are key parts of Poe's reception and legacy in popular culture. Noël Carroll has noted that:

> sometimes ... theories of comedy look ... equally serviceable as theories of horror. Freud ... identifies the object of wit with what can be called the

jokework, which manifests repressed modes of unconscious thinking. But, at the same time, in his celebrated essay 'The Uncanny' – which is as close as Freud comes to a theory of horror – the object of uncanny feelings is also the manifestation of repressed, unconscious modes of thinking . . . Thus, in Freud's theory, the road to comic laughter and the road to feelings of uncanniness are unaccountably the same. (Carroll 1999, 146)

This chapter follows Carroll; it is difficult to separate Poe's comedy from his horrors because they operate so similarly.

The author's engagement with comedy is not a major theme in Poe studies. Discussions of his comedy often confine themselves to discussing a small number of his stories as examples of a tendency which is supposed to be absent from his work taken more widely. 'Hop-Frog' and 'Tarr and Fether' (1845) are probably the two most often discussed. The impression remains that, as John Bryant observes, 'Poe stands alone among comic writers for his pointed *lack* of humor' (Bryant 1996, 17). This chapter instead argues a comic turn shapes much of Poe's work, but that this turn is often grotesque and horrific. Certainly, there can be tonal differences between his comic works and his horrors. In 'Never Bet the Devil Your Head' (1841), Toby Dammit is entertainingly decapitated before unsuccessful attempts are made to revive him. 'The Man That Was Used Up' (1839) ends with a comic reveal of the dismemberment of war hero John A. B. C. Smith. These are written with a knockabout energy and embrace the absurd in the service of making a joke – we know that the headless cannot be helped, and that it is not possible to survive being cut into several pieces. On the other hand, Poe's horror tales, such as 'The Cask of Amontillado' – where Montresor lures the unlucky Fortunato to his doom in the catacombs – maintain a po-faced tone, and most often describe action which is unlikely-yet-possible, with some exceptions. However, it is easy to make too much of these distinctions. Both 'Never Bet the Devil Your Head' and 'The Man That Was Used Up' rely on the mutilation of the human body as a gag, and while their scenarios might not raise a laugh, we understand that readers are being invited to do so. On the other hand, 'The Cask of Amontillado' is not funny, but nevertheless invokes the stuff of comedy, narrating a fatal prank and ending with Gothic laughter. Andrew Stott notes that 'comedy . . . allows us to stand back and look upon human misfortune from an emotional distance, sometimes even deriving great pleasure from it' (Stott 2005, 12). Read together, these tales seem to confirm this premise.

The idea of the carnivalesque – which can suggest both comedy and the grotesque – has been used to characterise Poe's Gothic comedy (Renza 2001, 11; Taylor 2015, 60; Jones 2015, 41–60), and Poe returns to images of carnival festivity. The events of 'Amontillado' take place as carnival is celebrated in the streets above, and the characters are in fancy dress; the last we hear of Fortunato is the jingling of the bells on his motley (Poe 1984, 854).[1] 'Hop-Frog' is a 'fool, or professional jester', valued 'in the eyes of the king, by the fact of his being also a dwarf and a cripple' (899); his love, Trippetta, a 'little less dwarfish than himself . . . and a marvellous dancer' (900) are both carnivalesque figures, people treated as spectacles to be observed and denigrated, in a court presided over by a king and a court who have 'grow[n] fat by joking' (899). The violent climax of the tale comes amidst a masquerade ball. Likewise, the 'The Masque of the Red Death' (1842) also features deaths at the peak of a costumed revel. These endings emphasise the idea of the carnival as a time of topsy-turvy and disruption. In 'Hop-Frog', the king is said to enjoy 'Rabelais's "Gargantua" . . . and upon the whole, practical jokes suited his taste far better than verbal ones' (899). Rabelais, of course, is the author who spurred Mikhail Bakhtin to provide his classic account of the carnival.

For Bakhtin, 'carnival celebrated temporary liberation from the prevailing truth and from the established order; it marked the suspension of all hierarchical rank, privileges, norms, and prohibitions' (Bakhtin 1984, 10). Both 'Hop-Frog' and 'Masque' seem to enact this, although in a nastier way than Bakhtin would have envisaged. For him, the carnival was radically inclusive and amiable, a period 'that it does not acknowledge any distinction between actors and spectators . . . Carnival is not a spectacle seen by the people; they live in it, and everyone participates' (Bakhtin 1984, 7). Poe's tales tend to emphasise the carnival's disregard for norms and prohibitions but are less interested in the carnival as an egalitarian and inclusive space. Instead, Poe seems unable to imagine the carnival as leading to anything other than violence – and not simply violence, but extraordinary, spectacular violence. To see the king and his councillors suspended above the gathered company in 'ourang-outang' costumes before they are set on fire and become a 'fetid, blackened, hideous, and indistinguishable mass' (907–8) perhaps is not what Bakhtin was thinking of.

While Bakhtin seems to celebrate the amities of the revelling crowd, Poe emphasises the agency of the individual. Philip McGowan proposes the notion of an American carnivalesque, distinct from the Bakhtinian. McGowan conceives of the carnival as a key development in a genuinely national form of American popular culture – both an actual site, but also a wider way of seeing which developed from the mid-nineteenth century and was shaped by 'minstrel shows, the explosion of sensationalised accounts of depravity and violence in reform literature and the national press, the growth of dime museums, the sprouting of traveling carnivals, and participation in international exhibitions [such as the World's Fair]' (McGowan 2001, 21). American carnival is focused on spectation more than participation. Moreover, it is a form of spectation which enacts 'policies of exclusion ... interspun with a particularised politics of exhibition and display' (McGowan 2001, 1). It diminishes and objectifies the object of its interest – the gimp, the minstrel, or the figure peeped on. Poe is acutely aware not just of violence, but the ways in which victimhood is both humiliating and spectacular.

Poe seems to juggle McGowan's American carnival with the Bakhtinian carnivalesque. He is, after all, an American writer, but one whose stories, through their settings, suggest a romanticised interest in the Old World. His carnivals might depose figures of authority, but they hardly elevate the common folk. Sometimes, death comes to the assembled crowd, but most often death arrives as something that is watched. We understand that Hop-Frog is doing the wrong thing by setting the king and his councillors on fire – but there is a sneaking sense – at least for readers who enjoy Poe – that this is the right kind of wrong thing, that actually we approve the act as a form of revenge against an abuser and a tyrant. Indeed, the same could be said of Prince Prospero and his thousand 'hale and light-hearted friends' in 'The Masque of the Red Death' who have shut themselves away to party while the rest of the kingdom suffers under the ravages of disease (485). Neither the Prince nor his guests are depicted in sufficient detail for us to have invested our sympathies in them, and perhaps death is a fair reward – although it is hard to tell.

American carnival holds much in common with the idea of the practical joke or prank – another idea Poe's stories return to with some regularity. Indeed, some of the most disturbing moments in Poe's stories emerge from dangerous pranking. The lengthy development and ghastly denouement of Hop-Frog's *'last jest'* (908) is one such. 'The Cask of Amontillado' is a narrative of elaborate pranking. '*At length* I would be avenged' vows Montresor before deceptively leading the hapless Fortunato down into the vaults, pretending to ask for his advice about sherry. We see Montresor perversely enjoying his own joke, expressing concern for Fortunato's health when he hears him cough in the cold subterranean air: 'we will go back; your health is precious. You are rich, respected, admired, beloved, you are happy, as once I was. You are a man to be missed' (850). A moment later, as Fortunato drinks to 'the buried that repose around us' Montresor drinks to the other's 'long life' (850). Sculley Bradley notes American humour's 'anti-romanticism. We love to puncture an illusion ... Pretensions of grandeur, false family pride, snobbishness, or conceit annoy us . . . we have chosen as our most comic figure the "sucker." He is the "goat," the victim of our practical jokes, the romancer who is fooled by the mere surface of things' (Bradley 1997, 48). Fortunato is just such a figure, both an admired patriarch who needs to be taken down a peg or two, and contemptibly foolish, unable to recognise he is the butt of Montresor's joke. It is only at the tale's climax that Fortunato sees he has been deceived and desperately pleads with the prankster. He pretends the joke is somehow friendly, saying it is 'an excellent jest' (854) and suggests he and Montresor return to the palazzo; but Montresor remains undeterred. Fortunato's death may be a joke, but it is not exactly funny. Poe acknowledges this slipperiness in 'William Wilson' (1839), where he describes banter and pranking as 'giving pain while assuming the aspect of mere fun' (343).

Poe often writes two-dimensional characters. This is the case in 'Amontillado'. We know very little about Fortunato. He has somehow wronged Montresor; he is obviously proud; he likes a drink. We have only the murderer's vague words to show his victim's guilt, rather than any account of what the unlucky Fortunato has actually done. In 'Hop-Frog', other than the fact the king is both jovial and unpleasant, we know little about him before he is tricked into meeting his end. David Carroll Simon describes how, especially in Rabelais, the prank is 'an expression of epistemological confidence' that must 'ensure the one-dimensionality of its target' (Simon 2019, 424, 425). The carnival works in broad strokes. Poe's victims are often presented in ways that make it difficult to invest much by way of readerly sympathy or concern in them. We might be disturbed by the ways these pranks end – that a man has been walled up, or that a group of men have been set alight; but our concern is not increased by knowing that this is Fortunato or the king and his court, because they are so thinly rendered.

The macabre 'jests' that occur in Poe's tales can also be read as grotesque slapstick. The death of the king and his court in 'Hop-Frog' is a bit like a Looney Tunes sketch. Slapstick

> treats the world as if it were capricious, unpredictable, and suddenly explosive. To think of a gag as an 'irreconcilable difference' [here, Donald Crafton's work is being referred to] is to emphasise its incompatibility with our understanding of how the world normally works. Slapstick, then, opens up the possibility of the world becoming inhospitable and strange to us. (Stott 2005, 95)

This describes a world in which pain or humiliation might befall us at any moment. We are hit in the face by a pie; we are hoisted before a crowd and set on fire. It is an uncanny world – the familiar is made strange, and repressed forces erupt without warning.

Slapstick typically relies on a broad approach to comedy and character. Poe's comedy can be very broad indeed. In 'Some Words with a Mummy' (1845), the narrator having just explained his *'light* supper' of five pounds of Welsh rabbit accompanied by five bottles of stout, receives an invitation to accompany Doctor Ponnonner (805), who has received permission from the directors of the city museum to unwrap their mummy. The tale again turns on spectacle – this time, drawing on the contemporary enthusiasm for public shows of mummy unwrapping, and the wider spectacularisation of Egyptian materials (see Luckhurst 2012, 87–151). Partway through this operation, the mummy is shocked with electricity and springs to life, explaining that his name is Allamistakeo, and he has, through the superior science of the ancients, merely been in a state of extended sleep. The names and the jovial routine about the narrator's dinner suggest the tenor of the comedy here (there is also a Captain Sabretash and a Silk Buckingham involved).

If the names are cartoonish, so too are the characters. At the close of the tale, the narrator notes that 'I am heartily sick of this life and of the nineteenth century in general. Besides, I am anxious to know who will be President in 2045. As soon . . . as I shave and swallow a cup of coffee, I shall just step over to Ponnonner's and get embalmed for a couple of hundred years' (821). This is a decision that emerges not out of character or any sense of the human body as a real thing, but out of a sense of the absurd and what might provide the tale with a punchline. When confronted with the ancient and living figure who has begun to converse with them, the assembled gentlemen initially think 'it might be as well to proceed with the investigation intended' and look to carry on with their dissection of the living, speaking man before them (812). If cutting into a mummy to discover it is alive is a scenario that operates around a comic upsetting of expectations, then continuing to cut into it once you know it is alive offers a second, horrifying, comic reversal.

'King Pest: A Tale Containing an Allegory' offers characters similarly underdeveloped in the service of comedy. Two drunken sailors, Hugh Tarpaulin and his friend Legs, run out of a London alehouse without paying. The pair are described in terms that are caricature more than character. Hugh has 'stumpy bow-legs' and a 'squat, unwieldy figure' with fists 'like the fins of a sea-turtle' (241). Legs, on the other hand, is 'exceedingly thin; and might . . . have answered, when drunk, for a pennant at the mast-head' (240). This emphasis on the ridiculous departs from literary realism; Hugh and Legs seem like figures in a joke rather than fully developed human beings, and readers are likely to remain somewhat distanced from them. This flatness of character is not a fault in the writing but an approach to depicting them that facilitates both the comedy – just as it does in 'Some Words with a Mummy' – and the coming horror of the text.

Legs and Hugh flee through the streets 'holding on their drunken course with shouts and yellings', and are 'drunk beyond moral sense' (243). This again suggests the excitement of the carnivalesque and its licentious tendencies; the carnival, at least for Bakhtin, operates beyond the norms of moral sense. The flight of Hugh and Legs, in fact, takes them out of bounds and into a part of the city that has been placed under ban due to the presence of the plague. There, the pair enter the court of King Pest, located in an undertaker's. The King presides over his court, who are seated around a table lit by a chandelier fashioned from a skeleton. If Hugh and Legs are caricatures, the court are virtually gargoyles. King Pest's face is 'yellow as saffron' and he has 'a forehead so unnaturally and hideously lofty, as to have the appearance of a bonnet or crown of flesh superadded upon the natural head' (244). The image offered is simultaneously ridiculous – a king who seems to wear a bonnet – and wildly grotesque. The rest of his court suffer from similar afflictions. There is a woman 'in the last stage of a dropsy' who resembles a 'huge puncheon of October beer', with a 'terrific chasm' of a mouth so large her earrings dangle into it (245). She wears a shroud. Another has 'galloping consumption', another's cheeks drop onto his shoulders like 'huge bladders of Oporto wine' (245–6). Another is wearing a coffin. They are given silly, punning names – 'His Grace the Duke Pest-Ilential' (248), etc. The protracted descriptions are repellent, but also framed in such a way that they are grossly amusing at the same time; Stott notes the grotesque dimensions of the comic body and its proximity to the corpse, construed in Kristevan terms (Stott 2005, 86–7). The scene perversely celebrates the ways disease distorts the human form. Wine is drunk from skulls. The elaborate costumes, together with the festivity, frame the undertaker's as a carnival site. The notion that a King and his court have moved into London, which ought more properly to be under the control of the 'chivalrous . . . third Edward' (240) closely follows the Bakhtinian idea that the carnival suspends the usual hierarchies. Poe imagines pandemic as a kind of festival, with King Pest as the lord of misrule.

Hugh suggests that the King is, in fact, 'Tim Hurlygurly, the stageplayer' (251). Some critics use this moment as a key to understanding what, exactly, is going on in the undertaker's – it is a kind of performance by unemployed actors (Renza 2001, 5, 16n), a reading which understands the episode as bizarre, although perhaps still connected to the real. Others tend to gloss over the identification (Atassi 2019), which accommodates the fantastic claims and images in the tale. Regardless of whether we think Hugh is correct in identifying the scene as a performance or is making a drunken mistake and is actually encountering genuinely supernatural or surreal figures, his suggestion threatens the sovereignty of King Pest; it is refusing to play his game, to participate in the sickly carnival. If, as Bakhtin has it, there are no spectators in the carnival, then Hugh's claim threatens this understanding, and he is refusing to properly participate. Hugh's suggestion is regarded as 'Treason!' (251) by the feasters, a melee ensues, and the sailors flee once more.

The tale has been read as holding an anti-Jacksonian warning; as describing various psychic and sexual maladies, including venereal disease; or as a riposte to contemporary critical habits (see Renza 2001). In each of these readings, meaning needs to be recovered through sophisticated hermeneutic manoeuvres, and may remain indecipherable to the non-professional reader. The idea that there is a secret meaning here, is of course encouraged by the tale's subtitle – perhaps this is what allegory suggests, in a literary sense? Yet, as Poe insists elsewhere, for allegory, 'there is scarcely one respectable word to be said', going on to argue that allegory, if used by the writer at all, must be an 'under-current' that will 'never . . . show itself unless *called* to the surface' where it can reinforce the 'upper' meaning of a tale (Poe 2003, 392). For Poe, readers should avoid interpretations which transform the surface-level meaning of a story. Poe's allegory in 'King Pest' may be simpler than some critics would have us believe; the tale operates 'beyond moral sense' because it is little concerned with what is right, what is wrong, with the act of interpretation or reflection. As they are in the carnival, spectacle, bodies, the surfaces of things are more important than deeper meanings. Allowing Poe to guide us as readers, perhaps the allegory 'King Pest' presents relates only to the disorienting powers of disease and the dangers of contagion. As the sailors flee back into the city outside the ban, Legs takes with him 'the fat lady in the shroud' and Hugh sneezes 'three or four times' (252). It does not matter if the man presiding over the table is Tim Hurlygurly putting on an act, or the king of disease. The sailors have already caught their deaths and are taking the infection back into the wider city. If the carnival, for Bakhtin, is a temporary period which proceeds towards the eventual restoration of order, 'King Pest' signals a carnival threatening to expand, to extend beyond its appointed place and season as the capital is gripped by the plague. Although they flee, in the end, Hugh and Legs cannot leave the court of King Pest. It is entirely of a piece with Poe's carnivalesque approach to the Gothic that this catastrophe is presented with a kind of zany energy.

Their revelry is captured in Hugh's laughter, a curious grunting chuckle he emits while parleying with Pest's court; '"Ugh! ugh! ugh! . . . ugh! ugh! ugh! – ugh! ugh! ugh! ugh! – ugh! ugh! ugh! . . ."' (250).

The noise suggests revulsion as much as delight. It might also depict further drinking – Hugh is already heavily intoxicated and looking for more. It is curious, too, that the sound is Hugh repeating his name, over and over, but without the first letter. He is diminished by the sound he makes, less than himself. The gulping sound he makes is laughter, but a laugh gone wrong. If Poe is most famous as a critic for his idea that the tale ought to create a '*single effect*' (Poe 2003, 396), it is possible to argue that his horrors in fact aim to create laughter, albeit laughter of a very specific – Gothic – sort. Paradoxically, this is laughter that is wildly ambivalent, suggesting a range of emotions and ideas that pull in different directions. It is striking that Poe should so frequently depict this laughter.

Poe was sensitive to the ways in which laughter potentially brings people together, but also to its potential to isolate and humiliate – both Bakhtin's and McGowan's notions of carnival are points of reference. 'The Oblong Box' (1844) is a tale of swapped identities at sea. The narrator comments that the woman supposed to be Mrs Wyatt 'amused us all very much', although she is 'far oftener laughed *at* than *with*' (647). That Mrs Wyatt seems less than ladylike is shown to bring the other passengers aboard the 'Independence' together as they recognise her vulgarity. While this recognition is reasonably good-natured, it isolates Mrs Wyatt as much as it helps constitute a shipboard society for the other passengers. Hop-Frog, recalling the difficulty of Mrs Wyatt's position, combines these forms of laughter in his role at court, 'a jester to laugh *with* and a dwarf to laugh *at*' (899). In Henri Bergson's classic account, 'laughter is always the laughter of a group' and 'humor arises from ... solidifying participation in a larger unit' (Boskin 1997, 17, 18). The idea of 'superiority theory' is sometimes associated with Poe's comedy (Taylor 2015, 58–9) – that is, the idea that the person doing the laughing recognises their superiority over another and, perhaps, enjoys that other's misfortune. Poe accepts these possibilities – but also sees laughter as an assertion of fear, pain and aloneness.

At the end of 'Amontillado', Fortunato, almost completely walled up, first screams and then laughs 'a low laugh that erected the hairs upon [Montresor's] head' before speaking 'in a sad voice' and then laughs again while suggesting that his killer is, after all, only joking (853–4). The laughter emerges from Fortunato's rapidly shifting feelings as he sobers, tries to grasp his circumstance and, perhaps, attempts to save himself. The second laugh can be seen as part of Fortunato's appeal to Montresor. He endeavours to show that he appreciates the comic dimension of what is being done to him, and that, in this, he and his killer are alike, part of a group. Yet the first laugh is alarming even to his killer. It does not bring the pair together; nor is it the laughter of superiority. Indeed, it is the exact opposite of both of these at the same time: a laughter of isolation and defeat, a laugh that seems as if it should take the place of a scream.

Many of Poe's tales feature a similarly negative laughter that emerges at moments of heightened emotion and forecasts disaster. In 'The Fall of the House of Usher', Roderick sings a ballad entitled 'The Haunted Palace' which chronicles the collapse of a happy and noble house. There are 'evil things, in robes of sorrow' that attack the palace and take possession of it, and the song ends with these spectral figures leaving the palace; 'A hideous throng rush out forever, / And laugh – but smile no more' (327). Sorrows, then, laugh, but it is an unsmiling laughter, a laughter which Poe defines by the absence of the expression which seems like a natural corollary of the laugh. This unsmiling laughter characterises Roderick's emotional state. The narrator finds him walking though the castle at night, sleepless, 'a mad hilarity in his eyes – an evidently restrained *hysteria* in his whole demeanour' (331). Roderick is well aware he has shut Madeline alive in her coffin, although the narrator is not yet aware that she lives. With this in mind when we read the passage, we can see that Roderick regards his ongoing abuse of his sister as a kind of joke; her interment is the source of the mad hilarity in his eyes. At the same time, the hysteria the narrator detects in Roderick suggests his excessive emotional state – but also laughter. This is distinct from the laughter described in 'Amontillado', in that it is amused by the violence done to Madeline, rather than an acknowledgement of victimhood. Perhaps Roderick is enjoying his moment of power over his sister – but equally there is a sense that he awaits the narrator's recognition of the elaborate and fatal prank he has pulled.

Like Usher, the narrator of 'The Pit and the Pendulum' (1842) runs a gamut of emotions. As his circumstances go from bad to worse he feels concern, despair and sometimes desperate hope. The tale is notable for its fraught emotionality as much as its imaginative tortures. While the narrator watches the great blade descend upon him he reaches a state of 'frenzied pleasure', then notes he 'alternately laughed and howled' (501). Laughter signals the excessive and perverse feeling of the moment, which cannot be captured by howls alone. This is torture construed as affectively sublime. However, laughter in Poe does not always have this dimension of excess, as it does in 'Usher' or 'The Pit and the Pendulum'. It may simply be cruel, suggestive of McGowan's notion of American carnival. Poe had rehearsed the scenario of 'The Pit and the Pendulum' in the 'A Predicament' segment of 'How to Write a Blackwood Article' (1838) four years earlier, but had framed it as slapstick. In the earlier story, Poe's heroine, Psyche Zenobia, manages to get her head caught in an enormous clockface and watches as one of the hands – or as she describes it, 'the ponderous and terrific *Scythe of Time*' (293) – descends upon her neck. Psyche does not laugh as she dies, but readers are encouraged to find her death amusing. After her eyeball has exploded out of its socket from the pressure, Psyche complains it looks back on her from where it has landed with 'an insolent air of independence and contempt' (295). 'The Pit and the Pendulum' describes laughter on the page but is not likely to be seen as funny; laughter is absent from 'A Predicament', but it might be supplied by readers who are amused by the comic violence meted out on the butt of the joke. The reader is placed in the position of Roderick Usher, knowing better and amused by the struggles of the female victim, although it is unlikely that we feel this as excessively as Roderick does. Both 'The Pit and the Pendulum' and 'A Predicament' chime with Henri Bergson's idea that one of the key tropes of comedy is seeing humanity reduced to, or encrusted in, the mechanical. Both feature helpless victims literally trapped inside machines. At the same time, the figure of the human caught inside the automation recalls the connection both Jentsch and Freud make between the automatic and the uncanny (see Carroll 1999, 146). Horror and comedy, treated like this, are very difficult to separate, and what are usually regarded as distinct affective registers grotesquely combine.

Fred Botting notes the connections between the Burkean sublime and the Gothic, speaking of 'a disrupted sense of order and a discombobulation of reason, imagination and feeling: intensities, magnitudes and violent contrasts overwhelmed mental faculties – evoking terror, awe, wonder – . . . threatened the eclipse of any subjective unity' (Botting 2014, 7). These are the qualities signalled by Poe's laughter. It is often associated with the realisation of one's own undoing, or the destruction of another figure. It has very little to do with human kindness. If laughter has not always been associated with the sublime, then Poe's tales – and the various films and texts that descend from them – suggest that in the context of the American Gothic, somewhere between terror, awe, wonder, nastiness and a disbelieving, sardonic campness, laughter emerges. As Eagleton noted, the carnival laugh 'is incorporative as well as liberating' (Eagleton 1981, 149). We join Poe's figures in their terrible and cruel laughter, or in their ghastly torments. At the same time, as readers we remain free to distance ourselves from whatever horrible scenario is being depicted. We participate in Poe's carnivals, but remain removed from them, watching and maybe laughing.

Note

1. Unless otherwise noted all Poe's tales are cited from this Quinn edition.

References

Atassi, Sami H. 2019. 'Playing with the Sovereign's Plague in "King Pest"'. *Studies in American Humor* 5, no. 2: 351–71.
Bakhtin, Mikhail. 1984. *Rabelais and His World*. Trans. Hélène Iswolsky. Bloomington: Indiana University Press.
Baudelaire, Charles. 2016. *Edgar Allan Poe: Sa Vie et Ses Ouvrages*, edited by W. T. Bandy. Toronto: University of Toronto Press.
Bonaparte, Marie. 1971. *The Life and Works of Edgar Allan Poe: A Psycho-Analytic Interpretation*. Trans. John Rodker. London: Hogarth.
Boskin, Joseph. 1997. 'History and Humor'. In *The Humor Prism in 20th Century America*, edited by Joseph Boskin, 17–27. Detroit: Wayne State University Press.
Botting, Fred. 2014. *Gothic*. Second edn. Abingdon: Routledge.
Bradley, Sculley. 1997. 'Our Native Humor'. In *The Humor Prism in 20th Century America*, edited by Joseph Boskin, 46–54. Detroit: Wayne State University Press.
Bryant, John. 1996. 'Poe's Ape of UnReason: Humor, Ritual, and Culture'. *Nineteenth-Century Literature* 51, no. 1 (June): 16–52.
Carroll, Noël. 1999. 'Horror and Humor'. *The Journal of Aesthetics and Art Criticism* 57, no. 2 (Spring): 145–60.
Corman, Roger, dir. 1961. *The Pit and the Pendulum*. Alta Vista.
Corman, Roger. dir. 1964. *The Masque of the Red Death*. Alta Vista.
Eagleton, Terry. 1981. *Walter Benjamin or Towards a Revolutionary Criticism*. London: NLB.
Jackson, Michael, perf., and John Landis, dir. 1983. 'Thriller'. Epic Records.
Jones, Timothy. 2015. *The Gothic and the Carnivalesque in American Culture*. Cardiff: University of Wales Press.
Luckhurst, Roger. 2012. *The Mummy's Curse: The True History of a Dark Fantasy*. Oxford: Oxford University Press.
McGowan, Philip. 2001. *American Carnival: Seeing and Reading American Culture*. Westport, CT: Greenwood Press.
Poe, Edgar Allan. [1846] 1984. 'The Cask of Amontillado'. In *Poetry and Tales*, edited by Patrick F. Quinn, 848–54. New York: Library of America.
Poe, Edgar Allan. [1839] 1984. 'The Fall of the House of Usher'. In *Poetry and Tales*, edited by Patrick F. Quinn, 317–36. New York: Library of America.
Poe, Edgar Allan. [1849] 1984. 'Hop-Frog'. In *Poetry and Tales*, edited by Patrick F. Quinn, 899–908. New York: Library of America.
Poe, Edgar Allan. [1838] 1984. 'How to Write a Blackwood Article'. In *Poetry and Tales*, edited by Patrick F. Quinn, 278–97. New York: Library of America.

Poe, Edgar Allan. [1835] 1984. 'King Pest: A Tale Containing an Allegory'. In *Poetry and Tales*, edited by Patrick F. Quinn, 240–52. New York: Library of America.

Poe, Edgar Allan. [1839] 1984. 'The Man That Was Used Up'. In *Poetry and Tales*, edited by Patrick F. Quinn, 307–16. New York: Library of America.

Poe, Edgar Allan. [1842] 1984. 'The Masque of the Red Death'. In *Poetry and Tales*, edited by Patrick F. Quinn, 485–90. New York: Library of America.

Poe, Edgar Allan. [1841] 1984. 'Never Bet the Devil Your Head'. In *Poetry and Tales*, edited by Patrick F. Quinn, 458–67. New York: Library of America.

Poe, Edgar Allan. [1844] 1984. 'The Oblong Box'. In *Poetry and Tales*, edited by Patrick F. Quinn, 643–54. New York: Library of America.

Poe, Edgar Allan. [1842] 1984. 'The Pit and the Pendulum'. In *Poetry and Tales*, edited by Patrick F. Quinn, 491–505. New York: Library of America.

Poe, Edgar Allan. [1845] 1984. 'Some Words with a Mummy'. In *Poetry and Tales*, edited by Patrick F. Quinn, 805–21. New York: Library of America.

Poe, Edgar Allan. [1845] 1984. 'The System of Doctor Tarr and Professor Fether'. In *Poetry and Tales*, edited by Patrick F. Quinn, 699–716. New York: Library of America.

Poe, Edgar Allan. [1839] 1984. 'William Wilson'. In *Poetry and Tales*, edited by Patrick F. Quinn, 337–57. New York: Library of America.

Poe, Edgar Allan. 2003. 'Review of "Twice Told Tales"'. In *The Fall of the House of Usher and Other Writings: Poems, Tales, Essays and Reviews*, edited by David Galloway, 387–97. London: Penguin.

Renza, Louis A. 2001. 'Poe's King: Playing It Close to the Pest'. *The Edgar Allan Poe Review* 2, no. 2 (Fall): 3–18.

Simon, David Carroll. 2019. 'Vicious Pranks: Comedy and Cruelty in Rabelais and Shakespeare'. *Studies in Philology* 116, no. 3 (Summer): 423–50.

Stott, Andrew. 2005. *Comedy*. New York: Routledge.

Taylor, Jonathan. 2015. 'His "Last Jest": On Edgar Allan Poe, "Hop-Frog" and Laughter'. *Poe Studies* 48: 58–82.

Chapter 5

Dickens and the Comic Gothic
Michael Hollington

Some years ago, I wrote a book on Dickens in relation to the idea of the Grotesque (listed below in the bibliography) – a concept, I believe, that can be considered as in close alignment with that of the Comic Gothic examined in these pages. They share in particular an essential hybridity, in which intrinsically contradictory generic modes fuse and interact. This is indicated by the obvious presence of apparent oxymoron in the case of the term 'Comic Gothic', and in that of 'Grotesque' by a body of theoretical writing which constantly points to hybridity as a defining feature of the tradition it examines. In my book I chose to single out for detailed consideration two major theorists, Mikhail Bakhtin and Wolfgang Kayser, both of whom – albeit with somewhat different emphases – focus on the Gothic elements of the hybrid artistic compound they identify as the 'Grotesque' – thereby exemplifying the connection between the two concepts.

Dickens – unlike, say, Henry James – was not a writer to concern himself unduly with conceptual generalisation or elaborate commentary on his artistic method. It is thus of significance that the word 'grotesque' occurs with relative frequency in his writing, both in the fiction itself and in his writing about it. A *locus classicus* of this is provided in a letter of September 1860, when he describes to his friend John Forster how the fundamental idea of *Great Expectations* first occurred to him: 'such a very fine, new, and grotesque idea has opened upon me' (Dickens 1979, 310) where the context clearly suggests that 'grotesque' had value for him as a term for an artistic tendency and as a method of working.

Turning to Dickens's explicit relation to the Gothic tradition, I should like to reiterate an assertion I made in the entry on Dickens in *The Encyclopedia of The Gothic*, that Dickens in the 1830s 'effected decisive and lasting change in the history of Gothic fiction' (Hughes, Punter and Smith 2016, 176). This can be called the 'inward turn of the Gothic', a decisive move away from exotic locations in time and space in order to focus on the marvellous and terrifying in everyday reality. *Sketches by Boz* provides the essential evidence for this significant change of emphasis: in 'Criminal Courts' the narrator passes Newgate prison and compares in his thoughts Elizabeth Fry the prison visitor and reformer with Ann Radcliffe the novelist: 'We have a great respect for Mrs Fry but she certainly ought to have written more romances than Mrs Radcliffe' (Dickens 1995a, 230).

In making this shift, Dickens clearly justifies his inclusion in the authors grouped as 'Romantic Realists' in Donald Fanger's influential *Dostoevsky and Romantic Realism*. Here, too, is hybridity, but Fanger does relatively little to explore the latent comic element in the compound – thoroughly on view already in *Sketches by Boz*, in which Dickens – from a 'Comic Gothic' perspective – perceives hackney cabs as equivalent to castles in Otranto or Udolpho: 'Cabs whizzed about, with the "fare" as carefully boxed up behind two glazed calico curtains as any mysterious picture in one of Mrs Radcliffe's castles' (Dickens 1995a, 541). Indeed, at all times the move away from the conventional medieval trappings of Gothic fiction to the mundanities of observed reality clearly invites deployment of comic bathos.

I believe that every one of Dickens's novels can yield rewarding insights from the perspective of the 'Comic Gothic'. However, I shall give priority in what follows to the first phase of his development as a writer, in which the separate elements that make up the amalgam are most clearly on view and I shall pay closest attention to the relevant detail of one novel only, *The Pickwick Papers* (1837). With *Gargantua* (1534) or *Don Quixote* or *Ulysses* (1922), Dickens's first book is often regarded as one of the great comic novels of the world, while at the same time, unlike these works, it is obvious to everyone that its inset stories owe much to the distinctive characteristics of Gothic fiction, whose first phase was beginning to fade as Dickens began to write.

This dual aspect of the novel is an initial reason for regarding *The Pickwick Papers* as a major specimen of the Comic Gothic mode. But interestingly, as the novel develops, the inset stories gradually decrease in number and frequency, especially after Pickwick's imprisonment, when we enter the world of Mrs Fry, where the horrors of everyday life exceed those of the writer's invention. It is as though we can trace the novelist feeling his way towards a fusion of disparate styles, and thus establishing what will become the essential mode of his writing. It is from this perspective that I approach *The Pickwick Papers* as a 'Comic Gothic' overture to his achievement.

Despite its comedy, *The Pickwick* Papers is in a very particular and peculiar way an extremely violent book, with references on almost every page to death, sadism and cruelty towards human beings and animals, to suicide and cannibalism, as well as to mere fisticuffs. I believe Dickens himself was quite conscious of this incongruity, and even foreshadowed it in his very first chapter by emphasising the essential adversarial character of Pickwickian meetings, modelled as they appear to be on what passes for debate in the Houses of Parliament at Westminster. Later, when Pickwick mistakenly invades a woman's bedroom at midnight, causing comic expressions of horror from her at the prospect of a duel between him and Magnus, the novel reminds us of this opening by remarking that

> if the middle-aged lady had mingled much with the busy world, or profited at all, by the manners and customs of those who make the laws and set the fashions, she would have known that this sort of ferocity is just the most harmless thing in nature; but as she had lived for the most part in the country, and never read the parliamentary debates, she was little versed in these particular refinements of civilized life. (Dickens 1999a, 318)

In other words, in this novel, we are in the world of Mrs Fry, where violence, despite contemporary pretensions about progress and the civilising effect of social manners, is shown in the 1820s and 30s to be as British as apple pie.

What is distinctive, though, in keeping with its intentions as comic writing, is that the novel contains no really significant deaths. All the Pickwickians and all the Wardles and Wellers are still alive and thriving at novel's end, despite whatever violent and humiliating experiences they may have been through in the course of it. Innumerable deaths are referred to anecdotally, or in the inset stories, but I can think of two examples only where these are of characters who appear in the main narrative, neither of them any more than as bit-part players. There is the significant death of the Chancery prisoner in the Fleet, who lets out his room to Pickwick, and that of Tony Weller's second wife, the landlady of the Marquess of Granby, stepmother of Sam.

The virtual absence of significant deaths in the book is all the more surprising when we take into account the not very frequently noticed fact that the book is humorously entitled in full as *The Posthumous Papers of the Pickwick Club*. 'Who has died, then?' the reader may well ask in puzzlement, and look for corpses, finding a logical answer to this comic whodunnit only at the very end of the novel, with the dissolution of the society: it must be the club itself rather than any particular member of it that has died. But there is another, even less frequently noticed feature of that full title: on the front page of the first, 1837 edition it is printed in Gothic script and set apart from the rest of the title.

What can be inferred from this, I believe, is that violence in *The Pickwick Papers* is a running joke, to be written in a special script, as it were, as an essential ingredient of the 'Comic Gothic'. It is above all comic violence and comic death, comic suicide and comic cannibalism, that form so important and so distinctive an aspect of *The Pickwick Papers*. Nowadays we might describe the book as an extended essay in black humour; but in Dickens's time, with the vogue for Gothic fiction gradually receding, or metamorphosing into variants that effected a blend with other modes, notably that of realist writing, the novel is best thought of, indeed, by means of this term. It is 'Comic Gothic' that I propose to examine here, starting from a particular focus on the idea of 'Gallows Humour', but radiating out from it in a manner that has resonance throughout Dickens's work.

'Gallows Humour' is a term translated from the German *Galgenhumor* and imported into English a century or so ago, according to the *Oxford English Dictionary*, and often employed by writers who have a special relationship to German culture – for instance, W. H. Auden, the author of a major essay on *The Pickwick Papers*. Whether or not Dickens was familiar with much relevant work from German language sources may be in partial doubt; he certainly, however, like many other writers of his time, including Edgar Allan Poe, thought of Germany as an important source of modern terror fiction, and he had through his friend Thomas Carlyle at least an acquaintance with some of its major representatives. What is absolutely clear is that on numerous occasions he employs it in *Pickwick* as a staple of Gothic comedy.

Perhaps the most telling instance is provided by Sam Weller's very first 'inimitable' Wellerism. Introduced as he cleans boots in the early morning in the courtyard of the White Hart Inn in London, he is asked to prioritise those that belong to room 22. 'No, no, reg'lar rotation, as Jack Ketch said, ven he tied the men up', is Sam's reply (Dickens 1999a, 131). Jack Ketch was the most prominent and famous public executioner employed by Charles II, notorious ever after the 1680s as an emblematic figure standing for all dispensers of officially sanctioned violent deaths, hangings and beheadings alike. He survived in popular culture in a variety of ways, including notably in Punch and Judy shows, which can be seen as an important source of much of the comic slapstick violence of *Pickwick*. Indeed, at one point Mr Pickwick is thought by bystanders to give his name as 'Punch', as he mutters 'cold punch' before falling asleep in the barrow that transports him to the shoot.

References to public execution through hanging are found, first, in a text that is not comic at all – the inset story entitled 'The Madman's Manuscript', that seems to reproduce 'horror Gothic' in its purest form, its 'mad' narrator gloating over the strength in his arms and hands that enables him to strangle his victims more decisively than either the hangman's noose or the executioner's sword. 'Show me the monarch whose angry frown was ever hated like the glare of a madman's eye', he asks, 'whose cord and axe were ever half so sure as a madman's gripe' (Dickens 1999a, 149–50). He takes concomitant sadistic pleasure in the idea of someone wrongly hanged for killing his wife as a result of a crime that he himself commits, 'some sane man swinging in the wind for some deed he never did' (Dickens 1999a, 152). Comic versions of the same motif may be said to culminate in an emblematic gargoyle of it in the Fleet prison. Asking directions to the lodgings originally assigned to him, Pickwick asks a potboy 'which is twenty-seven, my good fellow', and receives the following reply: 'five doors further on ... There's the likeness of a man being hung, and smoking a pipe the while, chalked outside the door' (Dickens 1999a, 560).

Here, the victim's apparent determination to enjoy minimal pleasures up until the very last moment of life illustrates a major principle of gallows humour – its focus from its chosen perspective on the inherent paradoxical absurdity of the very last moments of a life. 'Yours until death', is the humorous caption to the frontispiece of Charles Whitehead's 1836 *Autobiography of Jack Ketch*, which Dickens certainly knew, because Whitehead was originally approached to write the text to accompany Seymour's illustrations to what was to become *The Pickwick Papers* and may have suggested Dickens to the publishers Chapman and Hall as the man to replace him. A commonplace phrase that is meant to signify long-standing fidelity is here made amusing in the context of imminent death – as is another in similar fashion in a characteristic Wellerism in Chapter 19: 'If you walley my precious life don't upset me, as the gentleman said to the driver, when they was a carryin' him to Tyburn' (Dickens 1999a, 251) – Tyburn being the site of all public hangings up until 1783. Conversely, however, humour may be derived from the notation of extraordinary behaviour in the hours before death on the gallows, as observed for instance by Mr Weller senior of a colleague who did something as strange as write poetry just before his execution: 'I never know'd a respectable coachman as wrote poetry, 'cept one, as made an affectin' copy o' werses the night afore he wos hung for a highway robbery' (Dickens 1999a, 437).

But then, as Weller senior observes to his son as he advises him to commit suicide rather than marry, and to choose poison rather than possible alternatives, 'Hanging's wulgar' (Dickens 1999a, 308). It is more noble, it would seem, to have your head chopped off – the paradigm of aristocratic victims being of course King Charles I, the only British monarch to have suffered this fate. Dickens was acutely aware of having been given his Christian name, and perhaps sensitive about this, judging from the numerous references in his work, notably in the case of mad little Mr Dick in *David Copperfield*, with the -ens of his creator's name chopped off in his own, who imagines his head stuffed with the contents of King Charles's. He is referred to very early on in *The Pickwick Papers* by Jingle, who exclaims 'Heads, heads, take care of your heads', as the coach party passes through the short archway of the Golden Cross Inn, and who tells the ludicrous story of the lady who forgot to duck hers while she was eating a sandwich, and so left her five children and a sandwich bereft, 'with no mouth to put it in' (Dickens1999a, 26).

Lewis Carroll's 'Comic Gothic' Queen of Hearts in *Alice in Wonderland*, with her knee-jerk command of 'cut off his head' or 'cut off her head,' may well owe something to a reading of *The Pickwick Papers*, where such impulses abound. These move, in fact, beyond joke gargoyle references to execution – as in such Wellerisms as that in Chapter 23 concerning the public sphere ('it's over, and can't be helped, and that's one consolation, as they alvays says in Turkey, ven they cuts the wrong man's head off' (Dickens 1999a, 307)) or that in Chapter 28 concerning the private ('There now ve look compact and comfortable, as the father said ven he cut his little boy's head off to cure him o'squintin' (Dickens 1999a, 370)) – to repeated expressions of an actual comic desire to knock off someone's head. There is, for example, Sam in relation to Job Trotter ('What have you got to say to me, afore I knock your head off?' (Dickens 1991, 310)), or Tupman in relation to Jingle, suffering the latter's 'cutting in' ahead of him with Rachel: 'when at last he laid his aching temples between the sheets, he thought, with horrid delight on the satisfaction it would afford him, to have Jingle's head at that moment between the feather bed and the mattress' (Dickens 1999a, 113).

Latent violence, at least, is indeed a feature even of the central benevolent patriarchs of the book, Wardle and Pickwick, and a lot of energy is devoted by themselves and others to restraining it from full expression, notably by Sam Weller, who manages to keep his master's violent outrage at the wrongs he surveys in some sort of check. But I shall consider this later; meanwhile, it is time to enjoy some of the many hilarious violent deaths that contribute so significantly to this book as a 'Comic Gothic' masterpiece.

The spinster aunt Rachel at Dingley Dell can be said to set the tone of these when she inquires about Tupman, who has been wooing her, and has been subsequently wounded by Winkle: 'Is he dead? Is he – ha, ha, ha! Here the spinster aunt burst into fit number two, of hysteric laughter, interspersed with screams' (Dickens 1999a, 97). But it is

Sam Weller, with his own philosophy of laughter at the misfortunes of others – 'avay vith mellincholly, as the little boy said said ven his school-missis died' (Dickens 1999a, 590) – who is the most prolific purveyor of death jokes, regularly linking in his trademark Wellerisms everyday banal cliché to violent or murderous extremes. The most famous of these may be his gloss on the phrase 'business first, pleasure afterwards' – 'as King Richard the Third said ven he stabbed the t'other king in the Tower, afore he smothered the babbies' (Dickens 1999a, 329), but there are many more, including 'wery sorry to 'casion any personal inconwenience, Ma'am, as the housebreaker said to the old lady vhen he put her on the fire; but as me and my governor's only just come to town, and is just going away agin, it can't be helped you see' (Dickens 1999a, 348).

But it is Sam's counterpart Jingle who is the first to tap this major humorous vein in a big way in Chapter 2, where almost all his comic inventions in response to the Pickwickian thirst for information are about death. These begin, as we have seen, with the orphaned sandwich, but quickly modulate into references to violence and death in France during the July revolution (which in 1827, the year in which the scene of this chapter is supposedly set, had not yet taken place) and above all in Spain, as the would-be Don Giovanni Tupman asks him to detail his 'conquests' there. Jingle claims to have travelled with a stomach pump in his luggage, in case any lady should have need of it as a result of taking poison after falling for him and being jilted. But alas, it is of no avail, or rather, itself merely serves to hasten the death of Donna Christina, who is supposedly hopelessly enamoured of him: 'never recovered the stomach pump – undermined constitution – fell a victim' (Dickens 1999a, 28).

Jingle's ingenuity in the matter of death jokes is such that, in order to gratify Winkle's sporting pretensions in the same manner as he does Tupman's would-be Don Juanism, he invents the counter instance of a miraculous dog he once kept who was able to read a notice announcing a gamekeeper's intention to shoot all dogs and so avoid the fate intended for him. But perhaps the greatest triumph of Jingle's genius as a death-joker in this chapter is the story he tells of Don Bolaro Fizzgig, the father of Donna Christina. He too dies, but not, as in the Mozart opera that enjoyed such a vogue in London in the 1820s – with Shelley and Mary Shelley for example – at the hands of his daughter's seducer. His body is nowhere to be found, in a manner not inappropriate to a book where we search in vain for the corpse of posthumous Pickwickians:

> sudden disappearance – talk of the whole city – search made everywhere – without success – public fountain in the great square suddenly ceased playing – weeks elapsed – still a stoppage – workmen employed to clean

it – water drawn off – father-in-law discovered sticking head first in the main pipe, with a full confession in his right boot – took him out, and the fountain played again, as well as other. (Dickens 1999a, 28)

Here, at one stroke, Jingle introduces two great Dickensian 'Comic Gothic' specialities – the comic suicide and the comic death by drowning. To take the former first, it is the subject of persistent gargoyles throughout the text, from Tupman's joke suicide note after the elopement of Rachel with Jingle onward. 'Life has become insupportable to me', he writes alarmingly to the Pickwickians, who rush to his side in Cobham, only to discover him in front of a roast fowl 'looking as unlike a man who has taken his leave of the world, as possible' (Dickens 1999a 144, 146). He is to be succeeded in the same chapter by someone who does indeed commit suicide, but for the most absurd reason, that is, his inability to decipher the Bill Stumps stone – 'one enthusiastic individual cut himself off prematurely, in despair at being unable to fathom its meaning' (Dickens 1999a, 157). Sam Weller has a repertoire of comic suicide stories that include poisoning oneself – 'there's nothing so refreshing as sleep, as the servant-girl said afore she drank the egg-cup full o' laudanum' (Dickens 1999a, 213) – or eating oneself to death, as in the Boswell-inspired story of the 'the man as killed his-self on principle' by eating three shillings worth of crumpets before blowing his brains out (Dickens 1999a, 584). The link to Gothic fiction is provided by the narrator of the *Tale of the Queer Client*, who tells the story of a man who rented an apartment in which he could not sleep and finds out why by opening a closet where 'sure enough, standing bolt upright in the corner, was the last tenant, with a little bottle clasped firmly in his hand, and his face livid with the hue of a painful death' – and who, on the conclusion of his tale looks round at the attentively listening Pickwickians 'with a smile of grim delight' (Dickens 1999a, 276).

But, of course, suicide and death by drowning are frequently linked in the work of a man who was apparently irresistibly drawn to the morgue in Paris to inspect the corpses regularly recovered from the Seine. That same 'Queer Client' narrator, a connoisseur and devotee of gruesome deaths, makes the connection quite explicitly and for once in a serious manner and tone, when he asks Pickwick 'how many vain pleaders for mercy, do you think have turned away heart-sick from the lawyer's office, to find a resting place in the Thames?' (Dickens 1999a, 274). His supposition of their frequency gains support from Dismal Jemmy in Chapter 5, as he asks Pickwick 'Did it ever strike you on such a morning as this, that drowning would be happiness and peace?', a question that quickly modulates back into comic mode: '"God bless me, no!" replied

Mr Pickwick, edging a little from the balustrade, as the possibility of the dismal man's tipping him over by way of experiment, occurred to him rather forcibly' (Dickens 1999a, 71).

And indeed, that assumption, stated at the beginning of *The Old Curiosity Shop* as a temptation for any down-and-outer who may 'have heard or read in old time that drowning was not a hard death, but of all means of suicide the easiest and best' (Dickens 1995b, 4), makes regular comic appearance in early Dickens. There is the tragicomic Watkins Tottle in *Sketches by Boz*, disappointed in love, his body found in the Regent's Canal with 'a matrimonial advertisement from a lady, which appeared to have been cut out of a Sunday paper' (Dickens 1995a, 535); the hilarious Alfred Muntle aka Mantalini in *Nicholas Nickleby*, who declares himself willing 'to fill my pockets with change for a sovereign in halfpence and drown myself in the Thames' (Dickens 1990, 430); and the comically feeble Mr Chuckster in *The Old Curiosity Shop*, who expresses his jealousy of Kit Garland by declaring 'If I hadn't more of these qualities that comically endear a man to man, than our articled clerk has, I'd steal a Cheshire cheese, tie it round my neck, and drown myself' (Dickens 1995b, 409). These find their counterpart on several occasions in *Pickwick*: Sam Weller, for instance, in pleading his cause to Arabella, says that Winkle 'vishes he may be somethin'-unpleasanted if he don't drown himself' if he cannot see her (Dickens 1999a, 525) – and when it comes to telling his father what he would do to Stiggins if it were him, Weller is at pains to stress his magnanimity in offering the 'easiest and best' of deaths: 'I wouldn't be too hard on him, at first; I'd just drop him in the water-butt, and put the lid on' (Dickens 1999a, 360).

In order to reserve space for brief consideration of at least one other of Dickens's early 'Comic Gothic' novels, I cannot consider more than a sample of the innumerable death jokes in *Pickwick Papers*. Two categories in particular get scant justice here – jokes about animal deaths and cruelty to animals on the one hand and cannibal jokes on the other – both of them worthy of further consideration.

The Pickwick Papers presents a living and speaking universe, in which not only humans but animals and plants and even things have voices – and where violence and cruelty reign too. In Sam Weller's discourse, for instance, old turkeys pun with stoic humour on the word 'tough' as they confront their own execution: 'I'm pretty tough, that's vun consolation, as the wery old turkey remarked ven the farmer said he was afeerd he should be obliged to kill him, for the London market' (Dickens 1999a, 433). He attempts to cheer up Pickwick with the prospect of Arabella's imminent appearance with an animal analogy that presents an opposite case in the animal kingdom: 'If you know'd who was near, Sir, I rayther think you'd change your note; as the hawk remarked to himself with a cheerful laugh, ven he heerd the robin redbreast a singing round the corner' (Dickens 1999a, 626). An anonymous ostler speciously recommends a horse to Mr Pickwick by claiming that 'he wouldn't shy if he was to meet a vaggin-load of monkeys, with their tales burnt off' (Dickens 1999a, 73). And we may close this section with a return to the theme of comic drowning by means of a delicious tidbit in another early novel, this time *Oliver Twist*, where Bumble woos Mrs Corney by declaring 'that any cat, or kitten, that could live with you, ma'am, and *not* be fond of its home, must be a ass . . . I would drown it myself, with pleasure' (Dickens 1999b, 181).

For cannibalism jokes, we need look no further than the 'Sawbones' episodes of the novel involving the trainee surgeons Bob Sawyer and Benjamin Allen – rich exemplars of 'Comic Gothic' in *The Pickwick Papers*. 'Nothing like dissecting, to give one an appetite', declares Bob as he tucks into a hearty repast in which the conversation, by means of a 'by the bye' from Ben, effects wholesale confusion between the body parts of the chicken being devoured and the items of human anatomy which they are learning to dissect. 'Have you finished that leg yet?' he asks, and Bob replies, with his mouth full, 'It's a very muscular one for a child.' 'I've put my name down for an arm, at our place', continues Ben, 'only we can't get hold of any fellow that wants a head. I wish you'd take it', and Bob replies by confessing he 'wouldn't mind a brain, but I couldn't stand a whole head' (Dickens 1999a, 392–3), employing the deliciously vague word 'stand' in a way that permits us to conclude that it is his stomach that cannot take it.

But the presiding genius of cannibalism in the novel is Joe the fat boy – he who says he 'wants to make your flesh creep' to the elderly mother of Mr Wardle (who reminds him that she has always provided him with plenty of food) as 'a very blood-thirsty way of showing one's gratitude' (Dickens 1999a, 114). He wears a perpetual 'leer' on his face that seems to signify a desire to devour everything and everyone about him – including Sam Weller himself when he praises Mr Wardle's bountiful provision of food. 'Don't he breed nice pork!' Joe chimes in, as if Wardle were himself a pig, as he bestows meanwhile 'a semi-cannibalistic leer at Mr Weller, as he thought of the roast legs and gravy' (Dickens 1999a, 374) – belonging to whom unspecified.

I close this discussion of *Pickwick* as a 'Comic Gothic' masterpiece by turning from the numerous humorous references to cannibalism in this book to a serious one. The comic reference to the giant Blunderbore in the scene which finds Pickwick in the lady's bedroom unwittingly making fee-fi-fo-fum noises in the manner of that cannibal monster 'expressing his opinion that it was time to lay the cloth' for his meal of human blood and bones (Dickens 1999a, 303), has its serious counterpart in the representation of the prisoner in Chancery who lets out his room in the Fleet for Pickwick's use. The prisoner's 'sharp and thin' bones are the consequence of his having been slowly devoured by the allegorical cannibal giants of contemporary social injustice: 'the iron teeth of confinement and privation had been slowly filing them down for twenty years' (Dickens 1999a, 564).

It is important to see that in *The Pickwick Papers* violence is as much a part of the disposition of positive, even heroic characters like Wardle, Sam and Pickwick himself, as it is of its numerous caricature-like sinners and villains. It is clear that Dodson and Fogg, for instance, regularly arouse this strain in Pickwick's make-up whenever they come into his orbit. We learn on one such occasion, when he is invited to strike them, that 'as Fogg put himself very temptingly within the reach of Mr Pickwick's clenched fist, there is little doubt that that gentleman would have complied with his earnest energy, but for the interposition of Sam' (Dickens 1999a, 265). Earlier, on the way to Dingley Dell, Pickwick had cursed the horse that overturns the Pickwickians' carriage, and 'more than once he had calculated the probable amount of the expense he would incur by cutting his throat', and as they arrive near their destination with 'torn clothes, lacerated faces, dusty shoes, exhausted looks ... the temptation to destroy him ... rushed upon his mind with ten-fold force' (Dickens 1999a, 78). Of Wardle, when it is discovered that Jingle has eloped with Rachel, someone screams out 'Don't let him go alone he'll kill someone', but it is an irony that it should be Pickwick who fulfils this role, for after they have caught up with him he too expresses murderous intent – 'If ever I meet that man again I'll ...' – which fortunately remains unrealised (Dickens 1999a, 122, 127). Once more Sam comes to the rescue, as 'in the frenzy of his rage, he [Pickwick] hurled the inkstand madly forward, and followed it up himself. But Mr Jingle had disappeared, and he found himself caught up in the arms of Sam' (Dickens1999a, 142).

However, in this context, the suspicion begins to dawn on the reader that the import of all the violence in the book is by no means entirely negative. *The Pickwick Papers* is a young man's book, begun when its author had just turned twenty-four, and in portraying the elderly man who is its hero Dickens by no means identifies age with decrepitude but, on the contrary, converts him into a comic version of a kind of theatrical juvenile lead. 'You're such a fiery sort of young fellow', says Wardle of Pickwick, whom Arabella in turn describes as 'wild and fierce' (Dickens 1999a, 712, 724). Climbing over walls to rescue maidens in danger of abduction, or to intercede on behalf of thwarted lovers ('the happiness of young people … has ever been the chief pleasure of my life', he declares at the end of the book (Dickens 1999a, 749)), Pickwick seems to have drunk of the fabled medieval *Jungbrunnen* (fountain of youth) depicted by Lukas Cranach. Out with Tupman on 'the sort of afternoon that might induce a couple of elderly gentlemen, in a lonely field, to take off their great coats and play at leapfrog in pure lightness of heart and gaiety … we firmly believe that had Mr Tupman at that moment proffered "a back," Mr Pickwick would have accepted his offer with avidity' (Dickens 1999a, 366).

Thus, *The Pickwick Papers* is a book of life, and it is clear that violence is shown in it as an ineluctable constituent of the energies that go into the making of vigorous life – purposeful, even, when it is steered into violent hatred of injustice. The innumerable comic variations it plays upon violence and death act as a kind of attempt at exorcising the inevitability of them. Thus it is that on the occasion of the one significant death scene contained in it – that of the Chancery prisoner – the dying man's command is to 'open the window', so that 'the noise of carriages and carts, the rattle of wheels, the cries of men and boys; all the busy sounds of a mighty multitude instinct with life and occupation, blended into one deep murmur, floated into the room'. Thus, as at the very ending of *Little Dorrit*, the streets of London make their 'usual uproar', and there is melancholy, but nonetheless 'above the hoarse loud hum arose from time to time a boisterous laugh' (Dickens 1999a, 594).

That 'boisterous laugh' is still very much in evidence in *Barnaby Rudge*, first conceived in 1836, more or less simultaneously with *Pickwick*, but not actually completed and published until five years later. I shall comment briefly by way of conclusion on the emblematic embodiment of 'Comic Gothic' to be found in the conception of Barnaby's pet raven, Grip. 'Always merry' (Dickens 1993, 447), according to his master, he represents a choric apotheosis of hybridity: natural, supernatural, human, avian, comic, Gothic – so much so that he also has a role in the later history of the genre through the impact he made on Poe. We are told that Grip is central to this tale, catering to the 'appetite for the marvellous and love of the terrible which have probably been among the natural characteristics of mankind since the creation of the world' (Dickens 1993, 420). His first appearance, at Varden's workshop where Edward Chester is taken after being attacked and wounded on the London streets, immediately establishes his essential ambiguous duality, for Varden is torn between 'admiration for the bird and fear of him'. 'Do you see how he looks at me, as if he knew what I was saying?', he asks, asserting not only that the raven has human attributes but that his leitmotiv 'I'm a devil,

I'm a devil, I'm a devil' can be taken as evidence of Grip's supernatural powers ('"I more than half believe he speaks the truth. Upon my word I do," said Varden'). For as he performs his assertion of diabolical agency he is shown to be possessed by a spirit of humorous supernatural delight in his own evil as 'he flapped his wings against his sides as if he were bursting with laughter' (Dickens 1993, 61).

Functioning as a humorous parodic commentator on the main events and characters, Grip will later be shown as a critical figure in a tableau in the eminently Gothic surroundings of the room where Reuben Haredale was murdered, 'dull, dark, and sombre; heavy with worm-eaten books; deadened and shut in by faded hangings, muffling every sound; shadowed mournfully by trees whose rustling boughs gave ever and anon a spectral knocking at the glass; [that] wore, beyond all others in the house, a ghostly, gloomy affair'. Here he takes his place with the trio of Geoffrey Haredale, Mrs Rudge and Barnaby: 'the very raven, who had hopped upon the table and with the air of some old necromancer appeared to be profoundly studying a great folio volume that lay open on a desk, was strictly in unison with the rest, and looked like the embodied spirit of evil biding his time of mischief' (Dickens 1993, 202) – a unison that clearly illuminates the scene from the perspective of the 'Comic Gothic'.

References

Bakhtin, Mikhail. 1965. *Rabelais and his World*. Trans. Hélène Iswolsky. Boston: MIT Press.
Dickens, Charles. 1990. *Nicholas Nickleby*, edited by Paul Schlicke. Oxford: Oxford University Press (The World's Classics).
Dickens, Charles. 1993. *Barnaby Rudge*, intro. Cedric Watts. Ware: Wordsworth Classics.
Dickens, Charles. 1995a. *Sketches by Boz*, edited by Dennis Walder. London: Penguin.
Dickens, Charles. 1995b. *The Old Curiosity Shop*, intro. Peter Preston. Ware: Wordsworth Classics.
Dickens, Charles. 1997. *The Letters of Charles Dickens: Volume 9*, edited by Graham Storey. Oxford: Oxford University Press.
Dickens, Charles. 1999a. *The Pickwick Papers*, edited by Mark Wormald. Oxford: Oxford University Press (The World's Classics).
Dickens, Charles. 1999b. *Oliver Twist*, edited by Kathleen Tillotson. Oxford: Oxford University Press (The World's Classics).
Fanger, Donald. 1965. *Dostoevsky and Romantic Realism*. Cambridge MA: Harvard University Press.
Hollington, Michael. 1984. *Dickens and the Grotesque*. London: Croom Helm. Reissued 2014 by Routledge in the Routledge Revivals series.

Hollington, Michael. 2016. 'Dickens'. In *The Encyclopedia of the Gothic*, edited by William Hughes, David Punter and Andrew Smith, 176–81. Chichester: Wiley Blackwell.

Hughes, William, David Punter and Andrew Smith, eds. 2016. *The Encyclopedia oft he Gothic*. Chichester: Wiley Blackwell.

Kayser, Wolfgang. 1963. *The Grotesque in Art and Literature*. Trans. Ulrich Weißstein. Bloomington: Indiana University Press.

Part II

From the 1890s to the Twenty-First Century

Chapter 6

Oscar Wilde: Performing the Gothic
Neil Sammells

Oscar Wilde's *The Picture of Dorian Gray* (1891), that 'tale spawned from the leprous literature of the French Decadents, [...] heavy with the mephitic odours of moral and spiritual putrefaction' (Mason 1971, 65), is a sustained admixture of popular Gothic fiction, caustic social satire and melodrama, combined with Wilde's distinctive verbal wit and a certain aesthetic portentousness. In it the threat and frisson of the Gothic *uncanny* (the supernatural presence of the ageing portrait; Dorian's own seemingly perpetual juvenescence) and the Gothic arc of the narrative are used by Wilde to interrogate the super-sophisticated surfaces of life in London, the imperial metropolis, at the century's end. Wilde's deployment of familiar Gothic motifs in *Dorian Gray* should not surprise us, as I shall explain; though the comic and stylistic uses to which he puts these motifs and conventions are distinctive. What is perhaps more surprising, and itself revealing, is that the novel emerges partly from Wilde's previous comic and knowing engagement with the Gothic in his 1887 short stories, *The Canterville Ghost* and *Lord Arthur Savile's Crime*: an aesthetic manoeuvre in which his comic strategies slide from the campy to the camp Gothic, recalibrating the genre's balance of laughter and terror.

Prefacing Camp

Susan Sontag's 1964 'Notes on Camp' and its companion piece 'On Style' (published a year later) remain among the best and most fertile brief introductions to Wilde's work, as well as to the dandyism which is performed so elegantly by Lord Henry Wotton in *Dorian Gray*. For Sontag, Camp is a precise mode of aestheticism, one which sees the world 'not in terms of beauty, but in terms of the degree of artifice, of stylization' (Sontag 1983, 106). Indeed, the style of a particular work of art is foundational to a degree that its 'content' is not: it is style, she says, which is the 'signature of the artist's will' (Sontag 1983, 150). The value of Camp lies in the way it undermines crudely ethical valuations of art and people: 'Camp is a solvent of morality. It neutralises moral indignation, sponsors playfulness' (Sontag 1983, 106). Camp is now a term deeply embedded in critical discourse, enlisted to account for the 'guilty pleasures' of a particular sensibility and the ways in which those pleasures – that playfulness – might enact a radical and, in particular, a feminist politics (Robertson 1996, Barreca 1992). Sontag has clear reservations about the political efficacy of Camp because of its air of imperious disengagement, but we now see its gestures as a refusal of the limiting, the normative, the 'authentic'; and, as such, potentially the style of a liberatory politics both engendered by and critical of (late? advanced?) capitalism. There is, of course, a paradox at work here: one of which Sontag was aware, and which Wilde, with his refined taste for paradox, might have enjoyed. By attempting to talk or write seriously about Camp, by subjecting it to orthodox analysis and the language of contemporary cultural theory, we deny and delete the very playfulness it seeks to embody, and so risk collapsing into a very un-Wildean 'earnestness'. Allan Pero seeks to resolve this paradox by writing about Camp in a distinctly camp fashion. His 'A Fugue on Camp' eschews the conventional essay form in favour of a series of atomised and provocative aphorisms, reminiscent of Wilde's Preface to *Dorian Gray*, 'Maxims for the Overeducated', and 'Phrases and Philosophies for the Use of the Young'. Camp, Pero tells us, sounding an appropriately Bracknellian note, 'is both a dangerous supplement and a needful weapon in a handbag of dazzling accessories'. It is 'a glittering bulwark against the twin forces of philistinism and utility'; it is 'an experience of the sublime, but seen from the perspective of the ridiculous'; like Sibelius, Camp 'asks only to be misunderstood correctly' (Pero 2016, 28–31). Camp, in effect, is *attitude*: a way of seeing the world and of presenting oneself to the world. It is a way of resisting and mocking the pressures of convention and conformity: it provokes, it dazzles, and it repels.

Dorian Gray is a camp novel. When it was published in volume form (after first being serialised the year before in *Lippincott's Monthly*) Wilde added the celebrated Preface in which he 'brilliantly vulgarizes' (Bloom 1974, viii) the ideas of his former Oxford tutor, Walter Pater (Camp, of course, loves vulgarity). The Preface declares from the outset that this is a novel which offers itself for aesthetic inspection rather than ethical judgement, and that what follows is an exercise in style: 'There is no such thing as a moral or an immoral book. Books are well written, or badly written, that is all' (Wilde 1966, 17). This sentiment is echoed by Sontag in her description of Camp when she says that 'A work of art, insofar as it is a work of art, cannot – whatever the artist's personal intentions – advocate anything at all' (Sontag 1983, 150). Part of the function of the Preface is to balance or counteract the apparent 'moral' of the narrative in which Dorian pays the price for his Faustian bargain: that all renunciation as well as all excess brings its own punishment. Wilde felt that he had failed to keep this moral in 'its proper secondary place'. What he was trying to achieve was a fictive design in which morality 'was simply a dramatic element in a work of art and not the object of the work of art itself' (Mason 1974, 72–3). He puts this most succinctly in the Preface: 'An ethical sympathy in an artist is an unpardonable mannerism of style' (Wilde 1966, 17). In other words, Wilde is aestheticising – *stylising* – the moral content of his novel. This refusal of the antithesis between the ethical and the aesthetic (an antithesis which Sontag argues always privileges the former over the latter, and which she traces back to Plato) is behind the loaded phrasing of a letter in defence of *Dorian Gray* to the *Scots Observer* which had criticised its 'immorality': 'You ask me, Sir, why I should have the ethical beauty of my story recognised. I answer, simply because it exists, because the thing is there' (Mason 1974, 113). There we have it: *'ethical beauty'*. The ethical and the aesthetic collapse into each other, in a camp embrace.

A Quare Fellow

An integral aspect of *Dorian Gray*'s campness is its attitude towards, and its deployment of, the Gothic. Wilde was drawn to the form for several reasons, and from several directions. W. J. McCormack, for instance, sees something distinctively Irish in Wilde's attraction to Gothicism. He is keen to emphasise the contribution of Irish writers to the development of what we now recognise as a Gothic aesthetic. He argues, for instance, that some of its most important underlying assumptions can be found in Edmund Burke's *A Philosophical Enquiry into the Origins of our ideas of the Sublime and the Beautiful* (1757) and that his seminal *Reflections on the Revolution in France* (1790) itself uses literary devices that 'might be termed Gothic': not least that in which 'terror', analysed as an aesthetic category in *A Philosophical Enquiry*, is projected onto Jacobinism. Burke, then, lays some of the philosophical and theoretical foundations for the Gothic fiction of his Irish countrymen and successors in the nineteenth century: in particular, Charles Maturin, Sheridan Le Fanu and Bram Stoker. This trio were, of course, members of the Anglo-Irish Protestant Ascendancy into which Wilde was born and their fiction, McCormack points out, has been interpreted as emerging from a profound sense of class guilt (McCormack 1998, 136). Seen from this perspective, there is a particular Irish colouration to Wilde's idiosyncratic reworking of the familiar doppelgänger motif in Gothic fiction. The relationship between Dorian and his portrait owes its Gothic ancestry less to Edgar Allan Poe and his influential story of doubling, 'William Wilson' (1839), for instance, than to his fellow Irishman, Le Fanu, and a story published in the same year as Poe's, his 'Strange Event in the Life of Schalken the Painter', which itself reframes the pictorial motif initiated by Horace Walpole in *The Castle of Otranto* (1764). Or perhaps another way of seeing this: American and Continental Gothicism (the Frenchness that so enraged the English conservative press when the novel was first published) is refracted for Wilde through an Irish prism. That prism, more specifically, is that of the Anglo-Irish Ascendancy whose 'hyphenated existence', Jarlath Killeen argues, attracted its writers to 'liminal states, such as vampirism, ghosts and the living dead'. Such attraction articulated 'the desperation and ennui felt in the face of their own waning power in colonial Ireland' (Killeen 2009, 116). Caught between Englishness and Irishness, divided in their cultural and political allegiances, Anglo-Irish writers were drawn to Gothic fiction as a means of expressing their sense of liminality and to the uncanny as an imagined disruption of a prosaic and uncongenial present. Nick Groom similarly sees the Irish Gothic as indicative of a fraught sense of Irishness. Charles Maturin's *Melmoth the Wanderer* (1820), is a case in point, as is evident in its Gothic form as much as its Gothic content. In the novel, Groom argues, 'Irish identity is fractured and crazed, and *Melmoth*'s snarled up chronology reflects the Protestant Ascendancy trying to unravel history' (Groom 2012, 90).

Given this Anglo-Irish context, it is then unsurprising that Wilde was also drawn to the Gothic: and its attractiveness was enhanced for him by the prospect of writing in a modish genre with proven commercial and market appeal. Yet, Wilde's own political allegiances did not sit easily with those of the Ascendancy he was part of by birth, and its characteristic concatenation of cultural nationalism and political unionism. His Irish nationalism, nourished no doubt by his formidable mother, is now well understood. Further, the sense of liminality that characterises his fellow Irish Gothic novelists opens for Wilde a liberating space for Sontagian playfulness, comedy and self-fashioning rather than political paralysis or personal ennui. This is clear in the way he forged his sense of national identity. On the banning of *Salomé* he announced, not untheatrically, 'I am not English, I am Irish, which is quite another thing' (Ellmann 1988, 377). Simultaneously he undercut any prospect of his being expected to adhere to a fixed and stable national identity by proclaiming his intention to take up French citizenship. In effect, Wilde's camp espousal of an Irished Frenchness, or a French Irishness, is a mode of play and performance which eludes and cancels the authenticity of an imposed national identity in favour of one he creates for himself. 'Camp', as Pero puts it 'is the enemy of identity' (Pero 2016, 29): to be more precise, it is the enemy of an identity which is bestowed rather than self-created or chosen. Englishness, Irishness, Frenchness: positions Wilde can adopt to declare his *difference*.

Similarly, Wilde's interest in and exploitation of the Gothic is best seen not as atavistic, or a symptom of 'desperation and ennui' occasioned by the waning colonial power of his political class. His use of it is both more playful and deliberate than that. He is attracted to it because of its inherent 'queerness'. William Hughes and Andrew Smith argue that the Gothic has always been queer inasmuch as it operates in a liminal space between 'the acceptable and the familiar' and the 'troubling and different' (Hughes and Smith 2009, 1) and tests the boundaries between them. Queer in this sense describes more than sexual behaviour and preferences. It is 'to be different' and 'may equally inform a systematic stylistic deviance from perceived norms in personal style or artistic preference' (Hughes and Smith 2009, 3). Wilde, the 'Quare Fellow', sees in the Gothic a potential for a degree of stylisation which other narrative forms do not offer: in effect a campness which 'proclaims, even humorously, both an awareness of difference, and an expression of the power to mock, surprise, and shock'. Such campness, they suggest, may well be a key to the 'elusive queerness of the [Gothic] genre' (Hughes and Smith 2009, 3). What I want to suggest is that Wilde seizes on that elusiveness and fashions the Gothic in a very particular way; or, rather, that he 'holds' it in a particular way. He uses it in a particular style, to express a particular set of attitudes. In short, Wilde *performs* the Gothic.

Performing Theory

'All fine imaginative work', Wilde says in his essay 'The Critic as Artist', 'is self-conscious and deliberate' (Wilde 1966, 1020). His use of the Gothic in *Dorian Gray* is self-consciously and deliberately part of his larger anti-naturalistic project inasmuch as it matches fictive practice with aesthetic theory. The novel deploys motifs, atmosphere, situations and figures from popular Gothic novels of the 1880s and 1890s by writers like Walter Herries Pollock (*The Picture's Secret*, 1883), Edward J. Goodman (*His other Self*, 1889) and Elizabeth Lysaght (*The Veiled Picture, or the*

Wizard's Legacy,1890), with their generic exploration of pictures and double identities. The relationship between the portrait and its subject (Dorian) provides a Gothic and supernatural twist to the central theoretical paradox of Wilde's 'The Decay of Lying' and the other theoretical essays collected as *Intentions* (1891); that 'art' is more lifelike than 'nature' and the 'real thing'. In effect, Wilde's aesthetic theories invert and deny the commonly understood relationship between Life and Art. The qualities we attribute exclusively to one to turn out to be equally, and perhaps more insistently, present in the other. Life imitates, Art creates: because it teaches us how and what to see. It is not a mirror held up to nature. Vivian, Wilde's alter ego in this playful Socratic dialogue, claims that this aphorism is 'deliberately said by Hamlet to convince bystanders of his absolute insanity in all art-matters' (Wilde 1966, 991). The picture ages, Dorian stays perpetually young: and the uncanny disrupts and transforms the gilded and complacent contemporary world of late Victorian Mayfair, rupturing its smooth surface like a knife cutting through canvas. Of course, the novel is not just an artistic manifesto in fictive action. It is also a social satire with a persistent and corrosive commentary on upper-class marriage, for instance, and the manners and mores of an urban aristocracy articulated by Lord Henry Wotton's epigrammatic insouciance and studied indolence. Yet there is no inconsistency here: the satiric humour of the novel is both caustic and camp. Wilde's satire is a form of self-display (Lord Henry's is an identifiably Wildean wit) and the satiric tone of the novel is that of the playfulness we associate with Camp: a playfulness which Wilde would have recognised as part of a classical tradition which, Dustin Griffin argues, encompassed both Menippean and Lucianic satire (Griffin 1994, 84–8) and in which Wilde, the consummate classicist, would have been well versed. The Gothic sanctions and enables Wilde's desire to write humorously and satirically about modern life and to address contemporary notions of cultural and ethical decadence ('*fin de siècle*, *fin du globe*') without holding a mirror up to it and contradicting his own rejection of naturalism and realism. So, in a characteristically paradoxical sense, the Gothicism of *Dorian Gray* is for Wilde, in absolute accordance with his aesthetic theories, more real than the Zola-esque naturalism he explicitly decries in 'The Decay of Lying'. (Zola features significantly and prominently in the essay; Wilde worked on it during the controversy surrounding the English translation of *La terre*, which saw its publisher imprisoned for three months when convicted of obscene libel.) Pero again: 'Camp is a histrionic Heisenberg delighting in realism's decay' (Pero 2016, 28).

Wilde pits Mind against Nature. 'Nothing' opines Vivian, is 'more evident than that Nature hates Mind. Thinking is the most unhealthy thing in the world, and people die of it just as they die of any other disease' (Wilde 1966, 971). 'The Decay of Lying' champions an 'unhealthy (leprous? putrefying?) art of the mind'; one, in effect, which is subversive of all political, cultural and social institutions and discourses which ossify into a 'natural' state of affairs. As Terry Eagleton puts it, in aligning Wilde with Barthes and Foucault and, consequently, alongside a postmodern preoccupation with the nature of power: 'Nature is the family, heterosexuality, stock notions, social conventions; and Wilde had only to be presented with a convention to feel the irresistible urge to violate it' (Eagleton 1995, 334). Wilde violates convention in this instance with a provocative displacement of the natural by the aesthetic: his difference, his queerness, expressing itself in a characteristically camp gesture: 'Life imitates Art far more than Art imitates Life' (Wilde 1966, 982). Instead of truth-telling *mimesis*, Vivian – and by extension Wilde – argue for the virtues and necessity of an art which is unhealthy, untruthful and *uncanny*.

Styling the Gothic

Of course, Wilde's use of the Gothic in *Dorian Gray* is not entirely abstract or cerebral. The Gothic elements are meant to engage at a visceral level; in particular, to excite the 'terror' that Burke identified as integral to an aesthetic experience capable of encompassing the sublime and the beautiful. The novel is camp, not 'campy'. It seeks to preserve a delicate balance between the arch and the innocent, and to give its readers an experience that is thrilling and disturbing, as well as amusing. In this sense, the novel 'reflects an ambivalence (affection contradicted by contempt, obsession contradicted by irony) toward the subject matter' which Sontag identifies with Godard, and with *stylisation* (Sontag 1983, 117). The generally sensational and stylised atmosphere of the book is maintained by Wilde's lurid and frequently overwritten descriptions of Dorian's mounting terror in front of his portrait, and of the denizens of the East End as menacing and murderous. The cultural and political geography of London is given a Gothic colouration, as Dorian journeys into the heart of the East End's darkness in pursuit of new sensations, opium and rough trade. In so doing he stylises the contemporary political obsession with the 'East End problem' discussed and dismissed in Chapter 3 of *Dorian Gray*.

Julian Wolfreys has argued that the 'various apparitions and manifestations' of the Gothic 'haunt' nineteenth-century literature in the work of ostensibly non-Gothic writers such as Dickens, Eliot, Tennyson and Hardy (Wolfreys 2002, 13). Yet Wilde is not haunted by the Gothic; he is knowingly exploiting it and holding it up for inspection, while attempting to thrill his readership. Characteristically, he wants it both ways: to immerse his readers and to hold them at a distance. He confessed – probably with an eye more to self-advertisement than self-criticism – that the novel was 'far too crowded with sensational incident' (Mason 1974, 50). The book then is an exercise in Gothic as well as a commentary upon it and a demonstration of its place in Wilde's anti-naturalistic practice. Richard Ellmann says of Wilde's fairy tales that in them he could cancel 'his nightmare of being found out with light-hearted dreams of pardon and transfiguration' (Ellmann 1961, viii). By the same token, Wilde's knowing and referential use of the Gothic devices, conventions, borrowings and atmosphere in *Dorian Gray* acquires a particular frisson in the light of his own personal circumstances. The thrills and terrors of the homosexual double life, which he likened to feasting with panthers, are both indulged and objectified – in effect *aestheticised* – by the Gothic manner as Wilde flirts with his readers and the possibility of confessional disclosure. The possibility of exposure was something Wilde became acutely aware of after the novel first appeared in *Lippincott's Monthly*. The subsequent revision for publication in volume-form the following year deliberately pared back the homoerotic subtext.

There is another sense in which Wilde's fairy tales provide a helpful analogy with his attitude to and use of the Gothic. The collections *The Happy Prince and other Tales* (1888) and *The House of Pomegranates* (1891) are contemporaneous with the composition and publication of *Intentions* and to a degree bear the same self-conscious relationship to those essays as does *Dorian Gray*. Indeed, Wilde talks about the fairy tales in much the same terms. In defending the novel against the charge of immorality, Wilde described it as 'an essay on decorative art. It reacts against the brutality of plain realism' (Hart-Davis 1962, 221). He also said that 'The Happy Prince' 'is a reaction against the purely imitative treatment of modern art' (Hart-Davis 1962, 221). What is clear is that the fairy tales were for Wilde an experiment in form, as he explained by reference to 'The Nightingale and the Rose': 'I like to think that there may be many meanings to the Tale – for in writing it [. . .] I did not start with the idea and clothe it in form, but began with a form and strove to make it beautiful enough to have many secrets and many answers' (Hart-Davis 1962, 218).

Ashis Nandy's psychology of colonialism is useful here. Nandy notes that one of the principal strategies of imperialism is the construction of a fantasy of hypermasculinity on the part of the colonisers and the projection of childishness and effeminacy onto the colonised (Nandy

1988). Ironically, it is Lord Alfred Douglas who expresses that identification most succinctly in his belligerently titled *Without Apology* (1938): 'Unless you understand that Wilde is an Irishman through and through, you will never get an idea of what his real nature is. In many ways, he is as simple and innocent as a child' (Douglas 1938, 75). So, Wilde is treading a dangerous line: laying himself open to the accusation that by writing fairy tales he has internalised the childlike qualities and awareness projected onto the Irish by a Celticism as much in the service of the imperial masters as of the cultural nationalists. However, Wilde was clear that no 'fairly-educated person' could really believe his stories were meant for children. As he told the *Pall Mall Gazette*, in responding to a review of *The House of Pomegranates*: 'I had as much intention of pleasing the British child as I had of pleasing the British public. Mamilius is as delightful as Caliban is entirely detestable, but neither the standard of Mamilius nor the standard of Caliban is my standard' (Hart-Davis 1962, 302). It is precisely the self-consciousness with which Wilde deploys the fairy-tale form that allows us to defend him against the accusation that his anti-imperialism is compromised by *genre*. After all, his identification of the British public with Caliban is a sly inversion whereby the distinction between the coloniser and Prospero's colonised subject is collapsed. Wilde does not internalise childishness, he stylises it – and gets his retaliation in first. Similarly, Wilde stylises the Gothic in *Dorian Gray*; as with the fairy tales, form is his starting point. By holding Gothic conventions and motifs in a certain way, with a certain knowing attitude, he is absolved of the potential 'desperation and ennui' reflected in its use by his Anglo-Irish countrymen. Wilde inhabits the form and acts upon it; he is not imprisoned by it.

Wilde puts the Gothic to complex, multiform and sophisticated use in *Dorian Gray*. Its self-conscious amalgam of the Faustian bargain with the motif of the doppelgänger results in an overdetermined contemporary Gothic which stylises the novel's fashionable concerns with Darwinism, genetics, psychology, science – 'Life is a question of nerves, and fibres, and slowly built-up cells in which thought hides itself and passion has its dreams' (Wilde 1966, 162) – astrology and cultural degeneration. These concerns make the novel an exemplar of what Victoria Margree and Bryony Randall characterise as '*Fin-de-siècle* Gothic' (Margree and Randall 2012, 217–33) and which Smith and Hughes regard as sufficiently distinctive to be regarded as a separate expression of late Victorian Gothic (Smith and Hughes 2012, 3). Wilde's overdetermined Gothic is a recognition of the elastic 'undecidability' of the form. He exploits its potential from the inside to create that admixture I described at the beginning of this chapter, one which melds terror and thrills with melodrama, satire and camp.

He was able to do this because he had already explored the Gothic, and pushed it to its limits, in *The Canterville Ghost* and *Lord Arthur Savile's Crime*, which are indeed *campy*. Matthew Sturgis reminds us that Wilde's breakthrough as a writer of fiction was not with a collection of fairy tales but via *The Canterville Ghost* when it appeared in two numbers of the *Court and Society Review* at the beginning of 1887 (Sturgis 2018, 346). Again, the date is important: the story was in gestation at the same time as the fairy tales and the theoretical essays which were to make up *Intentions*. The *Court and Society Review* is a sophisticated context for what presents itself as a 'trivial' and humorous story of the supernatural, for the 'serious' people who read the *Review*. As Sturgis notes, the magazine covered such relatively esoteric cultural topics as contemporary opera and French 'decadent' writing (Sturgis 2018, 436). The story is characterised by what McCormack calls the 'violent sentimentality inherent in Gothicism' (McCormack 1998, 136). The ghost is freed from his obligation to haunt and terrorise by the compassion of a young, innocent and fearless American girl. The comic elements of the story are somewhat laboured, as the Elizabethan ghost's attempt to perform his role in the Gothic narrative and setting are constantly and consistently thwarted by American rationalism, pragmatism and modernity. In short, the histrionics of the ghost are repeatedly defused by American Cool. This dynamic is, argue Horner and Zlosnik, characteristic of the Comic Gothic text which 'frequently recuperates the "supernatural" Other into the material' (Horner and Zlosnik 1998, 4). As the new transatlantic owner of Canterville Chase puts it: 'if there were such a thing as a ghost in Europe, we'd have it at home in a very short time in one of our public museums, or on the road as a show' (Wilde 1966, 193). In this respect, Wilde takes his place among several writers who recognised that the Gothic ghost story was losing its edge and thus offering itself up for parody. Nick Freeman places *The Canterville Ghost* alongside Jerome K. Jerome's *Told after Supper* (1891), Rudyard Kipling's 'My Own True Ghost Story' (1888) and H. G. Wells's 'The Red Room' (1896) as examples of such mocking parodies. Fictional conventions might have become outdated, Freeman notes, 'yet the public appetite for ghost stories remained ravenous: why else go to the bother of ridicule?' (Freeman 2012, 100). Ridicule, however, is too crude a term to describe what Wilde is attempting in *The Canterville Ghost*. He is not dismissing the form of the ghost story, but responding to it, with an affectionate playfulness characteristic of camp, and a persistent and determined comic treatment which means it spills over into the campy. In so doing it delivers 'the laughter of accommodation rather than the terror of disorientation' that for Horner and Zlosnik defines the Comic Gothic text (Horner and Zlosnik 1998, 35).

Oddly, W. J. McCormack congratulates Wilde on 'inventing Gothic comedy' (McCormack 1998, 136) in this story and its successor, *Lord Arthur Savile's Crime* (published later in 1887, again in *Court and Society Review*). However, the comic potential of Gothic fiction was apparent from the outset, and certainly to Jane Austen in *Northanger Abbey* (1818) who makes affectionate fun of Catherine Morland's susceptibility to Gothic fantasy and, as Killeen points out, parodies the 'traditional Gothic fear of continental Catholics and their nefarious activities' (Killeen 2009, 11). Nick Groom also notes that from its very emergence in the late eighteenth and early nineteenth century the style of Gothic novels was 'instantly recognisable and frequently parodied' (Groom 2012, 76). What Wilde is doing is exploring the form and inhabiting it – in such a way as to heighten the inherent comedy in much Gothic fiction as it teeters so frequently on the edge of the ludicrous, rather than inventing a new comic subgenre. Wilde's playful engagement with Gothic fiction is not as simple as a 'subversion' of the form, because much Gothic fiction is self-conscious to the point of self-subversion. This is Wilde as Critic as Artist, commenting on the very material he is playing with. He is putting the Gothic in inverted commas.

Wilde's exercise in the campily Gothic is continued in *Lord Arthur Savile's Crime*. There is a sense here of Wilde hitting his stride. With its aristocratic Mayfair setting, the story feels very much like a proving ground for the Society Comedies of the next decade, and of course for *Dorian Gray* itself. For Sturgis, Wilde's distinctive and personal voice is very much in evidence here 'in the romantic unreality of its emotions, the playful absurdity of its plot, and the profligate scattering of its paradox' (Sturgis 2018, 348). The story is subtitled 'A Study in Duty', but of course the notion of 'duty' is emptied of all ethical significance by the 'playful absurdity' in which Lord Arthur seeks to fulfil it by committing a murder before his marriage. He ends up enacting the cheiromantist's prophecy by killing him, in an atmosphere of pervasive levity that anticipates the quintessentially English and camp Ealing Comedy, *Kind Hearts and Coronets* (1949). What the story does, however, is also depict a London that is replete with a violent potential, where dynamite is available from a celebrity terrorist who lives 'entirely for my art' (Wilde 1966, 187) and can be consulted on matters of domestic violence, where poisoned bonbons and exploding clocks are available for a price, and (as in the fate of Podgers), execution is summary and contingent. That violent potential however is distanced, ironised, refracted through the stylistics of wit: in short, by Camp. This is recognisably the world of *The Importance of Being Earnest* (1895), where Lady Bracknell speaks of potential acts of violence in Grosvenor Square and asks if, when the fiction of Algy's double life has been 'exploded', Bunbury has been the victim of a revolutionary outrage. So, Wilde deploys Gothic material in a deliberate undercutting of the complacent and mannered contemporary aristocratic scene to create an atmosphere of suppressed violence and irrationality. In *Dorian Gray* that suppressed violence is surfaced as Dorian turns to murder, and irrationality is dramatised by his tormented encounters with the uncanny. In *Lord Arthur Savile's Crime* the uncanny is at first indulged and then countered by the eponymous hero's stolid and task-orientated common sense. Finally, it is laughed at when Podgers the palm-reader meets his serio-comic end, and a temporarily disorientated Lord Arthur is accommodated once again into the comfortable future mapped out for him.

Conclusion

Earlier I suggested that Wilde holds the Gothic in a particular way, in a style that allows him to express a particular set of attitudes. That style, those attitudes, can perhaps best be summed up by the way that, on his release from prison Wilde adopted 'Sebastian Melmoth' as an alias as he sought exile in Europe. By adopting the name of Maturin's wandering 'hero', Wilde, in effect, 'Gothicises' himself: by playing a role, with rather more conviction than the Canterville ghost. In other words, Wilde enjoys a performative relationship with the Gothic which allows him to exploit it, enjoy it, and laugh at and with it. In *The Canterville Ghost* and *Lord Arthur Savile's Crime* Wilde did not invent a comic subgenre of the Gothic but pushed the form to its logical limits, exploiting the comic potential inherent in it: or as Horner and Zlosnik would have it, releasing its comic doppelgänger (Horner and Zlosnik 2005, 4). In other words, both stories are commentaries upon and exercises in Gothic fiction, and not simply mocking dismissals of it. There is a clear difference here. The short stories are examples of the Comic Gothic. *Dorian Gray* is a Gothic novel, and a camp novel, but it is not a comic novel, despite the elements of satiric comedy in it. Working through the Comic Gothic in this way enabled Wilde then to put the form to such sophisticated use in *The Picture of Dorian Gray* where his Gothicism performs the pyrotechnic aesthetics of his theoretical essays and the uncanny slices through the self-satisfied metropolitan milieu of his aristocratic dramatis personae.

All this is achieved in an atmosphere of self-conscious theatricalisation, which is a key element in Sontag's understanding of Camp. In *The Canterville Ghost* the drama of crime, shame, sin and expiation so incompetently performed by the sixteenth-century relic is dissolved by the aesthetic playfulness of the narrative and by what Wilde would later call in *The Importance of Being Earnest* 'the more than usually revolting sentimentality' of the ending, and its laughter of accommodation. The ghost's insistent theatricalisation of his predicament – 'with the enthusiastic egotism of the true artist he went over his most celebrated performances' (Wilde 1966, 197) – is the epitome of Camp. Moving from the short story to the novel, Wilde intensifies this theatricalisation and signals his intentions in the Preface when he declares that 'From the point of view of feeling, the actor's craft is the type' (Wilde 1966, 17). *Dorian Gray* is full of references to the theatre and to acting, most obviously in Dorian's ill-fated obsession with the young actress Sybil Vane. Dorian himself plays many parts: Prince Charming, drug addict, murderer, the most fashionable and desirable man in London. In this respect, he lives up to Lord Henry Wotton's aphorism: 'being natural is simply a pose, and the most irritating pose I know' (Wilde 1966, 20). Lord Henry's function is not simply to act as a counterweight to the painter Basil Hallward's ethical misgivings about the life Dorian is leading, but to emphasise repeatedly the potential for inauthenticity, for transforming oneself and others into a liberating theatrical spectacle: 'Suddenly we find we are no longer the actors, but the spectators of the play. We watch ourselves, and the mere wonder of the spectacle enthrals us' (Wilde 1966, 80). Sybil Vane is of interest to Dorian and Lord Henry only insofar as her precariously maintained abilities as an actress allow her many roles and personalities. She is an object of desire precisely because of her lack of a real, stable, graspable identity. When Sybil attempts to authenticate herself through love the results are embarrassing and disastrous. In some respects, *Dorian Gray* is a peculiarly Wildean parody of the nineteenth-century *Bildungsroman*: Dorian does not learn through experience who he is (like other literary 'orphans' before him such as David Copperfield or Oliver Twist), rather he tries to act out a narrative of self-definition and ends by living one of self-destruction.

What Dorian demonstrates to the reader is that identity is performative, it is playing a part: just as the Canterville ghost attempts to perform the role the Gothic script has written for him, and Wilde performed a new identity, that of the wandering, homeless outcast, after his release from Reading Gaol. By playing that part, Wilde was able to exert precarious control over his straitened and mostly friendless circumstances. Similarly, his camp Gothic novel fashions its own identity as a theatrical and liminal space, in which Wilde is at liberty to exploit the 'mingling (of) emotional opposites' which Horner and Zlosnik (2005, 8) see as integral to the Gothic project: in this case, that Wildean interplay of visceral thrills and abstract theory; esoteric literary Decadence and popular Gothic fiction; satire and melodrama; terror and laughter.

References

Barreca, Regina. 1992. *They Used to Call me Snow White . . . but I Drifted: Women's Strategic Use of Humour*. Harmondsworth: Penguin.
Bloom, Harold, ed. 1974. *Selected Writings of Walter Pater*. New York: Signet.
Douglas, Lord Alfred. 1938. *Without Apology*. New York: Secker.
Eagleton, Terry. 1995. *Heathcliff and the Great Hunger: Studies in Irish Culture*. London: Verso.
Ellmann, Richard, ed. 1961. *Selected Writings of Oscar Wilde*. Oxford: Oxford University Press.
Ellmann, Richard. 1988. *Oscar Wilde*. London: Hamilton.
Freeman, Nick. 2012. 'The Victorian Ghost Story'. In *Victorian Gothic*, edited by Andrew Smith and William Hughes. Edinburgh: Edinburgh University Press.
Griffin, Dustin. 1994. *Satire: A Critical Reintroduction*. Kentucky: University of Kentucky Press.
Groom, Nick. 2012. *The Gothic: A Very Short Introduction*. Oxford: Oxford University Press.
Hart-Davis, R., ed. 1962. *The Letters of Oscar Wilde*. London: Hart-Davis.
Horner, Avril and Sue Zlosnik. 1998. *Comic Gothic*. European Studies Research Institute: Salford.
Horner, Avril and Sue Zlosnik. 2005. *Gothic and the Comic Turn*. Basingstoke: Palgrave Macmillan.
Hughes, William and Andrew Smith, eds. 2009. *Queering the Gothic*. Manchester and New York: Manchester University Press.
Killeen, Jarlath. 2009. *Gothic Literature 1825–1914*. Cardiff: University of Wales Press.
McCormack, W. J. 1998. 'Irish Gothic'. In *The Handbook of Gothic Literature*, edited by Marie Mulvey Roberts, 135–7. London: Macmillan.
Margree, Victoria and Bryony Randall. 2012. '*Fin-de-Siècle* Gothic'. In *Victorian Gothic*, edited by Andrew Smith and William Hughes. Edinburgh: Edinburgh University Press.
Mason, Stuart. [1908] 1971. *Oscar Wilde, Art and Morality*. London: Haskell House.
Nandy, Ashis. 1988. *The Intimate Enemy: Loss and recovery of Self under Colonialism*. Oxford: Oxford University Press.
Pero, Allan. 2016. 'A Fugue on Camp'. In *Modernism/Modernity* 25, no. 1: 28–36.

Robertson, Pamela. 1996. *Guilty Pleasures: Feminist Camp from Mae West to Madonna*. Durham, NC and London: Duke University Press.

Smith, Andrew and William Hughes, eds. 2012. *The Victorian Gothic*. Edinburgh: Edinburgh University Press.

Sontag, Susan. 1983. *A Susan Sontag Reader*, edited by Elizabeth Hardwick. Harmondsworth: Penguin.

Sturgis, Matthew. 2018. *Oscar: A Life*. London: Head of Zeus.

Wilde, Oscar. 1966. *The Complete Works of Oscar Fingal O'Flahertie Wills Wilde*. New edition. London: Collins.

Wolfreys, Julian. 2002. *Victorian Hauntings: Spectrality, Gothic, the Uncanny and Literature*. Basingstoke: Palgrave Macmillan.

Chapter 7

The Comic Gothic of Edith Wharton's Witches
Sarah Whitehead

When Edith Wharton's novella *Ethan Frome* was first published in 1911, reviewers were struck by the tragedy of her New England tale of a miserable marriage and failed suicide attempt, with *The Saturday Review* claiming that it was a story 'too terrible . . . to be told' (Anon. 1911a, 650). The tragedy itself lay not so much in the unhappiness of a wretched marriage, but in the botched job Ethan makes of leaving it. Ethan falls in love with his wife's young cousin Mattie and, when the girl loses her position as a home help with the Fromes, he decides that death would be better than the bleak futures awaiting them if they have to live apart. Their suicidal plan to sleigh together down a dangerous slope into an ancient tree fails when Ethan is confronted by a vision of his wife's face, with its 'twisted monstrous lineaments' (Wharton 1995, 124) and swerves off course. Ethan survives to live on as a bent and twisted figure in constant pain and Mattie, now an invalid, is taken back to the Frome homestead, where she will spend the rest of her days under the care of the woman they wronged. Twenty-five years later, the once bright-eyed Mattie Silver has become a complaining drone with a 'bloodless and shrivelled face' (127) and is now virtually indistinguishable from her witch-like cousin, Zeena Frome.

Although Zeena is betrayed by her husband and the cousin who had supposedly come to help her, she is vilified by the narrator, who focuses on her cold, querulous nature and her aged, sickly appearance. In the year of the novella's publication, an anonymous *New York Times* reviewer, while moved by the tragic nature of events, echoed this view, finding Zeena the villain of the piece, describing her as 'a whining slattern who hugs her imaginary ailments to her flat and barren breast' and a selfish wife who spends the little money her husband has on 'quacks and patent nostrums' (Anon. 1911b, 603). In 1980 Elizabeth Ammons re-examined this demonised figure and convincingly identified the ugly, withered, toothless Zeena as the archetypally 'terrifying and repulsive' witch (1980, 77), an argument continued by later critics, including Judith Saunders (2018, 117) and Joanna Gill (2001, 17), who read Zeena's cat as her familiar. Indeed, such is the narrator's hatred for this 'evil' woman (Wharton 1995, 87) that his layers of grotesque portraiture can appear overdone at times, lending what Geoffrey Walton argues is a 'decided element of caricature' to this figure (1982, 86). While the notion that Zeena is the witch of the story has remained a popular one, to my knowledge no extended study has been made of the comic effect of this character. I read Zeena Frome as a comic witch and argue that she is one of various examples of Wharton's ludic dialogue with witchlore and its literary heritage, found in her fictional portraits of lonely, ageing women. It is, I argue, precisely the grotesque comedy of these figures that challenges the cultural frames of the texts in which they appear and which serves to parody the misogyny of witchcraft narratives in a comic riposte to a tradition of fear of female agency and ageing.

Zeena Frome (née Pierce) first meets Ethan when she comes to care for his ill mother. After old Mrs Frome's death, the fear of being alone on a silent farm prompts Ethan to ask Zeena to stay as his wife and we are left to surmise why she accepts – a lack of any other option for a woman of her socio-economic background seems the most likely reason. Shortly after they are married it becomes clear that Zeena's skill as a nurse 'had been acquired by the absorbed observation of her own symptoms' (53) and within a year Zeena develops 'the "sickliness"' which has since made her notable in 'a community rich in pathological instances' (53). Jennifer Travis reads her as a 'model of the hysteric' (1997, 46) and, according to Marlene Springer, her illness 'affords her a viable identity and antidote to her isolation' in the lonely New England countryside (1993, 61). Zeena's preoccupation with her illnesses and the barren atmosphere of the Frome household and its surrounding environs makes the arrival of pretty, cheerful Mattie a welcome change. Ethan's subsequent infatuation with her is presented sympathetically, seeming inevitable.

Reading *Ethan Frome* as a fairy tale, Ammons finds parallels with *Snow White* in the frozen New England landscape and the physical appearance of the young Mattie Silver ('black hair, red cheeks, white skin') and also in Zeena's stepmother role towards her orphaned cousin (Ammons 1980, 63). She argues that Wharton's physical description of Zeena clearly signals her as the witch of the story:

> Zeena's face alone would type her as a witch – sallow complexioned and old at thirty-five, her bloodless countenance is composed of high protruding cheekbones, lashless lids over piercing eyes, thin colorless hair, and a mesh of minute vertical lines between her gaunt nose and her granite chin. (Ammons 1980, 63)

Wharton's portrait of Zeena, with its Gothic blurring of the boundaries between life and death in the form of a woman who has the facial features of a corpse, and who lives in a house that has 'the deadly chill of a vault' (40) overlooking the Frome gravestones, is darkly comic. She is given a black cat, an owl and a high 'hard perpendicular bonnet' (46). The cat breaks her cherished pickle dish; the owl is stuffed and sits in the parlour in front of the match-safe; and she saves her smart hat for special occasions, such as trips to the doctor. Wharton's references to illness evoke much comic irony, making Zeena both disturbing and ridiculous as a reworked folkloric witch who heals the sick with herbs (Ringel 2009, 261). Wharton also fuses this figure with the more traditionally malignant witch. Rather than turning to a book of spells, Zeena prefers to read her copy of 'Kidney troubles and their cure' (106) along with the other very welcome gems of wisdom the patent medicine companies regularly send her. As Diana Price Herndl notes, it is an ironic twist to have Zeena use her own illness as a weapon against Ethan (1993, 168) and when Zeena delivers the latest doctor's diagnosis, she is both proud and powerful. Wharton writes:

> [She gazed] at him through the twilight with a mien of wan authority, as of one consciously singled out for a great fate. 'I've got complications,' she said.
> Only the chosen had complications. To have them was itself a distinction, though it was also, in most cases, a death warrant. People struggled on for years with 'troubles' but they almost always succumbed to 'complications'. (81)

Wharton positions the conversation in the traditionally Gothic liminal hour of twilight and, via a tone of wry detachment, encourages a humorous reading – signalled by the inverted commas around the vague labels of 'complications' and 'troubles', and by the discordant hyperbole of the phrase 'a great fate' and the word 'distinction' she uses to describe her condition. Directly after this announcement, there is one of the various 'sharp reversal[s] of sympathy' Pamela Knights identifies in the novella (2004, 84), and Zeena is described as looking 'so hard and lonely, sitting there in the darkness with such thoughts' (81). That is, until she starts her nightly routine, wrapping her head in some yellow flannel (43) dropping her false teeth into the tumbler by the bed and falling into a noisy sleep, with her mouth open (39). Partly repellent, partly clownish, but also evoking some sympathy, Zeena's dilapidating body and home cures make her a figure of both ridicule and pity. As Julian Wolfreys argues in his study of Dickens's use of the Comic Gothic, this humorous mode 'delegitimizes narrative's pretensions to speak in a single voice' (2000, 53), and Wharton's use of comedy certainly defies any straightforward witch reading of Zeena.

In a typically renovative manner, Wharton uses both cultural and literary heritage in her comic reworking of the witch archetype. Zeena's full name, Zenobia, is a good example of Wharton's playful engagement with precursive texts – whether it be a nod to Hawthorne's beautiful heroine Zenobia in *The Blithedale Romance* (1852) who regularly wears an exotic flower in her hair (as argued by various critics including Wolff (1977, 159); Ammons (1980, 76); Fryer (1986, 181)), or the famously beautiful and courageous third-century Queen Zenobia of Palmyra (as noted by Robin Peel (2005, 137) and Ammons (1980, 24)). Sadly, Zeena is not beautiful and, as for wearing an exotic flower in her hair, she cannot even get her geraniums to grow, never mind the cucumber vine around the front door. Either way, she is a comic inversion of her precursive namesakes. Zeena's lack would have been ironically framed in the first printing of 'Ethan Frome' in *Scribner's Magazine* from August through October 1911, which also carried advertisements for Cuticura soap to 'maintain the youthful freshness' of a 'schoolgirl complexion' (64d), White Rose glycerine soap to 'prevent the coming of premature wrinkles' (64e), not to mention the Keeley Cure, 'a scientific remedy [for neurasthenia and addiction] which has been skilfully and successfully administered by medical specialists for years' (69). (All references are to the September 1911 edition.) Janet Beer and Avril Horner note that while parody responds to heritage texts and values, it also enables the author 'to engage critically with the contemporary world' (2003, 270). The paratextual frame selling female beauty, youthfulness and mental health would have accentuated the comic excess of Zeena's premature ageing, ill health and vituperative grumpiness.

In Wharton's later story 'Bewitched' (1926), the witch is Prudence Rutledge, who, as one critic notes, has the defining features of indeterminate age, wasted appearance and sinister expression, and accordingly can be read as the agent of the story's title (McDowell 1970, 148). Like Zeena Frome, Mrs Rutledge lives with her husband in a remote farmhouse, near the aptly named 'Cold Corners' (Wharton [1926] 2001, 348). The story's focaliser is Orrin Bosworth, a young farmer, who is called to the Rutledge homestead along with another neighbour, the older Sylvester Brand and the local churchman Deacon Hibben. Mrs Rutledge has summoned the three to deal with the haunting of her husband, Saul Rutledge, by the ghost of his former sweetheart, Ora Brand, Sylvester's dead daughter. Mrs Rutledge demands the girl's coffin should be opened and a stake driven through her heart. Her husband Saul Rutledge, now a 'haggard wretch' (353) confirms, to his visitors' horror, that he is haunted by Ora, and that she regularly meets him at the abandoned house by Lamer pond. The three visitors agree to visit the place the next day, but a detour on their way home takes them down to the very spot that evening. When Sylvester Brand sees footprints in the fresh snow, leading up to the old house, he charges in, and is followed by the two other men. What happens next is unclear; Bosworth seems to see 'something white and wraithlike surge up' (365) out of the darkness and then hears a shot, followed by a cry. The traumatised Brand leaves the house, holding a revolver, followed by the two men who hold him down and get the gun out of his hand. The next day, Venny Brand, Sylvester Brand's younger daughter (and Ora's sister) is reported to have pneumonia and two days later she is dead; her death and the footprints suggest that she was the (live) girl Saul has been meeting.

Mrs Rutledge, like Zeena, is described as being closer to death, or in this case, stone, than life. Wharton writes:

> The inner fold of her [eye] lids was of the same uniform white as the rest of her skin, so that when she dropped them her rather prominent eyes looked like the sightless orbs of a marble statue. The impression was unpleasing. (350)

But even here Bosworth finds a dark humour. Watching her at Venny's funeral, as she 'glided past him', he muses that she looked 'as if the stone mason had carved her to put atop of Venny's grave' (367); Mrs Rutledge makes his flesh creep but she is also an object of mockery. Like Zeena, she is startlingly ugly, with 'a brow that project[ed] roundly over pale spectacled eyes' (350) and a peculiarly reptilian quality created by her abrupt twists of her head (352) and her narrow face which 'sway[ed] on a long thin neck' (367). Like Zeena, she has the prerequisite witch's hat which she wears to Venny's funeral: a 'monumental structure' (367) which she usually keeps safe in her trunk. At the funeral the bonnet is described as 'a perpendicular pile' (367), the alliteration creating a comic detachment, preparing the reader for the conclusion of uneasy bathos which is to come. After the end of the service, when everyone leaves the churchyard, Mrs Rutledge's final remark (and last line of the story) is '"'S long as we're down here I don't know but what I'll just call round and get a box of soap at Hiram Pringle's"' (368). Wharton's conclusion is a mixture of the symbolic Gothic of the funeral in its graveyard setting with the everyday consumerist and mundanely domestic. The darkness of the freshly dug grave and the whiteness associated with soap create an incongruous combination at the close of the narrative, leaving the reader unsettled and unsure how to react to this woman.

Both Zeena and Mrs Rutledge are witch figures with vampiric qualities. As Benjamin Fisher notes, Zeena's transformation of Mattie into a replica of herself is a typical outcome in vampire narratives, as is the choice of a close relative for her victim (1996, 30). In 'Bewitched', the local community is familiar with such supernatural menaces and how to deal with them. Mrs Rutledge cites the case of Lefferts Nash and Hannah Cory. She recalls that driving a stake through Cory's (presumably dead) breast cured Nash. She is sure that this method alone is the way to save Saul and cries out '"A stake through the breast! That's the old way; and it's the only way"' (358). Whether the vampire in this tale is the living dead Mrs Rutledge, or the young Venny Brand who is in a sexual relationship with Saul, or her dead sister Ora (Saul's former sweetheart), 'Bewitched' is a tale that is suffused with sexual desire, and its vampiric elements reinforce the heavy undercurrent of lust and its effects. The tradition of the witch as a 'vampire, a literal or spiritual life-drinker' is noted by Ringel who cites 'Carmilla' (1872) by Le Fanu (an author whose work Wharton much admired) as an example of this type of figure (Ringel 2009, 260). William Hughes notes the long history of the link between vampire, blood and its 'subtle cultural equation' of semen, and the eroticism of vampire texts, concluding that 'erotic encodings and imagery . . . now constitute an almost invariable accompaniment to any act of vampirism' (2009, 253, 256). The phallic imagery of the stake in 'Bewitched', as noted by McDowell (1970, 146) and Kathy Fedorko (1995, 110), makes an interesting contrast to the equally phallic missing cucumber that should be dangling on Zeena's dead vine round her door, creating an image of comic absence in the reader's mind.

The link between witches and sexual desire is unsatisfactorily and condescendingly explained by the first-person narrator in Wharton's last short story, 'All Souls' (1937). The tale opens one Halloween evening, when his cousin, the elderly Sara Clayburn, bumps into a woman in the grounds of her house. The stranger has apparently come to visit Agnes, one of the servants. This 'middle-aged, plain and rather pale' individual was, according to the narrator's later deductions, a fetch or 'a living woman inhabited by a witch' coming to take the servants to a midnight coven, and this was why they disappeared that weekend (Wharton [1937] 2001, 801, 820). According to the narrator, such is the licentiousness of a coven, he can only make oblique references to an orgiastic ritual, citing an 'uncontrollable longing . . . which breaks down all inhibitions'; he explains that 'once having taken part in a Coven one would move heaven and earth to take part again' (820). Read by Horner and Beer as an example of Wharton using supernatural forces 'to express the inexpressible about the sexual appetites of the older woman' (2011, 165), the story is an ironic one, told by a narrator who resorts to misogynistic witchlore to solve the mystery of the disappearance of the servants that weekend. In his introduction he states that the various explanations of what had happened were 'so exaggerated and ridiculously inaccurate' that he felt it was necessary to 'record the few facts actually known' (789); yet his own version is just as speculative, based solely on the absence of the servants and Sara meeting (twice) with an unknown woman. Furthermore, there is no mention of witches in Sara Clayburn's account of the weekend. The narrator's recourse to witchcraft reflects his own fears about female ageing and sexuality, and his unease about his elderly aunt's choice to live independently in her grand house in the countryside, rather than move to a flat in the city where he can keep an eye on her.

One of the most sexually predatory witchlike figures in Wharton's oeuvre is the eponymous Miss Mary Pask who practises an unnerving 'clumsy capering coquetry' when visited one night by the narrator (Wharton [1925] 2001, 315). The elderly spinster Mary plays with the young visitor when she realises that he thinks she is a ghost. (There had been a death notice mistakenly sent the previous autumn.) Not only does she remark, '"I've had so few visitors since my death"' (316), and comments on how much she likes the darkness as '"the dead . . . naturally get used to it"' (317), but she then goes on to lock him in and tries to seduce him. Wharton writes:

> And her way of sidling nearer to the door made me distinctly want to reach it before she did. In a rush of cowardice I strode ahead of her – but a second later she had the latch in her hand and was leaning against the panels, her long white raiment hanging about her like grave-clothes. She drooped her head a little sideways and peered at me under her lashless lids. (318)

Having captured her man, the elderly Mary behaves like a young girl, with the coquettish tilt of her head, and its demure invitation, lending an incongruous comedy to the scene. By leaning against the door and putting her body between him and his escape, she makes it clear that her desires are physical. She then makes this even more explicit in a direct request to the terrified narrator, who is now fixed on her 'blue-nailed hand that grasped the latch'. She says '"Oh, stay with me, stay with me . . . just tonight"', adding '"no one need know . . . no one will ever come and trouble us"'(318). In his horrified response Wharton creates a comic reversal of gender and age relations with a young, wealthy American man at the mercy of a lonely woman on the periphery of society. Once a forgotten and unimportant old woman, she is now an invincible one, exercising an almost supernatural power over him, with hands that can pull him into a room 'like a steel cable' (315). Apart from her deathly appearance, Mary's witch credentials are multiple: she lives in Brittany in the Baie des Trépassés – the Bay of the Dead – alone in a silent, isolated house; she is visited on a stormy night in a heavy fog; she has a 'shrivelled', 'wrinkled' appearance (315); when she moves she 'flit[s] spectrally' (316); when she walks her steps are 'soundless' (315); she lights three candles (one of which the narrator blows out, believing superstitiously that bad things come in threes); she has some cauldron-like 'copper pots' and the prerequisite dried plants ready to make her potions (316). However, unlike Zeena and Mrs Rutledge, we are not so much encouraged to laugh at her, but with her, enjoying the young man's terror as a result of his imagination and his 'New England conscience' (309). Indeed, in this story she laughs at him on four separate occasions. And with the final section of the story filling in the picture, when the narrator learns that Mary Pask had in fact not died last year but suffered a cataleptic trance, the joke really is on him.

Much of the comedy (for the reader, but not for the narrator) is rooted in the account of Mary's grotesque appearance. The narrator dwells in particular detail on her hands. When she puts a hand on his arm, he recalls 'And there, unmistakably, it lay on my sleeve: but changed and shrivelled – somehow like one of those pale freckled toadstools that the least touch resolves to dust . . .' (315). The description is abhorrent and funny in its excess. There is a play on the poison associated with toadstools and witches, and on the phrasing from the funeral service in this description of an apparently dead body part. In his study of the grotesque in the works of Rabelais, and as a response to Kayser's *The Grotesque in Art and Literature* (1963), Mikhail Bakhtin refutes Kayser's view of the grotesque as solely the 'gloomy, terrifying', 'hostile, alien and inhuman', arguing that he overlooks its association with the carnival spirit and laughter (Bakhtin 1984: 47). Philip Thomson agrees that there is 'almost always a comic element in the grotesque' and notes how Ruskin found the genre the product of a 'strong urge to play, invent and manipulate' (Thomson 2017, 29, 14). On perceiving the comedy, the reader, Thomson argues, delights in 'seeing taboos flouted, a sense of momentary release from inhibitions, intellectual pleasure at seeing the joke' (2017, 31). In the case of 'Miss Mary Pask' (1925), it is Mary herself who exploits the misunderstanding, and the reader who enjoys the metafictive version of the same joke. In linking this masculine narrative version of events to his New England conscience, Wharton shifts the object of ridicule to a mindset rich in the misogyny of a witchcraft heritage. She also centralises the age difference between visitor and host, so that, as Melanie Dawson argues, Mary's malicious playfulness serves to 'ironically counter the narrator's dismissive ideas about elderly women' (Dawson 2020, 309).

Taking its name from a series of 'fanciful' paintings found in the Golden House of Nero, the 'grotesque' became, by the sixteenth century, a term for 'bizarre' 'imaginative' and 'strange' fantastical designs (Barasch 1968, xxiii, xxv). The grotesque image was often a biologically deviant one, early examples including human mutations of beasts or plants, or biologically impossible forms such as the living dead, as found in the long tradition of the Dance of Death or *danse macabre* – an image of dancing skeletons greeting a living individual who will soon join their number. As Thomas Wright notes in his study of fifteenth-century versions of these images, the skeletons have a 'mirthful countenance' (1968, 215) and this grimly comic vision is reinforced by their dancelike movement. The incongruity, or embodied catachresis (Wolfreys 2000, 47) of the grotesque (a skeleton which is alive, for example) is where the heart of the humour lies, and it is in her playful use of seemingly dead or inanimate living witches where much of Wharton's grotesquerie can be found. Zeena Frome seems dead with her 'drawn and bloodless' countenance, her 'pale opaque eyes' and lips 'the same sallow colour as her face' (Wharton 1995, 48, 127) and Prudence Rutledge appears to be made of stone with her 'white', 'bloodless . . . clasping hands', 'like a stony paperweight' and eyes that look 'like marble eyeballs' (Wharton [1926] 2001, 350, 358, 367), yet both are living women whose bodies, according to the onlooker, appear to defy biological laws. The grotesque's association with excess can also be found in both Mary Pask and Zeena Frome; Mary's lustful behaviour towards her gentleman caller is, to him, frighteningly inappropriate and Zeena's unedifyingly 'vivid descriptions of intestinal disturbances among her friends and relatives' during suppertimes is revoltingly funny (Wharton 1995, 92). The two women break the taboos of polite society, simultaneously appalling and amusing the reader in their comic grotesquerie.

In her writing on the female grotesque, Julia Kristeva links the body's changing shape and functions to the abject, arguing that its state of flux and rejection or separation of elements such as fluids blur the borders of the inside and outside, creating a revulsion and horror borne of this physical ambiguity. In her study of the abject, Mary Russo writes that whereas the classical body is 'closed, static, self-contained', the grotesque body is 'open, protruding, irregular, secreting . . . changing, challenging the boundaries and symmetry of the idealised human form with a gothic liminality or in-betweenness' (Russo 1995, 8). The narrative focus in Wharton's witch stories is regularly on their grotesque bodies; neat, classical, idealised female symmetry is disrupted by protuberances such as Mary Pask's and Prudence Rutledge's bulging eyes (Wharton 2001, 310, 350), or orifices such as Zeena's 'open mouth' (Wharton 1995, 39) when she sleeps. Wharton's witches also have their abject, detachable parts and secretions; the most memorable being Zeena's false teeth extracted by night, which she adjusts by day via 'the familiar gesture' before she eats (Wharton 1995: 91).

The young male narrators' tendency to link the grotesque to female ageing follows a tradition of the witch figure being a powerful, often childless, older woman. Avril Horner and Sue Zlosnik note how Gothic texts often bring to the surface age-related misogyny and argue that in the case of the Comic Gothic, rather than continuing the negative stereotypes of older women found in folklore and literature, writers humorously critique the cultural rejection and abjection of female ageing. They place 'Miss Mary Pask' in a long line of women's critique of patriarchal attitudes towards the ageing woman (2016, 193) and I argue here that Wharton's use of a young, unreliable male narrator to comically challenge negative stereotyping found in this story is a feature of all of Wharton's witch narratives. The use of fairy-tale horror in a seemingly realist register and a regular recourse to stereotypes / witch tropes both create humour and prompt a satirical reading of these male visions of grotesque female ageing. In 'Miss Mary Pask', the woman's hands are like toadstools (fusing echoes of the Cumaean Sybil withering away with the association between witches and poisoning) and in 'Bewitched', Prudence Rutledge's gaunt face seems to be that of a tortoise, reminding the reader of her reptilian and therefore diabolical nature. The young man's hyperbolic abjection of female ageing lends an entertaining drama to his narration, but his unwitting comic response makes him a target of the reader's mockery.

In his study of the grotesque in Rabelais's *The Life of Gargantua and of Pantagruel*, Bakhtin argues that 'laughter has a deep philosophical meaning, it is one of the essential forms of truth concerning the world', adding that 'the world is seen anew, no less (and perhaps more) profoundly than when seen from the serious standpoint' (Bakhtin 1984, 66). Noting laughter's long-standing association with truth, he considers how medieval fabliaux, 'opened men's eyes' and 'uncovered' the realities of the world around them, concluding that laughter defended people against fear and falsehood, liberating them from (internal and external) prohibitions, unveiling the material bodily principle (of death and regeneration) (Bakhtin 1984, 94). The notion that the comedy of the grotesque presents the real world has remained a popular one. In his study of Robert Browning's poetry, G. K. Chesterton notes that caricature comes from nature itself, where 'all things top-heavy, lop-sided and nonsensical' can be found (Chesterton 1904, 149). Chesterton argues that the function of the grotesque in literature is to encourage the reader to look at the object attentively again 'from the outside' (1904, 151). If we read the grotesque as a prompt to revision the world around us, Wharton's witches become portraits of the real lives of many women at the time. Ammons reads Zeena as 'twisted' by the 'poverty and isolation and deadening routine' typical of poor women's lives in this region (1980, 77). Springer finds hypochondria 'typical of women in the late nineteenth century who used it as a means to control their environment and the gruelling demands of housework' (1993, 65) and Herndl describes Zeena as an 'invalid produced by the culture' she lives in (1993, 168). McDowell finds Prudence Rutledge's exaggerated 'belief in an implacable God' and 'cheerless' view of the future the result of 'the hardships of ordinary living' (1970, 149). Wharton's comic grotesques delineate both the effects of the living conditions of many women at the time and how the consequent damage to their physical and mental health led to their demonisation.

As Horner and Zlosnik note, much of the comic turn lies in the telling of the tale (2005, 9) and the narrative voice is the foundation of the comic in Wharton's witch stories. In *Ethan Frome*, 'Bewitched', 'Miss Mary Pask' and 'All Souls'', the narrating consciousness is that of a young man. Indeed, the story of Zeena is, as Wolff points out, virtually completely imagined by the narrator; he only meets her for a few minutes and has to rely on just the odd comment from Ethan and a neighbour to construct his tale (1977, 173). The narrative lens of these witch stories is also a modern one. Bosworth (the focaliser in 'Bewitched') is in 'contact with the modern world' (Wharton [1926] 2001, 358); the narrator of *Ethan Frome* is an electrical engineer visiting the region for work and the narrators in Miss Mary Pask and All Souls' are both younger men based in New York city. Their vision of these women as witches is founded upon a culture which aligned the feminine with youthful beauty. The men's recourse to witch clichés offers the reader a familiar literary milieu. However, their comically grotesque portraits turn the tradition of the horror of female ageing on its head by making it risible; here the objects of humour are not only the women, but also their narrators' ageism and lazy use of stereotypes. Furthermore, Wharton signals that these witches are not simply fairy-tale figures; she regularly includes modern, contemporary touches, such as the crimping pins Zeena uses to set her hair at night and Prudence's washing powder, to root these women in the real world. Advertisements for such products sat alongside the magazine editions of these texts, reminding readers how fear of ageing, or being perceived as slatternly, were the foundations of the profitable trade of marketing ideal womanhood in consumerist America.

Finally, it is not only the physical effects of female ageing, but also the power that these women wield that terrorises their male narrators.

Zeena, with her illnesses, has the motive and moral right to travel around the region visiting doctors, unlike her stay-at-home husband. She is also the sole decision maker when it comes to hiring or firing the home help – as an ill woman she sacks Mattie in order to give her room to a more experienced and useful girl and she can be read as 'the principal author of the suffering' (Saunders 2018, 121) in the tale. In the night-time encounter, Miss Mary Pask takes control by harnessing the young man's misunderstandings, revelling in her visitor's fear and making inappropriately forthright demands of him. Prudence Rutledge clearly rules the roost and successfully eliminates her husband's love interest and, until that fateful weekend, Sara Clayburn defies her young relative's injunctions to live in New York, preferring to live independently in her grand house in the countryside. Through comedy Wharton uses the tradition of the witch figure to present lonely, powerful women who provoke sympathy, disgust and laughter, in tales that can be read as horror stories, comic caricatures or satirical considerations of continuing misogynistic traditions. In her witch stories Wharton uses laughter, in the form of the Comic Gothic, to interweave these competing narrative purposes to engage with both a rich literary heritage and contemporary culture, to entertain and challenge, conform and subvert. While we ridicule and pity these women, the comedy in Wharton's portraiture demands that we question our own role in perpetuating these witch stereotypes. As Bakhtin writes of carnivalesque laughter, 'he who is laughing also belongs to it' (Bakhtin 1984, 12).

References

Ammons, Elizabeth. 1980. *Edith Wharton's Argument with America*. Athens: University of Georgia Press.
Anon. 1911a. *The Saturday Review* 112, 18 November: 650.
Anon. 1911b. 'Three lives in Supreme Torture', *New York Times*, 8 October: 603.
Bakhtin, Mikhail. [1914] 1984. *Rabelais and His World*. Trans. Hélène Iswolsky, Bloomington: Indiana University Press.
Barasch, Frances K. 1968. 'Introduction'. In Thomas Wright, *A History of Caricature and Grotesque in Literature and Art*, vii–lvii. New York: Frederick Ungar Publishing Co.
Beer, Janet and Avril Horner. 2003. '"This isn't exactly a ghost story": Edith Wharton and the Parodic Gothic'. *Journal of American Studies* 37, no. 2: 269–85.
Chesterton, G. K. 1904. *Robert Browning*. London: Macmillan.
Dawson, Melanie V. 2020. *Edith Wharton and the Modern Privileges of Age*. Gainesville: University Press of Florida.

Fedorko, Kathy A. 1995. *Gender and the Gothic in the Fiction of Edith Wharton*. Tuscaloosa and London: University of Alabama Press.

Fisher, Benjamin. 1996. 'Transitions from Victorian to Modern: the supernatural stories of Mary Wilkins Freeman and Edith Wharton'. In *American Supernatural Fiction from Edith Wharton to the 'Weird Tales' writers*, edited by Douglas Robillard, 3–42. New York: Garland.

Fryer, Judith 1986. *Felicitous Space: The imaginative Structures of Edith Wharton and Willa Cather*. Chapel Hill: University of North Carolina Press.

Gill, Joanna. 2001. '"The absorbed observation of her own symptoms": Ethan Frome and Anne Sexton's "The Break"'. *Edith Wharton Review* 17, no. 2: 14–22.

Hawthorne, Nathaniel. [1852] 2011. *The Blithedale Romance*. New York: Norton.

Herndl, Diana Price. 1993. *Invalid women: figuring feminine illness in American fiction and culture*. Chapel Hill and London: University of North Carolina Press.

Horner, Avril and Janet Beer. 2011. *Edith Wharton: Sex, Satire and the Older Woman*. Basingstoke: Palgrave Macmillan.

Horner, Avril and Sue Zlosnik. 2005. *Gothic and the Comic Turn*. Basingstoke: Palgrave Macmillan.

Horner, Avril and Sue Zlosnik, eds. 2016. *Women and the Gothic*. Edinburgh: Edinburgh University Press.

Hughes, William. 2009. 'Vampire'. In *The Handbook of the Gothic*, 2nd edn, edited by Marie Mulvey Roberts, 252–7. Basingstoke: Palgrave Macmillan.

Knights, Pamela. 2004. 'Introduction'. In Edith Wharton, *Ethan Frome*, 6–24. Ware: Wordsworth Editions.

Kristeva, Julia. 1982. *Powers of Horror: An essay on Abjection*. Trans. Leon Roudiez. New York: Columbia University Press.

McDowell, Margaret. 1970. 'Edith Wharton's Ghost Stories'. *Criticism* 12, no. 2: 133–52.

Peel, Robin. 2005. *Apart from Modernism*. Madison, NJ: Fairleigh Dickinson University Press.

Rabelais, François. 1944. *The complete works of Rabelais. The five books of Gargantua and Pantagruel in the modern translation of Jacques Le Clercq*. New York: Random House.

Ringel, Faye. 2009. 'Witches'. In *The Handbook of the Gothic*, 2nd edn, edited by Marie Mulvey Roberts, 259–61. Basingstoke: Palgrave Macmillan.

Russo, Mary J. 1995. *The Female Grotesque: Risk, Excess, and Modernity*. New York and London: Routledge.

Saunders, Judith P. 2018. *American Classics: Evolutionary Perspectives*. Boston: American Studies Press.

Springer, Marlene. 1993. *Ethan Frome: A Nightmare of Need*. New York: Twayne Publishers.

Thomson, Philip. 2017. *The Grotesque*. London: Routledge.

Travis, Jennifer. 1997. 'Pain and Recompense: The trouble with *Ethan Frome*. *Arizona Quarterly* 53, no. 3: 27–64.

Walton, Geoffrey. 1982. *Edith Wharton: A Critical Interpretation*. Rutherford, NJ: Fairleigh Dickinson University Press.

Wharton, Edith. 1911. 'Ethan Frome'. In *Scribner's Magazine*, August, 151–64; September, 317–34; October, 431–44. New York: Charles Scribner's Sons.

Wharton, Edith. [1911] 1995. *Ethan Frome*. London: Penguin Books.

Wharton, Edith. [1937] 2001. 'All Souls''. In *Collected Stories II*, 798–820. New York: Library of America.

Wharton, Edith. [1925] 2001. 'Miss Mary Pask'. In *Collected Stories II*, 309–23. New York: Library of America.

Wharton, Edith. [1926] 2001. 'Bewitched'. In *Collected Stories II*, 347–68. New York: Library of America.

Wolff, Cynthia Griffin. 1977. *A Feast of Words: The Triumph of Edith Wharton*. New York: Oxford University Press.

Wolfreys, Julian. 2000. 'I wants to make your flesh creep: Notes towards a reading of the Comic Gothic in Dickens'. In *Victorian Gothic*, edited by Ruth Robbins and Julian Wolfreys, 31–59. Basingstoke: Palgrave Macmillan.

Wright, Thomas. [1864] 1968. *A History of Caricature and Grotesque in Literature and Art*. New York: Frederick Ungar Publishing Co.

Chapter 8

Rational Rickets and Reluctant Canadians: Gothic Colonial Cringe in Robertson Davies's *High Spirits*
Cynthia Sugars

It seems there has always been something inherently ludicrous about the idea of a Canadian ghost. Not only is early Canadian literature replete with accounts of the impossibility of ghosting the landscape, culminating in 1962 with Earle Birney's claim that 'it's only by our lack of ghosts we're haunted' (1962, 18) but Canadian hauntings have been regarded as strategically advantageous, since ghosts and monsters bring with them an implied sense of cultural ancestry and history, which an emergent white colonial society found itself sorely lacking.[1] It is not surprising, then, that Canadian writers have consistently contorted the Gothic to supply local colour in the form of ambivalent cultural nostalgia. Yet the culture in question – white settler Canada – is bound by a reflexive contradiction: on the one hand it appears to take itself too seriously (Who are we? What are we haunted by?), while on the other it is known for its proficiency in belittling self-irony (we are nobodies, we are ridiculous, we are dull).[2] This is where the comic edge of the Gothic makes it a perfect fit for Canadian self-perception. As Avril Horner and Sue Zlosnik note, 'the comic within the Gothic offers a position of detachment and scepticism towards such cultural nostalgia' (2005, 3), which 'foregrounds a self-reflexivity and dialectical impulse intrinsic to the modern subject' (4) . . . or, one might add, the prototypical settler Canadian.

Ironic hauntings seem to proliferate the passageways of Canadian literature – from Stephen Leacock's parodic stories about ghosts who are not taken seriously, to Robertson Davies's novels and stories in which the Gothic makes its appearance as a comic device to puncture the pretensions of small-town middle-class Canada, to contemporary stories by Margaret Atwood and André Alexis. In this chapter, I will focus on Davies's collection of comic ghost stories, *High Spirits*, published in 1982. As Master of Massey College at the University of Toronto, Davies wrote a ghost story every year for the Massey College annual 'Gaudy

Night' celebrations each Christmas from 1963 to 1980. These stories are collected in *High Spirits*. Davies's introduction to the volume encapsulates the dilemma of the Canadian ghost tradition as a whole. As he puts it in his introduction to *High Spirits*, 'Canada needs ghosts, as a dietary supplement, a vitamin taken to stave off that most dreadful of modern ailments, the Rational Rickets' (1982, 2). Yet in addition to this Gothic infusion, it would seem that Davies is arguing for something more: a way for Canadians to laugh at their Anglophilic pretensions and colonial inheritance, a way of accommodating their embarrassed predilection for Gothic cultural affirmation. In these stories, we see Davies comically working through two of his (and many settler Canadians') obsessions: his sense of colonial 'secondhandness' in relation to British cultural and historical traditions, and his view that the newness of Canada rendered it at once *inhospitable to* yet *desperately in need of* local hauntings.

The Canadian cultural nationalists of the 1960s and 1970s knew this longing for Gothic infusion well. Indeed, Canadian Gothic fictions became so prevalent during the nationalist revival period in Canada that critics applied the term 'Southern Ontario Gothic' to describe the predominance of this mode in the writings of Margaret Atwood, Alice Munro, Robertson Davies, Graeme Gibson, Matt Cohen, James Reaney, Timothy Findley, and others. The term was coined in the early 1970s by Findley in an interview with Graeme Gibson (1973, 138) as a way of conjuring the shared 'sense of distinct regional, even mythological, place' of Southern Ontario (Hepburn 1997, 1085), an area that extends from Windsor to Toronto to Ottawa. In particular, these writings turn up the invisible Gothic underside of placid – indeed stereotypical – Canadian proprieties, offering glimpses of the supernatural and irrational, which persist as tantalising hints of unacknowledged inheritance. The Southern Ontario Gothic tradition testifies to authors' attempts to invigorate the conventionally realist and mainstream Canadian settlement landscapes with Gothic potential. By exploring the invisible Gothic underlay of conservative Ontario societies, authors were both writing within and writing back to the widely proclaimed Canadian 'lack of ghosts'.

This attempt to refute the stereotype of an unhaunted Canadian social landscape also played a role in the growing impetus to 'decolonise' Canadian culture from British and American influences. Writing during the period of early postcolonial consciousness in Canada – amidst the drive to resurrect forgotten local histories and celebrate white settler history – most of these authors sought to forge a Gothic presence amidst the seemingly unhistoried Canadian communities they inhabited. In doing so, many of these works sought to construct postcolonial ghosts that would help found settler history as part of a spiritually reinvigorated

Canadian landscape. Of the writers listed above, Robertson Davies stands out for his relentlessly comic take on this process of Canadian self-Gothicisation.[3]

Throughout his literary career, Davies was known for his derisive portrayals of small-town Canadian society. His piercing renditions of the paralysing proprieties and petty snobberies of provincial Ontario were often expressed in comically Gothic terms (or sometimes as a spoof on the absence of Gothic presence). For Davies, Canadians inhabited 'a delayed cultural tradition' (1973, 32), existing in a kind of uncomprehending stasis unaware of the changing modern world. The parochialism and conservatism of this fossilised society, for Davies, meant that Canada was 'wretchedly under-monstered' (1967, 68). Davies was ardent in his repeated pronouncements that Canadian culture lacked a suitably fulfilling Gothic pedigree, which translated into a conviction that, in his view, Canada – and Canadians – lacked imagination.

Although a central member of small-town Ontario society (Davies's family, and Davies himself, ran a series of local newspapers before Davies took up the post of Master of Massey College), Davies was nonetheless embarrassed by the company he was condemned – by the whims of history and inheritance – to keep. Davies's biographer, Judith Skelton Grant, terms this his 'reluctant Canadianism' (1994, 632). In many instances, Davies lamented Canada's failure to accommodate Old-World ghosts. Yet Davies's accounts are themselves haunted by the very Old-World spirits he so mourns. To conjure such ghosts is to affirm the lack of 'local' candidates, yet to not have such ghosts is to be forever condemned to lament their absence. His comic tour de force was to make Canadian ghosts *appear* old before their time.

This ambivalent relation to Canadian culture (or lack thereof) has its counterpart in Davies's conflicted sense of the underlying Gothic tenor of Canadian life. On more than one occasion, Davies accused Canada of being dowdy and prosaic; yet at other times, he emphasised the Gothic underlay of Canadian experience (take, for example, the catalysing snowball in his well-known novel *Fifth Business*, in which the throwing of an iconic snowball brings with it an unravelling and unearthing of the Gothic underpinnings of the town of Deptford). By filling in for our lack of ghosts, Davies's work could claim to be putting us in touch with ghosts that were already there. This gets complicated when European – or more specifically British – cultural traditions are used to instill a sense of Gothic density. For Davies, using Old-World ghosts becomes a way of reconciling Canadians to their colonial inferiority complex, their Gothic colonial cringe. Yet the paradox in Davies's work seems to be this: if Canadians have no recognisable ghosts, and no intuitive sense of the numinous, the fact that they are haunted by self-created imported ghosts is a symptom of their inability to be adequately haunted (or inspired) on Canadian soil. Or is it that they are haunted by this very perceived inadequacy – haunted, in other words, by their reluctant Canadianism? Jerrold E. Hogle writes of the Gothic as being 'torn between the enticing call of aristocratic wealth' and 'a desire to overthrow the past orders of authority' while seeking to attain the power of the orders it sought to dethrone (2002, 4). In many ways, the Canadian Gothic predicament is just this, seeking the aura and power of a distant (and now foreign) past while attempting to overthrow it. Indeed, Davies's fashioning of Massey College as a place of both transcendent antiquity and liberal modernity embodied this Gothic colonial dilemma.

This yields a potentially comic paradox: is an authentic Canadian haunting to be haunted by a figment of the past, or to *cease* to be haunted by the past? This 'reluctant Canadianism' – perhaps better termed a 'reluctant Canadian Gothicism' – finds expression in two intertwined denunciations lobbed by Davies against his fellow Canadians: on the one hand, he accuses Canadians of having no sense of history (and, by extension, no sense of ancestry/lineage); on the other, he sees Canadians as being strangled by their history and the bourgeois pretensions that come with it. In his 1971 interview with Donald Cameron, Davies lamented the fact that Canadians 'never talk about ourselves as a country with a sort of living past' (1973, 33). Yet in the same interview he asserted that Canadians are plagued by an 'uncomprehending clinging to the past' (34). This echoes his argument in 'A Country without a Mythology', in which he faults Canada for having dressed in 'cultural cast-offs' from older countries (1996, 282). In a nutshell, Davies's question would seem to be this: although Canada's past is derivative, colonial, unoriginal, indebted – how does one make of the derivative something rejuvenating and authentic? How does one simultaneously Gothicise and ironise colonial belatedness?

This is precisely the dilemma explored in Davies's writing (and, one might argue, in his self-fashioned persona as a public figure). Davies's characters (and, in his view, Canadians) seek to shed their embarrassing colonial origins and transform themselves, yet they also need to connect with these origins in order to avoid being culturally and imaginatively marooned. In *High Spirits*, it is a joyful rejection of these terms – an 'I do not give a damn' response as uttered by the ghost of John A. MacDonald in Davies's story 'The Charlottetown Banquet' (1982, 51) – that is the Comic Gothic solution. The British ghosts are not the embarrassment; it is the colonial response to those ghosts that is so. This confrontation requires a battle of wits – between ghosts, between living and dead, between modern-day Canadians and their forebears, between author and reader – in which the historical contingencies of ancestry and diaspora are acknowledged and shed; embraced and absorbed; rendered ghostly, one might say, but familiarly so. Only by engaging the ghosts in convivial repartee can characters overcome their Gothic colonial cringe.

In *High Spirits*, each of the ghost sightings takes place in the buildings and grounds of Massey College, and it does not take long to realise that Massey is a microcosm for Canada as a whole. Throughout, the newness of the college – like Canada generally – is described as making it an unlikely location for Gothic visitations. Massey College was built in 1962 from the substantial donation to the University of Toronto by Vincent Massey. Massey himself was heralded as emblematic of Canada's emergence from colonial artifice and British influence. Not only was he the first Governor General of Canada who was Canadian-born, but he was also an active supporter and patriotic advocate for the Arts in Canada, chairing in 1949 what has since become known as the 'Massey Commission', a Royal Commission that investigated the state of the arts and culture in post-war Canada. It was Massey who personally appointed Davies to be the first master of the new college, in part, paradoxically, because he liked the Old-World flamboyance of the man. In effect, Davies was something of a Gothic anachronism himself. His appointment to the college was somewhat controversial because Davies – a novelist, playwright and newspaperman – had no academic qualifications. And yet, like the ghosts who come to haunt the college in *High Spirits*, Davies brought with him a whiff of Old-World aristocratic validation. His endeavours to make Massey a lesser Oxford (specifically Balliol College, where Davies was a student in the late 1930s) included a heraldic coat of arms granted from the College of Arms in England (Skelton Grant 2015, 54) and the wearing of university robes at all college meals. Many of Davies's elitist trappings, including the restriction of the college to men only, came under criticism during the college's early years; one trustee was concerned that 'the possible charge of self-consciousness' would expose the college to ridicule (Skelton Grant 2015, 56).

This trait of exaggerated, Anglophilic self-consciousness is evident in the narrator of *High Spirits*, who is an ironic version of Davies himself – each story tells of a ghost encountered by the college master. In his introduction to the book, Davies notes that his ghost stories are intended both to 'amuse' and 'to add a new dimension to a building and a community that was brand-new' (1982, 2). Massey College, he notes, 'is a building of great architectural beauty, and few things become architecture so well as a whiff of the past, and a hint of the uncanny' (2). That the college, and arguably Canada, saw itself as being painfully in need of the cultural cachet that ghosts would bring with them, becomes a source of comedy in the stories, as the narrator in effect has to 'vet' various ghosts for their suitability as authentic haunters.

In the stories, the narrator presents himself as a reluctant medium. He believes in ghosts, he knows they are out there, but he wishes they would just leave him to get on with his work. This ironic protesting-too-much pervades the collection and contributes to much of its humour. 'It was never my intention that these [real-life ghost] stories should multiply', the narrator states in the third story of the collection. 'The last thing I desire for Massey College is the shabby notoriety of being haunted' (1982, 23). And yet, we are told, the hauntings began shortly after the college was opened, so the college itself, in its aspiration to be like comparable university colleges in Britain, required an authenticating ghost as much as it did the other conventional trappings of Old-World institutions (that is, the various paraphernalia that Davies gathered for it: a Latin motto, a coat of arms, a chapel, a college bell, staircases with Latin names, commissioned works of art, etc. (see Skelton Grant 2015)). Davies, as literary medium, will devise the college a ghost as well. Yet even though the building does not lend itself to traditional hauntings – for its newness precludes the existence of a home-grown ghost[4] – there is nevertheless something about Massey that makes it a lightning rod for the Comic Gothic. As the narrator remarks, 'I never saw a ghost till I came here – came to a brand-new building, every brick of which I had seen set in place, and all the furnishings of which have been known to me since they came from the makers' (23). Despite the master's protestations that 'being haunted is considered unseemly in an institution dedicated to truth and scholarship' (33), the college persists in attracting spectral candidates. Indeed, it appears to be plagued by a form of spectral overcompensation, for the youthful condition of being constitutively *unhaunted* demands more substantial ghosts who will make their haunting count. And throughout, the master-impresario performs his role as discerning bouncer and host. The very qualities for which Davies was hired – his persona as a literary magus and theatrical Gothic master of ceremonies – become the stuff of self-irony, as these characteristics, which elevate the college and its master to national fame and attract the ghosts in the first place, are also what risk propelling the place into tawdry melodrama. 'Massey College is troubled with ghosts', the master laments, 'much as lesser fabrics are troubled with mice; the most resolute determination is powerless to keep them away' (139).

This predicament reaches a peak in 'The Xerox in the Lost Room', in which the narrator laments the surfeit of ghosts with which the college is haunted: 'I cannot explain how a new building in a new country . . . comes to be so afflicted with what our university sociologists call "spectral density"' (1982, 163). He attributes the problem to 'a housing shortage in the World Beyond, just as there is here below' (163). The population explosion in the world at large has led to a parallel overcrowding in the afterlife. 'Where are they to put themselves?' the narrator asks. 'Many of them are emigrating from the lands of their origin and coming to Canada, which is still comparatively open, especially in the spiritual aspect of things' (163). Mirroring the influx of immigrants from Ireland and Britain in the early and mid-nineteenth century, the ghosts of dead Brits are similarly in need of a place to haunt. However, the narrator is quick to mention that the college seeks ghosts of the better class, ghosts from 'the upper ranks of the spirit world' (163), which will in turn lend the college a degree of cultural credibility. Because of this bias, the college has been charged with 'ectoplasmic elitism of the most disgusting kind' (53).

Wishing to be haunted by the ghost of Henrik Ibsen, who will nevertheless sneer at the debased nature of Canadian theatrical pretensions, the narrator reluctantly accepts the visitation of the college's most recent spectral applicant, the ghost of 'that particular type of gentleperson called a Poor Relation' (1982, 166). That the college is condemned to accept this lesser-class of British gentleman gnaws at the narrator, whose snobbish pretensions lead him to regard 'failure in the spirit world' as 'particularly chilling' (166). That the Poor Relation died an ignominious death by being hit over the head by the house butler only adds to the embarrassment: '[H]e had the gall to haunt Massey College!' It emerges that the Poor Relation has in fact gained status and respect after his death by being elevated to the position of Family Ghost, and as a result of a Canadian business venture, he 'emigrates' when his original homestead is transported over the ocean in a local attempt to reconstruct a little bit of England on Canadian soil. At first, the ghost puts up with the déclassé Canadians who work on his former home, but the last straw is when the house is opened as a public museum: 'Servants I will frighten – yes, gladly. Gentlefolk of my own kindred I will provide with the thrill of a true family phantom . . . But appearing to people who have paid admission on behalf of a charity – no, no, the thing is not to be thought of' (171). The ghost proves himself to be as snooty as the Massey College master, and together they find an inconspicuous spot for him in the college, which now houses an over-abundance of spectres. They settle on a room that was once in the construction plans but was removed – a room that is not there – and the ghost happily takes up his liminal abode, there and not-there, like an embarrassing relative hidden in the attic. Moreover, as a second-tier college spirit, our Poor Relation will be given extra college duties, including working as a copyist to supplement the inadequate Xerox machine (173). Having accomplished this task, the narrator excitedly spies the impatient ghost of Ibsen outside in the college quad, who immediately sneers at the parochialism of the place and promptly disappears.

This comic rejection of mediocre ghosts has its counterpart in what Davies often identified as Canadians' propensity to dismiss their humble origins. Davies often claimed that Canadians had inherited a kind of ancestral unconscious, defined by a note of resignation at having been forced to emigrate; they had inherited a 'reluctant Canadianism'. In this sense, Canadians were influenced not only by the tales of their ancestors and an outward-directed gaze towards the Old World, but also by an inherited disaffection with Canada. 'Virtually all of us are descended from people who never wanted to go to Canada, and who did so under the lash of grim necessity' (1996, 48), Davies writes in 'Literature in a Country without a Mythology'. 'Modern Canada is a prosperous country, but the miseries of its earliest white inhabitants is bred in the bone, and cannot, even now, be rooted out of the flesh' (49). The weighty influence of undesirable ancestors can thus be considered a form of haunting: 'That is part of what heredity means' (1996, 40). In his story 'The Pit Whence Ye Are Digged', a luxurious dinner at the college morphs, by an act of ghostly transformation, into a gathering of unappealing forebears. As if to suggest that all Canadians are but a reincarnation of their less-than-illustrious ancestors, the table is crowded by the riff-raff of eighteenth-century British society. The Fellows of Massey College thus become an ancestral parody of themselves – a Highland chieftain, a Russian peasant, a Welsh shepherd. The reluctant lesson the narrator takes away from the vision is that 'even from Gin Lane in the eighteenth century the modern Ph.D. may arise' (1982, 125), belittling his Canadian colleagues and students in the midst of celebrating the allure of the college's propensity for the supernatural.

This ambivalent response to Canadian ancestors extends to the figures of Canadian history, as when the narrator finds himself attending a ghostly version of the famous Charlottetown meeting of 1864, at which the deal for Canadian Confederation was hammered out under the leadership of the man who was to become Canada's first prime minister, John A. MacDonald. The college dining room becomes transformed into the Charlottetown banquet hall (in the Halifax Hotel), and our college master is seated at the table beside the great man himself. Applying himself to the meal by eating 'patriotically' (1982, 47), the narrator, as a former journalist, is intent on asking MacDonald one question:

'Sir John, may I enquire what you see in store for Canada, the land which you brought into being?' (50). Sir John's answer lets the narrator in on a secret for Canadians wandering the afterlife, for the former prime minister has found freedom at last. The 'heartlifting secret' about the next life is this: Canadians are allowed 'not to have to give a damn' (51) – about inheritance, about history, about colonial dependence, about national unity. The plague of Canadian earnestness – the rational rickets and colonial cringe – is rendered in the afterlife nothing but a mortal colonial preoccupation. In this moment, MacDonald epitomises that comic position of detachment and scepticism toward cultural nostalgia identified by Horner and Zlosnik. His nickname 'Old Tomorrow' (46) signals this contrived antiquity, both authenticating and out of place. He is a new ghost who appears old, and with tell-tale colonial manners, his spectral attentions are primarily focused on consuming the sherry.

Throughout the collection, Davies confronts the paradox of colonial cultural nostalgia head-on. Reluctant to relinquish the transplanted ghosts of the Old World, and urgently seeking to give them a locally grounded validity, he also recognises the inherent colonialism of this need. This is his challenge: if the Gothic looks back to ancestral inheritance, how can a colonial author render this inheritance authentic or foundational except through self-mockery? Two of the best stories in the collection have a comic postcolonial edge and feature Canadian ghosts coming face to face with British monarchs. In 'The Night of the Three Kings', George V and George VI appear as they attempt to retrieve a valuable stamp that was affixed to a letter sent to Vincent Massey. In laying claim to Massey property, the two kings are confronted by the ghost of Canadian prime minister William Lyon Mackenzie King, who insists that the stamp is Canadian property. In a humorous parody of Canadian autonomy and repatriation, George V belittles the Statute of Westminster as 'frightful bilge' (1982, 38) and demands that his stamp be returned. The narrator turns the situation to his colonialist advantage by allowing the two British Georges to visit the stamp once a year on the condition that they agree to lend their aristocratic allure to Massey's unenviable crop of less illustrious ghosts: 'We have had some ghosts here – shabby, detrimental spooks who ran the place down . . . All I ask is that for some part of your yearly visit you will permit yourselves to be seen. It would do so much to establish a good College tone' (39).

Ultimately, the story gives the Canadians the upper hand. If Canadian culture has long been haunted by British traditions, this story sets the haunting on Canadian terms by limiting the degree of British cultural influence (they can visit only once a year), and consigning them to the guidance of the '"third king"', the former prime minister Mackenzie

King, famous for his Gothic seances to revive his dead mother and his dog, but also the leader who guided Canada through the trials of the Great Depression and World War 2.[5] In the end, Mackenzie King is placed on an equal footing with the British monarchs (in fact, he is there to ensure they do not renege on their promise), thus symbolically overturning the rule that 'Canadians are not permitted to accept titles, even posthumously' (1982, 39),[6] since Mackenzie King is able to become a 'king' by association, and the three will thereafter haunt the college every year on 6 January, the Feast of the Three Kings. Thus has a Canadian ghost comically found its way into the ranks of British royalty.

In the humorous ghost story 'The Great Queen Is Amused', the ghosts of deformed Canadian authors haunt the college library, 'shaken with grief and despair' (1982, 24) at their misfortune in having been consigned to the shelves of Canadian literature. The college's pride in its Canadian literature collection is parodied in the unhappy condition of the 'insubstantial' authors whose books line the shelves (26). Conjured by the wife of a famous Canadian literature anthologist (Claude Bissell, who was also then president of the University of Toronto), the contorted and naked spectres of Canadian authors are 'clamouring to be reborn' in the hope that 'this time they might be born American authors' (28). Because they all appear naked, the narrator comically notes that the 'Canadian authors appeared . . . to have been neglectful of their physiques' (28). It is only a royal ghost who can put them to rest, but lacking such homegrown lineage, Canada must turn to Queen Victoria, who, it turns out, as the former Queen of Canada, is also, by default, a Canadian author. The ghost of Queen Victoria is less than amused by the Massey master, who despite his claims to be a 'democrat' is awed by her presence, genuflecting at her feet and enacting the very Anglophilia that informs the need for imported hauntings in the first place. When he offers her advice, the queen chastises him for his sycophancy: '"[D]o not presume to teach the great-great-grandmother of your Sovereign how to . . . lay ghosts"' (30). She then proceeds to quell 'the disorderly group of [her] colonial subjects' (30) and peremptorily dismisses the 'rabble of middle-class Canadian ghosts' (29). At the end, the master, too, is dismissed by the queen; nevertheless, his colonialist needs are satisfied by the knowledge that his humble college has provided amusement to her majesty and has been graced by her (albeit spectral) presence. As for the Canadian writers, well, they are consigned to the dusty shelves once again, unlikely to be revivified until another fusty CanLit critic seeks material for his next lacklustre book (Davies was never very kind to literary critics).

The self-reflexive nature of the comedy, augmented by the stories' origins in Davies's Gaudy Night recitations for college fellows, is enhanced by Davies's awareness of the ridiculous nature of his pretensions – pretensions to British ancestry and psychic polymathy. The master in the stories repeatedly cites texts of ancient lore and wisdom, and yet he seems strangely inept at ghost-hunting. Much as Massey College needs the ghosts to enhance its reputation, the ghosts, as we have seen, appear to use the master for their own ends. And because he is awed by them, he becomes their dupe. The book opens with Davies's own riposte to the Gothic motif of the sceptical narrator, whose initial disbelief in ghosts is proven mistaken by the circumstances to be relayed. Instead, Davies's narrator, through a form of Gothic deflation, identifies himself as a 'fanciful person' whose terror of ghosts is superseded only by the 'horrifying' spectre of the MA thesis he is condemned to read late at night in his college rooms. When a ghost appears in his room that is an uncanny mirror of himself, our master, with wounded vanity, behaves with effrontery and manages to bungle the occasion. The ghost in question is a ghost of a future master of the college who responds to the narrator as though *he* (Davies) were the ghost haunting his chamber. But his accusation is even more dismissive than this, for it emerges that the ghost from the future barely recalls our master at all and does not even remember that he *was* a master. In the course of their exchange, we learn that our master has become ghostly in more ways than one, as he has been lost to the history of the college and is presumably condemned never to haunt it since he would not be recognised as one of their own.

This self-mocking use of the Gothic to at once shake up and uphold the foundations of Massey College – and the famous author associated with the college's beginnings – is threaded throughout the book. The accumulation of Massey ghosts (though never of Vincent Massey himself) builds as the stories proceed, so that by the end of the collection, the college is seen to be haunted by too many spectres – that is, until the concluding story, the last of Davies's Gaudy Night tales before his real-life retirement as master. In this tale, there is no present ghost, but the rejection of a future one. Given the opportunity to have himself frozen by a leading alchemist and cryonics expert and to return to Massey a hundred years into the future to see how the college is faring, the soon-to-be-former master is given a word of advice by his wife: '"Don't be a Massey College ghost; it would be most unbecoming"' (1982, 197). This would place the master in a position similar to John A. MacDonald and Mackenzie King, whose ghosts the master had appealed to for a comment on the future of Canada. They, too, rejected the summons, refusing to play the part of Old Tomorrows prophesying what was to come. '"Don't you remember the line from our theatre days"', Davies's wife persists, '"Superfluous lags the veteran on the stage?"' (197). In other words, the master must resist the temptation to become another outmoded Gothic spectre, an Anglophilic bore haunting the shelves of Canadian cultural history. This is where colonial belatedness and nostalgia turn on ironic self-parody. We have come full circle: a tongue-in-cheek refusal to haunt and be haunted by a colonial holdover. What is left, in the end, but to laugh?

Notes

1. Note that my argument in this chapter does not apply to Indigenous storytelling traditions in Canada. Many Indigenous writers do use stories of magic and the supernatural, but their engagement with what we might term the Gothic is notably different from the writings of white settlers. See my chapter on Indigenous Gothic in *Canadian Gothic: Literature, History and the Spectre of Self-Invention* (2014).
2. Linda Hutcheon has frequently argued that irony is particularly well suited to Canadian expression. See, for example, her introduction to *Double Talking: Essays on Verbal and Visual Ironies in Canadian Contemporary Art and Literature*, in which she observes that 'there is a structural and temperamental affinity ... between the inescapable doubleness (or even multiplicity) at the base of irony as a trope and the historical and cultural nature of Canada as a nation' (1992, 12). Similarly, in *Splitting Images: Contemporary Canadian Ironies*, she notes that 'self-deprecating irony' is 'typical of the inhabitants of Canada' and argues that 'Canada [sic] often speaks with a doubled voice, with the forked tongue of irony' (1989, 1).
3. That Davies had a penchant for the Comic Gothic early on is evident in his well-known sequence of novels, The Deptford Trilogy, from the 1970s. It is also no surprise that Davies was influenced by the comic stories of the famed Canadian ironist Stephen Leacock; Davies edited a collection of Leacock's fiction, *A Feast of Stephen*, in 1970.
4. This has echoes in Susanna Moodie's famous pioneer narrative *Roughing It in the Bush* (1852), in which a Yankee settler proclaims, 'There are no ghosts in Canada! ... The country is too new for ghosts' (2007, 286). Davies was well aware of this scene in Moodie's book: 'No ghosts in Canada?' he retorted. 'The country which too vigorously asserts its normality and rationalism is like a man who declares that he is without imagination; suddenly the ghosts he has denied may overcome him' (1981, 234). It is no surprise that the ghost of Moodie appears as a forlorn and naked spectre in another story in the collection, 'The Great Queen is Amused'.
5. King is a favourite target for the Comic Gothic, namely because, after his death, it emerged that he held regular seances and crystal-ball sessions to communicate with his dead mother and pet dog. Rumour has it that he consulted his mother, and other historical figures, for advice about political matters. In another story in *High Spirits*, 'Conversations with the Little Table', the spirit of King communicates with the narrator through

table-rapping. His concerns in the afterlife prove to be as competitive and politically motivated as they were when he was alive.
6. This is an allusion to an incident that occurred in Vincent Massey's lifetime and to which Davies responded. Massey learned that the queen wanted to recognise his service as 'her first native-born governor general in Canada by making him a Knight of the Garter' (Skelton Grant 2015, 46), but the Canadian government was opposed to the granting of titles. This incident sparked Davies to write a critique of the policy in *The Peterborough Examiner* of 18 January 1960. According to Skelton Grant, it was Davies's position on this issue that in part led Massey to consider him for the Massey College post a few years later.

References

Birney, Earle. 1962. 'Can. Lit.' In *Ice Cod Bell or Stone*, 18. Toronto: McClelland and Stewart.

Davies, Robertson. 1967. *Samuel Marchbanks' Almanack*. Toronto: McClelland and Stewart.

Davies, Robertson. 1973. 'Robertson Davies: The Bizarre and Passionate Life of the Canadian People'. In *Conversations with Canadian Novelists I*, 30–48. Interview by Donald Cameron. Toronto: Macmillan.

Davies, Robertson. 1981. 'Canadian Literature: 1964'. In *The Well-Tempered Critic: One Man's Views of Theatre and Letters in Canada*, edited by Judith Skelton Grant, 228–37. Toronto: McClelland and Stewart.

Davies, Robertson. 1982. *High Spirits: A Collection of Ghost Stories*. Toronto: Penguin Books Canada.

Davies, Robertson. 1996. 'Literature in a Country without a Mythology'. In *The Merry Heart: Selections 1980–1995*, 40–63. Toronto: McClelland and Stewart.

Findley, Timothy. 1973. 'Timothy Findley'. In *Eleven Canadian Novelists Interviewed by Graeme Gibson*, 115–49. Toronto: Anansi.

Hepburn, Allan and Michael Hurley. 1997. 'Southern Ontario Gothic'. In *The Oxford Companion to Canadian Literature*, edited by Eugene Benson and William Toye, 2nd edn, 1085–6. Don Mills: Oxford University Press.

Hogle, Jerrold E. 2002. 'Introduction: The Gothic in Western Culture'. In *The Cambridge Companion to Gothic Fiction*, edited by Jerrold E. Hogle, 1–20. Cambridge: Cambridge University Press.

Horner, Avril and Sue Zlosnik. 2005. *Gothic and the Comic Turn*. Basingstoke: Palgrave Macmillan.

Hutcheon, Linda. 1989. *Splitting Images: Contemporary Canadian Ironies*. Oxford: Oxford University Press.

Hutcheon, Linda. 1992. 'Introduction'. In *Double Talking: Essays on Verbal and Visual Ironies in Canadian Contemporary Art and Literature*, edited by Linda Hutcheon, 11–28. Toronto: ECW Press.

Moodie, Susanna. [1852] 2007. *Roughing It in the Bush; or, Life in Canada*. Toronto: McClelland and Stewart.

Skelton Grant, Judith. 1994. *Robertson Davies: Man of Myth*. New York: Viking.
Skelton Grant, Judith. 2015. *A Meeting of Minds: The Massey College Story*. Toronto: University of Toronto Press.
Sugars, Cynthia. 2014. *Canadian Gothic: Literature, History and the Spectre of Self-Invention*. Cardiff: University of Wales Press.

Chapter 9

Laughter through Tears: A Jewish Perspective on the Comic Gothic
Faye Ringel

Jews have not been treated well in the Gothic genre. They may be shown as Christ-denying sinners, cursed to eternal exile, that Wandering Jew who can be a sorcerer and exorcist as in *The Monk* or a despised beggar.[1] Jews in Gothic fiction can be objects of ridicule, as in George du Maurier's *Trilby* (1895) with its mesmerist villain Svengali ('so offensive to the normal Englishman') and the 'dirty . . . Jewess "Mimi la salope"' (58).[2] *Dracula* has been read as encoding antisemitic tropes, and Jews and vampires have been linked in history as well as in Gothic fiction and film.[3] Whether dangerous or ridiculous, male or female, Jews represent the Other and the Outsider.

But from the inside, things can look different. When Jewish writers first in Yiddish and later in English began creating their own Gothic fiction, they accomplished a comic turning of the tables, making light of their own texts and traditions. Tales collected in ancient times in the Talmud, by medieval commentators, in the chronicles of Hassidic wonder rebbes, and in Israel's folklore archives can yield a surprisingly comic vision of the supernatural. When post-Enlightenment writers in Yiddish, Hebrew and English apply their perspective to these taproot texts, the result can be satiric or darkly comic.[4]

The most immediately recognisable example of the Jewish Comic Gothic is Tevye's dream in *Fiddler on the Roof*. In the Broadway musical by Bock and Harnick (1964), Tevye narrates these visitations to his wife Golde, while ghosts benevolent and revengeful throng the stage. This scene is taken almost verbatim from its source, Sholem Aleichem's story 'Today's Children', in which Tevye's oldest daughter Tsaytl insists on marrying the tailor Motl Kamzoyl instead of the butcher Lazar Wolf. Tevye convinces Golde this is the right decision through an invented nightmare in which Grandma Tsaytl and the butcher's first wife come from the next world to bless Motl and curse the promised new bride. It's no wonder that Tevye concludes the narrative, 'Why make a short story long? I must be made of iron if I could manage to lie there under the blankets without bursting from laughter' (Aleichem 1987, 52). This episode is emblematic of the ability of the Gothic to juxtapose parody, hilarity and terror. Tevye's readers and viewers are invited to laugh at outmoded superstitions while acknowledging their power to arouse fear and thus enthral us. As Walpole argues in the preface to *The Castle of Otranto*:

> Belief in every kind of prodigy was so established in those dark ages, that an author would not be faithful to the manners of the times, who should omit all mention of them. He is not bound to believe them himself, but he must represent his actors as believing them. (Walpole 1794, v)

The nineteenth-century creators of modern Yiddish literature had a similar relationship with Jewish religious beliefs as the writers of the English Gothic revival a century earlier had with Roman Catholicism: enlightened scepticism and fascination mingled with distaste. The audience for Sholem Aleichem and the other Yiddish modernists might have been living in the nineteenth and early twentieth centuries, but in some ways they were still in their own Middle Ages, subject to the terror of unreasoned persecution, with some following spiritual leaders who were seen as miracle workers. Walpole's outmoded beliefs – 'miracles, visions, necromancy, dreams, and other preternatural events' (v) – were matters of daily life in the Pale of Settlement as they remain today in Hassidic enclaves in New York or Jerusalem. This clash of cultures creates an uneasy tension between comedy and tragedy. Readers and viewers were expected simultaneously to suspend disbelief and accept the reality of supernatural happenings – and to laugh at the antics of demons and those they possessed.

Yiddish writers of fiction reflect the maxim of the Yiddish theatre – 'laughter through tears' – dealing with the most tragic subjects through comedy. There is even a robust tradition of humour about the Holocaust, surely the most tragically Gothic of historical events.[5] Sholem Aleichem, 'Father of Yiddish Literature', known for his ironic wit as the 'Jewish Mark Twain', composed his own epitaph, 'And just as the people were laughing . . . he cried alone, so that no one would see' (quoted in Glaser 2012, 19).[6] Canadian Yiddish scholar Ruth R. Wisse in *No Joke: Making Jewish Humor* reminds us that 'Sholem Aleichem's humor, often called "laughter through tears," is more accurately understood as laughter through fears' (2013, 63).[7] What better definition of the Comic Gothic? As Van Helsing puts it in *Dracula*, laughter can triumph over the most tragic of circumstances: 'it is a strange world, a sad world, a world full of miseries, and woes, and troubles. And yet when King Laugh come, he make them all dance to the tune he play' (Stoker 1897, 191).

To vastly over-simplify, Jewish attitudes toward the supernatural unite the extremes of acceptance and scepticism. As Joachim Neugroschel, foremost anthologist of the Jewish fantastic, observes, 'The two traditions, rationalism and fantasy, are so intergrown . . . and still dialectical. They will only be fused into one when the Messiah comes' (1991, x). The eleventh-century sage Maimonides, famed for his scepticism about and rationalisation of biblical miracles, nevertheless believed without question in the coming of the Messiah. Orthodox Rabbinic commentators still favour legal reasoning over miracle working, without denying the existence of the supernatural. How, then, do Jews distinguish between belief in God, the Torah and 2,000 years of rabbinic exegesis and belief in demons, golems, the evil eye – beliefs we post-Enlightenment postmoderns refer to as the fantastic or Gothic?

The Yiddish word *bobbe-meyse* conveys this dialectic. It means folktale, tall tale – or lie. Most Yiddish speakers believe it derives from *bobbe or bubbeh* (old woman, grandmother). In actuality, the term comes from the earliest printed example of secular Yiddish, the *Bovo-Bukh*, (1541), the Arthurian romances of Bevis of Hampton translated into Yiddish, stories which even in the Middle Ages were seen as happening long ago. The chivalric adventures contained therein are Gothic (literally) and undercut by parody. The term was then transferred to equally unbelievable stories. Such *bobbe-meyses* are by their very nature and definition inherently absurd and thus comic.

The supernatural themes most often found in Jewish Gothic folklore and most often satirised and deconstructed in twentieth-century and contemporary Gothic fiction are possession by dybbuks and demons and the creation of golems. The 'dybbuk' (from the Hebrew verb meaning 'to be attached') can be found most frequently in Ashkenazi Jewish legends from the late Middle Ages to the present. According to Howard Schwartz, accounts of possession by the spirit of a dead person became common from the sixteenth century (1988, 11). Jews who lived in Muslim cultures were more likely to tell stories of possession by demons. In all cultures, such possession narratives are usually tragic. It is conceivable, however, that some earlier dybbuk stories might have been played for laughs. For instance, in a tale from the sixteenth-century *Shivhei ha-Ari* (collected legends of Kabbalist Rabbi Isaac Luria of Sfat), a dybbuk enters a fish. The fish is caught, and the dybbuk promptly possesses the body of the woman who eats it. Rabbi Luria pronounces the Holy Name, and out pops the dybbuk, like a spiritual Heimlich manoeuvre removing a fish bone from her throat (Schwartz 1988, 12).

Other types of demons and the tales of their origins are found in Rabbinic sources: the majority are deadly serious. Gershom Scholem, the great modern scholar of Kabbalah, describes a class of demons who resemble poltergeists and enjoy mocking people. They were known as 'jesters' – *letzim* or *letzonim*. Typical is this tale collected in Romania in the nineteenth century, 'Mocking Devils', about a wagoner fooled by a demon in the shape of a buck. The wagoner hesitates but finally prays, and the apparition disappears, having mocked this insufficiently pious Jew (Schwartz 1988, 237). Isaac Bashevis Singer recounts this story in the voice of the mocking demon in 'From the Diary of One Not Born' (1985). Stories such as these are meant to evoke laughter, since the victim of the jester demon gets away with nothing more than a good scare. Another supernatural creature related to these *letzonim* is the *lantukh* or Yiddish hobgoblin. Singer devotes one of his *Stories for Children* to this being, similar to the English brownie or J. K. Rowling's house-elf.

In a completely different voice, Singer's Gothic short stories and novels for adults tell of possessions, lust, demonic infestations, visits from Satan and the dreadful punishments for yielding to his temptations. These stories evoke far more tears than laughter, though 'The Mirror' (1956), whose narrator is an imp, employs comic exaggeration and revels in its Rabelaisian excess. The imp hides in the mirror and tempts the vain wife Zirel to fly off with him to Hell, where Lilith and other devils torment her while the imp laughs (Singer 1985, 87).

In the 1930s in Warsaw and in New York, Singer was criticised by Yiddish-speaking intellectuals for these forays into the Gothic, for writing about the superstitions of the Old Country rather than the social problems of his times. In 1978, he was awarded the Nobel Prize for Literature for preserving these fragments of a vanished world. As the Nobel biographical note states, 'These demons are not only graphic literary symbols, but also real, tangible beings – Singer, in fact, says he believes in their physical presence. The middle ages rise up in his work and permeate the present' (Nobel n.d.). The word 'Gothic' does not appear in this note, but no better definition can be found than this last sentence. Singer's speech at the Nobel Banquet amplifies the definition, answering the question of 'Why do you write in Yiddish?' with 'I like to write ghost stories and nothing fits a ghost better than a dying language . . . Ghosts love Yiddish and as far as I know, they all speak it' (Nobel n.d.).

Though the writers who created nineteenth-century secular Yiddish literature were male, the language itself is affectionately known as 'mame-loshn' (mother tongue). In the twentieth century, women's voices finally began to be heard in print, in Yiddish and English. Ruth Bienstock Anolik argues that these Jewish women writers of fiction:

engage in a Bloomian misreading of the powerful texts of their tradition, particularly the folktales of the golem and the dybbuk. In appropriating and recreating these narratives in their own image, Jewish women writers open up a narrative space for the figure of the creative, powerful, and vocal woman. In revising and feminizing these narratives, Jewish women write themselves back into their tradition, appropriating the tradition and making it truly their own. (2001, 40)[8]

Ghosts of thousands of years of persecution, from the Romans to the Nazis, haunt Jewish Gothic drama and fiction. The most famous Jewish ghost story must be the play *The Dybbuk, or Between Two Worlds*, first performed in 1920. Its author, who wrote in Yiddish as S. Ansky, claimed that he had based it on an exorcism he witnessed while collecting folklore in the Russian Pale of Settlement just before World War 1. This tragic and profoundly Gothic play has themes of betrayal, thwarted love and vows that endure beyond life.

In the past few decades, there has been an increase in what might be termed 'Jewish magical realism', literature that accepts the ghosts, demons and monsters and uses them as agents of and occasions for satiric commentary. Deconstructing Ansky's drama, Ellen Galford's novel *The Dyke and the Dybbuk* (1994) is a Lesbian feminist picaresque romp set in contemporary London and the other world. In this novel, winner of the 1994 Lambda Literary Award for Best Lesbian and Gay Humour, Galford transforms the heterosexual pairing at the centre of Ansky's play into a series of lesbian relationships between mortals and immortals. This novel exemplifies Horner and Zlosnik's observation that in the Comic Gothic text, 'the diabolic energy of the Other is frequently translated into laughter and sexuality' (2000, 243). The novel's first thwarted lesbian romance leads Anya the Apostate to invoke a curse on the woman she loves who has left her for a husband: not only will Gittel be possessed by a dybbuk, but the curse will alight on her daughters for thirty-three generations. In the Old Country, a rabbi exorcises Gittel's possessing demon and imprisons her in a tree for several hundred years. Freed by a lightning strike, she discovers that all the Jews have disappeared. Eventually, this demon finds her way to London where the irreverent 'Dyke' of the title, Rainbow Rosenbloom, is Gittel's direct descendant.

The narrating voice of the dybbuk Kokos is learned and humorous – she knows the entire spectrum of Jewish demon-lore, as does her antagonist, the Rabbi ben Issachar, who would 'entrap us, paralyse us, make us appear, disappear, or generally jump through hoops for his greater glorification' (10). The rabbi gives the possessed bride Gittel an amulet in a glass of wine which he has blessed, but the dybbuk forces her to spit it out and tell the would-be exorcist 'Won't you ever learn, Shmuel? White wine with fish, red wine with incantations!' (11).

The dybbuk is (as befits such a being) well acquainted with the Gothic concept of the dead hand of the past. The shadow of the Holocaust lies over this novel: Rainbow Rosenbloom (*née* Rosalind) is a survivor, as is the Orthodox daughter of this generation's ben Issachar with whom Kokos causes Rainbow to fall in love. Their families have ended up in England instead of the gas chambers because they 'may have sniffed blood on the wind, or may have been looking for the golden city, but who, for whatever reason, took their future generations out of danger's way in time' (90). Rainbow knows enough dybbuk lore to be frightened, as does her friend Naomi, who says, mentioning the very example of Jewish Comic Gothic with which this chapter began, 'I'm a nice Jewish girl with one grandmother who sat through *Fiddler on the Roof* twenty-seven times and another who used to scare me to death with bedtime stories about the Evil Eye' (74). As Wisse notes, Jewish humour could cause those nightmares – and soothe them: Jewish writers and comedians were believed to possess 'an innate capacity for transmuting humiliation, subjugation, misery, and dread into funniness' (2013, 65). Kokos – and Galford – perform those very transmutations.

The Sheol (Hell) of Galford's novel is a capitalist world of competing corporations. The dybbuk emerges from her exile to find that she is now a low-level employee of Mephistco. Lilith, mother of demons in Jewish legend, is an executive: 'Lil, the magnificent, many-talented, shape-shifting demon queen' whose corporate garb is the seven-headed dragon of Revelations (145). The novel has a comic ending. In postmodern fashion, Kokos, (Old) Nick and Lil, finding themselves cast out of Hell in a hostile takeover by the Japanese afterlife, head for Hollywood to lend their talents to making horror films and comedies.

This postmodern narrator is doubly aware that she is a character in her own story. Rainbow's Orthodox love object Riva cites the taproot texts, demon stories from biblical to early modern sources, tragic and – more often – comic, attempting to warn Rainbow of her possessed state. Kokos reminds us of the tears beneath the laughter: 'Has our charming storyteller forgotten . . . the Christian world made no distinction between Jews and demons – knowing both had horns?' (182). Even in modern London, memories of persecution are never far from the minds of Jews.

Jewish Gothic folklore and the modern fiction that draws upon it rely on the mystical teachings of Kabbalah. While rationalist Judaism eschews speculation about the afterlife, Kabbalah encompasses the doctrine of reincarnation or the transmigration of souls. Such a soul in the process of being reborn is called a *gilgul*. The soul may be reborn in the body of a 'lesser creation' – even a rock or a plant, though a horse is a common incarnation. In *gilgul* tales, whether collected from oral tradition or from sixteenth-century manuscripts, the soul is harried from one life to the next by angels with rods, ever longing to escape these endless returns. However, when the soul occupies an animal body, even this tragic theme can yield a comic ending: in one Eastern European Jewish tale, 'The Wizard's Apprentice', the eponymous protagonist transforms himself into a horse and from there into other forms, bests his master in a wizard's duel, and all ends well (Schwartz 1988). Legends of reincarnation are made the vehicle for high comedy and biting satire on Hassidism by nineteenth-century Yiddish writer A. B. Gotlober in 'The Gilgul, or The Transmigration'.[9] This hilarious story is narrated by one such reincarnated soul, with humorous asides worthy of a Borscht Belt comedian; it is also a vicious satire on Hassidism from a sceptical writer of the Jewish Enlightenment or Haskalah. The narrator, now a ghost, recounts his many past lives, including one as a leech who sucks blood from a pious rabbi's haemorrhoids and next returns as a moneylender who sucks the life from his clients (1991, 427).

In *The Dyke and the Dybbuk*, Anya the Apostate becomes a *gilgul* who eventually repents of her actions. She exorcises and punishes Kokos, whose sarcastic voice contrasts with Anya's more serious tones. Anya reminds us of Lewis's Wandering Jew in *The Monk* – never permitted to rest in any place or age of the world. Anya compares being Jewish and lesbian to her present liminal status: 'women like me – and you – who walk like ghosts through a world that tries not to see us. Talk about lost tribes' (Galford 1994, 225).

The golem, the best-known supernatural figure in Jewish folklore, also derives from the teachings of Kabbalah. Mastering the art of manipulating the unpronounceable Hebrew letters of God's name would be to approach the condition of God, to create life. Thus, the golem: an artificial being of supernatural strength, created from clay and animated by the practical magic of a Kabbalist. Legends about wonder-working rabbis with mute, hulking servants spread throughout the Old World; many such legends attached themselves to one historic figure, Rabbi Jehuda Loew ben Bezalel of Prague (c. 1525–1609). This master of Kabbalah published many Talmudic commentaries and other books, but never did he claim to have created a golem. Legends grew about him in his lifetime, based on his friendship with the Emperor Rudolf and the circle of alchemists at the Hapsburg court, including Dr John Dee of Great Britain, as well as the astronomer Tycho Brahe. In folklore, Rabbi Loewe is remembered as a wizard (Ringel 1998, 256).

The characterisation of the Golem of Prague as heroic protector of the Jews dates only from 1904, when Jehudah (Yudl) Rosenberg claimed to have discovered a manuscript by the son-in-law of the Maharal (an acronymic title given to Rabbi Loew meaning 'great rabbi'), in which this rabbi creates the Golem expressly to shield the Jews in the Prague Ghetto from the Blood Libel of child sacrifice. The pamphlet, which Neugroschel calls 'grade-B Gothic' (1991, 701) was widely read: it became the source for most twentieth-century golem narratives. Its popularity is not surprising, given the resurgence of Blood Libel accusations in the Russian and Austro-Hungarian Empires, culminating in the infamous Mendel Beylis trial. The Gothic device of the lost and rediscovered manuscript frames the narrative of the sixteenth-century events and lends them the authority of a secret history.

Earlier golem stories – some of which were collected in Rosenberg's pamphlet along with the Blood Libel story – tended to be more comic, following the folkloric pattern of Dukas's 'The Sorcerer's Apprentice'. These folktales utilise the comic devices of gigantism, inflation and excess, emphasising the golem's stupidity and literal-mindedness. The golem is ordered to draw water, and he floods the town. He is ordered to bake matzo, and he uses all the wheat in the country. Typically, the golem is soulless and silent. Though the created being's actions may appear comic, they are nevertheless threatening, exemplifying laughter through tears. Only the golem's creator can stop his creation by removing the name of God from its mouth or by other methods.

While the most famous twentieth-century retellings of The Golem of Prague are tragic, in more recent transformations of the golem legend, this monstrous figure may inspire laughter as in Cynthia Ozick's collection of linked stories *The Puttermesser Papers* (1997) – or romance, in Marge Piercy's *He, She and It* (1991) and Helene Wecker's *The Golem and the Jinni* (2013). 'Puttermesser and Xanthippe' (1982), later included in *The Puttermesser Papers*, features a female golem with a female creator. Through the Gothic folklore of the golem, Ozick satirises the most serious subjects: feminism, ageing, municipal government. She names the corrupt Mayor of New York 'Malachy Mavett' – that is, 'Malach Ha-Mavet' – the Angel of Death. When Puttermesser becomes mayor, New York is transfigured – all is peace, honesty, utopia. But the creator begins to wonder about the ethics surrounding her own creation: 'Xanthippe did not exist before Puttermesser made her: that is clear enough. But Xanthippe made Puttermesser mayor, and Mayor Puttermesser too did not exist before. And that is just as clear. Puttermesser sees that she is the golem's golem' (Ozick 1982, 208). Eventually, the created being rebels against her mother, and Puttermesser is forced to uncreate her. Ozick uses the rhetorical devices of comic irony: deflation, exaggeration, juxtaposition. Xanthippe departs from the male golem tradition by developing an insatiable sexual appetite: though she cannot procreate, she can attract males – including her mother's lover.[10] The medieval Jewish commentators, however, were much clearer on the concept of sex with a golem. In the records of Talmudic disputation, one point of argument was whether golems could be counted in a minyan, the quorum of ten males required for communal prayer. The consensus of opinion was that golems could not be counted because they were uncircumcised, lacking any thing that could *be* circumcised.

The golem theme may have reached its peak of popularity with the success of *The Golem and the Jinni* by Helene Wecker (2013), which has received awards given for mainstream, fantastic, and Jewish fiction. Like Puttermesser's Xanthippe, this novel's female golem feels sexual desire. Her interspecies, interfaith romance with a Muslim Jinni comments on religion, illegal immigration and assimilation in early twentieth-century Manhattan. Like other immigrants, the golem Chava gazes at the Statue of Liberty, 'a gray-green woman standing in the middle of the water . . . she stood so still: was it another golem?' and concludes 'This, too, . . . was a constructed woman' (Wecker, 15). What a brilliant observation about the icon whom the Jewish poet Emma Lazarus first dubbed 'The New Colossus'. There are moments of comedy as the awkward and naïve Chava learns to navigate her strange new world.[11]

These deconstructions of the golem legends ask, 'What is the responsibility of the parent for the life she creates?' The works of Ozick and Wecker remind us inescapably of another novel by a woman about a created being abandoned by its creator. In Wecker's novel, Chava has two parents: Schall, a monstrous wizard, and the Rabbi, who names her after the first created woman (Chava is a Hebrew variant of Eve). Unlike Victor Frankenstein, the rabbi does not run away from this creature.

The transformation of the golem from object to subject is part of the process in postmodern popular culture of making the monstrous both heroic and comic. Like vampires and zombies, golems have been 'mainstreamed', losing their specific folkloric or historical associations in the Western (and Eastern – there are golems in Japanese games and texts) imaginary. The golem has become a benevolent protector, whether in children's books and video or in the online game of Minecraft which features Snow Golems and Iron Golems (Minecraft Wiki n.d.). Deracinated from its Jewish origin, golems have joined the collection of supernatural beings formerly monstrous, now cute and cuddly – Dracula, Cthulhu, zombies, Frankenstein's Creature. Hanukah 2014 brought children the 'Gelt-Giving Golem', a stuffed golem with Velcro hands that appears to be the Jewish equivalent of the creepy Elf on the Shelf. The marketing material shows Rabbi Loewe creating a Hanukah Golem who loves chocolate.

Ashkenazi folklore contains many comic tales not of monsters but of fools. Do they belong in a discussion of the Comic Gothic? Of course, they do. Fools are ridiculous and human with an aspect of the fantastic. They may be connected to the divine (the 'Holy Fool' found in Christian and Jewish traditions) or to the demonic (like Peter Schlemihl, who sold his shadow to the Gray Man). Since about the seventeenth century, Jewish tradition has assigned them a special home: the Polish village of Chelm, a real place, like Gotham, England's town of fools. In one origin tale, the angels emptied a bag containing the world's supply of fools over Chelm. By coincidence, one of the legendary golem-makers was Rabbi Elijah of Chelm who died in 1583. One legend said that he met his death while removing the crucial letter from his creation's forehead, 'when the golem became mud again, his whole weight fell on the rabbi, . . . and crushed him' (quoted in Scholem 1965, 201). Perhaps he was a Fool of Chelm.

The folktales about the fools of Chelm were originally designed for an adult audience who would appreciate their parodies of rabbinic wisdom literature; they were also satiric commentaries on conditions in the *shtetl*. Yiddish writer Menakhem Kipnis, who perished in the Warsaw Ghetto, wrote in 1930 of con men and fools in 'What Became of the Fools of Khelm?' but the laughter turns quickly to tears as one con artist convinces the entire town to drown themselves in order to reach *Yenne Velt* – the afterlife – from which they could return with gold and jewels. 'And that was how they perished and vanished – those old and beloved fools of Khelm, about whom the world tells so many . . . wonderful folk legends' (Kipnis 2002, 607). The message seems to be that only in the afterlife can there be a happy ending for the fools of Chelm. Isaac Bashevis Singer's 'Gimpel the Fool', translated from Yiddish by another Nobel laureate, Saul Bellow, is a parable narrated by a *tam*, a natural fool, the butt of everyone's jokes, everyone's victim. Gimpel's hope is also in the afterlife. Readers laugh through tears as he declares on his deathbed, 'When the time comes, I will go joyfully. Whatever may be there, it will be real, without complication, without ridicule, without deception . . . there even Gimpel cannot be deceived' (Singer 1985, 21).

When Singer began to write for children, he naturally turned to the comic folktales of Chelm. Since then, authors and illustrators have retold the supernatural tales Singer collected in *Stories for Children* (1966). For example, Francine Prose collaborated with David Podwal on *The Angels'*

Mistake, an attempt to explain the origin of the village of Chelm; their sequel, *The Demons' Mistake*, transports the Chelmites' demons to contemporary New York. These stories of Chelm are haunted by the other world, the world to come. Tragically, we know the fate of the actual inhabitants of Chelm who were sent to that other world by the Nazis. For today's audience, Jewish history and Yiddish folktales seem equally unreal – what could be more fantastic than the Holocaust, which wiped out fool and sage, unbeliever and pious Hassid alike? Or as in Singer's story 'The Last Demon', maybe even the demons as well, with no one left to fear them. 'Why demons, when man himself is a demon?' (1999, 90). The legendary monsters – golems, dybbuks, demons – lose their power to frighten us next to the banal evil of Hitler, Stalin and their all-too-human followers.

In reviewing contemporary writers of the Jewish Comic Gothic, it is no coincidence that so many women appear. These women writers have turned ancient patriarchal traditions upside down, resisting the Jewish Orthodoxy that to this day sees in a liberated woman the shadow of Lilith, mother of demons. They have also confronted the orthodox vision of the Gothic that demands a tragic ending, especially for the female characters. As Cixous states in 'The Laugh of the Medusa', women 'take pleasure in jumbling the order of space, in disorienting it, in changing around the furniture, dislocating things and values, breaking them all up, emptying structures, and turning propriety upside down' (1976, 887); feminine texts, claims Cixous, 'break up the "truth" with laughter' (888). Cixous never mentions Jewish writers in this groundbreaking essay. In *Portrait of Jacques Derrida as a Young Jewish Saint* (2004), however, she reclaims her Algerian Jewish origins. Of Derrida, her childhood friend, she says, 'And that laughing is another philosophical way of learning to die, this too he whispers to us in tears' (7). She asks, '*That's Jewish, you think?*' (7). Of course, it is.

The word 'Israel' (*Yisroel*) derives from one who wrestles with divine beings (Genesis 32: 29). Writers of Jewish heritage, female and male, have had more than enough Gothic history and superstition to struggle against, like Jacob wrestling the unnamed being who might be an angel. From the Middle Ages to the nineteenth-century Golden Age of Yiddish to present-day America, Britain and other countries not covered in this chapter, Jewish writers of the Comic Gothic have turned tears into laughter, and through that laughter conquered fears.

Notes

1. The Wandering Jew (Lewis 1796, 185) is 'doomed to inspire all who look on me with terror and detestation' (179).
2. See Horner and Zlosnik's serious treatment of this Comic Gothic text (2000, 243–8).
3. For analysis of the conjunction of Jews and vampires, see Malchow (1996); Lampert-Weissig (2015).
4. Most compilations of Jewish humour neglect the supernatural. Ausubel (1948); Novak and Waldoks (1981), Wisse (2013) and Krasny (2016) briefly mention supernatural folklore.
5. See Wisse (2013, 143–81); Steir-Livni (2017); Patt (2016).
6. See also Oring (1983, 268).
7. Ausubel (1948, xx).
8. For a feminist reading of Galford and other women's revisionist fictions of dybbuks, see Legutko (2010).
9. Originally published as *Der gilgl, humoristishe ertseylung, aroysgegebn fun dem gabes eynikl* [The Reincarnated Soul, a Humorous Story, Published by the Synagogue Warden's Grandson] (Gotlober 1871).
10. The golem as possible love-object is the theme of several popular contemporary novels: Marge Piercy's *He, She, and It* (1991) uses Gothic tropes but is not comic, while Frances Sherwood's *The Book of Splendor* is neither comic nor particularly Gothic. Anolik (2001, 41) lists other women's golem stories.
11. Wecker's sequel to this novel, *The Hidden Palace* (2021), leans more to adventure and the tragic Gothic rather than the comic or satiric.

References

Aleichem, Sholem. [1899] 1987. *Tevye the Dairyman and The Railroad Stories*. Trans. Hillel Halkin. New York: Shocken Books.

Anolik, Ruth Bienstock. 2001. 'Appropriating the Golem, Possessing the Dybbuk: Female Retellings of Jewish Tales'. *Modern Language Studies* 31, no. 2 (Autumn): 39–55. https://www.jstor.org/stable/3195336.

Ausubel, Nathan, ed. 1948. *A Treasury of Jewish Folklore*. New York: Crown.

Cixous, Hélène. 1976. 'The Laugh of the Medusa'. Trans. Keith Cohen and Paula Cohen. *Signs* 1, no. 4 (Summer): 875–93. https://www.jstor.org/stable/3173239.

Cixous, Hélène. 2004. *Portrait of Jacques Derrida as a Young Jewish Saint*. Trans. Beverley Bie Brahic. European Perspectives: A Series in Social Thought and Cultural Criticism. New York: Columbia University Press.

Du Maurier, George. 1895. *Trilby: A Novel*. London: Osgood, McIlvaine. https://books.google.com/books?id=HBMNrf-ULasC&newbks=1&newbks_redir=0&dq=Trilby&source=gbs_navlinks_s.

Galford, Ellen. 1994. *The Dyke and the Dybbuk*. New York: Seal Press.

Glaser, Amelia. 2012. *Jews and Ukrainians in Russia's Literary Borderlands: From the Shtetl Fair to the Petersburg Bookshop*. Chicago: Northwestern University Press.

Gotlober, A. B. [1871] 1991. 'The Gilgul or The Transmigration'. In *Great Tales of Jewish Occult and Fantasy*, edited and translated by Joachim Neugroschel, 386–434. New York: Outlet Books.

Horner, Avril and Sue Zlosnik. 2000. 'Comic Gothic'. In *A Companion to the Gothic*, edited by David Punter. 242–54. Oxford: Blackwell.

Kipnis, Menakhem. [1930] 2002. 'What Became of the Fools of Khelm?' In *No Star Too Beautiful: Yiddish Stories from 1382 to the Present*, edited and translated by Joachim Neugroschel, 600–7. New York: W.W. Norton.

Krasny, Michael. 2016. *Let There Be Laughter*. New York: William Morrow.

Lampert-Weissig, Lisa. 2015. 'The Vampire as Dark and Glorious Necessity in George Sylvester Viereck's *House of the Vampire* and Hanns Heinz Ewers's *Vampir*'. In *Open Graves, Open Minds: Representations of Vampires and the Undead from the Enlightenment to the Present Day*, edited by Sam George and Bill Hughes, 79–95. Manchester: Manchester University Press.

Legutko, Agnieszka. 2010. 'Feminist Dybbuks: Spirit Possession Motif in Post-Second Wave Jewish Women's Fiction'. *Bridges* 15, no. 1 (Spring). Special Issue: Fable, Folklore, and Legend: 6–26. https://doi.org/10.2979/bri.2010.15.1.6.

Lewis, Matthew G. [1796] 1952. *The Monk*. New York: Grove Press.

Malchow, H. L. 1996. *Gothic Images of Race in Nineteenth-Century Britain*. Stanford, CA: Stanford University Press.

Minecraft Wiki. n.d. 'Golem'. https://minecraft.fandom.com/wiki/Golem.

Neugroschel, Joachim, ed. and trans. 1991. *Great Tales of Jewish Occult and Fantasy: The Dybbuk and 30 Other Classic Stories*. New York: Outlet Books.

Nobel Prize. n.d. 'Isaac Bashevis Singer: Biographical'. https://www.nobelprize.org/prizes/literature/1978/singer/biographical.

Nobel Prize. n.d. 'Isaac Bashevis Singer: Banquet Speech'. https://www.nobelprize.org/prizes/literature/1978/singer/speech.

Novak, William and Moshe Waldoks, eds. 1981. *The Big Book of Jewish Humor*. New York: Harper.

Oring, Elliott. 1983. 'The People of the Joke: On the Conceptualization of a Jewish Humor'. *Western Folklore* 42, no. 4 (October): 261–71.

Ozick, Cynthia. 1982. 'Puttermesser and Xanthippe'. *Salmagundi* 55 (Winter): 163–225. https://www.jstor.org/stable/40547491.

Patt, Avinoam. 2016. 'Jewish Humor Before and During the Holocaust'. In *A Club of Their Own: Jewish Humorists and the Contemporary World*, edited by Eli Lederhendler and Gabriel N. Finder, 113–31. *Studies in Contemporary Jewry: An Annual*, vol. 29. Oxford: Oxford University Press.

Prose, Francine (author) and Mark H. Podwal (illustrator). 1997. *The Angel's Mistake: Stories of Chelm*. New York: Greenwillow.

Prose, Francine (author) and Mark H. Podwal (illustrator). 2000. *The Demons' Mistake: A Story from Chelm*. New York: Greenwillow.

Ringel, Faye. 1998. 'Wizards'. In *The Handbook to Gothic Literature*, edited by Marie Mulvey-Roberts, 256–8. London: Macmillan.

Rosenberg, Yudl. [1909] 1991. *The Golem*. In *Great Tales of Jewish Occult and Fantasy: The Dybbuk and 30 Other Classic Stories*. Trans. Joachim Neugroschel, 162–225. New York: Outlet Books.

Scholem, Gershom. 1965. *On the Kabbalah and its Symbolism*. Trans. Ralph Mannheim. New York: Schocken.

Schwartz, Howard. 1988. *Lilith's Cave: Jewish Tales of the Supernatural*. New York: Oxford University Press.

Singer, Isaac Bashevis. 1966. *Stories for Children*. New York: Farrar, Straus, Giroux.

Singer, Isaac Bashevis. 1985. *Gimpel the Fool and Other Stories*. New York: Farrar, Straus and Giroux.

Singer, Isaac Bashevis. [1964] 1999. 'The Last Demon'. Trans. Martha Glicklich and Cecil Hemley. *More Wandering Stars*, edited by Jack Dann, 89–98. Woodstock: Jewish Lights Publishing.

Steir-Livni, Liat. 2017. *Is It OK to Laugh About It?: Holocaust Humour, Satire and Parody in Israeli Culture*. London: Vallentine Mitchell.

Stoker, Bram. [1897] 2011. *Dracula*, edited by Roger Luckhurst. Oxford: Oxford World's Classics.

Walpole, Horace. [1764] 2014. *The Castle of Otranto: A Gothic Story*, edited by Nick Groom. Oxford: Oxford World's Classics.

Wecker, Helene. 2013. *The Golem and the Jinni*. New York: Harper.

Wecker, Helene. 2021. *The Hidden Palace*. New York: Harper.

Wisse, Ruth. 2013. *No Joke: Making Jewish Humor*. Princeton, NJ: Princeton University Press.

Further Reading

George, Sam and Bill Hughes, eds. 2015. *Open Graves, Open Minds: Representations of Vampires and the Undead from the Enlightenment to the Present Day*. Manchester: Manchester University Press.

Neugroschel, Joachim, ed. and trans. 2002. *No Star Too Beautiful: Yiddish Stories from 1382 to the Present*. New York: W.W. Norton.

Chapter 10

The Comic Gothic in Youth Literature: From the Explained Supernatural to the 'Whimsical Macabre'

Karen Coats

The presence of Gothic themes in children's literature has been fraught with controversy and questions at least since the emergence of Gothic literature itself in the mid-eighteenth century. In fact, Dale Townshend (2008) makes a compelling case that modern children's literature, which arguably began 'in the 1740s, [when] a cluster of London publishers began to produce new books designed to instruct and delight young readers' (Grenby 2014), developed largely in a direction that aimed to draw a sharp line between what was considered appropriate and beneficial for children and the Gothic melodramas that were becoming popular for adults at the time. While Avril Horner and Sue Zlosnik (2005) argue that the Gothic has always had the ability to both appal and amuse, children's literature operates, as Grenby notes, under a different mandate: to instruct and delight. In what follows, I trace the ways in which the Comic Gothic in literature for young readers has responded to this latter imperative. The relative weight of instruction and delight has certainly shifted over the years as literature for young readers has developed from its primarily educative and protectionist roots into a complex genre characterised by multimodal aesthetics and a more inclusive subject matter that has blurred the lines between adult and child reading that Townshend shows were so carefully and conscientiously drawn in the seventeenth and eighteenth centuries. Especially in recent years, crossover Gothic franchises such as the Harry Potter and Twilight series have attracted multi-age global fan bases, indicating an enormous appetite for stories that transform traditional figures and scenarios of horror into the redemptive if somewhat compromised endings readers have come to expect from children's literature. The result is a robust and varied approach to contemporary Comic Gothic that highlights increasingly ambiguous and ambivalent feelings about contemporary childhood. But those feelings have a history that began with a proto-version of the Comic Gothic in children's literature.

Before the Beginnings of Children's Comic Gothic

As Horner and Zlosnik (2005) note, a comic tendency in Gothic literature has been latent in the genre since its emergence in 1764 with Horace Walpole's *The Castle of Otranto*. This is certainly the case in texts explicitly written for children. Given the undeniable and persistent appeal of scary stories for children, it became clear quite early to children's authors that the explained supernatural offers a way to balance entertainment with the requirement that children's literature should also instruct children in accordance with the best educational theories of the day. Beginning in the seventeenth century, Reformationist and Enlightenment world views adumbrated new philosophies of childhood. The Reformers constructed the child as inherently poised on a precariously thin line between diabolical evil and saintly goodness and therefore in need of a frank disclosure of the consequences of their freely willed choices. European Enlightenment thinkers followed John Locke's claim that children are 'blank slates', innocently open to experience and thus in need of protection from anti-rational folk superstitions and fearful imaginings. Both perspectives had come to recognise that children's physicality, circumstances and capacities for affect and cognition would win out, however, resulting in a seemingly innate preference for literature that narrates vulnerability and gives material substance to existential anxieties and fears of being small in a big world, of the unknown and unknowable, of unruly desires regarding consumption and concomitant fears of being consumed. Heavily influenced by religious thinkers and rationalists alike, then, creators of literature for children increasingly sought to divert children's interests away from the sensational tales of horror and dark desires that they were naturally drawn to by crafting their own ideological agendas into works that would appeal to children.

Townshend (2008) points to two proto-Gothic scenes in John Newbery's *The History of Little Goody Two-Shoes* (1765) that mark a clear distinction between children's and adult literature in terms of what was considered acceptable in each: 'The same month in late 1764 which saw, with [*The Castle of*] *Otranto*, the hard-earned admission of the ghost to the pages of adult romance, the spectre – or, more accurately, the mere ghost of a ghost – was expelled from the realms of respectable literature for children' (Townshend 2008, 16). In the first scene, the villagers are awakened at four o'clock in the morning by the tolling of the church bells. Many are convinced that the bells have been pulled by the ghost of Lady Ducklington, whose funeral had been held in the church the previous day. The level-headed rector, refusing to countenance such a notion, opens the church door to a very relieved, very cold Little Margery Two-Shoes, who had fallen asleep after the funeral and awakened to find herself locked in. In the second scene, Margery has now become a teacher, and has used a barometer to advise her neighbours when they might take in their harvest to avoid wet weather. For this service she is accused of being a witch by people in neighbouring villages who have lost their own harvests to unseasonable rain. In her defence, she produces the barometer, at which point 'All the Company laughed and *Sir William Dove*, who was on the Bench, asked her Accusers, how they could be such Fools, as to think there was any such Thing as a Witch' (Part II: Chapter VI).

Townshend notes that these scenes are representative of the 'explained supernatural', which aimed to shift the direction of oral storytelling away from 'feminine forms of knowledge' (17) towards the Enlightenment goals of an 'anti-oral, anti-supernatural' (18) rationality. I would add that these scenes were likely very funny to their eighteenth-century readers even without the character laughter narrated in the second scene. In addition, they exhibit how Gothic themes would be treated throughout the course of children's literature, and their presentation is instructive with respect to how they construct the child Margery as more rational, and therefore more enlightened, than the adults around her. This is particularly true in the case of the first scene. The frightened adult villagers are called 'Blockheads' by the rector, indicating an inability to think for themselves. The church clerk, Will Dobbins, justifies his fear by insisting that his father has seen a ghost 'in the Shape of a Windmill, and it walked all round the Church in a white sheet, with Jack Boots on, and had a Gun by its Side instead of a Sword' (Part I: Chapter VI). This incongruous, absurd description would probably have been viewed as comical even if the rector had not responded in what was likely a sarcastic tone: 'A fine Picture of a Ghost truly, says Mr. *Long*, give me the Key of the Church, you Monkey.' The woodcut illustration that accompanies the episode shows a diminutive Margery standing apart from a group of adults huddled together, one bearing a cane, one a tankard; her hand is outstretched in a gesture that suggests she is beseeching them to be calm as she explains how she happened to get locked in the church and used the bells to summon help.

It is only when the rector leaves, however, that the ashamed parishioners are bold enough to ask her for the whole story. Her explanation is as much a sermon as a well-crafted tale of delicious suspense. Finding herself in pitch dark, she feels hands on her shoulders, a cold touch on her neck, a 'pit pat, pit pat, pit pat' sound following her down the church aisle; finally, she is bumped by something that almost knocks her down. All along, she comforts herself by praying and remembering that nothing can harm her as she is under the protection of God. She shuts herself into the enclosed pulpit, but a rustling noise prevents her from sleeping until it reveals itself to be a dog. She concludes her tale:

> As to my Part, I would as soon lie all Night in the Church as in any other Place; and I am sure that any little Boy or Girl, who is good, and loves GOD Almighty, and keeps his Commandments, may as safely lie in the Church, or the Church-yard, as any where else, if they take Care not to get Cold; for I am sure there are no Ghosts, either to hurt, or to frighten them; though any one possessed of Fear might have taken Neighbour *Saunderson's* Dog with his cold Nose for a Ghost; and if they had not been undeceived, as I was, would never have thought otherwise.

In the later scene, there is no appeal to religion at all. Margery's defence and wit have been inspired by the rational application of science and technology. The narrator intrudes with an injunction against sharing stories of the supernatural with the young: 'Mercy upon me! People stuff Children's Heads with Stories of Ghosts, Fairies, Witches, and such Nonsense when they are young, and so they continue Fools all their Days', adding that 'it is impossible for a Woman to pass for a Witch unless she is *very poor, very old*, and lives in a Neighbourhood where the People are *void of common sense*', and repeating that such people must be '*very stupid*' (Part II, Chapter VI).

Both scenes demonstrate the desire for the ascendency of rationality over superstition, positioning an orphaned child as its harbinger. Margery and her brother's orphaned and abused status is not accidental. Rather, it indicates a desire to break from a past that has kept people in subservience to outmoded ideas of the supernatural. And although there is no attempt to deceive the naïve populace by a supernatural ruse, the rest of her story is not unlike a typical plot in the *Scooby-Doo* franchise (1969–present). The villains of *The History of Little Goody Two-Shoes* are a pair of greedy men, who, through land grabs and the corrupt dispensing of justice, have displaced, impoverished and indirectly caused the death of Margery's parents. When the avaricious pair attempt to do yet another shady deal, Margery and her brother, now older, are able to expose and bring them to justice; in other words, they would have got away with it had it not been for those meddling kids.

At the same time, however, this proto-Gothic tale also shows how the entanglement of titillating dread, religious doctrine and rationality in eighteenth-century children's literature could deploy superiority humour to showcase the absurdity of certain beliefs. Earlier religious writers like John Bunyan (1628–88), James Janeway (1636–74) and Isaac Watts

(1674–1748) took a more serious approach by drawing upon the hellish imagery of their faith for their quest narratives, melodrama and memorable poetry. There is no humour in *The Pilgrim's Progress* (Bunyan 1678), *A Token for Children: Being an exact account of the conversions, holy and exemplary lives, and joyful deaths of several young children* (Janeway 1671–2), or Watts's injunctive poetry. Instead, the overbearing earnestness of their presentations of virtue and prudence as the condition for a good and prosperous life made them ripe for parody as the speculative economy of the nineteenth century and after displaced such a simple view of cause and effect. Instead of Janeway's naturally pious or repentant children rewarded with early death as a means to inspire religious feeling in readers, Heinrich Hoffmann offered an anthology of humorously grim and grisly fates for children who would not listen to their elders in *Der Struwwelpeter* (1845, expanded and translated into English in 1847). Lewis Carroll's parodic treatment of Watts's poetry in his Alice books is well known. Edmund Gorey, inspired by such stories, severed the connection between misbehaviour and death altogether with *The Gashlycrumb Tinies* (1963). And allusions to Bunyan's text appear in countless children's books producing serious or humorous effects, most recently perhaps in Chris Riddell's Goth Girl series (2013–17), where Bunyan's Slough of Despond is part of Metaphorical Smith's Hobbyhorse Racecourse on the grounds of Ghastly-Gorm Hall. While these and other parodies and allusions can be experienced as humorous even without detailed knowledge of the originals, they represent an assertion of superiority over previous ways of thinking about the education of children. They cast the reader as knowing, transgressive and self-aware rather than naïve, well able not only to recognise absurdity and distinguish fantastic exaggeration from real world violence and natural consequences, but also to find such incongruous and hyperbolic literary treatments funny.

Writers more committed to the expulsion of folk superstitions (even if they believed in the truth of religious doctrines), such as Sarah Trimmer (1741–1810), Anna Laetitia Barbauld (1743–1825) and Maria Edgeworth (1768–1849), sought to craft quotidian stories and dialogues that relied on rational explanations and natural consequences of human behaviour for engaging the interests of their readers. Their work was undeniably popular and influential for a significant period, but their focus on real-world social reform through exclusively rational education led to their expelling not just the Gothic but also any kind of fantasy from children's reading. However, their attempts to impose rational goodness by excluding wild flights of fancy and anarchist desire from the literature children read were bound to fail eventually for at least two reasons: first, because unalloyed, everyday goodness is boring, and second, because good children rewarded for their rational decisions set against bad children punished for transgressive desires alienates readers from themselves. It may be true enough that 'superiority humour' depends on the assertion of rationality over those who are intellectually inferior, but the use of real child characters may cut too close to the bone for the distance required to make such naivety consistently funny for readers. Hence, Gothic themes once banned from childhood reading returned to literature by way of the Romantics, who championed the unfettered intensity of their own childly imaginations which they claimed were fed by wild tales of the supernatural. As a result, efforts to exalt the dominance of rational instruction over the fears and tenebrous interests of childhood worked, but in a paradoxical way. Belief in the supernatural, extreme emotional displays, mysteries of the body and fear of the dark began to be represented more often in children's books, but as a world apart, a rabbit hole to go down, a realm of animated toys, or a neverland to fly away to before growing up and leaving such folly behind. The Comic Gothic thus returned to its roots as 'the means through which we reify our own enlightenment' (Spooner 2006, 25) as mature grown-ups.

Children's Bodies and the Comic Gothic

Critical explorations of the Comic Gothic often focus on defending the value of particular texts or motifs (for example, Cross 2008; McGillis 2009) or critiquing the ways in which individual texts or series confront cultural ideologies (for example, Nodelman 1997; Dahlen and Thomas 2022). This granular focus is understandable, given that the proliferation and variety of contemporary Comic Gothic texts make it extremely hard to give a big picture overview or theory that would explain how the genre works. However, I will attempt to advance some general ideas about functions and patterns rather than close read individual texts to suggest how we might conceptualise not only Comic Gothic's acceptability but arguably its dominance as an aesthetic literary experience for young readers.

The popularity of the Comic Gothic in children's literature may have waxed and waned over time, but like any good monster, it always returns. Part of the reason for that, I argue, is because of the role it plays in the development and affirmation of a child's sense of self. Peter Hollindale (1997) argues that every children's book stages an encounter with its readers that demonstrates a construction of what he calls 'childness' – the quality of being a child in a certain place and time – offering them the opportunity to consider how they are situated within that construction. While some aspects of these constructions vary by time and place, certain tropes of the Gothic, including the vulnerability of small and weak protagonists facing looming adversaries, heightened emotions, unfixed dread, forbidden spaces and knowledge, secrets, morphing bodies, etc., are features of everyday life for children no matter what era or culture in which they live. Comic interludes and resolutions offer release from the anxiety engendered by these material conditions through vicarious immersion in the plight of the characters.

The duality of affects in the Comic Gothic thus speaks to child readers of their own childness in a very distinctive way. Jerry Griswold (2006) argues that there are five dominant themes in children's literature that correspond to the experience of childhood itself: snugness, aliveness, smallness, lightness and scariness. Of course we might map these onto dominant themes in Gothic literature: snugness can alternately imply cosy enclosure or a fear of entombment; aliveness speaks to the sense of a fully animate universe, from talking animals to live dolls to spectres to the undead; smallness evokes the vulnerability of a mere human in contrast to the shape-shifting, grotesque bodies of monsters; and lightness calls to mind the construction of the child at play as analogous to how the denial of depth in the Gothic plays within and against the Romantic 'desire for plenitude, for interiority and depth' (Spooner 2006, 28).

The fact that the Comic Gothic inclines toward humour rather than horror when addressing each of these themes highlights the childly focus of the texts. Contemporary constructions of childhood have come to acknowledge the depth and intensity of both positive and negative feelings of which children are capable, but there is nonetheless a tendency to promote positive and prosocial affects to the point of pathologising sadness and anxiety in children. So what to do about scariness in their literature? Whence its undeniable appeal for children, and how does a comic intrusion or reversal function for its readers? Griswold argues that children like to read scary stories because they 'evoke a more intense feeling of being alive and a heightened recognition of being an individual' (2006, 49). For cosseted children in reasonably safe and affluent cultures, this opportunity to experience existential danger vicariously can be an awakening to a more meaningful sense of being a self in negotiation with a wider world. Since the fear-invoking stimulus comes from outside and is perceived as threatening, in other words, it makes developing children more aware that there is in fact an inside, an inner self, as it were, that needs protecting; it shows children their boundaries, and prompts a response of 'self-preservation' (49). The result of such encounters, Griswold notes, is visceral as well as cerebral: alongside the characters in the stories, readers' breath quickens, hearts beat faster, goosebumps rise. These physical sensations are the result of the adrenal gland secreting cortisol, which causes increased glucose production that fuels the brain and muscles to deal with stress. This makes a person feel physically strong and gives an energy boost. Moreover, the physical coordination of various parts of the brain working toward the same end makes a person feel more coherent and focused. As the stimulus is safely contained within the finite reality of a fictional setting and is for that reason already encoded for them with the appropriate cognitive labels or the physical responses they are having, the reader can enjoy the physical sensations of mounting tension. A comic intrusion or perspective within the story itself, then, not only enables a physical release of tension through laughter, but also implies and encourages children to further develop an 'intellectual resistance in the form of keeping a distance to all that is going on around us' (Zupančič 2008, 4).

Such cognitive distancing is also important for understanding how the Comic Gothic functions for children. The success of the comic turns not only on this embodied experience of tension and release, but also on the cognitive ability to imagine something otherwise without feeling threatened in oneself. For children in modernity, developing a stable sense of self that enables such detachment is an achievement, often hard won and consistently in danger of challenge to the point of dissolution, such that Gothic moments of horror/humour must be carefully staged and managed. Alenka Zupančič argues that this way of thinking about comedy as a distancing mechanism, is made possible through a 'metaphysics of finitude' (48); in other words, the secular-scientific world view has defanged comedy itself by positioning belief in anything beyond the phenomenal world as merely a carnivalesque excursion into absurdity, fun for a while, but not relevant to real life. She suggests that the insistence that there are enclosed finitudes – a real world and an unreal world safely contained in the temporal enclosure of a joke or fiction – denies the possibility of transcendence and foregrounds a sense of safe distance from what can't be explained in rational terms. The existence of multiple but separate finitudes is a point elaborated as essential to comedy by Peter Berger (2014) as well, though he suggests that encountering an alternate reality may open a path to religious belief rather than foreclose upon it. In fact, Victoria Nelson (2012, xi) goes so far as to suggest that contemporary Gothic(k) offers young readers an opportunity, 'even the only allowed one, a predominantly secular-scientific culture such as ours has for imagining and encountering the sacred, albeit in unconscious ways'. Like Zupančič, Berger draws on Hegel to suggest that comedy relies on the idea of 'a parallel world – somehow weightless, made of air, in which actions can be lightly begun and just as lightly ended' (Berger, 25). In this way of thinking, children's Comic Gothic fits snugly into the humanist-Romantic view of the self that dominates contemporary constructions of childhood. But conversely, the fact that children return to the Comic Gothic over and over again may highlight 'a *failed finitude* . . . a finitude with a leak in it' (52) that modern secularists are at pains to insist isn't there in the end; in other words, the educative quality of these texts doesn't seem to take hold without continual reinforcement. Zupančič argues that this failed finitude is where the really subversive quality of comedy lies; Berger goes further to suggest that recognising the leakiness of finitudes in the comic intrusion is a necessary but not sufficient or inevitable prelude to acknowledging realities only accessible through faith. Children are not as sure as unbelieving adults that the empirically perceptual world is all there is; by adding the Comic to the Gothic, adult authors open doors to the supernatural but may also seek to close them by encouraging children to see the absurdity of belief and retreat to the safety of a rationally explained supernatural. In the end, censorious adults, whether believers or not, who are worried about the effects of the Comic Gothic on questing young readers would do well to consider that comic objections to or parodies of the unsatisfactory aspects of everyday realities highlight injustice and enable new perspectives and possibilities for positive change to become thinkable.

The Way We Live, and Laugh, Now

Still, however, the burdens imposed upon children's literature to educate its readers into the values of a culture, or at the very least to do no harm, have continued to haunt the genre in general, and the Gothic in particular. In contemporary global cultures, these values include, of course, developing both literary competencies and the ability to accommodate shifting social values. The ability to locate the humour in a story, as in life, depends upon a perception of incongruity, which in turn relies on a deeply structural awareness of what has been presented as 'normal' or schematic through iterative practice. As deeper understandings of children's cognitive and affective development change and combine with adult ideologies about what makes a good life now and what will bring about better social futures, creators and publishers must strike a new balance between education (broadly conceived) and entertainment in the literature they share with children. Contemporary children's Comic Gothic participates in this project by taking many forms for various purposes. For instance, it may stage what appears to be a supernatural mystery that is later explained as a human ruse or simple misunderstanding; think of the *Scooby-Doo* franchise (1969–present) as a continual replay of the former, and Frances Hodgson Burnett's *The Secret Garden* (1911) as an example of the latter. It may weaponise the blithe innocence or unexpected talents of a vulnerable childlike character to defeat an evil villain. This is often the trajectory of Roald Dahl's Comic Gothic tales as well as Lemony Snicket's *Series of Unfortunate Events (*1999–2006) and picture books such as Susannah Lloyd and Ellie Snowdon's *The Terribly Friendly Fox* (2019). The latter is itself indebted to Beatrix Potter's many tales which can seem to fall into the Comic Gothic due to the sinister incongruity of cheerfully naïve animal characters lured to, but ultimately saved from, their deaths. Jon Klassen's Gothic vision is less redemptive, more in the tradition of the comic cautionary tales of Hoffman; his small animals who steal from larger ones suffer offstage deaths as a result of their transgressions. These Comic Gothic picture books also teach multimodal literary competencies of dramatic irony and attention to detail through a mismatch between the verbal texts and the illustrations.

Alternately, children's Comic Gothic may be deployed in the service of specific ideological agendas relevant to a wished-for real world by metaphor or analogy. In literature for middle grade or young adult readers, for instance, Gothic themes have been leveraged in the service of promoting gender fluidity, critiquing the effects of capitalism, patriarchy and colonialism, and championing posthuman and new materialist responses to environmental damage; many of these stories deploy horror leavened with irony, wit and dark humour. M. T. Anderson's *Thirsty* (1997), for instance, links the onset of awakening sexual desire to vampirism in cleverly campy ways, while Lynn Messina's *Little Vampire Women* (2010) exposes the creepy comic undertones latent in the original Victorian coming-of-age tale it parodies. Countless zombie novels satirise teen conformity and consumer culture while sparkly, reformed vampires just want to find love and live normal suburban lives. Comic Gothic literature for younger children, however, almost always stages and responds to threats closer to home and to the specificities of child embodiment, and uses humour, festive comedy, or reintegration to reassure child readers that they will survive whether by luck or by pluck. The first book in Jim Benton's Franny K. Stein series (2003–20), for instance, takes sharp aim at gender expectations as his eponymous protagonist makes a potion to transform herself from a girl who loves bats, flying piranhas, and dolls with steel teeth that can 'easily munch the heads off other dolls' (Benton 2003, 25) into a girly girl her classmates would not be afraid of. Her reverse Jekyll-Hyde transformation does not take, however, as her classmates continually need her outré skills and mad-scientist creativity to make their lives more interesting, as well as to rescue them from gruesomely comical monsters.

Such comic tales, whether redemptive or not, draw on the perennial fascination children and young adults have with scary stories while responding to contemporary adult concerns of their era, offering consolation to young readers and challenge to teens. As a result, these contemporary exemplars of the Comic Gothic for young readers may be too obvious in their metaphors to realise any real social or psychological change. Spooner (2006, 8) suggests that 'as a genre deliberately intended to provoke horror and unease, [contemporary Gothic] plays to audience expectations and therefore is rather too self-conscious to illuminate our most secret fears'. Enclosed in a carnivalesque world apart from the real one, such texts thus may have limited psychological effect and no evident prosocial reach. However, Julie Cross (2008) argues that they do have an educative purpose as they entertain and delight their readers with sophisticated intertextual wordplay. Beyond caricatures and pratfalls that serve to ameliorate fear, the Comic Gothic challenges readers by introducing aspects of irony and parody that encourage cognitive growth. Chris Riddell's Goth Girl series (2013–17) offers an example of this possibility with copious puns that require a lot of general and local knowledge. In *Goth Girl and the Fete Worse than Death* (2014), for instance, knowledge of British poets and baking celebrities is required for readers to recognise the clever spoofs on the personal styles of William Flake, The Hairy Hikers, Nigellina Superspoon, Gordon Ramsgate, Mary Huckleberry, Paul Hollyhead and Heston Harboil. Also making appearances are Alfred Lord Tennislesson and William Wordsworthalot. The footnotes broaden and deepen the allusions to British literature and culture (the poets, for instance, regularly sail across a lake in a pea-green boat), using humour to create insiders who get the jokes and challenge outsiders to remedy their ignorance so that they won't feel like they have missed something that was supposed to be funny.

Despite its references, the Goth Girl series does not seem to be making any commentary on the real world or the values of past literature. Instead, Catherine Spooner (2017) names the Goth Girl series as a prototype of the 'whimsical macabre'. This aestheticised version of the Comic Gothic:

> deliberately fuses the cute, fanciful and quirky with the gloomy, gruesome and morbid. It brings together images of, or associated with, childhood, often filtered through a retro or neo-Victorian lens, with Gothic and horror iconography, to create a genuinely comic effect ... defined principally through its playful, quirky manipulations of Gothic style and imagery. (104)

A version of the whimsical macabre is also evident in J. Patrick Lewis and Jane Yolen's poetic picture book, *Last Laughs: Animal Epitaphs* (2012) and the Comic Gothic concept books published by BabyLit, which ask babies to count tombstones (Adams 2012) or name the parts of Frankenstein's body (Adams 2014), inuring even very young children to the more horrific aspects of death and the monstrous by incorporating their incongruity into the normal flow of everyday experience. In *Frankenstein Makes a Sandwich* (2006) and *Frankenstein Takes the Cake* (2008), Adam Rex plays all the Gothic monsters for laughs in his illustrated anthologies of hilarious parodies of both classic and contemporary forms, highlighting the blur of genres, styles and time periods in the Comic Gothic as well as the 'complex playing off of fear against fun in twenty-first century Gothic, ultimately resulting in the containment of horror and disgust and prioritisation of consumption and pleasure' (Spooner 2017, 25). In the case of the Comic Gothic for children, I might argue against the containment of horror and disgust in favour of their leakiness into our contemporary notions of what is useful in drawing and keeping the attention of young readers. The humour in Rex's blog posts, comics, advertisements and illustrated poems taps a rich vein of knowledge of what adaptation theorists call culture-texts (Rose 1996). But children do not necessarily need to know the original stories of Dracula, Frankenstein, the Phantom of the Opera, or the Headless Horseman to appreciate the humour of Frankenstein using the rotten vegetables villagers throw at him to make a towering sandwich, witches advertising buckets of water as diet aids, or the Phantom not being able to get 'It's a Small World' out of his head. Rather, 'through the processes of consistent readaptation in popular media, and through the reusage and augmentation of motifs first appearing in earlier adaptations, a body of popular-cultural memories and associations is created' (Rose 1996, 3). When these associations are combined with everyday childhood experiences, the comic incongruity of the sons of Frankenstein and Dracula being more afraid of going to the dentist than of their monstrous dads both validates children's fears and renders them absurd.

A browse through the children's and young adult sections of any library or bookstore will reveal the enormous popularity of the Comic Gothic in contemporary literary aesthetics of youth literature. And while it is easy enough to say that this is a response to what children want and what we believe they need to develop a strong sense of self, questions remain as to how these texts construct our contemporary notions of childhood. Spooner also draws attention to what Maja Brzozowka-Brywczynska (2007, 214) specifies as the monstrous/cute, 'a cute as read through its thesaurus (endearing, loveable, delightful, darling, pretty) and then re-read through the notion of strangeness and marvel (something that is not as it seems, that suffers from innate contradictions)', arguing that the whimsical macabre 'is closely aligned ... but not reducible to it' (Spooner 2017, 104). Perhaps we might locate this difference in the attitude a text appears to take toward its intended readers. Whereas texts such as those by Hoffman, Gorey and Klassen expose the contradictions of the monstrous/cute by perpetrating extreme violence against child bodies, Rex's and Benton's texts sympathise with their powerlessness, as does Mo Willems in *Leonardo the Terrible Monster* (2008) by creating a monster whose attempts to be scary fall pathetically flat. The former may exercise, and exorcise, a certain amount of ambivalent aggression against the condition of childhood itself; its demands and desires *are* monstrous, transgressive, endlessly acquisitive, and thus they need to be contained or eliminated. The latter, by contrast, come alongside their quirky child and adult characters, acknowledging their existential difficulties, fears and desires, and proposing creative solutions and redemptive outcomes even for the most monstrous. That both these and other constructions of childhood within the Comic Gothic find room on contemporary bookshelves attests to the enduring need for a genre that will continue to adapt to shifting cultural ideologies in the face of the enduring qualities of childhood experience.

References

Adams, Jennifer. 2012. *Little Master Stoker: Dracula: A Babylit Counting Primer*. Illustrated by Alison Oliver. Layton, UT: Gibbs Smith.
Adams, Jennifer. 2014. *Little Miss Shelley: Frankenstein: An Anatomy Primer*. Illustrated by Alison Oliver. Layton, UT: Gibbs Smith.
Anderson, M. T. 1997. *Thirsty*. Somerville, MA: Candlewick.
Benton, Jim. 2003. *Franny K. Stein Mad Scientist: Lunch Walks Among Us*. New York: Simon & Schuster.
Berger, Peter L. 2014. *Redeeming Laughter: The Comic Dimension of Human Experience*, 2nd edn. Berlin: De Gruyter.
Brzozowka-Brywczynska, Maja. 2007. 'Monstrous/Cute: Notes on the Ambivalent Nature of Cuteness'. In *Monsters and the Monstrous: Myths and Metaphors of Enduring Evil*, edited by Niall Scott, 213–26. Amsterdam and New York: Rodopi.
Cross, Julie. 2008. 'Frightening and funny: Humour in children's Gothic fiction'. In *The Gothic in Children's Literature: Haunting the Borders*, edited by Anna Jackson, Karen Coats and Roderick McGillis, 57–76. New York: Routledge.
Dahlen, Sarah P. and Ebony E. Thomas, eds. 2022. *Harry Potter and the Other: Race, Justice, and Difference in the Wizarding World*. Jackson: University Press of Mississippi.

Grenby, Matthew O. 2014. *The Origins of Children's Literature*. British Library. https://www.bl.uk/romantics-and-victorians/articles/the-origins-of-childrens-literature.

Griswold, Jerry. 2006. *Feeling Like a Kid: Childhood and Children's Literature*. Baltimore: Johns Hopkins University Press.

Hollindale, Peter. 1997. *Signs of Childness in Children's Books*. Stroud: Thimble Press.

Horner, Avril and Sue Zlosnik. 2005. *Gothic and the Comic Turn*. Basingstoke: Palgrave Macmillan.

Lewis, Patrick and Jane Yolen. 2012. *Last Laughs: Animal Epitaphs*. Illustrated by Jeffrey S. Timmins. Watertown, MA: Charlesbridge.

Lloyd, Susannah and Ellie Snowdon. 2019. *The Terribly Friendly Fox*. London: Simon & Schuster.

McGillis, Roderick. 2009. 'Humour and the body in children's literature'. In *The Cambridge Companion to Children's Literature*, edited by Matthew Grenby and Andrea Immel, 258–71. Cambridge: Cambridge University Press.

Messina, Lynn. 2010. *Little Vampire Women*. New York: HarperTeen.

Nelson, Victoria. (2012). *Gothicka: Vampire Heroes, Human Gods, and the New Supernatural*. Cambridge, MA: Harvard University Press.

Newbery, John. [1765] 1881. *The History of Little Goody Two-Shoes*. https://www.gutenberg.org/files/13675/13675-h/13675-h.htm.

Nodelman, Perry. 1997. 'Ordinary monstrosity: The world of Goosebumps'. *Children's Literature Association Quarterly* 22, no. 3: 118–25.

Rex, Adam. 2006. *Frankenstein Makes a Sandwich*. Boston: Houghton Mifflin Harcourt.

Rex, Adam. 2008. *Frankenstein Takes the Cake*. Boston: Houghton Mifflin Harcourt.

Riddell, Chris. 2014. *Goth Girl and the Fete Worse than Death*. London: Macmillan Children's Books.

Rose, Brian A. 1996. *'Jekyll and Hyde' Adapted: Dramatizations of Cultural Anxiety*. Westport, CT: Greenwood.

Spooner, Catherine. 2006. *Contemporary Gothic*. London: Reaktion Books.

Spooner, Catherine. 2017. *Post-Millennial Gothic: Comedy, Romance, and the Rise of the 'Happy Gothic'*. London: Bloomsbury.

Townshend, Dale. 2008. 'The haunted nursery: 1764–1830'. *The Gothic in Children's Literature: Haunting the Borders*, edited by Anna Jackson, Karen Coats and Roderick McGillis, 15–38. New York: Routledge.

Willems, Mo. 2008. *Leonardo the Terrible Monster*. London: Walker.

Zupančič, Alenka. 2008. *The Odd One In: On Comedy*. Cambridge, MA: MIT Press.

Part III

Comic Gothic and the New Millennium

Chapter 11

Post-Apocalyptic Film and TV Capers: The Comedy Zombie, Capitalist Realism and the (End of the) Neoliberal World

Linnie Blake

For upwards of seventy years, the American zombie apocalypse narrative has enabled readers and viewers to explore the ways in which they think of their nation and themselves (Blake 2016b).[1] Since the 1980s, moreover, the zombie has become a mainstay of a form of politically engaged mass cultural product that I have termed 'Neoliberal Gothic' (Blake 2015, Blake and Monnet 2016). This eponymous sub-mode emerges from, and is explicitly critical of, free-market capitalism, that model of economic organisation that since the 1980s has promoted massive cuts to spending on health, education and welfare while championing heavy investment in the military and trade agreements that inherently favour the transnational corporation over the political desires and material needs of actual people. Reshaping global societies along aggressively Social Darwinist lines, the neoliberal neo-imperialists of the present have undertaken a number of measures, ranging from economic sanctions to regime change, that refashion global selfhood in the image of the market: precarious employment turning workers into endlessly mutable denizens of an ever-evolving global economy. The result has been not only the marked polarisation of global populations in terms of wealth but 'the erosion of democratic governance, the pulling apart of social cohesion, and the vanishing of equal opportunities for all' (OXFAM 2014). Stumbling through the ruined infrastructure of the neoliberal state, then, the zombie has become both the dehumanised incarnation of the 99 per cent of us who have been failed by free-market economics, and an abject embodiment of the avaricious appetites that neoliberalism embodies and enacts. Meanwhile, the post-apocalyptic landscapes zombies inhabit encapsulate, in Jameson's words, the core tenet of neoliberal life: that it is 'easier to imagine the end of the world than to imagine the end of capitalism' (Jameson 1994, vii). For, as my body of work on Neoliberal Gothic has argued (Blake 2016a, 2018), such monsters enable us to explore both the material changes wrought by neoliberalism and our psychosocial response to it as human beings while attempting, again in Jameson's words, 'to imagine capitalism by way of imagining the end of the world' (Jameson 1994, vii). This, in Jodi Dean's words, is because 'capitalism *is* the end of the world', its 'exploitation, dispossession, and confinement' of global populations being that which we 'witness and endure' every day 'in the ruins of everyday life', ours being 'lost lives, lives of loss' (Dean 2019).[2]

Given such a bleak prognosis for humanity, it is perhaps unsurprising that in recent years a lighter and self-consciously amusing form of zombie narrative has emerged, transforming neoliberalism's monster of choice into a pratfalling buffoon, a winsome romantic or an absurdist extra in narratives that privilege comedy and romance over horror. Such a figure, this chapter will argue, offers neoliberal audiences both escapist entertainment and comfort by undertaking a recuperation of the Gothic's subversive potentiality. Thus retaining the Gothic's modal deconstruction of the key binaries of enlightenment rationality (self and other; the socially acceptable and the transgressive; the predictable and the shocking; the normative and the aberrant, for example), these comedic narratives deploy laughter as a means of neutralising the neoliberal zombie's capacity for social and economic critique and proffer instead an amusingly 'gothicky' surface that, in Horkheimer and Adorno's formulation, merely reconciles us to the horrific conditions of everyday life in a profoundly unequal and inveterately unjust world.[3] In the first instance this chapter will examine such a cultural turn as it manifests in the films *Fido* (2006), *Warm Bodies* (2013), *Zombieland* (2009) and *Zombieland: Double Tap* (2019). It will argue that all these texts posit laughter as the only available response to the neoliberal condition and, in so doing, underscore our own entrapment within that state of passive acceptance of the late capitalist status quo that Mark Fisher has termed Capitalist Realism. Contrapuntally, however, it will subsequently explore the low-budget independent film *American Zombie* (2007), as Neoliberal Gothic refutation of Capitalist Realism that reaffirms both the zombie as agent of political analysis and the zombie narrative as exhortation to radical social change. Both texts are very funny and they deploy a brutal form of satire that is self-reflexively aware of comedy's ideologically regressive function and yet seeks to transcend the genre's reactionary potentiality to reaffirm the zombie's ongoing capacity for economic analysis and ideological critique.

***

While successive Republican and Democrat administrations had adopted an inveterately neoliberal agenda since Reagan, the events of September 11, 2001 precipitated the emergence of a new and unashamedly bellicose phase of global neoliberalisation. Distracting the American people from the fact that the object of attack was American corporate capitalism's imperialistic ambitions, the then President George W. Bush reconceptualised the day's events as an attack on 'freedom' itself: giving the red scare rhetoric of the 1950s an orientalist twist in the process (Blake 2011). Thus, as Naomi Klein explored at length in *The Shock Doctrine* (2007), fear was weaponised as a means of rolling back civil liberties at home and expanding markets abroad: as first the military destruction of Iraq and then its contractor-led reconstruction amply demonstrated. And so, in Marcuse's formulation, 'under the rule of a repressive whole, liberty [was] made into a powerful instrument of domination' (Marcuse 1964, 21), the simplistic rhetorical opposition between the rationalist democracies of the West and the primitive religious oligarchies of the East enabling a de facto privatisation of the Iraqi state while radically destabilising the entire Muslim world.

It was against this background of shrinking civil rights at home and militarised neoliberal expansion abroad that the comedy zombie narrative first came into being, the Canadian film *Fido* of 2006 best encapsulating the zeitgeist. A Sirkian melodrama with zombies, *Fido* offers an entirely historically apposite satire of the culture of fear on which disaster capitalism is predicated, undertaking an extended exploration of its impact on both the psychology of the frightened individual and the communities he or she inhabits. It is set in a re-imagined American 1950s, the 'mesmerizing lost reality of the Eisenhower era' that, in Jameson's words, was fixed in the national imagination as a period of 'peace and plenty, sunny suburbs and family-oriented social stability' (Jameson 1984, 67). And it satirises, accordingly, the ways in which American mass culture has configured the 1950s as 'lost object of desire', most recently as a conceptual escape from economic precarity and communal fragmentation of the neoliberal present while offering just enough social critique to satisfy liberal audiences aware that something has gone wrong but unsure as to how an alternative may be found.

Set some years after the zombie wars, the film thus opens with a black-and-white propaganda piece that captures admirably the style and tone of red-scare era public information films. An 'evil' radioactive dust cloud once engulfed 'our great planet', we are told, causing the dead to reanimate. It was neither the might of the state nor the inventiveness of the citizenry that rescued humanity, the newsreel pompously intones, but the amusingly named Dr Geiger, a Frankensteinian scientist and founder of the Zomcon Corporation. It is this extraordinary individual who is credited with discovering that to control a zombie's brain is to put it to productive use. And it is the corporation he founded that now encircles the small towns of the United States, the 'protective wall of steel' betwixt zombies and humans being both highly reminiscent of the securitisation of the American state in the years following 9/11 and foreshadowing Trump's 'build a wall' rhetoric on the 2016 election trail. With Geiger's invention of the 'domestication collar', moreover, a device highly redolent of the means historically deployed to subdue enslaved African Americans, the undead themselves have been transformed into commodities 'as gentle as a household pet'. Their surplus value may now be extracted as they are set to work in menial service-sector roles – packing shopping in supermarkets, working as crossing guards or as 'local colour' characters – waving to people entering or leaving the town.[4] For *Fido*, in other words, the comedy zombie exemplifies workers under capitalism, being deemed 'productive members of society' because they can become whatever the corporation needs them to be at any given moment, untroubled by the need for safe working conditions, mandatory hours of rest or a living wage. The world they inhabit, moreover, is that of the privately securitised state: Zomcom's alarm buttons peppering the neighbourhood and guaranteeing that any zombie who acts authentically and shrugs off its slave collar is effectively terminated. 'So thank you Zomcon', says the voice-over, 'for winning the zombie wars and giving us the company of tomorrow that gives us a safer future today.' It is a piece of self-consciously garbled rhetoric, of course. And it is funny: encapsulating as it does the obfuscatory nature of class relations under capitalism and the work of the media in assuaging the fear that the media itself promotes. So, just as the idyllic 1950s were themselves a highly oppressive decade of communist witch-hunts and wholesale infringements of civil liberties, the ostensibly idyllic town of Willard (named for a location in Romero's totemic *Night of the Living Dead*) is thus revealed as an oppressive surveillance society in which children are trained to shoot for the head and encouraged to join the Zomcon Scouts in preparation for life in service of the securitised corporation. Where it differs from the 1950s is that the business of oppression has been privatised, neoliberal style. Now the citizenry pay directly for their own protection: Zomcom's security alarms being installed, for a price, in family homes throughout the town.

Fido is a very funny film, Billy Connolly's performance in the title role (a combination of slapstick hilarity and befuddled romantic yearnings) enabling a very liberal affirmation of the inherent value of all Americans and a championing of their right to a life of sorts, a sensible degree of liberty, and the pursuit of happiness within the strictures of the heterosexual middle-class nuclear family. But while the satire is on point, the solutions offered to structural oppression under capitalism are reactionary at best. The zombies held in Zomcom's infernal headquarters may break free of their bounds in a spontaneous act of revolution. But they are rapidly and comprehensively crushed. The most an enslaved zombie can hope for, it seems, is incorporation into the neoliberal hegemony: Fido becoming an attentive surrogate father to the young Timmy while the now-undead Zomcom executive and patriarch Jonathan Bottoms gets his comeuppance by being brought under the control of his daughter. But there is no structural change deemed possible. The humanity of the zombie may have been affirmed within certain tightly controlled parameters but the nameless undead remain both enslaved by the economic and moral norms of the corporate state and happy in their enslavement. Any other form of living is as unimaginable, as is any form of life that is not suburban, middle class, capitalist and predominantly white. Even the taboo-busting romance between Timmy's mother and Fido is recuperated – offering considerably more than it delivers in terms of a radical revisioning of interpersonal relations under capitalism. Thus, Mark Fisher's Capitalist Realism is actualised in Willard and the satirical dimensions of the film are lost under a series of affirmations that it is heterosexual romance that has the capacity to curb the excesses of neoliberal securitisation: love can save us all. It is a profoundly regressive trope, of course, and one that is revisited in Jonathan Levine's *Warm Bodies* (2013) to similarly liberal effect.

Like *Fido*, *Warm Bodies* is a comedy zombie film that undertakes a sustained exploration of the ways in which undeath, like capitalism, reifies the individual – the protagonist-narrator's monologue pointing to the disjunction between his rich inner life and his social persona: a behoodied zombie shuffling through an unnamed airport in the company of numerous others differentiated mainly by their former jobs. For the post-apocalyptic world still bears the traces of its predecessor's division of labour, the zombies destined to walk for eternity bearing the signifiers of their former roles as cogs in the wheel of an advanced industrial society: a janitor, a personal trainer, the rich son of a corporate CEO. Some, like a chef complete with hat, or our hero, who imagines he was probably unemployed because he is wearing a hoodie, betray their past in their clothing or actions. Others, like the security guard who continues to scan those walking dead who pass through his metal detector, endlessly repeat the mechanised actions that dominated their working life. His repetitive action echoes, of course,

Marx's theorisation of the alienation of the worker under industrial capitalism, a paradigm that found its most famous filmic expression in the United States in Charlie Chaplin's *Modern Times* of 1936. But while preapocalypse class groupings may appear to have been swept away by the great leveller that is death, the post-apocalyptic world has instituted its own hierarchy: the ruling class here being the aggressive 'boneys' who 'eat anything with a heartbeat' and rule over the more recognisably human zombies who do the same but, in classic liberal mode, are said to have the decency to 'feel conflicted about it'.

This conflict is that of all neoliberal subjects who, like our hero, may know themselves to be unhappy, lonely and entrapped but have no idea as to what, if anything, may be done about it. For a while, it seems, the consumption of brains has given our hero the illusion of escape into the lives of others, offering a certain sense of intersubjectivity and a symbolic representation of our own consumption of mass culture under capitalism in the process. But this is a temporary expedient and, of course, it is not real. What *is* real, the film argues, are the comforts of heterosexual romance: *Warm Bodies* eschews the political critique of the Neoliberal Gothic for a kind of romantic comedy that is profoundly ideologically regressive. Enhancing the romantic dimensions is the soundtrack, including Bob Dylan's 'Shelter From the Storm' (whereby our hero expresses his desire to protect his human love object) and Bruce Springsteen's 'Everybody's got a Hungry Heart' (whereby he rejects the literal consumption of organs for something more intangibly dreamy). The comedy is neatly furnished both by Nicholas Hoult's winsomely startled performance and his voice-over, which reinforces the disjunction between his physical deadness and his yearning to be alive. Only when he begins to dream of his love object, then, does he begin the journey towards full sentience. And it is notable that in these dreams she whispers not sweet nothings in his ear but neoliberal ideology: 'You can be whatever you want to be', she opines, in much the same way as the language of unlimited free-market opportunities has affirmed unlimited possibilities to us all regardless of escalating inequalities. He wakes to find her gone and to realise, as many of us have realised before him, that he is in fact a 'slow, pale, dead-eyed, hunched-over zombie' in thrall to mystified social relations and reified to the bone.

This is not to imply, however, that *Warm Bodies* proffers a radical or liberatory message. It does not. Instead, like *Fido* before it, it recoups the revolutionary potential of both popular discontent with the status quo and the Gothic mode itself by reincorporating the abject within the cultural norms of the living. For our hero is not, it seems, as isolated as he believed. His friend Marcus and a group of inveterately romantic undead also 'want more' and their desire to become fully sensate leads them, inexorably, to realise their dreams, becoming human once more. It is a message that purports to be revolutionary, but on closer inspection is far from radical. The alliance of heavily militarised humans and human-aspirational zombies may take on the boneys who are, as has been established, 'too far gone to change'. And in victory, the undead may become free to 'learn how to live again' in an orgy of sunsets, baseball, hide and seek, and tolerant, connected acceptance. The film may even end with the giant wall that protected humanity from the zombie horde being demolished. But this is little more than a liberal fantasy that promises the unification of an increasingly polarised nation without meaningful analysis of the workings of power in the world. *Warm Bodies* reveals itself, accordingly, as an amusing exemplification of the obfuscatory nature of mass culture under capitalism, proffering a momentary distraction from the seemingly insurmountable horrors of the real world while evading any calls for structural change. For the filmic world has not been healed by economic justice but by the bourgeois imperatives of heterosexual romance, a romance that erases or absorbs difference and magically returns the world to its pre-zombie state.

The mega-hit zombie-comedy crossovers *Zombieland* (2009) and *Zombieland: Double Tap* (2019) offer a very similar vision, both being device-foregrounding, ideologically conservative road movies that function less as a critique of the present and more as an elegy for a lost way of life and its cultural products. There may be an intimation at the start of the first film that the 'pre-z' world had its flaws: the narrator observing of Garland, Texas, that 'it may look as if zombies destroyed it, but that's just Garland'. But this is as far as the film's engagement with, and critique of, our present moment goes. *Zombieland* does not, in other words, expand on the fact that like whole swathes of industrial America, the real Garland, Texas met its productive end long before the apocalypse, global shifts in manufacturing transforming the city into a service-sector economy where retail and the financial sector came to replace manufacturing and construction as agents of wealth generation. The film has no interest in rust-belt decay, community breakdown or economic precarity in other words. Instead, the dominant tone is a kind of late capitalist nostalgia, as Jameson defined it, for an America that has been lost and to which our protagonists long to return. 'Oh America!' proclaims our narrator at the start of the first film, as the Capitol burns:

> I wish I could tell you that this was still America. But I've come to think you can't have a country without people. And there are no people here. No, my friends. This is now the United States of Zombieland.

Accordingly, it comes as no surprise that our protagonists spend the two films that follow questing after symbolic objects from the American past – the Twinkie in the first film and Elvis Presley ephemera in the second – while reconstituting the American nuclear family from a motley collection of strangers who now name themselves after the towns they have come from or are heading to. Certainly, there is an intimation in this that in the post-zombie world people have become things but there is no exploration of the fact that as inhabitants of rust-belt cities they were reified by capitalism long before the first zombie took its first bite. This is because these inveterately American heroes, whose blacktop adventures draw heavily on both road movie and western conventions, are terminally invested in the ideology of American nationhood: exemplified by the confectionary of the first film and the blue suede shoes of the second. Like the 1950s suburbia satirised so ably by *Fido*, these objects embody the ways in which capitalism seeks to assuage our discontent with sweet treats and mass cultural products respectively. The billions of global dead, one notes, exist only as de-individuated antagonists that stand in the way of our heroes' nostalgic quest to recoup a lost America. For in true Capitalist Realist style, the end of the world may have destroyed capitalism, but it has not destroyed the yearning for its cultural products. The cultural nostalgia that pervades the diegetic world of the *Zombieland* films, in other words, is itself part of the neoliberal zeitgeist. For while the post-war consensus vanished under a global pandemic of neoliberal individualism, the dream of intergenerational social mobility upwards, communal cohesion and national economic pre-eminence remained. And, ironically, it was those very presidents who owed their public recognition to mass culture (B-movie actor Ronald Reagan and reality television star Donald Trump) who would escalate the advancement of the global free market while appealing to such dreams: both promising to somehow 'make America great again'.

Having established the ways in which the comedic reappropriation of the zombie functions as a means of defusing that figure's radical potential, this chapter considers texts that go beyond the nostalgic liberalism of films like *Warm Bodies* to offer an explicitly political critique of the economic factors that led to the increasingly authoritarian and xenophobic nature of American life. The television series *Z Nation* (2014–18), for example, is an often-surrealist blacktop adventure that lays the blame for the utter polarisation of the United States under Trump squarely at the feet of neoliberal corporatism and its agents. I conclude my argument with *American Zombie* (2007), a pitch-perfect parody of the documentary form that satirises that genre's tendency to spectacularise inequality while failing to provide coherent political analysis.

In *American Zombie* two documentary film-makers, Grace and John (the latter a rather sleazy tabloid type who dresses up in scrubs to pick up women), set out to chronicle the lives of LA County's resident undead – estimated by the Centre for the Study of the Living Deceased to stand between five and seven thousand. These range from the barely functional 'ferals' who live in tents in makeshift camps about the city, to those who can look after themselves but have little cognitive ability, to those who have most of their mental facility intact and can pass as human. From intercut interviews with characters like Dr Gloria Reynolds, epidemiologist, and the historian Roderigo Weiss we learn that the undead have at some point been infected with the R428 virus, which transforms them into zombies should they die violently. We then get to know several of the infected. These include the precariously employed Ivan who works the nightshift at the minimart and lives in a shared apartment with other undead and one human. This because 'it's impossible to get credit as a zombie' so it's either 'a shitty apartment or the bus stop'. Eating expired food from the minimart, Ivan tries 'to get as many preservatives in [his] body as possible' for obvious reasons. Judy, by contrast, is of a higher socio-economic class. She works for a health food company, enjoys scrapbooking, loves cats, is vegan and keeps an organic refrigerator. She is in utter denial about her zombie status ('it's not something I like to advertise') and wants to marry a human and adopt children. Thus the proletariat and the aspirational middle classes of the zombie world are encapsulated.

The most ostensibly political of the undead, though is Joel, being founder of the Zombie Advocacy Group ('we're here, we're dead, get used to it'), an organisation that clearly echoes the struggles of various identity groups under neoliberalism: class-based analysis having given way since the 1980s to a more issue-led politics that promotes the interests of marginalised groups without always being connected, in Cornel West's words,

> to deep political solidarity that hones in on a financialized form of predatory capitalism. A capitalism that is killing the planet, poor people, working people here and abroad. (Blakely 2020)

As such, Joel may demand that zombies secure the right to vote, marry and hold a driving licence, receive better health care, better jobs and ascend the social ladder 'to the top'. But he thinks this is best achieved by placing the 'untapped labour pool' in exploitative employment conditions where their utter 'flexibility' (a concept beloved of neoliberal employers) makes them an 'ideal workforce'. Taking no breaks, receiving virtually no wages and no overtime pay at all, they now work the city's very worst jobs formerly taken, it is acknowledged, by Mexicans. Thus, the cornerstone of national ideology – that aliens may be appropriately Americanised by working hard without complaining in the face of exploitative employment conditions – is revisited through the figure of the zombie. And Joel reveals himself as a liberal apologist for injustice in thrall to the self-same ideology that underpinned eighteenth-century discourses of America's democratic exceptionalism: personal advancement through hard work and social compliance. Indicted alongside him are this impotent civil rights activist, the heartless employer and the film-makers Grace and John themselves, who are aware of their responsibilities as documentarians and fail to do a thing.

Meantime, as is always the case in neoliberal societies, a zombie service sector has emerged – a range of specialists owing their roles and their income to the undead. Apart from Joel's legal counsel, whose motive is clearly sexual, none work towards the actual liberation of their client base. They include the Revenant Psychologist who counsels those confused by their new identities, the priest who sees the undead as 'an untapped market for spiritual enlightenment' claiming 'Jesus was the original zombie', and the art critic who asserts that 'the emergence of zombie art is singularly the most important thing to happen on the Los Angeles art scene in the last 20 years' and gleefully asserts that they and he are 'going to make a mint'. More viscerally, there's Esperanza McNunn – a faith healer who has marketized Native American and Caribbean folk practices to treat zombie hair loss, skin decay and maggots. Thus, the reification of people by capitalism is very much present in *American Zombie* the movie, but Grace and John's documentary opts instead to focus on the sensationalist events of the 'Live Dead' festival – where mysterious blue vials are taken by the zombie festival goers and a living person is ostensibly, and willingly, consumed. Hence, Grace and John's film is reappropriated by dominant ideologies of national identity and individual subjectivity, losing sight of the economics of zombie subsistence and focusing on the Zombie Advocacy Group's links to domestic terrorism instead.

In a downbeat, low-budget way *American Zombie* is certainly a very funny film. It gives us a soundtrack of socially aspirational zombie rap: 'I know we're half dead; we're just like you (tryna get ahead).' It gives us a film-maker so culturally tone-deaf that he incessantly enquires as to whether these very human zombies have fridges full of human brains. It paints a hysterical picture of heterosexual human-zombie sex, which is predictably terrible but with interestingly bitey foreplay. And in so doing it echoes how inadequate many American film-makers are when it comes to drilling down into the root causes of contemporary social disadvantage and the ramifications, for social stability, of escalating inequalities. It is significant, then, that the film closes with John being savaged by former health-freak assimilationist Judy, who has now embraced her zombie-self and turned John into that which he most fears: a zombie. Uniquely, the film closes with hope not for the re-humanisation of the zombie or his assimilation into human society but for his victory over the living. As zombie activist Joel, abandoning his liberal civil rights persona says: 'Day's gonna come; we're gonna rise; and you guys are gonna be fucked.' It is a profoundly revolutionary message.

The films considered in this chapter can all be seen to embody the Gothic's tendency to borrow from other texts, genres and modes to express what Victor Sage termed 'epistemological doubt [...] in the presence of death' (Sage 1994, 193). In this case, this includes not only the mortality of the individual but of the self under capitalism and, moreover, the death of both the post-war consensus but also the Enlightenment project's commitment to rationality and to rights. They also function, in Jerrold E. Hogle's words, as 'repositor[ies] of the newest contradictions and anxieties in western life' (Hogle 2002, 247), specifically the growing awareness that we have been enslaved by an economic system that teaches us to believe we are free. As we have seen, films like *Fido*, *Zombieland* and *Warm Bodies* echo the seemingly inevitable recuperation of radical energies by capitalist ideology. Others, like *American Zombie*, undertake a highly self-aware exploration of the role of mass culture in the promotion of Capitalist Realism, existing on what Avril Horner and Sue Zlosnik have called 'the unstable boundary between humour and horror', a boundary they set about transgressing 'in both directions' (Horner and Zlosnik 2005, 165). Thus, I have argued that the comical pratfalls, explosive pyrotechnics and parodic social milieux of the comedy zombie can be seen to provide a certain light relief from neoliberalism's insistent rush to planetary annihilation even as the sub-mode puts an amusing spin on the alienation of the individual under capitalism. But this is not necessarily a radical impulse, these films functioning far too often as a means of stitching audiences ever more tightly into dominant ideologies of identity – capitalist individualism, bourgeois heterosexuality and normative whiteness. Laughter, many comedy-zombie films posit, is the only available response to the horrors of the neoliberal world: a profoundly reactionary vision. But this, as we have seen, is not the entire story, for as *American Zombie* attests, the sub-mode of zombie comedy can be seen on occasion to offer a radical, potentially revolutionary, message. Once more, it seems, the Gothic can be seen to proffer revolution and reaction in equal measure, its liminal protagonists standing on the border of life and death, radical energies and reactionary recuperation and in this instance, in William Paul's formulation: screaming and laughter.

Notes

1. Such texts would include the communist-inflected plant people of *Invasion of the Body Snatchers* (1956) and Richard Matheson's *I am Legend* (1954), and George A. Romero's original 'Dead' trilogy: *Night of the Living Dead* (1968), *Dawn of the Dead* (1978) and *Day of the Dead* (1985).
2. Dean is writing specifically of the work of the late critic and theorist Mark Fisher who very much made Jameson's observation his own in his 2009 work *Capitalist Realism*, in which he writes specifically about the ways in which neoliberalism forestalls our ability to imagine a way out of the horrors of the world the so-called free market made.
3. I deploy Alexandra Warwick's term 'gothicky' here to distinguish between Neoliberal Gothic's mission to expose and critique the failings of late capitalism and the mass cultural deployment of Gothic signifiers to evoke the Gothic while retrenching that sense of the inescapability of late capitalism and its preferred modes of social organisation: the individual, the family, the market.
4. It is notable that Edgar Wright's *Shaun of the Dead* (2004) was the first to garner a laugh from putting zombies to work in poorly paid service-sector capacities, such as trolley collectors in supermarkets. It is a trope much used subsequently both to prompt laughter and foster a sense of audience identification with these mindless modalities of capital.

References

Blake, Linnie. 2011. '"I am the devil and I'm here to do the devil's work": Rob Zombie, George Bush and the Limits of American Freedom'. In *American Horror after 9/11*, edited by Aviva Briefel and Jay McRoy, 186–99. Austin: University of Texas Press.

Blake, Linnie. 2015. '"Are We Worth Saving? You Tell Me": Neoliberalism, Zombies and the Failure of Free Trade'. *Gothic Studies* 17, no. 2: 26–41.

Blake, Linnie. 2016a. 'Catastrophic Events and Queer Northern Villages: Zombie Pharmacology in the Flesh'. In *Neoliberal Gothic: International Gothic in the Neoliberal Age*, edited by Linnie Blake and Agnieszka Soltysik Monnet, 104–21. Manchester: Manchester University Press.

Blake, Linnie. 2016b. 'Consumed Out of the Good Land: The American Zombie, Geopolitics and The Post-War World'. In *American Gothic Culture: An Edinburgh Companion*, edited by Jason Haslam and Joel Faflak, 222–36. Edinburgh: Edinburgh University Press.

Blake, Linnie. 2018. 'Max Brooks's *World War Z* (2006) – Neoliberal Gothic'. In *The Gothic: A Reader,* edited by Simon Bacon, 195–201. London: Peter Lang.

Blake, Linnie and Agnieszka Soltysik Monnet, eds. 2016. *Neoliberal Gothic: International Gothic in the Neoliberal Age*. Manchester: Manchester University Press.

Blakely, Grace and *Tribune*. 2020. 'A World to Win: Liberation and Domination, An Interview with Cornell West', 1 October. https://blubrry.com/jacobin/68304940/a-world-to-win-liberation-and-domination-an-interview-with-cornel-west/

Dean, Jodi. 2019. 'Capitalism is the End of the World'. *Mediations: Journal of the Marxist Literary Group* 33, no. 1–2: *Realism Re-evaluated*. https://mediationsjournal.org/articles/end-of-world

Fisher, Mark. 2009. *Capitalist Realism: Is There No Alternative?* London: Zero Books.

Hogle, Jerrold E. 2002. 'Introduction: The Gothic in Western Culture'. In *Gothic Fiction*, edited by Jerrold E. Hogle, 1–20. Cambridge: Cambridge University Press.

Horkheimer, Max and Theodor Adorno. 1972. *The Culture Industry: Enlightenment as Mass Deception. The Dialectic of Enlightenment*, 120–67. New York: Herder and Herder.

Horner, Avril and Sue Zlosnik. 2005. *Gothic and the Comic Turn*. London: Palgrave Macmillan.

Jameson, Fredric. 1984. 'Postmodernism, Or, The Cultural Logic of Late Capitalism'. *New Left Review* 146 (July-August): 59–92.

Jameson, Fredric. 1994. *The Seeds of Time* New York: Columbia University Press.

Klein, Naomi. 2007. *The Shock Doctrine*. Toronto: Knopf Canada.

Marcuse, Herbert. 1964. *One-Dimensional Man: Studies in the Ideology of Advanced Industrial Society*. Boston: Beacon Press.

OXFAM. 2014. 'Working for the Few: Political Capture and Economic Inequality', 20 January. https://www-cdn.oxfam.org/s3fs-public/file_attachments/bp-working-for-few-political-capture-economic-inequality-200114-en_3.pdf

Paul, William. 1994. *Laughing Screaming: Modern Hollywood Horror and Comedy*. New York: Columbia University Press.

Sage, Victor. 1994. 'Gothic Laughter: Farce and Horror in Five Texts'. In *Gothick Origins and Innovations*, edited by Allan Lloyd Smith and Victor Sage, 190–201. Amsterdam: Rodopi.

Warwick, Alexandra. 2007. 'Feeling Gothicky?', *Gothic Studies* 9, no. 1: 5–15.

Wright, Edgar, dir. 2004. *Shaun of the Dead*. Universal Pictures. StudioCanal.

Further Reading

Blake, Linnie. 2002. 'Another One for the Fire: George A Romero's American Theology of the Flesh'. In *Shocking Cinema of the 1970s*, edited by Xavier Mendik, introduced by Michael Winner, 151–66. London: Noir Publishing.

Blake, Linnie. 2008. *The Wounds of Nations: Horror Cinema, Historical Trauma and National Identity*. Manchester: Manchester University Press.

Blake, Linnie. 2016. 'Gothic Rapture in the Hysterical Sublime?: *Twin Peaks* and the Origins of Neo-Liberal Gothic TV'. In *Return to Twin Peaks: New Approaches to Materiality, Theory, and Genre on Television*, edited by Catherine Spooner and Jeffrey Andrew Weinstock, 229–46. Basingstoke: Palgrave Macmillan.

Blake, Linnie. 2019. 'Neoliberal Gothic'. In *Twenty First Century Gothic: An Edinburgh Companion*, edited by Xavier Aldana Reyes and Maisha Wester, 60–71. Edinburgh: Edinburgh University Press.

Elliott, Kamilla. 2008. 'Gothic – Film – Parody'. In *The Routledge Companion to Gothic*, edited by Catherine Spooner and Emma McEvoy, 223–33. London: Routledge.

Holm, Nicholas. 2017. *Humour as Politics: The Political Aesthetics of Contemporary Comedy*. Basingstoke: Palgrave Macmillan.

Hutcheon, Linda. 1989. *The Politics of Postmodernism*. New York: Routledge.

Jowett, Lorna and Stacey Abbot. 2013. *TV Horror: The Dark Side of the Small Screen*. London: I. B. Tauris.

Lockyer, Sharon and Michael Pickering. 2009. 'Introduction: The Ethics and Aesthetics of Humour and Comedy'. In *Beyond a Joke: The Limits of Humour*, edited by Sharon Lockyer and Michael Pickering, 25–44. Basingstoke: Palgrave Macmillan.

Rancière, Jacques. 2009. 'Contemporary Art and the Politics of Aesthetics'. In *Communities of Sense: Rethinking Aesthetics and Politics*, edited by Beth Hinderliter, William Kaizen, Vered Maimon, Jaleh Mansoor and Seth McCormick, 31–50. Durham, NC: Duke University Press.

Tsakona, Villy and Diana Elena Popa. 2011. 'Humour in Politics and the Politics of Humour: An Introduction'. In *Studies in Political Humour: In Between Political Critique and Public Entertainment*, edited by Villy Tsakona, and Diana Elena Popa, 1–30. Amsterdam: John Benjamins.

Winthrop, John. 1630. 'A Modell of Christian Charity'. Collections of the Massachusetts Historical Society (Boston, 1838). 3rd series. 7: 31–48. https://history.hanover.edu/texts/winthmod.html

Wollin, Sheldon. 2008. *Democracy Incorporated: Managed Democracy and the Specter of Inverted Totalitarianism*. Princeton: Princeton University Press.

Chapter 12

Haunting Me, Haunting You: Gothic Parody and Melodrama in Thai Popular Horror

Katarzyna Ancuta

Making a case for Thai Gothic inevitably takes us beyond the confines of the genre as envisioned by traditionalists. While it is possible to find Thai literature that employs Gothic conventions, it is rarely imitative of Western texts and its 'Gothicism' needs to be demonstrated on home ground. Things are not easier in cinema, even though in this case Gothic has never been defined as a coherent genre and tends to be approached as either a subcategory of horror, or a broader visual aesthetics. Thai horror may have gained some recognition on international markets, but a significant part of local production never makes it abroad, as it is seen as incompatible with what global audiences have come to understand as the horror genre. In fact, Thai cinema does not even have a name for horror, designating the films into one of two groups: *nang phi* (films about ghosts, animistic spirits and magic, which constitute almost the entire local cinematic horror repertoire) and *nang sayong khwan* (films meant to terrify you with non-supernatural action). Thai horror cinema has benefited from the demand spurred by the global success of Japanese and Korean horror productions, winning the hearts of regional audiences with a new brand of pan-Asian urban middle-class vengeful ghost stories that have become the export face of the genre since the early 2000s. These new films, however, are not entirely representative of what Thai audiences recognise as horror, a category which, for better or for worse, is seen as the core of Thai popular cinema.

Thai popular cinema can be broadly described as locally (and often cheaply) produced films targeting lower-class urban and rural audiences. In the past, they were mostly screened at temple fairs and open-air markets by mobile cinemas and offered an alternative to the foreign productions that played in Bangkok's air-conditioned theatres to more elite viewers. The films were shot in a conventional style derived from popular performances, most notably *likay* – a dance-drama form of folk theatre. This translated into a rather static presentational style of cinematography and editing, meant to create an illusion that the events had been staged in front of the live audience, and affected the narrative structure (Ainslie 2012, 55). Just like *likay* performances, which tend to abandon structured storytelling in favour of improvisation and rely mostly on extravagant costumes, exaggerated acting and the audience's imagination, popular cinema assumes that the audience is already familiar with the story and enhances the plot with stock numbers – repetitive fixed scenes adding to overall entertainment (Ainslie 2012, 61). Patsorn Sungsri stresses the conventionality of the popular cinematic narrative, realised through the use of stock characters, including genderfluid ones, a 'flavoursome' blending of emotional states like excitement, melancholy or romance, and overall lack of realism (2004, 53–7). Thai popular cinema went through its golden age between the 1950s and 1970s, the period often referred to as the 16-mm era, leaving behind hundreds of cheaply produced movies made on 16-mm film stock with non-synchronised sound, many of which were ghost films. This is not to say that popular cinema is fully a thing of the past, as its conventions are very much alive in contemporary horror, comedies and action films, the three genres which, in the Thai context, frequently blend into one.

Humour has always been an integral part of Thai popular horror, to the extent that such films are often categorised in Thai as *talok-phi-kathoey*, the term referring to the obligatory 'unholy trinity' of ghosts, slapstick comedy and the *kathoey* – a Thai third gender category, typically reduced in such productions to its exaggerated loudmouth transsexual/drag representation, depicted in terms of the Gothic body which is simultaneously the site of ridicule and fear. This chapter attempts to distinguish between a horror comedy (a comedy film that purposefully uses horror elements to create a comic effect) and a popular horror film (a horror film which includes comic stock numbers to offset the scary parts). The chapter examines the work of two directors whose films allow us to illustrate this difference – Yuthlert Sippapak and Poj Arnon. Both directors are key figures of Thai popular cinema, even though they are associated with marginally different audiences. This chapter focuses on two longer film series – *Buppah Rahtree* (currently five films) by Sippapak, a tale of a very stubborn female ghost that refuses to leave her apartment, and *Hor Taew Tak* (currently seven films) by Arnon, which introduces a group of ghost-fighting drag queens. While *Hor Taew Tak* films are clearly horror comedies targeting LGBTQ+ audiences, *Buppah Rahtree* stays closer to conventional horror using humour to offset its Gothic content. Despite these differences, the article argues that the comic elements of these films are an indispensable part of their Gothic framework and intrinsic to Thai popular horror film in general.[1]

Her Name was Buppah, She Lived on the Sixth Floor: Thai Popular Horror as Comic Gothic Melodrama

Released in 2003, *Buppah Rahtree*, directed by Yuthlert Sippapak was one of the first Thai horror films that made waves at international festivals, for the most part leaving viewers and critics equally baffled. Mark R. Leeper, for instance, wrote about the film on *Rotten Tomatoes* in 2004: 'This ghost story goes in eight different directions at once, from tragic social message to slapstick comedy. Chilling, but the film is too unfocused', while Jon Condit of *Dread Central* speculated in 2005 that 'It's almost as if director Yuthlert Sippapak ... filmed three separate movies; a romantic drama, a comedy and a supernatural horror, and edited them together in post-production.' Perhaps partially in response to such criticism, in 2021, Sippapak uploaded his director's cut version of the film to YouTube. The new version removed over thirty minutes of original material but this did not affect the film's overall narrative structure, where the main plot is constantly interrupted by an inclusion of extended comic sequences built around stock characters and numbers. Today *Buppah Rahtree* and its sequels tend to be labelled as 'comedy horror' and left at that, but the film's apparent hybridity is inherent in Thai popular horror and needs to be addressed as such.

Buppah Rahtree tells the story of a lonely female student, Buppah, who dies and becomes a ghost terrorising the tenants of a Bangkok apartment complex. Buppah falls victim of a cruel prank when a rich boy, Ake, seduces her to win a bet and then 'ghosts' her without an explanation. Right on cue, she discovers she is pregnant, although the cause of her pregnancy is slightly obscured by the subsequent revelation of her being also sexually abused by her uncle. When Ake reappears apologising for his conduct and learns of Buppah's predicament, his parents help the couple arrange an abortion and promptly ship Ake to England to avoid further trouble. Abandoned once again, Buppah suffers a haemorrhage and dies in her apartment's bathroom all alone. Her body is discovered one month later when the landlady attempts to evict her for not paying rent.

This is when things begin to take a comic turn as Buppah's ghost resists the attempts to have her body removed from the room by the coroner, police, priests and a variety of shamans called to the rescue. Annoyed by their continuing efforts, Buppah reciprocates by turning into a tenant from hell – stalking her neighbours and shrieking all night long, until the building is left almost empty. When Ake returns to Bangkok and seems to reunite with Buppah, the remaining tenants are too scared to tell him that he shares the room with a ghost. Since Buppah wants to keep their relationship platonic, Ake cheats on her with the daughter of the porridge vendor, for which he gets promptly punished. Buppah burns his private parts with hot gruel and proceeds to amputate both of his legs (a nod to Takashi Miike's *Audition*). At the end of the film, we discover that Ake had actually died a while ago, and the person we saw with Buppah was already a ghost. Buppah is almost exorcised by a Khmer shaman but escapes and returns to her apartment unharmed. She continues to live in room 609 with her now legless ghost-boyfriend who seems to have accepted his fate.

Despite its fragmented plot, the first film in the series is certainly the most coherent. The sequel, *Rahtree Returns* (2005) focuses mostly on Ake, who strikes up a friendship with a blind tenant and mischievously torments a gang of pathetically incompetent bank robbers hiding from the police in one of the apartments. Exorcised at the end of the film, Buppah returns in part three (3.1) – *Rahtree Reborn* (2009) – where she is physically reborn as an abused schoolgirl and then, after the girl is raped and killed, is also spiritually reborn as the ghostly Buppah we know. From that point onwards, rather confusingly, she exists as two spectral presences – the ghost of little Buppah who seems bent on revenge and the ghost of adult Buppah who rekindles a relationship with her former student, Rung. In the fourth part (3.2), *Rahtree's Revenge* (2009), the murderous man-hating little Buppah takes over and goes on rampage leading to a massacre.[2]

Buppah Rahtree films follow a classic pattern of an Asian ghost story in which the corporeal manifestation of the ghost leads to situations where she is mistaken for a living person. The landlady, for instance, is shown having a conversation with Buppah about her rent after the girl has already died; similarly, Ake's ghost is shown interacting with the tenants throughout the film. The material condition of the ghosts allows them also to act as romantic partners and even engage in sexual acts with humans without raising any suspicion, a motif already present in the Chinese *zhiguai* (stories of the strange) – short writings seen as literary prototypes of the ghost story in the region, some of which, for instance Ban Gao's *Sou Shen Ji* ('In Search of the Supernatural'), date back to the fourth century. In the Thai context, *Buppah Rahtree* can be seen as a modern retelling of the famous Thai ghost story of Mae Nak Phra Khanong. As I have argued elsewhere (Ancuta 2020, 88–9), Mae Nak is a Thai version of a 'ghost-wife' – a category of spectral 'waiting women' frequently found in Asian folklore and its literary reiterations, for instance in the Japanese *kaidan* tales, like Ueda Akinari's *Ugetsu Monogatari* (*Tales of Moonlight and Rain*, 1778). The stories often share a similar theme of a man who resumes a relationship with a woman he previously abandoned only to discover that he has been living with a corpse. They are often told from the perspective of the woman who continues waiting for her wayward husband even after her death, ready to forgive him and take him back.

Mae Nak, who dies in childbirth awaiting the return of her husband from war, incorporates also the belief shared across Southeast Asia that ghosts of pregnant women, or those who died in childbirth, return as violent and powerful spirits. Known in Thai as *phi tai tham klom*, these ghosts are supposedly so fearsome that historical records refer to a barbaric practice of sacrificing pregnant women and burying them alive under buildings and city walls with load-bearing posts driven through their bellies in order to turn their spirits into guardians (Guelden 1995, 56–7). Although, unlike those women, Mae Nak does not get murdered but simply dies giving birth to a stillborn baby, she refuses to leave her house, guarding it in the absence of her husband. When the man finally comes home, she resumes her duties of a wife and a mother as if nothing has happened. The domestic bliss of the couple is interrupted by the villagers who try to warn the husband that he has been living with a ghost. Enraged, Mae Nak turns her anger against them. She then suffers the ultimate betrayal when the husband joins the villagers in appealing to a famous monk to have her exorcised. This final exorcism is sometimes depicted as a punishment of the unruly spirit, but most often it is portrayed as an act of love, since the Buddhist framing of the story makes us see ghosts as souls that need help to let go of their suffering.

The parallels between Buppah and Mae Nak are clear. Buppah dies as a result of a botched abortion. Waiting for Ake, she refuses to leave the apartment, because he promised he would be back. When Ake finally returns, she scares people to prevent them from revealing to him that she is dead. Like a dutiful ghost-wife, she takes care of her man, bringing him food and clothes. But Buppah also fits the description of another Thai ghost stereotype, that of an excessively possessive (and potentially deranged) girlfriend unwilling to let go of her boyfriend even after her death.[3] To prevent Ake from leaving her for another woman, she amputates his legs and keeps him tied to a bed where she tortures him on a whim. When he strikes up a conversation with a blind female tenant, she sews his mouth shut with a thread. Buppah's desire to control Ake is also emphasised in the film by the fact that she does not allow him to revert to his original form even when we already know he is a ghost. Unlike Buppah, who alternates between a scary version reflecting the condition of her corpse and her human form, Ake's ghost never regains his legs. If Buppah has no problem leaving the building to go on various errands, Ake is stuck in a wheelchair, confined to the apartment, and can make it as far as the rooftop at best. While the reason why he remains in this condition is never openly addressed, his appearance symbolises the unequal power balance in the couple's relationship. In that sense, Buppah clearly resembles other Asian female ghosts – women who lacked agency and were abused in life but became angry and powerful in death.

Buppah Rahtree films resist orderly narrative structure in favour of a kaleidoscopic display of Gothic and comic moments. It would be futile to suggest that they encapsulate Gothic on a generic level, as the internal hybridity of Thai popular horror makes it difficult to discuss as a coherent genre. Gothic tropes and conventions in the films tend to be employed in scenes meant to evoke terror (generating psychological responses related to anxiety and fear) and horror (through graphic displays of body horror, frightening and disgusting in equal measures). They are often used to produce a melodramatic effect, particularly in the context of the films' social commentary on class and gender inequalities at the roots of domestic violence. The affinity between Gothic and melodrama is well documented. Michael Gamer has argued that 'Gothic was the first language of melodrama' (2018, 32) since melodrama was keen to emulate the visual and sonic effects of Gothic novels and plays. Pointing to the links between melodrama and Gothic sensation novel, Lisa Schmidt has argued that 'melodrama [. . .] turns out to be a constituent of the Gothic experience of horror' (2013, 162). Peter Brooks's criteria for melodrama which include '[t]he indulgence of strong emotionalism; moral polarisation and schematisation; extreme states of being, situations, action; overt villainy, persecution of the good, and final reward of virtue; inflated and extravagant expression; dark plottings, suspense, [and] breathtaking peripety' (1995: 11–12), can simultaneously be applied to many Gothic tales. They work equally well in Thai popular horror.

On some level then, the internal hybridity of films like *Buppah Rahtree* can be explained by their reliance on genre-crossing Gothic melodrama. Gamer notes that the appeal of melodrama lies in its tendency 'to consume other genres into itself' (2018, 37), adding that Gothic melodramas are known to fervently cannibalise an abundance of sources 'to create highly wrought scenes of action and suspense' (37), and that their impact is measured by their ability to thrill and confound the audiences by transforming familiar materials into something new and exciting. Avril Horner and Sue Zlosnik have argued that Gothic's incongruity and hybridity also open up 'the possibility of a comic turn in the presence of horror or terror' (2005, 3), a quality that should not be dismissed as merely 'the hysterical laughter of comic relief' (3) but rather understood as 'an exploitation of the stylised theatricality of the Gothic device, which is always teetering on the edge of self-parody' (12). Thai popular cinema provides us with two possible methods of combining comic and Gothic elements in a film: by creating a linear narrative structure with (at least) two independent plot lines, where scary, serious or tragic scenes that belong to the main plot line are interrupted by loosely related (or unrelated) comedy skits, or by resorting to predictable Gothic/horror tropes and formulae for a comic effect, mostly through pastiche and parody.

Buppah Rahtree is a clear example of the first option, with its main plot line focusing on the relationship between Buppah and Ake supplemented by a variety of peripheral sequences that act as a distraction. These short interludes focus on an abundance of stock characters representing popular comic types: swindlers, gamblers, fake shamans and exorcists, weak men and bossy women, cowardly police offices and guards, and loudmouth gossiping *kathoeys*. In Thai figurative art and drama, such lower-class characters are considered complementary to noble dramatic characters the story focuses on. They are also represented differently: positioned on the margins of Buddhist murals, not stylised or ornamented, considered vulgar characters, portrayed in mundane everyday situations often foregrounding actions inseparably tied to their bodies (e.g. eating, smoking, making love or giving birth), and expressive of emotions. Their clothes, possessions, even the colour of their skin mark them as 'ordinary' and therefore having no real dramatic importance (Sungsri 2004, 42). In popular cinema narratives, aimed at the 'ordinary' audience, such scenes can often take up a significant portion of screen time as they afford their viewers a specific vantage point from which they can enjoy, interpret and even interact with the film, and encourage empathic identification.

Berys Gaut (2010) distinguishes between imaginative and empathic identification in cinema, with the former requiring the viewers to imagine themselves in the position of the characters they identify with, and the latter which suggests that identification with fictional characters triggers actual emotional responses in the viewers. Like other forms of communal entertainment, popular cinema promotes participation and films are meant to be part of the shared experience. Popular cinema audiences are encouraged to watch films in groups and respond affectively, and one way to ensure that is to provide opportunities for the audience to claim the narrative as their own. Gaut divided imaginative identification into perceptual, affective, motivational, epistemic and practical aspects, or imagining what the character sees, feels, wants, believes in and does (258, 263). In Thai popular cinema, the practical aspect is of primary importance – the more detailed and authentic the films' reconstruction of everyday reality known to the audience, the easier they are to identify with.

Popular films gain credibility by ensuring that their characters wear 'authentic' clothes, eat the right food and travel on buses that stick to their regular routes. Buppah's condominium is even identified by its actual name and address, Oscar Apartment in Bangkok's central area of Makkasan, the now demolished location supposedly haunted in real life and on film. *Buppah Rahtree* films spend a staggering amount of time on their 'ordinary' characters shown eating, reading newspapers, getting a haircut, gambling, arguing, gossiping, consulting fortune tellers and sleeping on the job. Humour is an integral part of these segments as the characters make light of their situation, make fun of one another, and respond to threats in an exaggerated manner. Comic elements alternate between language jokes, subtle irony and crude slapstick. These may seem disconnected from the rest of the film, but the comical framing of acts and behaviours that can clearly be described as violent and discriminatory serves as a chilling commentary on socially sanctioned misogyny, ableism, and exploitation of the vulnerable individuals that result in horror.

The Queer and the Dead: Kathoey Gothic as Horror Comedy

If *Buppah Rahtree* uses comedy to offset horror and connect with the film's audiences, Poj Arnon's *Hor Taew Tak* films explore the comic potential of Gothic and the genre's eagerness to parody itself. Currently on its seventh instalment, the series introduces an ensemble of ageing *kathoeys* in loosely structured plots that involve confrontation with various supernatural phenomena. The Thai title seems impossible to translate as it relies heavily on word play. The word *hor* indicates a school dormitory and indeed the film's heroines tend to rent rooms to students in most films. *Taew* is the name of the main protagonist but the word functions colloquially to refer to cross-dressing boys or young *kathoeys*.[4] The last word, *tak*, describes an act of breaking or blowing something up but in the context of the previous two words may also imply the idea of 'coming out of the closet'. Made by and for the members of the widely diverse Thai LGBTQ+ community, the films are known for their highly coded language, rich in sexual allusions, regionalisms and slang words that make them amusing to the locals but also partially incomprehensible.

The series elevates confusion to an art form. The first *Hor Taew Tak* film, made in 2007, introduces four *kathoey* 'aunties', Jae-Taew, Cartoon, Mot-dum and Songkram, who run a boarding house for boys that just happens to have a ghost problem. The apartment complex is haunted not by one but two ghosts – that of Pancake, a *kathoey* student who slipped, hit her head on a toilet and died during a date, and the more tragic character of Num Ning who was raped and fell off the roof trying to destroy the recording of her rape. The two ghosts linger around the building, although for different reasons. While Pancake is bored and finds it rather amusing to peep on boys in the bathroom or annoy the aunties, Num Ning is controlled by a shaman and used in unfair competition, as she is meant to scare the tenants into moving to a newly built condo run by the mother of the boy who killed her. Under the leadership of Jae-Taew, the drag queens solve the mystery of the haunting, bring the guilty parties to justice and strike a friendship with Pancake who decides to stay after Num Ning moves on.

The sequels follow repetitive plot lines with Pancake (the ghost) joining Jae-Taew, Cartoon and Mot-dum on ghost-hunting adventures and Songkram being reduced to an occasional supporting character. In the second film, made in 2009, the team confront two *phi nang lum* – ghosts of Thai traditional dancers who are a frequent motif in Thai horror – and a practitioner of black magic, another *kathoey* character who happens to be connected to the ghosts through their past life. The third film, made in 2011, is a spoof of the *Twilight* saga as amidst the usual medley of ghosts and black magic Pancake has to deal with an emotional dilemma of whether she prefers to date a vampire or a werewolf. The fourth film (2012) takes the action to Oscar Apartment in a parody of *Buppah Rahtree*. The fifth one (2015), set in a posh private school for boys that looks like it is stuck in the 1930s, makes fun of Thai ghost *lakorns* (soap operas). The sixth film (2018) takes on Bollywood Gothic, as the protagonists are lured into an old mansion where they have to battle ferocious Indian ghosts, and the most recent instalment, *Hor Taew Tak Hak Covid* (2021), puts everyone, including ghosts and zombies, in quarantine.

If there is one word to describe the *Hor Taew Tak* universe it has to be pandemonium – the world of unrestrained disorder, wild uproar and chaos. Its protagonists are larger than life, sporting impossible outfits that turn them into exaggerated caricatures of themselves, blurting out their incomprehensible lines with a speed of light, constantly cursing and using profanities, turning every second word into a sexual innuendo, and hurling insults at one another so steeped in sexist, racist and ableist stereotypes that it feels somewhat disturbing to find them funny.

The films offer a localised version of the Bakhtinian carnival – a festive life organised around laughter, militant anti-authoritarianism, and a joyful acceptance of the materiality of the body (Dentith 1995, 64), expressed in this case through a combination of *kathoey* vernacular culture with exuberant Gothic grotesque. The carnivalesque aspect of *Hor Taew Tak* films is realised through their reliance on folk humour with its predisposition for pageantry, parody and foul language, and their affirmative attitude towards the grotesque bodies of their protagonists, which in the context of the films double as Gothic bodies.

Bakhtin observes that the grotesque body 'is a body in the act of becoming. It is never finished, never completed; it is continually built, created, and builds and creates another body' (quoted in Dentith 2010, 226). The *kathoey* body as portrayed in the films is the body in flux, characterised by its ontological indeterminacy and ongoing reinvention through drag performance. The characters shift between male and female identities, adjusting their pronouns depending on situations, referring to themselves as 'ladies' but dissing others for being 'ugly men'.[5] Jae-Taew demands obedience from her son Koy asserting that he owes her double respect as she used to be his father and is now his mother. Pancake's manly ghost-vampire ex-husband, Tangtong, reappears in one of the later films as a *kathoey* and a wife to another man. The characters take their drag performance to the extreme going through hundreds of glamorous outfits, unbelievable wigs, boots and accessories, fake eyelashes and tons of make-up, the result of which makes them simultaneously ridiculous and divine. But the *kathoey* body, especially that of the aging *kathoey*, is always on the verge of being perceived as corrupt and deformed, a connection strengthened in the films by its frequent comparison with corpses, ghosts and monsters.

The *kathoey* characters in *Hor Taew Tak* can be fairly described as 'men in drag', since none of them exhibits any traces of androgynous or feminine physique, which is often the case with real-life *kathoeys*. The actors chosen for the roles are professional comedians, many of whom identify as heterosexual men, despite the fact that they are known mostly for performing non-binary characters. Under the clothes and make-up, then, they appear to be old men. Their bulky, sagging, dark-skinned and otherwise unremarkable bodies stand in stark contrast with those of desirable heroes and heroines of regular Thai movies. The films' framing of these *kathoey* bodies as objects of desire is used to produce a comic effect. If we were to assume that all the fashion accessories are meant to help the protagonists emulate women, as the films' scripts would make us believe, their performance must be deemed a failure. The mis-gendered body is thus always potentially a monstrous body and it appears in scenes that generate laughter or fear. As repetitively demonstrated in the films, our protagonists are more likely to be confused for female ghosts than living women.

Thai popular cinema has long history of using non-normative bodies as a site of fear and laughter, the borderline between the two often appearing blurry. This applies in equal measures to bodies that do not meet conventional beauty standards, defy gender norms and bear markers of physical or mental disability. Many Thai comedians have made their careers out of their unusual physique. Kohtee Aramboy, who plays Pancake in *Hor Taew Tak* films, was reputedly born with too many female hormones, which gave him the appearance of a man-child. Tep Seesai, who plays the school principal in the fifth film, is well known for his toothless grin. *Buppah Rahtree* films feature two comedians with disabilities, Sayan Doksadao Muangcharoen, diagnosed with Down syndrome, and Aang Terdterng (Suthon Vejkama) who seems to have a speech disorder. Usually cast in minimal supporting roles, it is apparent that most of these actors have been hired for their unusual looks. The actors seem quite aware of that as well. Sudarat Butrprom (Tukky) who appeared in two *Hor Taew Tak* films, commented on being known as an actress with an 'ugly face': 'I'm not pretty. My fans like me because I'm not. They take pity on me because I'm not pretty and probably teased me for that matter' (Duangkamol 2014).

Hor Taew Tak films draw their humour from deliberately breaking established horror conventions. In doing so they expose the extent to which horror, or indeed Gothic (reduced in this case to an aesthetic or narrative mode used within the films) relies on repetitive motifs, clichéd characters and predictable plot lines, and creates a Gothic parody. Gothic parodies, however, are imitations that also embody critique. Gothic parody evolved parallel to Gothic literature, and given Gothic's tendency to parody itself, the line between the two is often blurred. Writing about the earliest examples of Gothic parodies, Natalie Neill concludes they were meant to critique the genre and profit from it, they were used as a vehicle of social satire, or were simply produced for entertainment (2016, 200). At first glance, *Hor Taew Tak* films appear to be focused entirely on the surface, delivering a spectacle devoid of deeper meaning. In that sense, they remind us of what Tom Gunning has called 'cinema of attractions' – a cinema that 'displays its visibility' (2006, 382) and 'directly solicits spectator attention, inciting visual curiosity, and supplying pleasure through an exciting spectacle' (384) rather than engaging the viewer through the narrative. Yet underneath their crass jokes and pageantry, we find stories of domestic abuse, sexual violence against women, class and gender inequality, abuse of power by the wealthy and privileged, and corruption of state and religious institutions, which form the backdrop against which Gothic and horror stories have been set for centuries.

Horner and Zlosnik have argued that 'the comic within the Gothic foregrounds a self-reflexivity and dialectical impulse intrinsic to the modern subject' (2005, 4) and that Gothic texts often resort to intertextuality and metafiction or engage with self-parody to respond critically to various aspects of the contemporary world (2005, 12). *Hor Taew Tak* films are highly intertextual, shaping their meanings through direct quotations, allusions and parody of other texts, creating interconnections between works of the genre, linking to films and other media texts, including the coverage of current social, cultural and political news. They function as a repository of 'classic' scenes from Thai horror films (e.g. a ghost of a Thai dancer appearing next to a spirit house, a female ghost lurking in a cramped space of a bathroom or an elevator) and imitate the style of successful productions (e.g. the *Twilight*-inspired episode that features an array of Victorian fashion and a lot more Christian symbolism than usual). The Comic Gothic framing of the films and the intertextual techniques they employ encourage the audience to see them as objects of play, as intertextuality demands both reflection and interaction.

Conclusions: No Laughing Matter?

Horner and Zlosnik write: 'it is perhaps best to think of Gothic writing as a spectrum that, at one end, produces horror-writing containing moments of comic hysteria or relief and, at the other, works in which there are clear signals that nothing is to be taken seriously' (2005, 4). Thai popular horror films and horror comedies fit comfortably at both ends of this spectrum. It is of course debatable to what extent we can see these films as clearly 'Gothic', given the fact that it is sometimes problematic to assign them even to the horror genre. But perhaps the inherent hybridity of such films should not be seen as a handicap, as it aligns them with Gothic melodrama or Gothic parody, two genres whose very existence depends on remixing, recontextualising and appropriating other sources. Thai horror films spin Gothic narratives focused predominantly on victimised heroines who then return as angry iterations of the monstrous feminine, powerful yet pitiful, as the roots of their anger lie in the pervasive misogyny of the country's patriarchal culture. While the more recent examples, made in an effort to increase the marketability of the genre outside of Thailand, take this formula seriously, a great majority of productions feel more at home with the conventional style of Thai popular cinema that relegates them to 'folk' entertainment. In one of the scenes from *Buppah Rahtree*, a customer complains that the restaurant in the apartment building sells only processed food. The man, identified by his appearance as a middle-class urbanite, concludes by saying that eating junk food can only appeal to the lower classes, and then clarifies – 'the kind of people who probably like watching Thai horror films'. Constantly laughing at their own expense, Thai horror films remind us that Gothic is always ready to take a comic turn but its laughter is anything but hollow.

Notes

1. This chapter uses the label of 'Thai popular horror' to distinguish between the films that align with the conventional aesthetics of Thai popular cinema and the newer productions which adopt foreign/global models of horror.
2. The fifth film, *Buppah Arigato* (2016), which rebooted the franchise, is omitted from discussion as it is unrelated to the main storyline.
3. Films like *My Ex* (*Fan Kao*, Choopetch, 2009), *Body 19* (*Sop 19*, Purijitpanya, 2007), or *I Miss U* (*Rak Chan Ya Khitthueng Chan*, Arayangkoon, 2012) are examples of this theme.
4. In the Thai context, these labels are seen as descriptors of gender rather than sexuality.
5. Despite the fact that traditionally Thais understand *kathoey* as a third gender category, officially, Thailand recognises only male and female genders.

References

Ainslie, Mary Jane. 2012. 'Contemporary Thai Horror Film: A Monstrous Hybrid'. PhD Diss. Manchester Metropolitan University.

Ancuta, Katarzyna. 2020. 'The Waiting Woman as the Most Enduring Asian Ghost Heroine'. *Gothic Studies* 22, no. 1: 81–97.

Arnon, Poj, dir. 2007. *Hor Taew Tak* (*Haunting Me*). Thailand: Phranakarn Film.

Arnon, Poj, dir. 2009. *Hor Taew Tak 2* (*Oh My Ghost*). Thailand: Phranakarn Film.

Arnon, Poj, dir. 2011. *Hor Taew Tak 3* (*Oh My Ghost 2*). Thailand: Phranakarn Film.

Arnon, Poj, dir. 2012. *Hor Taew Tak 4* (*Oh My Ghost 3*). Thailand: Phranakarn Film.

Arnon, Poj, dir. 2015. *Hor Taew Tak 5* (*Oh My Ghost 4*). Thailand: Phranakarn Film.

Arnon, Poj, dir. 2018. *Hor Taew Tak 6* (*Oh My Ghost 5*). Thailand: Phranakarn Film.

Arnon, Poj, dir. 2021. *Hor Taew Tak 7* (*Oh My Ghost 6*). Thailand: Phranakarn Film.
Brooks, Peter. [1976] 1995. *The Melodramatic Imagination: Balzac, Henry James, Melodrama, and the Mode of Excess*. New Haven, CT: Yale University Press.
Condit, Jon. 2005. 'Buppah Rahtree'. Dread Central. https://www.dreadcentral.com/reviews/3795/buppah-rahtree-2003/
Dentith, Simon. 1995. *Bakhtinian Thought: An Introductory Reader*. London: Routledge.
Duangkamol, Panya. 2014. 'Confessions of an Ugly Duckling'. *Bangkok Post*, 8 June. https://www.bangkokpost.com/life/social-and-lifestyle/414116/confessions-of-an-ugly-duckling
Gamer, Michael. 2018. 'Gothic Melodrama'. In *The Cambridge Companion to English Melodrama*, edited by Carolyn Williams, 31–46. Cambridge: Cambridge University Press.
Gaut, Berys. 2010. *A Philosophy of Cinematic Art*. Cambridge: Cambridge University Press.
Guelden, Marlane. 1995. *Thailand: Into the Spirit World*. Bangkok: Asia Books.
Gunning, Tom. 2006. 'The Cinema of Attraction[s]: Early Film, Its Spectator and the Avant-Garde'. In *The Cinema of Attractions Reloaded*, edited by Wanda Strauven, 381–8. Amsterdam: Amsterdam University Press.
Horner, Avril and Sue Zlosnik. 2005. *Gothic and the Comic Turn*. Basingstoke: Palgrave Macmillan.
Leeper, Mark R. 2004. 'Critic Reviews for *Rahtree: Flower of the Night*'. Rotten Tomatoes. https://www.rottentomatoes.com/m/rahtree_flower_of_the_night
Neill, Natalie. 2016. 'Gothic Parody'. In *Romantic Gothic: An Edinburgh Companion*, edited by Angela Wright and Dale Townsend, 185–206. Edinburgh: Edinburgh University Press.
Schmidt, Lisa. 2013. 'Television: Horror's "Original" Home'. *Horror Studies* 4, no. 2: 159–71.
Sippapak, Yuthler, dir. 2003. *Buppah Rahtree* (*Rahtree: Flower of the Night*). Thailand: Mahagan Pictures.
Sippapak, Yuthler, dir. 2005. *Buppah Rahtree 2* (*Rahtree Returns*). Thailand: Mahagan Pictures.
Sippapak, Yuthler, dir. 2009. *Buppah Rahtree 3.1* (*Rahtree Reborn*). Thailand: Mahagan Pictures.
Sippapak, Yuthler, dir. 2009. *Buppah Rahtree 3.2* (*Rahtree Revenge*). Thailand: Mahagan Pictures.
Sungsri, Patsorn. 2004. 'Thai Cinema as National Cinema: An Evaluative History'. PhD Diss. Murdoch University, Perth, Australia.

Chapter 13

The 'Inverse Uncanny': Humour and Tim Burton's Gothic Parodies
Monica Germanà

Introduction

Tim Burton's oeuvre to date has included films as diverse as *Bat Man* (1989), *Mars Attacks* (1996), *Planet of the Apes* (2001) and *Charlie and the Chocolate Factory* (2005). A representative part of these works may be best described as Gothic '*bricolage*' (Carver 2013, 119) or 'parodies' (Spooner 2017; Weinstock 2013) because, as Catherine Spooner notes, they are rewritings of pre-existing Gothic stories such as Mary Shelley's *Frankenstein* (1818) and the penny dreadful series *The String of Pearls* (1845–6), or Gothicised adaptations of European fairy tales (Ray 2010) and children's classics such as Lewis Carroll's *Alice's Adventures in Wonderland* (1865) and *Through the Looking Glass* (1871). While speaking to the hybridity of Gothic and its monsters, Burton's Gothic parodies, which include *Corpse Bride* (2005), *Alice in Wonderland* (2010) and *Frankenweenie* (2012), produce a reverberation of cultural antecedents, the playful interaction of which is, in itself, a source of entertainment for the spectator familiar with the tropes. Simultaneously, in playing with familiar themes and points of references, Burton's diversions from the original narratives signal the *uncanny* interplay of familiar/unfamiliar categories. As they defamiliarise recognisable characters and interrogate well-known themes and storylines, the parodies undermine the 'serious' business of fear while drawing attention to the frightening aspects of 'funny'.

The manifest combination of horror and laughter in Burton's works has prompted Jeffrey Weinstock to define them, rather than purely (and seriously) Gothic, as 'Gothic' and 'Gothic-lite', because in their derivative self-reflectiveness 'the horror of the Gothic mode' is somewhat diluted or 'persistently undercut' 'through humor and sentimentality' (Weinstock 2013, 26). Gothic has, however, always been 'a form without an original, a series of citations and revivals' (Spooner 2017, 53), its narratives persistently revolving around 'fakery' and 'counterfeits' (Hogle 2000). There is, moreover, little doubt that Burton's self-conscious use of Gothic, his frequent returns to certain tropes – the death of the aristocracy, female resistance against patriarchy, the affect of loss and mourning – and even the image he and his former wife, Helena Bonham Carter, have cultivated for themselves (Spooner 2017, 51), point to distinctly self-conscious strategies of what we may call 'meta-Gothic', a Gothic that reflects upon its own conventions, themes and preoccupations. This, however, does not undermine the 'authenticity' of Burton's Gothic, but, as this chapter demonstrates, amplifies Gothic's ability to create unease; in particular, it is the use of humour, the key narrative strategy of Burton's meta-Gothic, that points to the distinctive affect of Gothic humour: the *inverse uncanny*.

Gothic Humour: The Inverse Uncanny

From the grotesque bodies of vampires, zombies and other undead creatures, to the hysterical reactions that human characters have to them and other Gothic scenarios, humour is, surprisingly perhaps, rarely absent from Gothic narratives. The peculiar adjacence of two apparently opposite affects has, in fact, frequently been identified in the Gothic tradition at large. Rather than considering 'serious' and 'comic' at odds with each other, as Avril Horner and Sue Zlosnik argue in their pioneering analysis, the Comic Gothic may be best conceived of 'as a spectrum that, at one end, produces horror writing containing moments of comic hysteria or relief and, at the other, works in which there are clear signals that nothing is to be taken seriously' (Horner and Zlosnik 2005, 4). Playfulness, comedy and humour are not, in other words, incongruent with the darker side of Gothic; they stand, in fact, in a dialectical and mutual relationship with the genre's more 'serious' narrative modes.

Gothic humour underpins Gothic's critical investigation of the darker shadows of modernity, human experience and so-called 'civilisation'. Frankenstein's sudden realisation that the Creature stitched up from the body parts of decomposing corpses is, predictably, not attractive, is a fitting example of unsettling proximity of the tragic and the comic exposed by Gothic:

> Beautiful! Great God! His yellow skin scarcely covered the work of muscles and arteries beneath; his hair was of a lustrous black, and flowing; his teeth of a pearly whiteness; but these luxuriances only formed a more horrid contrast with his watery eyes, that seemed almost of the same colour as the dun-white

sockets in which they were set, his shrivelled complexion and straight black lips. (Shelley [1818] 2012, 35)

Telling of its affective strength, the humorous quality of Frankenstein's hubristic project has regularly emerged in the 'hideous progeny' of Shelley's novel, from James Whale's earlier productions (*Frankenstein* (1931); *The Bride of Frankenstein* (1935)) to the more 'modern' parodies of *Young Frankenstein* (Brooks, 1974) or *Frankenhooker* (Henenlotter, 1990). In the novel, however, humour is, without a doubt, at the expense of Victor Frankenstein, whose self-absorption makes him comically blind to the horrific consequences of his 'Enlightened' education and 'progressive' practice.

Equally complex is the use of humour in Emily Brontë's *Wuthering Heights* (1847), a haunting narrative that deals with the most perverse deviations of desire, from domestic violence and child abuse, to incest and necrophilia. At the beginning of the story Lockwood's use of a biblical reference to reproach Heathcliff's hostility deploys hyperbolic humour to complain about the latter's lack of hospitality: 'The herd of possessed swine could have had no worse spirits in them than those animals of yours, sir. You might as well leave a stranger with a brood of tigers!' (Brontë 1990, 6). Although applied to Lockwood's fastidious intolerance of the shortcomings of Heathcliff's hospitality, the hyperbolic humour in fact foreshadows the much darker secrets the plot later unveils.

In other texts, the presaging of later revelations deploys ambiguous language, which, upon a second reading, or to a reader already familiar with the storyline, will emphasise the funny qualities within the apparently serious scene. The double meaning concealed in Count Dracula's welcoming words, for instance, is particularly entertaining to the discerning reader of Bram Stoker's novel:

> 'Welcome to my house! Enter *freely* and of your own will!' He made no motion of stepping to meet me, but stood *like a statue*, as though his gesture of welcome had fixed him into stone. The instant, however, that I had stepped over the threshold, he moved impulsively forward, and holding out his hand grasped mine with a strength which made me wince, an effect which was not lessened by the fact that it seemed *as cold as ice* – more like the hand of a dead than a living man. Again he said:
>
> 'Welcome to my house. Come *freely*. Go safely; and leave something of the *happiness* you bring!' (Stoker 2011, 15–16, my italics)

That the count stands 'like a statue' and that his hand is 'as cold as ice' ought to alert Harker, invited to the castle in his capacity as solicitor, that this is no ordinary client or business transaction. Dracula's emphatic repetition of the word 'freely', and especially his jovial invitation to 'leave something of the happiness you bring', an implicit and ironic reference to Dracula's appetite for Harker's blood, amplify the playful treatment of the most sinister themes in this Gothic narrative.

Using the examples quoted above, it is possible to identify four specific areas of correspondence between Gothic and humour. First, as a quintessentially derivative genre, Gothic revels in the constant reworking of its own formulas; always a parody of itself, Gothic invites its own rewriting. The particularly fecund corpus of *Frankenstein* adaptations, pastiches and spoofs, which Burton has repeatedly contributed to, demonstrates, perhaps more than any other Gothic text, the appeal of Gothic imitation. Secondly, Gothic's inclination for excess finds its correspondence in humour's deployment of the hyperbolic to exaggerate the ordinary for comic effect: Lockwood's biblical reference to express his distress brings this to the fore. Thirdly, Gothic's resistance to closure frequently exploits semantic ambiguity to accommodate multiple interpretations; puns and wordplay similarly exploit language ambivalence for comic effect: Harker's warm welcome to Castle Dracula is comically ironic, given that Harker's 'happiness' has a different meaning for the two interlocutors. Finally, Gothic's exploration of the strange, the weird and the inexplicable bears similarities to nonsense as a way of using absurd and impossible scenarios to mock, and simultaneously push, the limits of rational logic: Frankenstein's dismay at the Creature's physical unattractiveness evidently falls within this form of Gothic humour. The hyperbolic humour, playful language and subversion of linear thinking that characterise Burton's Gothic parodies, it will be seen, exemplify these points of contact between Gothic and humour and signal the subversive function that Gothic humour plays in these narratives.

The multiple forms and stylistic devices of Gothic humour operate collectively to close the gap between the serious and the facetious, signalling, concurrently, an affective overlap of that which may incite fear

Table 13.1 'Gothic' and 'Humour' Correspondences. Created by Monica Germanà.

Gothic	Humour
Formula	Parody
Excess	Hyperbole
Ambiguity	Puns
Uncanny	Nonsense

and horror, and that which, instead, triggers comic relief and laughter. Romantic writer Jean Paul Richter defined the comic as '*umgekehrte Erhabene*' (1804), which Thomas Carlyle translated as 'inverse sublimity' and defined as that which elevates 'into our affections what is below us, while sublimity draws down into our affections what is above us' (1869, 6.21). Instead of experiencing a sense of awe in relation to the universe's grand and inscrutable designs, humour raises apparently trivial things to a higher level of significance: '[b]y lifting up low things, rather than bringing exalted conceptions down into our awareness, the humorist, like the sublime poet, renders objects vivid to the imagination' (Sutton 1966, 179). The 'inverse sublimity' of Victorian pantomimes, cartoons and literary illustrations, where humour blurs the line between the ordinary and the fantastic, and debunks hierarchies between humans and animals, animate and inanimate creatures (Sutton 1966, 181), bears resemblance to the subversive hybridity of Gothic monsters from the doppelgänger of Robert Louis Stevenson's *Strange Case of Dr Jekyll and Mr Hyde* (1886) to the insect horror of Richard Marsh's *The Beetle* (1897). Yet, there is a sense in which hierarchies and categorical boundaries are only, in fact, temporarily subverted or broken down by the 'inverse sublimity' of certain Victorian texts which, eventually, reinstate structure and order. To take the example of one of the texts Burton has Gothicised, the ending of Carroll's *Alice's Adventures in Wonderland* returns both sisters to the 'dull reality' of their ordinary lives (Carroll [1865] 1998, 110), even though memories of the nonsensical Wonderland may accompany Alice – and her sister – into adulthood. The strangeness of wonderland, in other words, is only a temporary disruption in Alice's ordinary and orderly life.

Significantly, in the anarchic Wonderland it is the grin of the Cheshire Cat that signals the ambivalence of humour: both impossible – '"I didn't know that cats could grin"', says Alice – and undeniable – the cat 'vanished quite slowly, beginning with the end of the tail, and ending with the grin, which remained some time after the rest of it had gone'. The disembodied grin is one the most memorable images of Wonderland's nonsense: '"I've often seen a cat without a grin, [. . .] but a grin without a cat! It's the most curious thing I ever saw in my life!"' Alice concludes (Carroll [1865] 1998, 52, 59). Though Carroll's *Alice* cannot be straightforwardly read as a Gothic novel, the Cheshire Cat's spectral grin helps locate the physical response to Gothic humour somewhere between hysteria and laughter. Mikkel Borch-Jacobsen argues that laughter, embodying humour's blurring of physical and psychological levels of human experience, signals 'the relativity of this "whole" which is the self, implies going beyond ourselves, in the most impossible excess of ourselves' (1987, 739). As well as pushing the boundaries of self, the disruption induced by the 'lacerating, intimately explosive' experience of laughter (Borch-Jacobsen 1987, 742), may be seen as a form of 'inverse abjection', an experience, which, in Julia Kristeva's words, also points to 'the fragile border [. . .] where identities (subject/object, etc.) do not exist or only barely so' (Kristeva 1982, 207). Symbolic of the subversively self-abasing laughter of Gothic, the grin is, arguably, the most fitting representation of the physical response to Gothic humour. Reminiscent of the toothy smile of the skull, a familiar icon in popular Gothic imagery, the grin is both visible and invisible, tangible and imagined, wicked and funny.

Rather than conservatively restoring a sense of stability after the temporary disturbance produced by humour, one could claim that Gothic humour persistently oscillates between order and disorder, pointing to the disquieting contiguity and coexistence of serious and comical. 'How funny it is [. . .] that a word ("funny") should mean both "amusing" and strange"', Andrew Bennett and Nicholas Royle note of the uncanny

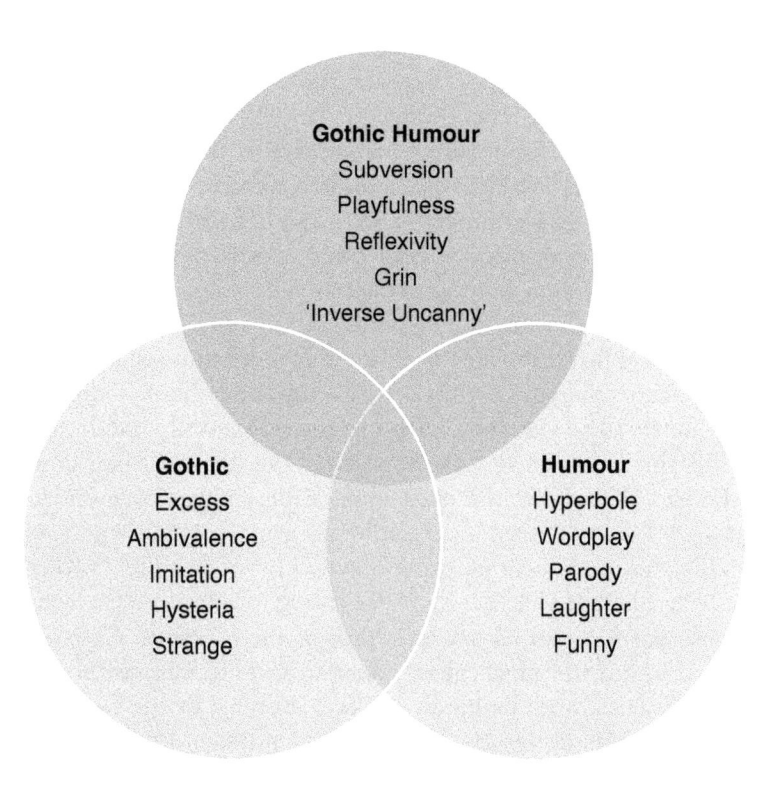

Gothic Humour
Subversion
Playfulness
Reflexivity
Grin
'Inverse Uncanny'

Gothic
Excess
Ambivalence
Imitation
Hysteria
Strange

Humour
Hyperbole
Wordplay
Parody
Laughter
Funny

Figure 13.1 In-Between: Gothic Humour. Created by Monica Germanà.

semantics of 'funny' and the 'intimate link between laughter and death' (2004, 93). Such semantic overlap between the strangeness of funny and the funniness of strange is historically embedded in the English language. Meanings of the word 'comical' include 'strange', 'odd', 'difficult to deal with', 'awkward' and 'disagreeable'; the term has also been associated with both the 'unintentionally' and the 'intentionally' humorous (*OED* 2022). Such semantic incongruity is akin to that identified by Ernst Jentsch (1906) and Sigmund Freud (1919) in the German word '*Unheimlich*' (uncanny), which forms the basis for their respective studies of the psychological and aesthetic complexities of the uncanny. What I would like to suggest, therefore, is that Gothic humour may be thought of as the *inverse uncanny*, which results from the playful juxtaposition of the familiar and the unfamiliar in a narrative that entertains and assuages anxiety and, at the same time, disturbs and creates unease. The disruption of familiarity central to the mechanics of the uncanny is intensified in the meta-Gothic of Burton's works, where habitual consumers of Gothic simultaneously experience comfortable entertainment in the acknowledgement of known themes, sources and characters, and disorientation in the subversive twists the parodies deliver.

Corpse Bride (2005)

Forced marriage, a staple theme in classic Gothic texts from Horace Walpole's *The Castle of Otranto* (1764) to Ann Radcliffe's *The Mysteries of Udolpho* (1794), is central to the plot of *Corpse Bride*. Villainous gold-digger Lord Barkis Bittern afflicts the parallel stories of two young women, Emily, the 'corpse bride' of the title, and Victoria Everglot, the daughter of a penniless aristocratic family looking for a marriage of convenience to solve their financial difficulties. After a series of comical blunders during the rehearsal, Victoria's fiancé, Victor van Dort, the clumsy son of nouveau riche fisherman William van Dort and his wife Nell, walks through a forest to practise his vows, and accidentally marries 'Corpse Bride' Emily, whose bony finger he puts a ring on, having mistaken it for a broken branch. This provides a renewed opportunity for Barkis, who, having eloped with and killed Emily in the past, and under false impressions about the Everglot family's assets, plans to take Victor's place as Victoria's husband-to-be.

Inspired by a traditional Eastern European fairy tale (Ray 2010), the film's critique of patriarchal misogyny and rigid social norms is set in a Victorian England visually depicted as the dreary Land of the Living; as one of the film reviewers observes, '[e]veryone in the film has a deathly grey pallor, a ghastly lack of colour in the cheeks' (Bradshaw 2005). The *mise en scène* of the initial tracking shot – ticking clocks in a shop, the repetitive actions of a man sweeping the ground and of two fishermen chopping the heads off fish – amplifies the gloominess that characterises Burton's vision of a repressed and cheerless Victorian England (Loutitt 2018, 280). The cavernous bareness of the Everglot mansion is ironically picked up in the phoney exchange of pleasantries between the two ladies: 'I love what you've done with the place; who's your decorator?' says Nell van Dort to please Maudeline Everglot (voiced by Joanna Lumley). Against the stiff sombreness of The Land of the Living stands the intoxicating exuberance of 'The Land of the Dead where an endless party – a Mexican Day of the Dead at the height of a carnival mood' (Warner 2005) – is going on in full colour; here the dead's psychedelic '*joie de mourir*' (Weinstock 2013, 8) vibrantly clashes with the cadaverous stillness of the 'breathers' overground. In contrast to the literally tight-laced body of Victoria, whose corset is tightened in preparation for the wedding, Emily's figure, albeit also kept in shape by a corset, paradoxically, looks more animated than Victoria's ever does. Emily's fraying bridal attire may evoke the 'withered' dress and countenance of the jilted Miss Havisham, the 'skeleton in the ashes of a rich dress' (Dickens [1860] 2008, 58), as Pip describes the old spinster in Charles Dickens's *Great Expectations*, but her verve articulates her agency more forcefully than Victoria ever dares to express her own desire.

The *danse macabre* performed by a quartet of grinning skeletons delivers a distinctly livelier display of vitality than the listless routines 'upstairs', exposing, simultaneously, the ontological fluidity of life/death and the inevitability of the latter:

> Die, die, we all pass away
> But don't wear a frown
> Because it's really okay
> You might try and hide
> And you might try and pray
> But we all end up
> The remains of the day. (Burton 2005)

That the dead are not quite dead – just like the living were not quite alive – is validated by the loose structure of the dancing skeletons, who can lose their heads only to be reassembled again in their routine. In the afterlife, bodies and minds are as unstructured as they are interchangeable. With no bodily constraints or unity of self, limbs and skulls may detach and reattach themselves to the original bodies, or those of others, without any significant consequence.

The hyperbolic paradoxes of the afterlife are reinforced by the nonsense jokes and puns which the script delivers with gusto. While Victor's language skills, already shaky among the living, seem completely lost – 'I want some questions. Now!' he demands of the dead – the tongue-in cheek dead never seem lost for words; 'Does he have a dead brother?' asks a woman; the cheeky maggot that keeps popping out Emily's right eye promises to 'keep an eye out for him', while when Victor runs away, a black widow spider addresses him flirtatiously: 'Married, ah? I am a widow' (Burton 2005). Emily's own ability to laugh at herself and her predicament – of the beautiful view across the cemetery she says, 'It takes my breath away. Well, it would if I had any' (Burton 2005; Ray 2010, 215) – exhibits 'the victorious assertion of the ego's invincibility' celebrated in Freud's essay on humour (1927, 2). Similarly, the song performed to comfort Emily for the loss of Victor to a living woman subverts the memento mori trope through yet another humorous paradox:

> The sole redeeming feature
> From that little creature
> Is that she's alive
> –Overrated
> –Overblown
> Everybody knows
> That's just a temporary state
> Which is cured very quickly
> When we meet our fate. (Burton 2005)

Replacing the commonplace *tempus fugit* with the idea that life is a condition 'cured very quickly' (by death), *Corpse Bride*'s afterlife extravaganza points to the inverse uncanny as a narrative mode that playfully challenges the boundaries between life and death, while its self-reflexive nods to a well-known Gothic tradition prompt a deeper reflection on the serious issues – forced marriage, sexual violence, female sacrifice – addressed in the parody with Gothic humour.

Alice in Wonderland (2010)

Although Lewis Carroll's Alice books – *Alice's Adventures in Wonderland* (1865) and *Through the Looking Glass* (1871) – are not conventionally read as Gothic texts, reviewers of Burton's 2010 adaptation have rightly drawn attention to the self-conscious Gothic aesthetics of Burton's adaptation:

> His new movie imagines Alice returning as a 19-year-old to this strange land, to find that it is plunged in gloom. The tea party is still going, but all the dishes are wrecked, the cups have sprung leaks and the event itself is sited in some wasteland, like a depiction of the Somme. It is difficult to tell if this is an intentional answer to Carroll's original joke or just part of the inevitable Goth darkness that Burton conjures up. Even Alice, played by Australian newcomer Mia Wasikowska, has dark shadows around her eyes. (Bradshaw 2010)

After the initial scene, the English tea party organised for Alice's imminent betrothal to a pompous young man of aristocratic stock, the film's realistic mode manifestly switches to recognisable Gothic aesthetics after her fall through the cavernous, birth-canal-like rabbit hole. The silhouettes of skeletal bare tree branches, the ghostly appearances and disappearances of the Cheshire Cat and its grin, and the pervasive use of a dark palette make 'Underland' a distinctly creepier space than the playful madness of Carroll's Wonderland. Juxtaposed with the dark natural landscape, a lavish decadence of red and gold accents similarly conveys the Gothic ambience of the Red Queen's castle, replete with turrets, stained-glass windows, velvet curtains and Gothic-arched door frames, not to mention a moat awash with the chopped heads of those who fell foul of the Queen's wrath. As with the kaleidoscopic portrayal of afterlife in *Corpse Bride*, 'Underland is visually crowded', notes Spooner, 'the screen filled with excessive ornamentation' (2017, 58), reflecting Burton's self-conscious use of the exaggerated aesthetics of Gothic.

It is within the barely contained boundaries of this excessive Underland, that the film offers a joint exploration of the ridiculous qualities of fear and the subversive function of humour to destabilise authority. The Red Queen's grotesquely large head is as much a source of humour as it is of fear. Out of fear, her courtesans' visible prosthetics enhance certain body parts in order to flatter the Queen's fragile ego with their fake grotesquery. While it seems obvious that the Queen with the enlarged heart-shaped head would rather be loved than feared, it also becomes apparent that the fear upon which her power rests is also a travesty. As the masquerade becomes manifest when a lady's prosthetic nose falls off, the playful tension of the inverse uncanny reveals the temporary alignment of fear and humour. No longer a solid foundation for power, fear itself is reduced to a frivolous appendage, a sartorial accessory that can be easily discarded when the wind of fashion changes its direction. Humour, as Freud argues, 'is not resigned; it is rebellious' (1927, 163); humorously, the scene raises serious questions about power, those who crave it, and those who become enslaved by it.

Humour's ability to destabilise the norm is not confined to the absurd power structures of Underland. Even before her fall down the rabbit hole, Alice's use of humour simultaneously diffuses tension and draws attention to her serious preoccupations with patriarchal control. While dancing the quadrille, Alice's vision of 'all the ladies wearing trousers and all the men wearing dresses' proves too piquant for her fiancé-to-be Hamish: 'It would be best if you kept your visions to yourself. When in doubt remain silent', he quips. Telling of her growing sense of agency, however, the cross-dressing vision reflects Alice's own sartorial resistance to corset and stockings: 'Who's to say what is proper? What if it was agreed that "proper" was wearing a codfish on your head? Would you wear it?' Alice retorts to her mother's accusations of impropriety (Burton 2010). Pale-looking, 'bonkers', and about to be forced into marriage, Alice fulfils many of the qualities of the Gothic heroine; unlike the (humourless) damsels in distress of Walpole and Radcliffe however, her wit sets her free.

As seen in *Corpse Bride*, humour points to laughter as an experience which simultaneously undermines and endorses the sovereignty of self. It is no accident then, that Alice's politely humorous rejection of Hamish's presumptuous proposal – 'I'm sorry Hamish, I can't marry you. You're not the right man for me. And there's that trouble with your digestion' – is followed by a brief performance of the 'futterwacken' dance. The wacky choreography performed by the Mad Hatter after Alice's defeat of the Jabberwocky in Underland and consequent banishment of the Red Queen to the Outlands, is a mocking statement defying authority, as Alice's inappropriate performance simultaneously ridicules upper-class etiquette and gender roles. The function of Gothic laughter, already placed in a dialectical relationship with horror by Victor Sage (Sage 1994, 190), may, according to Fred Botting, be 'either rationally open and liberating or devilishly, anarchically irreverent' (2005, 112). Taking Burton's Alice as an example, one could go further and argue that Alice's grin is in fact *both* 'liberating' and 'anarchically irreverent'. Ironically, while the futterwacken dance may signal Alice's temporary loss of sense and self, it also reclaims her agency, as instead of settling for an unhappy union, her professional involvement in Hamish's father's international trading company means Alice has, quite literally, the last laugh.

Frankenweenie (2012)

As with his previous 1984 short film of the same title, Burton's stop-motion feature-length animation *Frankenweenie* returns to a favourite Gothic narrative, that of Shelley's *Frankenstein* (see Spooner 2017, 50), with a storyline familiar even to audiences with the least knowledge of the Gothic tradition. After Victor Frankenstein, a gifted schoolboy, successfully revives his bull terrier Sparky, his schoolmates, whose appetite for science has increased since the arrival of a new teacher, Mr Rzykruski, choose to experiment with resuscitation with drastic consequences for the quiet community of New Holland.

Frankenweenie's engagement with *Frankenstein* is mediated by – and visually indebted to – Whale's 1931 iconic adaptation of Shelley's novel: the square-top hairstyle of one of Victor's schoolmates, Nassor, whose name also means 'The Victorious' (Corrigan et al. 2016, 199), and the pitchfork-bearing mob at the end of the films, are among the details viewers familiar with Whale's iconography would easily recognise. As a parody of a parody, therefore, the self-reflexive quality of *Frankenweenie* further expands the ever-satisfying web of familiar threads of Burton's meta-Gothic. The high density of such intertextual connections also produces an inverse uncanny affect; while it creates a sense of comfort and reassurance by way of the familiar elements a knowing audience would enjoy identifying, the film also challenges the viewer to identify the points of departure from the 'originals', or even question the existence of any original *tout court*. The meta-Gothic reverberation is further enhanced by the plethora of references to monsters external to the Frankenstein mythology, including Godzilla, which inspires Sparky's performance in Victor's amateur films, but also the Japanese *kaiju* Mothra, besides vampires, mummies and wererats (Weinstock 2013, 26).

As already seen in *Corpse Bride* and *Alice in Wonderland*, Gothic humour lowers the life/death, natural/supernatural barriers in a way that is simultaneously entertaining and disquieting. Placed at the start of *Frankenweenie*, the meta-cinematic credit sequence at the end of Victor's amateur film-within-the-film, 'The End or is It?', foreshadows the thematic interrogation of the life/death boundaries in *Frankenstein*. The dialogue between the Burgermeister and his niece, the appropriately named Elsa van Helsing, playfully points to death as a desirable option, when the latter is forced to sing on stage wearing a hat adorned with lit candles:

> ELSA: I don't think this is safe.
> BURGERMEISTER: Nonsense. We have the fire chief over here.
> BURGERMEISTER: You know, a lot of girls would kill to be in your place.
> ELSA: I'd welcome death.

The scene points to death as both feared and desired by Elsa on the one hand, and concurrently made more likely by the presence of the decrepit and skeletal fire chief, on the other. The hyperbolic humour and irony here simultaneously endorse and mock the serious business of death.

As well as interrogating conventional understandings of life and death, and the permeable boundaries between the two conditions, *Frankenweenie*'s Gothic humour addresses the film's moral exploration of the acknowledgement of death, the management of loss, and mourning among children. Rather than dismissing these as taboos in children's literature and film, Gothic humour successfully conveys the least pleasant themes to a younger audience through a series of devices that carefully tread on the edge between serious and funny (Cross 2008, 59; Reynolds 2001, 3). While not diminishing the emotional impact of pet bereavement, *Frankenweenie*'s treatment of the animals' deaths and subsequent resurrections presents many opportunities for comic relief. From the cemetery architecture, which features cute, animal-themed adornments instead of the more sombre memento mori ornamentation of human graveyards, to the pets' names – Nassor's diminutive hamster is named 'Colossus' – death is presented through a less frightening lens.

The humour generated by the ensuing pet resurrections takes this further, pointing – like Shelley's *Frankenstein* – to human interference and arrogance as worse evils than mortality and mourning: 'Science is not good or bad', Mr Rzykruski reminds Victor, 'but it can be used both ways. That is why you must always be careful' (Burton 2012). The misunderstanding of what science is, and what it is for, similarly emerges when Bob's mother asks her son and Toshiaki, who are testing a dubious flying device for the school's science fair, what they are doing on the roof. Their simple answer – 'Science' – is both factually correct and unquestionably funny because it foreshadows the consequences of uncontrolled scientific experimentation. The less troubling, though not less humorous, effects of the resuscitation process – Sparky's body leaking water from his suture holes – lead to a crescendo of mishaps, as the children all decide to dabble in animal resuscitation, using the principles of galvanism demonstrated in class by Mr Rzykruski and initially adopted by Victor to bring Sparky back to life. Thus, Weird Girl's cat, Mr Whiskers, contaminated by a recently revived bat, turns into a vampire cat of gigantic proportions; Edgar's dead rat turns into a wererat; Colossus rises from his monumental mausoleum as a diminutive, but very aggressive, mummified rodent; Bob breeds small, but particularly lethal, water creatures from a box of Sea-Monkeys, which escape into the town fair to cause chaos; Toshiaki's turtle, playfully called Shelley, is transformed into an enormous monster: 'my problem is bigger', he admits in a hilarious understatement of the large-scale disaster he is responsible for, including the death of Colossus, which Shelley mercilessly squashes underfoot.

Paradoxically, death becomes the only solution to restore order after the chaos of resurrection; while osmosis makes the fresh-water monsters explode after eating salty popcorn, Edgar's wererat and Shelley are both electrocuted. Finally, Mr Whiskers is impaled by a stray piece of wood from the windmill set on fire by the angry townsfolk in order to kill Sparky, whom they erroneously deem responsible for the post-resurrection pandemonium. Although the story's happy ending allows Victor to revive Sparky – with the help of his family and the community of New Holland – one more time, the deadly consequences of bad science, made more vividly memorable through Gothic humour, will stay with characters and audiences long after the film's ending.

Conclusion

While Gothic humour has led some critics to underestimate the serious implication of 'funny', the self-reflexivity of meta-Gothic and Gothic parody has played a significant role in the changing paradigms of Gothic and its consumption by popular audiences. As exemplified by the works of Tim Burton examined in this chapter, familiarity with the themes, characters and stock motifs of traditional Gothic allows, arguably, for a more – rather than less – intense experience of Gothic's most frightening and even taboo themes. As the 'inverse uncanny', Gothic humour emerges precisely from the playful intersection of the familiar with the unfamiliar, whereby the temporary pleasure of ludic entertainment intensifies the more long-lasting unease of the 'serious' *unheimlich*.

References

Bennett, Andrew and Nicholas Royle. 2004. *Literature, Criticism and Theory*. London: Pearson Longman.
Borch-Jacobsen, Mikkel. 1987. 'The Laughter of Being'. *MLN* 102, no. 4 (September): 737–60.
Botting, Fred. [1996] 2005. *Gothic*. London and New York: Routledge.
Bradshaw, Peter. 2005. 'Tim Burton's Corpse Bride'. *The Guardian*, 21 October. https://www.theguardian.com/culture/2005/oct/21/3?CMP=gu_com
Bradshaw, Peter. 2010. '*Alice in Wonderland*'. *The Guardian*, 4 March. https://www.theguardian.com/film/2010/mar/04/alice-in-wonderland-review
Brontë, Emily. [1847] 1990. *Wuthering Heights*. New York and London: W.W. Norton.
Brooks, Mel, dir. 1974. *Young Frankenstein*. Fox.
Burton, Tim, dir. 2005. *Corpse Bride*. Tim Burton Productions and Laika Entertainment.

Burton, Tim, dir. 2010. *Alice in Wonderland*. Disney.
Burton, Tim, dir. 2012. *Frankenweenie*. Walt Disney Pictures.
Carlyle, Thomas. 1869. *Collected Works*, 30 vols. London: Chapman and Hall.
Carroll, Lewis. [1865 and 1871] 1998. *Alice's Adventures in Wonderland* and *Through the Looking Glass*. London: Penguin.
Carver, Stephen. 2013. '"He wants to be just like Vincent Price": Influence and Intertext in the Gothic Films of Tim Burton'. In *The Works of Tim Burton*, edited by Jeffrey Weinstock, 117–31. London: Palgrave.
'comical, adj. and n.'. 2022. *OED Online*. Oxford University Press. https://www.oed.com/view/Entry/36912?redirected From=comical.
Corrigan, John, Frederick Denny, Martin S. Jafee and Carlos Eire. 2016. *Jews, Christians, Muslims: A Comparative Introduction to Monotheistic Religions*. London and New York: Taylor and Francis.
Cross, Julie. 2008. 'Frightening and Funny: Humour in Children's Gothic Fiction'. In *The Gothic in Children's Literature*, edited by Anna Jackson, Roderick McGillis, Karen Coats, 57–76. New York: Routledge.
Dickens, Charles. [1860] 2008. *Great Expectations*. London: Penguin.
Freud, Sigmund. 1927. 'Humour'. *The International Journal of Psycho-Analysis* 9.
Freud, Sigmund. [1919] 1953. 'The Uncanny'. In *The Standard Edition of the Complete Psychological Works of Sigmund Freud*, vol. 17, 218–253. Trans. James Strachey. London: Hogarth Press.
Henenlotter, Frank, dir. 1990. *Frankenhooker*. Shapiro-Glickenhaus Entertainment.
Hogle, Jerrold E. 2000. 'The Gothic Ghost of the Counterfeit and the Progress of Abjection'. In *A Companion to the Gothic*, edited by David Punter, 293–304. Oxford: Blackwell.
Horner, Avril and Sue Zlosnik. 2005. *Gothic and the Comic Turn*. Basingstoke: Palgrave Macmillan.
Jentsch, Ernst. [1906] 1997. 'On the Psychology of the Uncanny'. *Angelaki: Journal of the Theoretical Humanities* 2, no. 1: 7–16.
Kristeva, Julia. 1982. *Powers of Horror: An Essay on Abjection*. New York: Columbia University Press.
Loutitt, C. J. J. 2018. 'Tim Burton's Pop-Victorian Aesthetic'. *Gothic Studies* 20, no. 1–2: 276–94.
Radcliffe, Ann. [1794] 2001. *The Mysteries of Udolpho*. London: Penguin.
Ray, Brian. 2010. 'Tim Burton and the Idea of Fairy Tales'. In *Fairy Tales Films*, edited by Pauline Greenhill and Sidney Eve Matrix, 198–218. Logan: Utah State University Press.
Reynolds, Kimberley, Geraldine Brennan and Kevin McCarron. 2001. *Frightening Fiction*. London: Continuum.
Sage, Victor. 1994. 'Gothic Laughter: Farce and Horror in Five Texts'. In *Gothick Origins and Innovations*, edited by Allan Lloyd-Smith and Victor Sage, 190–203. Amsterdam and Atlanta: Rodopi Press.
Shelley, Mary Wollstonecraft. [1818] 2012. *Frankenstein: The 1818 Text, Contexts, Criticism*, edited by J. Paul Hunter. New York: W. W. Norton.
Spooner, Catherine. 2017. *Post-Millennial Gothic: Comedy, Romance and the Rise of Happy Gothic*. London and New York: Bloomsbury.
Stoker, Bram. [1897] 2011. *Dracula*, edited by Roger Luckhurst. Oxford: Oxford World's Classics.

Sutton, Max Keith. 1966. '"Inverse Sublimity" in Victorian Humour'. *Victorian Studies* 10, no. 2: 177–92.
Walpole, Horace. [1765] 2008. *The Castle of Otranto*. Oxford: Oxford World's Classics.
Warner, Marina. 2005. 'Dark Arts'. *The Guardian*, 14 October. https://www.theguardian.com/film/2005/oct/14/1?CMP=gu_com
Weinstock, Jeffrey. 2013. *The Works of Tim Burton*. Basingstoke: Palgrave Macmillan.
Whale, James, dir. 1931. *Frankenstein*. Universal Pictures.
Whale, James, dir. 1935. *The Bride of Frankenstein*. Universal Pictures.

Chapter 14

'Your Girlfriend is a Bloody Ghost!': Indian Horror / Gothic Comedy Cinema
Deimantas Valančiūnas

Indian popular cinema, despite being better known for its melodrama-framed love stories, has also produced over the years a vast number of films in the Gothic and horror genres. The first experiments with supernatural themes began in 1949 with the release of the film *Mahal* (*The Palace*, dir. Kamal Amrohi), which can be considered as the first Indian Gothic film (Mishra 2002). *Mahal* contained a number of narrative and aesthetic conventions attributed to the genre, such as ancient mansions harbouring secrets from the past and the new owners haunted by a (usually) female ghost. The enormous popularity of *Mahal* spawned several other films sharing very similar narrative and aesthetic features, resulting in the formation of a specific genre of Bombay Gothic (Dwyer 2011) which continued throughout the 1950s and 1960s. The horror genre took some time to develop and is associated with the Ramsay family (usually referred to as the Ramsay brothers), who started making films in the early 1970s in the manner of the Gothic/horror aesthetics of the British Hammer Horror films. The Ramsay brothers' horror films, however, were categorised as B-grade movies, as were many other horror films (with several exceptions) by other film-makers throughout the period. The horror genre did not reach the mainstream Indian film industry until the early 2000s, when it became associated with several notable Bollywood film directors, like Ram Gopal Varma, Mahesh Bhatt and others.

It has to be noted though that generic conceptualisation of Indian horror or Gothic films is notoriously problematic. Since its beginning, Indian cinema for years resisted the logic of genre classification. Adopting melodrama with inclusive song and dance sequences as its preferred format, Indian popular cinema was following the *masala* structure – an 'omnibus form' (Iyer 2022) which incorporated a variety of different moods and emotions. Therefore, even those films which would be labelled as either 'Gothic' or 'Horror' usually included elements of romance, action and comedy. Because of that, the definite line which would separate Gothic/horror from comedy/romance was incredibly thin. However, as noted by Mithuraaj Dhusiya, even though the Ramsay brothers' films incorporated many elements of comic relief and slapstick, 'neither are they advertised nor consumed as horror-comedies' (Dhusiya 2018, 142). Despite this generic fluidity, even from the beginning of the development of the Gothic/horror genre in India there were films which were identified more as 'comedy', rather than 'ghost' or 'horror' films. One of the earliest attempts to blend these two cinematographic genres was made in 1965 with Mehmood's film *Bhoot Bungla* (*Haunted House*), followed by other films, like Mehra's *Chamatkar* (*Miracle*) in 1992 or Kothare's *Zapatlela* (*Possessed*) in 1993 in the Marathi language. However, these were rather scattered examples and it was only from around the mid-2000s that we witnessed the surge of a particular body of films which are consciously marketed as 'horror comedies', indicating not only the possible changes in the Indian film market, but also the changes in the cinema consumption habits of the audience. Since both Gothic and Comedy are genres which may function as a definite social and political critique, the emergence of a 'collision of laughter and terror' (Carroll 1999, 146) in India as a separate (and very popular) genre in the mid-2000s may also signal certain sociocultural transformations and national tensions which required a novel cultural expression and exposure. Caroline Joan Picart too sees horror comedy as a 'hybrid genre' which allows exploration of the 'new realms of narrative possibilities' (Picart 2003, 191). Contrary to some other Asian countries (like Japan), India never employed the term 'Gothic' to describe its cultural production (and even the Gothic films of the 1950s and 1960s were labelled as such mostly by the academicians and critics much later). However, films falling under the 'horror-comedy' category quite often employ some of the most important Gothic features and tropes (such as physical or psychological haunting, transgression, doubles, otherness, to name but a few). As Gothic is always concerned with boundaries and their instabilities, 'its characteristic features can easily be turned to comic effect', as Avril Horner and Sue Zlosnik contend (2005, 17). This strategy may also be associated with the very nature of the Gothic/horror-comedy genre's narratives, which 'take their characters' initially stable reality and steadily, relentlessly unravel it around them', as Cynthia J. Miller and A. Bowdoin Van Riper suggest (2016, xv). This subversive, carnivalesque nature of the horror-comedy genre creates a potential space for political critique. Picart notes that juxtaposition of such comic elements as slapstick, impersonation and parody on the one hand, and horror elements on the other, in the horror-comedy genre creates a generic expression that 'allows for a simultaneous destabilisation of the boundaries of power, gender, and sexuality' (Picart 2003, 191).

Indian horror comedies, even if incorporating some of the strategies discussed above, retain their certain cultural specificity in relation to other cinematographic cultures. For example, in many of the well-known horror-comedy films in American or British production (e.g. Mel Brooks's *Dracula Dead and Loving It*, Edgar Wright's *Shaun of the Dead*, John Landle's *An American Werewolf in London* and so on), the comedy is achieved through playing around with horror and Gothic conventions – characters, environments and situations. Indian horror-comedy genre, however, is on the contrary firm in its clear separation of the comic and the horrific in horror-comedy films. In many cases, slapstick, parody, intertextuality and over-the-top dialogues comprise the comic aspect, while the horrific narrative line in many cases functions separately, often tied with the melodramatic mode. The logic of this may be rooted in classical Indian aesthetics, which are based on the theory of *rasa* – a particular emotion, conveyed by a performer and felt by the audience (Jones 2010, 37). The ancient Sanskrit text *Natyashastra* lists eight fundamental *rasas* (aesthetic flavours), amongst them *hasya* – laughter and *bhayanaka* – terror, which function independently, yet may work in tandem in the same performance. It may be argued that it is this division of spectators' responses, united into one genre, which not only draws different audiences to watch the film, but also enables a stronger articulation of the sociopolitical commentary and critique that the comedy horror genre has potential to express. Therefore, by looking at some of the most important Comic Gothic / horror films of Indian cinema this chapter will investigate these films as a certain cultural platform where the Comic Gothic / horror mode is evoked in order to address and discuss the anxieties of modern India about modernisation, memory, gender and sexuality.

Ghosts and Indian Horror-Comedy Films

The figure of the ghost in Indian cinema has been present from the very beginning of the Gothic genre and almost all the Gothic films throughout the 1950s and 1960s engaged in haunting narratives. Therefore, it is not surprising that one of the first films attributed to the horror-comedy genre – *Bhoot Bungla* (1965) – also had a ghost angle. However, even though the film accumulated some of the conventional Gothic aesthetics (the murder mystery, secrets from the past, a haunted ancient mansion), it also followed a particular narrative strategy, typical of Gothic films in India at that time. That is: not having actual ghosts, as the apparent ghost narrative would be rationalised and explained at the end of the film, thus changing the Gothic narrative into the whodunnit mystery. This strategy was very characteristic of the Indian Gothic cinema of the period and can be linked to the Nehruvian era and a certain ambiguous attitude towards independent India's strategy of rationalisation and modernisation led by India's first prime minister, Jawaharlal Nehru (Sen 2017; Valančiūnas 2021). Therefore, in *Bhoot Bungla* most of the ghostly appearances were in the song sequences and functioned more as a space to experiment with special effects, creating a certain spectacle and excitement for the spectators, rather than inducing fear. After *Bhoot Bungla* there were several other ghost comedy films; however, it was not until the mid-2000s that the horror-comedy genre was elevated to a new ground with the release of Sharma's film *Bhoothnath* (*Lord of Ghosts*, 2008), which is based on Oscar Wilde's story 'The Canterville Ghost'. The film is set in an old mansion in Goa which is rented by a young family and the story revolves around the developing friendship between the elderly ghost Kailash (played by Indian superstar actor Amitabh Bachchan) and the boy Banku. Aesthetically, the film incorporates some of the staples of the Gothic, especially in the first half of the film, where a towering colonial mansion, lightning storms and the unidentified presence of the ghost create a mysterious atmosphere. As the story progresses, the ghost, however, does not evoke much fear, and is presented as sympathetic and rather mischievous. Most of the comic elements in *Bhoothnath* are achieved through Kailash's competitions with Banku, various tricks he plays on other characters and by his visit to the school Banku attends. However, during the second half of the film the narrative moves into a much more dramatic mode with the introduction of Kailash's son Vijay, who has just returned to India from the US and is willing to sell the house and transform it into a holiday resort. At this point in the film we learn the story of Kailash and how he died, tripping on the staircase and falling to his death while trying to stop his son and grandson from leaving the house and going to the US for good.

The horror-comedy genre here creates a sensitive platform for the film to draw attention to such themes as displacement and migration, as seen through the two similar narrative lines – children leaving their elderly parents behind (in the case of Vijay) and parents leaving their families behind (in the case of Banku, whose father works on a long-distance cruise ship and is usually gone for a long period of time). Loneliness becomes one of the major factors that unites Banku and Kailash, as both are the victims of globalisation, transnational travels and migration. All of these issues have been prevalent in Indian popular cinema since the economic liberalisation of 1991, from which time films have often dramatised the idea of Indian identity in transition, associated with endangered cultural values represented mainly through the institution of the joint family system (Uberoi 2006). *Bhoothnath* also pays attention to the theme of the importance of heritage and familial memory, since Kailash refuses to move to the US and leave his house, because it is connected to a sense of stability, memories and family history. This attitude is challenged by the rapidly growing modernisation of India, with urban development, growth of leisure venues and the expansion of the consumption sector, which is presented as a danger to Indian identity since it pays little or no attention to familial heritage and memory, as exemplified by Vijay's indifference to his family house. This generational gap and indifference to the family is most obviously dramatised when Vijay refuses to perform the *antyeshti samskara* (funerary rites) for his father, leaving it to Banku's parents to perform them. In the end, however, the film restores faith in the institution of the family as Vijay finally arrives to perform the funerary rites, thus achieving a reconciliation with his father. Vijay finally acknowledges the house as a site of continuity of familial heritage and this is what informs his final decision not to sell it.

The association between the (haunted) house, memory and heritage is also explored in another example of horror-comedy genre – the Bengali film *Bhooter Bhabishyat* (*Future of the Past*, 2012), directed by Anik Datta and remade in the Hindi language in 2014 as *Gang of Ghosts*. *Bhooter Bhabishyat* operates on similar premises as *Bhoothnath* but explores and expands the concept of Indian identity. In the film, an aspiring film-maker, Ayan, arrives at a supposedly haunted mansion to shoot a commercial advertisement. Here he encounters a mysterious stranger, Biplab, who on learning about Ayan's ambitions to become a film-maker, relates to him a potential story for a film. In this story, most of the heritage and old buildings in the city of Kolkata are being demolished, which renders many of the 'inhabitants' of the houses (that is, ghosts), homeless. Having no place of their own, the ghosts are attempting to settle in one of the last remaining palaces of the city – Chowdhury mansion, which, unfortunately, has a limited capacity and only selected ghosts are allowed to stay in it. Because all of the ghosts come from very different periods of time, and from very diverse social and cultural backgrounds, many clashes and skirmishes arise. However, the ghosts have to start working together to withstand the demolition plans for this remaining mansion drawn up by the ruthless real estate developer Bhutoria.

Bhooter Bhabishyat employs the site of a haunted mansion and the figure of a ghost to raise a critical commentary on several key sociopolitical issues in India (and the region of Bengal, where the film's narrative is set). Firstly, as in *Bhoothnath*, it draws our attention to the rapidly growing urbanisation and commercialisation in India as a result of global financial flows, the expansion of consumer culture and a rapidly growing middle class. However, as the film suggests, this rapid growth and modernisation of the city is made at the expense of the heritage and cultural sites, as many ancient houses and palaces are being demolished in order to transform them into commercial venues, like shopping malls. The film also emphasises the unequal power relations visible in this process of urban growth, associated with the black market, local gang lords, illegal land acquisitions and the eviction of people. As Nishi Pulugurtha (2021) suggests, the film refers extra-textually to similar resonant instances in West Bengal, such as the Nandigram dispute, where land acquisition for building a chemical plant resulted in many violent clashes with local people. *Bhooter Bhabishyat* creates a parallel between the helpless ghosts which are rendered homeless as their houses are destroyed and the villagers of Nandigram (and numerous similar towns) who experience the same fate, becoming 'ghosts' in a certain sense of the word: their invisibility being a result of unequal power relations.

In addition, *Bhooter Bhabishyat* offers a strong social commentary on the role and importance of historical memory and heritage for contemporary identity. The film employs the figure of the ghost to highlight the cultural and social diversity of the region. The comic aspect of the film is activated by placing the ghosts together who belong not only to different historical periods and events of national importance (for example, the eighteenth century, British Empire, Partition, Kargil War) but also to different social and cultural backgrounds (Muslims, Hindus, refugees, Naxalites, untouchables and so on). The comic aspect of the film is achieved through numerous instances when these different identities clash with one another, enabling the film also to highlight a number of issues associated with class, caste, language and religion which are prevalent in India. The cultural, religious and linguistic diversity that these ghosts represent is especially relevant for India in the twenty-first century, when growing Hindu nationalism attempts to represent India as culturally homogenous through revisionist readings of India's past. The ghosts, however, despite their differences and conflicting interpretations arising due to different historical periods they belong to, begin to learn to live and work in tandem. The film makes a point about the importance of accepting every bit of history, no matter how contentious that may be, as in one way or another it reveals the foundation of the country's social and cultural present moment. The acceptability and integration of difference is achieved through the comic sequence in the film when the ghosts decide to do a fashion show, where each ghost dresses up as the opposite of their religious/cultural identities. Therefore, the Gothic conventions of the ghostly presence, the haunted mansion, and transgression are activated and accumulated in order for *Bhooter Bhabishyat* to draw attention not only to the threatening expansion of urbanisation and commercialisation, but also to the endangered distinctive cultural and religious diversity of Bengal.

Monstrous-Feminine and its Subversion in Indian Horror-Comedy Films

While ghost films are some of the most popular in the Gothic/horror genre, the other strand of narratives in Indian horror and Gothic production is concerned with female monsters. In constructing these female monsters, Indian horror films have been drawing not only from Western horror cinema, but also taking inspiration from vernacular folk traditions, as evident from the so called '*chudail* films'. *Chudail* (sometimes spelled as *churail* or *churel*) is a bloodthirsty and malevolent female ghost popular in the North Indian folk tradition. She is believed to be a ghost of a woman who died during pregnancy or childbirth and who assumes the form of a beautiful young woman to seduce men into having sexual intercourse with her and then draining their blood (Mcclintock 1990). This dangerous, monstrous female fiend (together with other similar local monstrous variations, like *daayan* or *petni*) has been a part of the Indian horror cultural production since the 1980s. Although *chudail* films have been more often than not confined to the low-budget and B-grade cinema circles, the sexual nature of the ghost has opened up numerous possibilities for the film-makers to engage in social critique by challenging conservative attitudes in Indian cinema. Traditionally, the female monster has been employed in low-budget and B-grade horror films primarily for the purpose of exploiting sexual content and as an opportunity to display the sexualised female body. However, I will argue that the recent trends in Indian horror-comedy films demonstrate that the pattern is changing and that the monstrous female characters have gradually been invested with more critical meaning so that there is a significant shift in representing and constructing the female monster. To understand these changes in Indian horror-comedy cinema, I draw on the conceptual framework of the 'monstrous-feminine' developed by Barbara Creed. Rather than talking about the 'female monster', Creed suggests the usage of the term 'monstrous-feminine', which emphasises the importance of gender in the construction of her monstrosity. The cultural production associated with the monstrous-feminine is thus concerned with what it is about woman that is shocking, terrifying, horrific and abject (Creed 1993, 1). In other words, the monstrous-feminine represents cultural anxieties associated with women. However, it may be argued that through these representations, horror-comedy genre films can become a site of critique of those very cultural assumptions, subverting not only their representation, but also certain power relations. Analysing two recent horror-comedy films *Stree* (*Woman*, 2018, directed by Amar Kaushik) and *Roohi* (2021, directed by Hardik Mehta) (both of which feature a *chudail*), I will therefore attempt to investigate how the monstrous-feminine is reinvented in contemporary horror-comedy genre in order to address and discuss contemporary national sociocultural anxieties such as the issues of women's safety, assault on the body, personal freedom and marriage, among others.

Stree's story line revolves around a small village of Chandrapore where every year, during a four-day religious festival, a *chudail* appears to terrorise the men of the village. *Chudail*, who is called simply a Stree (or a woman) in the film, is the ghost of a courtesan of the Mughal era, who was killed by the villagers for her illicit love affair. Since then, every year she reappears to take vengeance on the village men, making them disappear, one by one. Therefore, for four nights in a row, villagers keep writing on their doors and walls *o stree kal aanaa* ('oh woman, come tomorrow') in order to trick the *chudail* to come another day, until the festival is over and *chudail* disappears for another year.

Taking into consideration the already discussed potential of the horror-comedy crossover to address and disrupt social and cultural boundaries, *Stree* can also be read as a commentary on certain sociocultural instabilities and anxieties in India. One of the first visible narrative features of *Stree* is the assault on the male body, as it is the men of the village in the film who are the prime target. However, this violence directed towards men in the film could be read as the opposite – as a commentary on the violence against women, because the horror-comedy genre allows this subversive shift of perspectives. Therefore, we may argue that the film uses the monstrous-feminine to comment, in a subversive and carnivalesque manner, on the assault on the female body. The discussions about female body, agency, security of public spaces in India has been driven forward enormously since the 'Nirbhaya case' (otherwise known as the Delhi gang rape of 2012), when a 22-year-old medical student was brutally gang raped, tortured and killed while travelling on the evening bus in Delhi. After this gruesome assault, the media, numerous NGOs and independent social networks and platforms continued exposing and reporting hundreds of cases of rape, mutilation and disappearances of women of different ethnic and social backgrounds (Bhattacharyya 2015). This has been taken further by the Indian film industry as well, and both commercial and independent cinema have addressed violence against women as their subject in a number of recent films (for example *Angry Indian Goddesses* (2015), *Pink* (2016), *Article 15* (2019) and so on.)

Stree contributes to these cultural discussions by commenting on safe spaces, paranoia and terror, but does that through the horror-comedy framework in a highly subversive way, disrupting and reversing power relations. It does so by first of all placing men in the victim position, making their anxiety the central aspect of the film, as their source of terror becomes the monstrous-feminine Stree, with her deadly, dangerous and terrifying abjection, represented through her decomposing body. By employing POV shots of the always present, but rarely seen *chudail*, the film recreates an atmosphere of constant surveillance, where the men become the objects of the lusty, but also potentially violent gaze of the Stree. The public space becomes threatening, and in the film men are trying to brace and protect themselves by walking in groups, dressing up as women or hiding behind the closed doors of their homes. But even the boarded private space does not guarantee protection and the men keep disappearing even from behind the locked door. The aspect of disappearance is also crucial in the sociopolitical commentary of the film. The invisible assault on the male bodies corresponds to the extratextual references to the numerous assaults on women, their kidnapping and rape, where the rapists are more often than not unidentified or mysteriously cleared of charges (Verma, Qureshi and Kim 2017). In the film, the men who are abducted by Stree leave nothing behind but their clothes, which is also an indication of physical assault and rape. And even when at the end of the film the power of *chudail* is allegedly damaged and dozens of men reappear from the ruins of an old mansion, finally set free, their nakedness showcases their persistent vulnerability and insecurity. *Stree* ends with the reappearance of *chudail* as she is riding on a bus, indicating that the violence against women is far from over. *Stree* is littered with witty dialogues, comic situations and amusing plot twists which primarily constitute the comedy segment of the film. The Gothic atmosphere of paranoia and terror and its association with the melodramatic narrative of the background story of Stree, however, constitute the serious aspect of the film, enabling a much stronger and effective critique.

The second film to be considered is *Roohi*. Here the story takes place in the small city of Bagadpur, which proudly retains the old custom of bride abduction. Two friends, Bhawra and Kattani, are hired by a local gang lord to kidnap a girl for a potential groom, but once they have done the kidnapping, the deal is suspended, and so the two friends have to bring the girl, Roohi, to an abandoned factory to wait for further instructions. As they transfer the girl to the factory, it appears that she is possessed by a *chudail*, Afza, who takes control of Roohi's body at certain times. As Bhawra starts to fall in love with Roohi, he attempts to free her from the possession of *chudail*.

If *Stree* tackles the issues of female body and safety, *Roohi* takes on the topic of female subjectivity and independence, especially in relation to marriage. As the film's lore explains, Afza, the *chudail* who possesses Roohi's body, is a malevolent and restless spirit of a girl who died prior to the consummation of marriage. Therefore, she possesses the bodies of young marriageable girls in the hope of achieving marriage herself through them. In this way, the marriage becomes the prime explanation of the haunting and the central theme of *Roohi*. In the film, Roohi exemplifies woman without subjectivity – she can be kidnapped for marriage, but also 'delayed' when the marriage deal is suspended. At the same time her possessor *chudail* Afza embodies the unwanted aspect of female liberty. Similar to the *Stree*, *Roohi* here too activates the imagery of the monstrous-feminine, expressed through the decomposing appearance of Afza's body. As Afza is the ghost of an unmarried woman, we may argue that her ugly, disgusting and abject decomposing body represents the cultural perception of an unmarried woman. In India, despite the rapid changes in social and cultural spheres of life, marriage remains a crucial staple of social organisation and has been promoted through popular culture and cinema in particular. As Rachel Dwyer observes, 'heterosexual romance, marriage, parenthood and the fulfilment of other family roles underpin the melodrama, as it is at its core about the private world of the home and the family' (Dwyer 2014, 186). In this way, even though remaining single may be seen as a visible choice of lifestyle in contemporary India, it comes not without problems, especially for single women. As Sarah Lamb contends in her anthropological research on Bengali women in India, 'many women's narratives highlighted the difficulties and kinds of structural violence single women face, including forms of gender inequality, social isolation, economic vulnerability, and feelings of not being recognised as a normal and valuable person' (Lamb 2018, 52). *Roohi* actualises many of these concerns through a subversive horror-comedy framework. The two female characters, Roohi and Afza, each exemplify the threatening and pitiful position of a single woman, while the narrative positions of the two male characters, Bhawra and Kattani, show the two men trying to save both women. The classical line of heterosexual fulfilment offering both romantic love and a consequent marriage is executed through Bhawra and Roohi's narrative while the comic mode is evoked when Bhawra's friend Kattani falls in love with the *chudail* Afza, as though indicating that there is always a man ready for saving even the abject, terrifying and unwanted women. However, the film presents us with a subversive ending. Instead of marrying Bhawra and, possibly, escaping the curse of the *chudail*, Roohi takes control by walking around the sacred fire and putting vermillion on her forehead – thus, marrying herself, or rather, her possessor, Afza. The ending can be interpreted so that, by doing this, Roohi accepts the abject monstrosity of an unmarried self and becomes unified with it. The last shot of the film depicts Roohi riding a motorcycle out of town. Bhawra and Kattani speculate that Roohi will stop and turn around, acknowledging her love for one of them (an intertextual reference to one of the most popular Bollywood romantic films, Chopra's *Dilwale Dulhania Le Jayenge*, 1995). And Roohi does stop but does not turn around and looks into the side mirror of the bike instead. The close-up shot of the mirror displays only Roohi's eyes, as she wants to see herself only, and, therefore, breaks the conventions of Indian popular cinema and popular cultural assumptions and expectations, by choosing independence and self-reliance. We still assume that the monstrous *chudail* is inside her, but she accepts her as a part of herself, and so her singleness becomes not a limitation, but a path to freedom at this point. As in the previously discussed example of *Stree*, *Roohi* builds its narrative on a twofold generic approach. The slapstick comic characters of Bhawra and Kattani and their attempts to save Roohi/Afza are filled with funny dialogues and intertextual references to other popular Indian films, while the terrifying and horrific narrative of the *chudail*, and especially the ending of the film, are conveyed through the melodramatic mode. This combination of twofold generic approach and subversive strategy enables the film's critical stance towards the fetishisation of marriage in Indian culture and its critical commentary on women's independence and gender-based roles in society.

Conclusion

In a 2020 film, *Laxmii*, directed by Raghava Lawrence and advertised as horror comedy, the narrative introduces us to Aasif, a sceptic of the supernatural, and his wife Rashmi. They lead an independent life, keeping minimal contact with Rashmi's parents, since her father opposed their marriage on religious grounds (Aasif is a Muslim).

Yet they decide to visit Rashmi's parents on their wedding anniversary despite the familial conflict. Rashmi's parents live in a neighbourhood which is considered to be haunted and it takes little time for Aasif to be possessed by a ghost – and, to be precise, by a female ghost. Much of the comedy in the first part of this film arises from Asif's strange manners, as in the moments of possession he behaves and dresses as a woman: much to the horror of the members of the family, and amusement of the spectators. However, towards the second half of the film, we learn that Aasif is actually possessed not by a female ghost, but by the ghost of a transgender activist, Laxmii, who together with his adoptive family were killed by a local rich man because Laxmii refused to let him take over her piece of land on which she planned to construct a hospital for transgender people. Through the perspective of the ghost, we learn about the difficult life of Laxmii – her non-supportive parents and the sympathetic schoolteacher who adopted and named her Laxmii after the goddess of wealth in Hindu mythology, Laxmii's long path to become a transgender activist and, finally, her lost battle with the local gang lords. Now we see her plea for revenge. This is a part of the film where the comic mode changes to melodrama, and this is where the sympathetic and critical dimension of a horror-comedy genre plays its part. *Laxmii*, together with other films discussed in this chapter demonstrate how the rise of horror comedies as a genre in Indian cinema initiated a way to address certain critical aspects of Indian social and cultural norms in a subversive, and hence pleasurable way. Similarly, catering to the audiences which are now much more concerned about the generic classification of media, the comedy-horror films draw a diverse audience, which may become sensitive to the expressed critique precisely through the conscious division of the film narrative into the comic/pleasurable and the horrific/melodramatic. This new generic expression, which has gained momentum since the mid-2000s, employs some of the most common Gothic tropes of haunting, transgression, possession and crossing of boundaries in an effective interrogation of persisting questions of gender, identity and nationhood. As the ghost narratives probe the questions of modernisation, belonging and memory, the monstrous-feminine narrative line interrogates gender norms and roles. Contrary to the previous portrayals of female ghosts (*chudails*) in many B-grade films, the films discussed in this chapter reverse this representation. Through the decomposing, rotting, abject and, most importantly, desexualised bodies of the monstrous-feminine, the films subvert the previous eroticised gaze on the female body. By evoking the horror-comedy mode, the films express a strong social and cultural critique in regard to the female body and women's liberty and sexuality.

References

Amrohi, Kamal, dir. 1949. *Mahal*. Bombay Talkies.
Bhattacharyya, Rituparna. 2015. 'Understanding the Spatialities of Sexual Assault against Indian Women in India'. *Gender, Place & Culture* 22, no. 9: 1340–56. https://doi.org/10.1080/0966369X.2014.969684.
Brooks, Mel, 1995. dir. *Dracula: Dead and Loving It*. Gaumont.
Carroll, Noël. 1999. 'Horror and Humor'. *The Journal of Aesthetics and Art Criticism* 57, no. 2: 145–60. https://doi.org/10.2307/432309
Chopra, Aditya, dir. 1995. *Dilwale Dulhania Le Jeyenge*. Yash Raj Films.
Creed, Barbara. 1993. *The Monstrous-Feminine. Film, Feminism, Psychoanalysis*. New York: Routledge.
Datta, Anik, dir. 2012. *Bhooter Bhabishyat*. Mojo Productions.
Dhusiya, Mithuraaj. 2018. *Indian Horror Cinema: (En)gendering the Monstrous*. New York: Routledge.
Dwyer, Rachel. 2011. 'Bombay Gothic: On the 60th Anniversary of Kamal Amrohi's A *Maha*'. In *Beyond the Boundaries of Bollywood. The Many Forms of Hindi Cinema*, edited by Rachel Dwyer and Jerry Pinto, 130–55. New Delhi: Oxford University Press.
Dwyer, Rachel. 2014. *Bollywood's India: Hindi Cinema as a Guide to Contemporary India*. London: Reaktion Books.
Horner, Avril and Sue Zlosnik. 2005. *Gothic and the Comic Turn*. Basingstoke: Palgrave Macmillan.
Iyer, Usha. 2022. 'Dance and Ludic Queerness. A Genealogy of Gestures from Bhagwan to Bachchan'. In *A Companion to Indian Cinema*, edited by Neepa Majumdar and Ranjani Mazumdar, 199–218. Chichester: Wiley Blackwell.
Jones, Matthew. 2010. 'Bollywood, *Rasa* and Indian Cinema: Misconceptions, Meanings and *Millionaire*'. *Visual Anthropology* 23, no. 1: 33–43. https://doi.org/10.1080/08949460903368895
Kaushik, Amar, dir. 2018. *Stree*. D2R Films, Maddock Films.
Kothare, Mahesh, dir. 1993. *Zapatlela*. Jenma Film International.
Lamb, Sarah. 2018. 'Being Single in India: Gendered Identities, Class Mobilities, and Personhoods in Flux'. *Ethos. Journal of the Society for Psychological Anthropology* 46, no. 1: 49–69. https://doi.org/10.1111/etho.12193
Landle, John, dir. 1981. *An American Werewolf in London*. PolyGram Pictures.
Lawrence, Raghava, dir. 2020. *Laxmii*. Cape of Good Films.
Mcclintock, Wayne. 1990. 'Demons and Ghosts in Indian Folklore'. *Missiology: An International Review* 18, no. 1: 37–47. https://doi.org/10.1177/009182969001800104
Mehmood, dir. 1965. *Bhoot Bungla*. Mumtaz Films.
Mehra, Rajiv, dir. 1992. *Chamatkar*. Eagle Films.
Mehta, Hardik, dir. 2021. *Roohi*. Jio Studios, Maddock Films.
Miller, Cynthia J. and A. Bowdoin Van Riper. 2016. 'Introduction'. In *The Laughing Dead: The Horror-Comedy Film from Bride of Frankenstein to Zombieland*, edited by Cynthia J. Miller and A. Bowdoin Van Riper, xiii–xxiii. Lanham, MD: Rowman & Littlefield.
Mishra, Vijay. 2002. *Bollywood Cinema. Temples of Desire*. London and New York: Routledge.

Picart, Caroline Joan. 2003. *Remaking the Frankenstein Myth on Film: Between Laughter and Horror*. Albany: State University of New York Press.
Pulugurtha, Nishi. 2021. 'The Past and the Present: A Reading of *Bhooter Bhabishyat*'. In *South Asian Gothic. Haunted Cultures, Histories and Media*, edited by Katarzyna Ancuta and Deimantas Valančiūnas, 49–61. Cardiff: University of Wales Press.
Sen, Meheli. 2017. *Haunting Bollywood: Gender, Genre, and the Supernatural in Hindi Commercial Cinema*. Austin: University of Texas Press.
Sharma, Vivek, dir. 2008. *Bhoothnath*. NH Studioz.
Uberoi, Patricia. 2006. *Freedom and Destiny: Gender, Family, and Popular Culture in India*. New Delhi and New York: Oxford University Press.
Valančiūnas, Deimantas. 2021. '*Rebecca* in India: The Appropriation of European Gothic in Indian Cinema'. In *South Asian Gothic. Haunted Cultures, Histories and Media*, edited by Katarzyna Ancuta and Deimantas Valančiūnas, 97–111. Cardiff: University of Wales Press.
Verma, Arvind, Hanif Qureshi and Jee Yearn Kim. 2017. 'Exploring the Trend of Violence against Women in India'. *International Journal of Comparative and Applied Criminal Justice* 41, no. 1–2: 3–18. https://doi.org/10.1080/01924036.2016.1211021
Wright, Edgar, dir. *Shaun of the Dead*. Universal Pictures, StudioCanal.

Chapter 15

Rural Hauntings and Black Sheep: Comic Turns, Violence and Supernatural Echoes in New Zealand's Gothic Comedy Films

Lorna Piatti-Farnell and Angelique Nairn

In his well-known critical overview over the defining characteristics of the Gothic, David Punter (1996) outlines three overarching components that underscore the mode: paranoia, the barbaric and the concept of taboo. Focused as it is on representational intersections of excess, the macabre, and uncanny atmospheres, it is not uncommon to see the Gothic mode rendering feelings of alienation, social separation, Otherness and, ultimately, fear, as these feelings are rendered in contexts of isolation that rely on terror as an overarching framework.

In their focus on the violent, immoral and supernatural (Mercer 2014) as it grapples with the sublime (Spooner 2017), representations of the Gothic – not only in traditional literary forms but in more recent manifestations found in film, television and popular culture – often evoke feelings of horror (Beville 2009) and disturb with their inclinations towards death and their disruption of the boundaries of social order (Horner and Zlosnik 2012).

Despite what can be construed as a penchant for the unfamiliar and the dire, Gothic narratives can act as a means of teaching about 'cultural and political oppression' (Horner and Zlosnik 2005, 1), and can address that which might trouble and perturb (Gildersleeve and Cantrell 2022). In the case of Aotearoa New Zealand, Gothic narratives offer an exploration of the insecurities of the nation and the anxieties that plague the country's cultural identity.[1] They can reveal much about a country that might have a short history but nevertheless is possessed of a savage and oppressive one. Taking this regionalised understanding of the Gothic as a point of departure, in this chapter we seek to explore what constitutes the Kiwi Gothic from a predominantly Pākehā perspective; specifically, we explore how the Gothic comic turn manifests in the internationally recognised horror-comedy films *Housebound* (2014) and *Black Sheep* (2006) as evocative examples of New Zealand Gothic horror comedies.[2]

Both films rely on what is often commonly referred to as 'Kiwi humour': a type of comedy that is attuned to local ways of life, while also drawing attention to the geographically and often culturally secluded nature of New Zealand as a country. Through the construction of multiple comic turns, both *Housebound* and *Black Sheep* exploit and subvert Gothic horror narratives and iconographies, while also crafting an uncanny and disaffecting, yet unavoidable humorous, representation of the twenty-first-century everyday. Ultimately, the result of this mixture is the creation of an Antipodean Comic Gothic mystique, where metaphorical horrors and fears become paradoxically tangible, yet hidden within the layers of the seemingly 'normal' New Zealand cultural context.

Approaching New Zealand Gothic

Unlike the European Gothic tradition, which is primarily and historically entangled with ancient architecture, folklore and a myriad of supernatural stories, New Zealand's Gothic tradition is reliant on the natural landscape as a source of tension, horror and isolation. As Ian Conrich (2012, 393) writes, 'New Zealand fiction, its literature and film, has repeatedly portrayed spaces of isolation, loss, and despair, of a rugged, wild, and treacherous land that can assail and entrap.' Echoing Conrich's perception, Mercer (2014) contends that it is unsurprising that New Zealand Gothic, or Kiwi Gothic as it is also known, is focused on the threat posed by the natural environment, given New Zealand is foremost a settler nation that was constructed by taming the land and colonising its Indigenous populations. This perceived subversion is reliant on the long-standing and culturally established view of New Zealand as a pastoral idyll, an image that was heavily advertised during British colonial times – in opposition to the 'dreary' conditions of Victorian Britain – and which proved to be instrumental in attracting waves of willing immigrants to the new colony. The idea of New Zealand as a pastoral paradise continues to serve as one of the central identity markers for both New Zealand and its people, at home and internationally. Accordingly, much of New Zealand's Gothic literature and film has portrayed the landscape as malevolent (Mercer 2014), remote and oppressive (Leotta 2016) with the potential to overpower its 'eccentric, disturbed, or disadvantaged' people, and as haunted by sinister and unseen threats (Conrich 2012, 397). Such depictions of the land in film and literature have sought to unpack the colonial anxiety that produces identity crises among Pākehā people. It attests to what Conrich (2012) considers a feeling of unsettlement and vulnerability that accompanies displacement and isolation from British heritage, especially for women, and has been evident in such cinematic offerings as Vincent Ward's *Virgil* (1984), Anna Maclean's *Crush* (1992), Jane Campion's *The Piano* (1993) and Curtis Vowell's *Fantail* (2013). Films such as these render the New Zealand landscape treacherous, and frightening, and anything but a utopia. The New Zealand Gothic commonly subverts the idealised notions of New Zealand as a pastoral idyll in order to channel the actual realities of both rural life and geographical and social isolation, which are commonly recharacterised through metaphorical representations of 'entrapment, violence and death' (Mercer 2014, 53).

In their utilisation of the Gothic mode, New Zealand literature and film are predisposed to explore 'the binary opposition of domestic/wild' (Conrich 2012, 403) by telling stories of domestic dysfunction. The land can be seen to contribute to the breakdown of families with homesteads in rural locations producing 'families afflicted by mental illness and violence, or homes invaded by external forces'. For example, the film *Heart of the Stag* (1984) tells the story of a sheep farmer who is sexually abusing his daughter, while *In My Father's Den* (1972/2004) penned by Maurice Gee and later adapted to film by Brad McGann, explores the unravelling of the Prior family which becomes intertwined by grief, betrayal, abuse and murder. Both texts emphasise the family traumas that are amongst the common themes of New Zealand Gothic stories, as well as the tendency towards the psychological and inner monster (Lawn 2002). Of course, Kiwi Gothic also engages with typical monsters such as vampires and zombies, but these are integrated into stories where the themes of repression, secrets, insanity, psychosexual stories and the spiritual realm are central. Admittedly, these examples of New Zealand Gothic reflect a Pākehā world view, and that is in part because as Kavka (2014) attests, the supernatural and departed spirits are not conducive to feelings of dread among the Māori population.[3] In fact, it has led Smith (2011, 115) to argue that 'Kiwi Gothic' is predominantly a 'Pākehā thing'.

Although New Zealand has produced several ostensibly 'serious' Gothic narratives – including literary examples such as Jean Devaney's *The Butcher Shop* (1926) and Janet Frame's *Faces in the Water* (1961), films such as *Jack Be Nimble* (1993), *Heavenly Creatures* (1994) and documentaries such as *Cinema of Unease* (1995) – a distinctive aspect of New Zealand's approach is the tendency of authors and film-makers to embrace both the Gothic and the comic in their work (Leotta 2010). Allan Cameron further supports Leotta's position by suggesting that there is a 'relative scarcity of straightforwardly generic horror films in the nation's cinematic corpus' (2010, 56). Horror, with its Gothic aspects

(Punter 1996; Spooner 2017) has been predisposed to hybridity producing horror-comedy films because both horror and comedy are underpinned by being affective genres that question social and cultural order (Abbott 2011). New Zealand film-makers have capitalised on such an amalgamation forging the 'Kiwi splatstick' genre pioneered by the likes of Peter Jackson in his films *Bad Taste* (1987) and *Braindead* (1992). 'Kiwi splatstick' relies on 'the excess of horror and splatter' (Leotta 2010, 303) combined with parody and slapstick, to create productions that Erin Harrington (2020, 91) suggests permit an 'interplay between the horrific, the abject, and the ludicrous'. Subsequent films such as *Fresh Meat* (2012), *What We Do in the Shadows* (2014) – and its television-based spin-off, *Wellington Paranormal* (2018–22) – and *Deathgasm* (2015) have continued the tradition, challenging 'the binary between "serious" and "comic"' (Piatti-Farnell 2022, 189) to elicit shock in unsuspecting viewers but also to lend cultural specificity that continues to shape the conceptualisation of the New Zealand Gothic. Two other films that have contributed to the horror-comedy approach of New Zealand film-makers are *Housebound* (2014) and *Black Sheep* (2006) and it is to those films we now turn to explore further understandings of New Zealand Gothic and its comedic undertones.

Rural Hauntings

Housebound (2014) is a Gothic horror-comedy film directed by Gerard Johnstone. It tells the story of Kylie Bucknell (Morgana O'Reilly) who is forced to live with her mother Miriam (Rima TeWiata) after being sentenced to eight months of house arrest having botched an ATM robbery. Confined to the house by an ankle monitor, Kylie regresses into teenage selfishness and is particularly frustrated by her mother's belief that the house they occupy is haunted. The mere fact that Kylie is constructed as a rebellious teen alludes to Conrich's (2012) argument that Gothic narratives produced from a New Zealand perspective tend to be developed through the lens of adolescence. Such an approach is perceived as metaphorical in that, compared to, for example, European Gothic depictions, New Zealand and its Gothic stories are 'new' and therefore films like *Housebound* contribute to learning more about what constitutes the country's cultural identity and Gothic leanings. Furthermore, the film explores the relationship between mother and daughter, which is typical of New Zealand Gothic texts, where families are depicted as 'dysfunctional and isolated' (Conrich 2012, 398). Yet it also sets the stage for a 'love story between a mother and her daughter'

(Heller-Nicholas 2015, 26) as the two work together to grapple with the haunted house.

After her own 'ghostly' experience, Kylie, Miriam and Amos (Glen-Paul Waru) – the security guard charged with monitoring Kylie – determine that the house was once the setting for a horrific murder and they seek to uncover more about the crime. Kylie's claims to her counsellor Dennis (Cameron Rhodes) that the house is haunted are ignored, attributed to hallucinations resulting from perceived substance abuse and lead Dennis to want Kylie to be institutionalised. Such a direction in the film alludes to the psychological and deranged forces that shape Kiwi Gothic monsters (Lawn 2006). However, Kylie is clearly not mentally unhinged and uncovers that the haunting presence in the house is a squatter, and furthermore, that Dennis is responsible for the past gruesome murder. Dennis tries to kill the squatter, Amos, Kylie and her mother but is thwarted when Kylie stabs him in the neck with a weapon that also links to a high voltage charge that inevitably blows up Dennis's head. As with many Gothic narratives that engage with comic elements (a point we will return to shortly), the demise of Dennis dabbles in gallows humour and ensures the comic and gore are emphasised 'with equal zest' (Kawin 2012, 200). The film won genre awards in both Scotland and Switzerland and was shown in film festivals around the world including those in Montreal, Melbourne and London (Heller-Nicholas 2015).

Housebound has many of the expectations of a Gothic offering but none so obvious as being a story of a haunted house where, in this case, at least one of the inhabitants is trapped. Although the haunted house of *Housebound* may not be an abbey, castle or graveyard common in Gothic fiction (Botting 2013), it does provide a setting steeped in the atmosphere expected of Gothic edifices. Known to channel distinct feelings of terror and alienation, the Gothic edifice also acts as a 'receptacle of history' (Georgieva, 109), providing a channel for the past and the present to blend and merge, through (among other things) notions of entrapment. Indeed, the house in *Housebound* creates what Aguirre (1990, 2) refers to as a 'closed space' where terror and dread are experienced as Kylie, Amos and Miriam respond to the unexplainable noises and navigate the gloomy, dark and, indeed, hidden passageways that exist within the walls of the house. Accordingly, the house contributes to the entrapment of the characters. As Talairach-Vielmas contends, Gothic narratives propose 'metaphors of entrapment and literal imprisonment', that 'frame the heroine's experience through powerlessness' (2007, 160). Kylie's powerlessness is clearly delineated by the ankle bracelet and the dismissal of her 'haunted house' claims by her counsellor and echoes

Spooner's (2019) perception that women's entrapment has been tied to the domestic space.

However, the film can be read as possessing a feminist edge as the daughter and mother work together to uncover the truth and seek accountability for the horrific murder. Such an approach to entrapment, while not uniquely that of New Zealand, does however highlight the capacity of Gothic narratives to possess political intentions, including 'feminist and other liberationist' (Edmond 2004, 115) motives. That is, rather than telling the traditional Gothic story of 'vulnerable heroines undergoing moral trials' (Lawn 2002, 49), which Horner and Zlosnik (2016) were perturbed to find perpetuated anxieties and anger towards women, *Housebound* does not dispossess Kylie of all her agency. Instead, she acts as what Ledoux (2011, 331) considers a 'defiant damsel' because her imprisonment in the house does not threaten her physical prowess and cunning. For example, Heller-Nicholas (2015, 26) in her review of *Housebound* claims that Kylie typifies the 'traditional female horror hero' because she acts with 'confidence and feisty audacity'. Kylie's approach to the unfolding drama also reveals much about the comic turn of New Zealand horror films.

According to Nicholas Holm (2017, 103), 'New Zealand humour has traditionally been characterised as dry and understated.' Indeed, it has been variously described as deadpan or laconic, because it often lacks emotion or affect (Holm 2017; 2019). The laconic approach was celebrated and promoted by comedian John Clarke and his famous persona Fred Dagg, with its 'cultivation of a naïve likability, the dry refusal of excess or even any excitement, and a studied performance of one's own apparent failure' (Holm 2019, 45) and is particularly apparent in *Housebound* in the portrayal of Miriam. For example, when the ankle bracelet is affixed to Kylie's leg, Miriam remarks: 'Gosh that is high tech, isn't it? Aren't you lucky Kylie having all that fancy technology on your foot?' Kylie's look of disgust and apparent frustration at her mother's 'brief, concise' and 'sententious' (Holm 2019, 40) comment not only sets up the troubled relationship between mother and daughter but highlights for the viewer that Miriam's naivety, silliness and in some cases farcical behaviour will continue to be a means of comic relief during times of heightened terror and tension. Miriam, therefore, acts as a juxtaposition to Kylie's no-nonsense, sarcastic approach. For example, when questioned on how she intends to deal with the 'ghost' in the house, Kylie asserts that she intends to 'smash it in the face', which captures the dry humour, stoicism and 'just get on with it' attitude that Harrington (2020) considers is a marker of New Zealander's national traits.

While Miriam might be considered laconic and Kylie sarcastic, the comic in *Housebound* is also apparent in the attitude and behaviour of security officer Amos. Amos's interactions with the family are typical of the New Zealand inclination towards deadpan humour. Holm (2017, 104) describes deadpan as 'a particular style of comic acting in which humorous content is performed with a blank face and an unenthusiastic demeanour' and typifies Berlant's (2015, 195) 'flat affect' where there is the underperformance of emotion. Take for instance the scene where Amos has been alerted to a ghostly presence in the house and decides to check it out. He promptly pulls a Dictaphone from his jacket pocket and begins trying to converse with the ghost, pausing after each question in the hopes that the recorder will pick up a response. When Kylie questions his approach by asking, 'Do you really think someone is going to answer?' Amos adopts a deadpan expression as he retorts, 'Maybe they already have.' Not only does this scene signal the New Zealand sense of humour, but it also does what several horror-comedy films do and that is engage in parody (Allen 2011; Horner and Zlosnik 2012; Miller and Van Riper 2016; Piatti-Farnell 2022; Spooner 2019). Director Gerard Johnstone has noted that he took inspiration from television programmes such as *Ghost Hunters* (2004–16) (Heller-Nicholas 2015) and, by drawing on such genre codes, was able to use exaggeration, inversion and misdirection (Harries, 2002) to as Yogerst (2016, 179) and Horner and Zlosnik (2005) put it, 'spoof' such shows. Such spoofing and parodying led reviewer Heller-Nicholas (2015, 27) to suggest that '[t]here's something incredibly funny about people who diagnose spiritual infestations like they're fixing a dishwasher'. The humour in *Housebound*, then, helps to conceptualise the film as New Zealand made and in so doing, contributes to the development and maintenance of the culture's 'aesthetic judgements, cultural politics and community building' (Holm 2019, 39).

Brutalised by Sheep

In their evaluation of the intersection between comedy and representations of the undead, Cynthia Miller and Bowdoin Van Riper contend that 'parody, satire, burlesque, irony, black humour, absurdity [and], farce all shine a spotlight on the human condition' (2016, xiv). Narrative combinations that join the undead – especially zombies – and the comedic everyday are both unnerving and unsettling precisely because of their referential power to the suggestively mundane existence of the living. This contextual relevance is indeed to be found in *Black*

Sheep (2006), a Gothic horror-comedy film directed by Jonathan King. Set in rural New Zealand, the film tells the story of the Oldfield brothers, Angus (Peter Feeney) and Henry (Nathan Meister). From the offset, the film identifies its Gothic underpinnings by being rooted in instances of trauma and fear (Spooner 2017). Both brothers grew up on the farm, but young Henry, having been traumatised by the death of his father while herding sheep, and his brother killing his beloved pet sheep and donning the fleece, develops 'ovinophobia' and chooses to settle in the city. As the story unfolds, Henry is forced to return to the farm fifteen years later to sell his share of the property, but unbeknownst to Henry, Angus has begun attempting to genetically engineer sheep (Cameron 2010). As Andrea Wright (2018, 139) puts it, the premise of the story centres on 'the most banal of creatures, sheep' being 'accidentally turned into terrifying rampant zombified beasts'. The sheep are inadvertently infected with botched genetic material by animal activists Grant (Oliver Driver) and Experience (Danielle Mason), who steal a failed experiment. Grant is bitten and begins to transform into a 'sheep-human hybrid' (McDonnell 2006, 118). It falls to Henry, Experience and Henry's childhood friend Tucker (Tammy Davis) to get the situation under control and thwart Angus's plans (Cameron 2010). What contributes to the film being a uniquely New Zealand offering in the horror-comedy genre, despite overseas investment in the production (Lavery 2018), is the terrain. Here, the land is constructed as an isolating and menacing force where '[t]alk of tradition, love of the land and kinship transform into depraved jabs about bestiality, accompanied by gory special effects that are somewhat reminiscent of the low-budget cult-horror films' (Lavery 2018, 118). As Leotta (2010) explains, what makes *Black Sheep* a New Zealand Gothic offering is its ability to construct the land, not as a pastoral idyll but rather as a place where danger and terror abound, a point we return to later in the chapter.

Central to the storyline, is the genetic modification of sheep by the introduction of human DNA into their genome. To transgress the boundaries of what is deemed appropriate behaviour can produce feelings of horror and terror in viewers of a film like *Black Sheep* (Horner and Zlosnik 2005; Edmond 2004), especially because the film ventures into the monstrous by destabilising what it means to be human (Och 2013). That is, the human-sheep hybrid is uncanny or *unheimlich*, and its unfamiliarity, yet real possibility – given the capacity to tamper with and clone sheep – ventures into an exploration of 'the hybrid, artificial or fragmented body that has been transformed, modified, or that has replacement parts that are not made of flesh and bone' (Conrich and Sedgwick 2017, 9). Yet, although the film functions as a social commentary on genetic manipulation and commercial greed (Leotta 2010), it is still a Gothic horror comedy, and such a comic turn can create what Horner and Zlosnik (2012) consider a dialogue around scientific advancement. The comedic elements offer 'a measure of detachment from the scenes of pain and suffering that would be disturbing in a different Gothic context' (Horner and Zlosnik 2005, 13), which can mitigate feelings of fear and anxiety that hamper social progress (Horner and Zlosnik 2012). Equally, however, the comedy and horror can establish the film as a political critique and as we contend here, *Black Sheep* operates as a questioning of the New Zealand settler identity and rhetoric of 'pure' New Zealand.

Much has been written about how New Zealand is considered a 'pastoral paradise or island sanctuary' (Glidersleeve and Cantrill 2022, 9), yet films such as *Black Sheep* permit an exploration of the underbelly of rural New Zealand. As Mercer (2017, 51) suggests, the depictions of New Zealand have often romanticised the country, but its social, cultural and economic progress is a product of agricultural slaughter and its accompanying 'violence, death and decay'. The farm, then, can act as a Gothic setting dominated by 'repressed terrors and guilt' (Mercer 2017, 54) and conjures up images of the 'sadistic pleasures' (63) and 'brutalised' (62) corrupting forces of the slaughterhouses that can drive a person to act inhumanly, as Angus does in *Black Sheep*. *Black Sheep* does not shy away from the dark underbelly of agricultural rule. Instead, in a comic twist, the zombie sheep enact their revenge on their unsuspecting victims, producing a role reversal that still highlights that New Zealand is a country of violence and violation despite the colonisers and settlers becoming the victims. For example, there are several scenes where the sheep are seen devouring the bodies of their victims, biting and infecting their prey, and terrorising the protagonists as they try to outwit the sheep to ensure their own survival. In its violence and brutality, *Black Sheep* can function as an allegory that constructs the settler identity as perhaps irreconcilably altered by colonial life and the resistance of the land to settler interference (Mercer 2014).

To encourage viewers to grapple with what constitutes humanity (Och 2013), *Black Sheep* relies on Antipodean humour such as excess, reversal and parody (Allen 2011). Much like the over-the-top satire and parody apparent in Peter Jackson's horror-comedy *Bad Taste* (Horton 2001), *Black Sheep* tends towards gross-out humour that exaggerates the portrayal of blood and other bodily liquids (Abbott 2011). Accordingly, it typifies the 'Kiwi splatstick' genre (Leotta 2010, 303), where the emphasis is placed on creating a visceral response in audiences through the incorporation of 'physical comedy and gross-out body horror' (Och 2013, 206). For example, Henry is forced to crawl through a herd of zombie sheep disguised as a sheep by wearing sheep skin. During his crawl across the field, he is mounted by a ram, and promptly sexually violated. Not only is this an intentional reference to the New Zealand stereotype of the people being 'sheep-shaggers', but it also uses bestiality for laughs and prompts cringe responses in viewers. Given its tendency towards splatstick, *Black Sheep* may be viewed less as a horror film with 'moments of comic hysteria or relief' and more as a work that, while underscored with political motivations, is clearly communicating signals that it is not to 'be taken [too] seriously' (Horner and Zlosnik 2005, 4).

Bruce Kawin remarks, '[m]any horror comedies depend on the final neutralising, civilising or expulsion of horror' and *Black Sheep* is no different (2012, 200). Although it is riddled with gore and the grotesque, and at times can be funny and horrific, the film inevitably ends on a positive note when a vaccine is administered to those infected and the zombie sheep are killed by lighting a fire off their methane gas expulsions and blowing them up. Despite the 'happy ending', the film still manages to end with a political consideration of the environmental implication of farming and perhaps successfully highlights that the New Zealand landscape can be a source of Gothic tension and disturbance.

Conclusion

Conrich (2012, 393) contends that '[t]he myths of New Zealand have presented a country that is clean and green, an environment of tranquillity and harmony, a principal landscape offering security and sanctuary', yet the New Zealand Gothic texts referred to in this chapter suggest that such a perception is idealistic rather than an accurate representation. The overwhelmingly positive depictions of New Zealand neglect to portray a country grappling with its isolation, the violence that accompanied British settlement of the place and people, and a land that continues to haunt and rebel against submission attempts. These New Zealand Gothic films, then, can function as a means of exorcising such national traumas (Gildersleeve and Cantrell 2022) for Pākehā people, by subtly and in some cases, overtly, addressing underlying social issues that continue to plague contemporary New Zealand society. For example, these Gothic films reflect on cultural concerns from genetic engineering, organic farming and methane gas omissions to family dysfunction, egalitarianism and Kiwi stoicism. In this way, the New Zealand Gothic aligns with the Gothic motivation to 'identify what is unfixed, transgressive, other, and threatening, in the hope that it can be contained, its threat defused' (Byron 2012, 187) and boundaries of order re-established.

Furthermore, these New Zealand concerns are explored in typical New Zealand fashion: deadpan, laconic, parody horror comedies. Illustrating Horner and Zlosnik's (2005) perception that the Gothic can be comical, New Zealand film-makers have sought to combine the grotesque and banal to create what Cameron (2010, 56) refers to as a 'cinema of unease'. Coupled with 'deadpan humour, absurdity, understatement (including litotes), and situational irony consistent with the key features of a stereotypically "Kiwi" sense of humour' (Harrington 2020, 91), these film-makers have developed a hybrid genre that is uniquely New Zealand. Alongside locally identifiable elements such as accents, attire and place markers (Piatti-Farnell 2022), they have consequently extended and maintained the local interpretation of that which can frighten but also invoke laughter.

Although the nation might be young and navigating its identity, what can be discerned is that the 'Kiwi Gothic' is not undefinable as previous scholars have suggested (Wevers 2004). The 'Kiwi Gothic' might be in nothing and anything (Lawn 2006) but much like other Gothic texts, it emphasises contemporary fears and cultural anxieties and does so by exploring disturbances, the supernatural, the violent and the uncanny, with a little humour thrown in.

Notes

1. Aotearoa is the word used by the indigenous people of the land to refer to New Zealand.
2. Pākehā is the word used to describe New Zealanders primarily of European descent.
3. Māori is the word used to refer to indigenous people of Aotearoa.

References

Abbott, Stacey. 2011. 'Rabbits' Feet and Spleen Juice: The Comic Strategies of TV Horror'. In *TV Goes to Hell: An Unofficial Road Map of Supernatural*, edited by Stacey Abbott and David Lavery, 3–17. London: ECW Press.
Aguirre, Manuel. 1990. *The Closed Space: Horror Literature and Western Symbolism*. Manchester: Manchester University Press.
Allen, Brenda J. 2011. 'The Man Alone, the Black Sheep and the Bad Apple: Squeaky Wheels of New Zealand Cinema'. *MEDIANZ: Media Studies Journal of Aotearoa New Zealand* 12: 87–109.

Berlant, Lauren. 2015. 'Structures of Unfeeling: Mysterious Skin'. *International Journal of Politics, Culture, and Society* 28: 191–213.
Beville, Maria. 2009. *Gothic-postmodernism: Voicing the Terrors of Postmodernity*. Amsterdam: Rodopi.
Botting, Fred. 2013. *Gothic*, 2nd edn. London: Routledge.
Byron, Glennis. 2012. 'Gothic in the 1890s'. In *A New Companion to the Gothic*, edited by David Punter, 186–97. Oxford: Blackwell.
Cameron, Allan. 2010. 'The Locals and the Global: Transnational Currents in Contemporary New Zealand Horror'. *Studies in Australasian Cinema* 4, no. 1: 55–72.
Conrich, Ian. 2012. 'New Zealand Gothic'. In *A New Companion to the Gothic*, edited by David Punter, 393–408. Oxford: Blackwell.
Conrich, Ian and Laura Sedgwick. 2017. *Gothic Dissections in Film and Literature*. Basingstoke: Palgrave Macmillan.
Edmond, Murray. 2004. 'How gothic is s/he? Three New Zealand Dramas'. *Australian Drama Studies* 44: 113–29.
Georgieva, Margarita. 2013. *The Gothic Child*. Basingstoke: Palgrave Macmillan.
Gildersleeve, Jessica and Kate Cantrell. 2022. 'Introduction: Please Check the Signal – Screening the Gothic in the Upside Down'. In *Screening the Gothic in Australia and New Zealand*, edited by Jessica Gildersleeve and Kate Cantrell, 7–20. Amsterdam: Amsterdam University Press.
Harries, Dan. 2002. 'Film Parody and the Resuscitation of Genre'. In *Genre and Contemporary Hollywood*, edited by Steve Neale, 281–93. London: British Film Institute.
Harrington, Erin. 2020. 'Policing through Parody with *Wellington Paranormal*'. *Continuum: Journal of Media & Cultural Studies* 34, no. 1: 88–101.
Heller-Nicholas, Alexandra. 2015. 'Revenge of the Cheese Grater: Housebound and the Domestic Horror-Comedy'. *Metro Magazine* 184: 24–7.
Holm, Nicholas. 2017. 'The Politics of Deadpan in Australasian Satire'. In *Satire and Politics: The Interplay of Heritage and Practice*, edited by Jessica Milner Davis, 103–24. Basingstoke: Palgrave Macmillan.
Holm, Nicholas. 2019. '"Fred, it's a mess": Fred Dagg and the Cultural Politics of the Laconic'. *Comedy Studies* 10, no. 1: 39–55.
Horner, Avril and Sue Zlosnik. 2005. *Gothic and the Comic Turn*. Basingstoke: Palgrave Macmillan.
Horner, Avril and Sue Zlosnik. 2012. 'Comic Gothic'. In *A New Companion to the Gothic*, edited by David Punter, 321–34. Oxford: Blackwell Publishing.
Horner, Avril and Sue Zlosnik. 2016. 'Introduction'. In *Women and the Gothic: An Edinburgh Companion*, edited by Avril Horner and Sue Zlosnik, 1–14. Edinburgh: Edinburgh University Press.
Horton, Andrew. 2001. '"Udderly Hilarious": New Directions in New Zealand Comedy as Seen in Harry Sinclair's "The Price of Milk"'. *Film Criticism* 25, no. 3: 59–69.
Johnstone, Gerard. dir. 2014. *Housebound*. New Zealand: Semi-Professional Pictures.
Kavka, Misha. 2014. 'Haunting and the (Im)possibility of Māori Gothic'. In *The Gothic and the Everyday*, edited by Lorna Piatti-Farnell and Maria Beville, 225–40. Basingstoke: Palgrave Macmillan.

Kawin, Bruce, F. 2012. *Horror and the Horror Film*. London: Anthem Press.
King, Jonathan, dir. 2006. *Black Sheep*. New Zealand Film Commission/ Daesung Group.
Lavery, Louise. 2018. 'Freaky Farmers and Sick Flocks: The Locals and Black Sheep'. *Metro Magazine* 197: 116–19.
Lawn, Jennifer. 2002. 'Domesticating settler Gothic in New Zealand literature'. *New Literatures Review* 38: 42–64.
Lawn, Jennifer. 2006. 'Introduction: Warping the Familiar'. In *Gothic NZ – The Darker Side of Kiwi Culture*, edited by Misha Kavka, Jennifer Lawn and Mary Paul, 11–21. Dunedin: Otago University Press.
Ledoux, Ellen. M. 2011. 'Defiant Damsels: Gothic Space and Female Agency in *Emmeline*, *The Mysteries of Udolpho* and *Secrecy*'. *Women's Writing* 18, no. 3: 331–47.
Leotta, Alfio. 2010. 'From Comic-Gothic to "slapstick": Black Humour in New Zealand Cinema'. In *Directory of World Cinema: Australia & New Zealand*, edited by Ben Goldsmith and Geoff Lealand, 296–303. London: Intellect.
Leotta, Alfio. 2016. 'Possum's Cinematic Space: Landscape, Alienation and New Zealand Gothic'. *Short Film Studies* 6, no. 1: 45–8.
McDonnell, Jenny. 2006. 'Black Sheep'. *The Irish Journal of Gothic and Horror Studies* 3: 118–19.
Mercer, Erin. 2014. '"Manuka bushes covered with thick spider webs": Katherine Mansfield and the Colonial Gothic Tradition'. *Journal of New Zealand Literature* 32, no. 2: 85–105.
Mercer, Erin. 2017. '"Shot at and slashed and whacked"': The Gothic Slaughterhouse in New Zealand Fiction'. *Journal of New Zealand Literature* 35, no. 2: 51–71.
Miller, Cynthia J. and A. Bowdoin Van Riper. 2016. 'Introduction'. In *The Laughing Dead: The Horror-Comedy Film from Bride of Frankenstein to Zombieland*, edited by Cynthia J. Miller and A. Bowdoin Van Riper, xiii–xxiii. London: Rowman & Littlefield.
Och, Dana. 2013. '"The Sheep Are Revolting": Becoming-Animal in the Postcolonial Zombie Comedy'. In *Transnational Horror Across Visual Media: Fragmented Bodies*, edited by Dana Och and Kirsten Strayer, 193–208. New York: Routledge.
Piatti-Farnell, Lorna. 2022. 'Dead, and Into the World: Localness, Culture, and Domesticity in New Zealand's *What We Do in the Shadows*'. In *Screening the Gothic in Australia and New Zealand*, edited by Jessica Gildersleeve and Kate Cantrell, 179–94. Amsterdam: Amsterdam University Press.
Punter, David. 1996. *The Literature of Terror Volume 2: A History of Gothic Fiction from 1765 to the Present Day*. New York: Routledge.
Smith, Jo. 2011. 'Aotearoa/New Zealand: An Unsettled State in a Sea of Islands'. *Settler Colonial Studies* 1, no. 1: 111–31.
Spooner, Catherine. 2017. *Post-Millennial Gothic: Comedy, Romance and the Rise of Happy Gothic*. London: Bloomsbury.
Spooner, Catherine. 2019 'Gothic Comedy'. In *Twenty-First-Century Gothic*, edited by Maisha Wester and Xavier Aldana Reyes, 189–202. Edinburgh: Edinburgh University Press.
Talairach-Vielmas, Laurence. 2007. *Moulding the Female Body in Victorian Fairy Tales and Sensation Novels*. London: Ashgate.

Wevers, Lydia. 2004. 'The Politics of Culture'. In *Writing at the Edge of the Universe: Essays from the Creative Writing Conference*, edited by Mark Williams, 109–22. Christchurch: Canterbury University Press.

Wright, Andrea. 2018. '"Vampires don't do dishes": Old Myth, the Modern World, Horror and the Mundane in *What We Do in the Shadows* (2014)'. *Journal of New Zealand & Pacific Studies* 6, no. 2: 137–49.

Yogerst, Chris. 2016. 'Rules for Surviving a Horror Comedy: Satiric Genre Transformation from Scream to Zombieland'. In *The Laughing Dead: The Horror-Comedy Film from Bride of Frankenstein to Zombieland*, edited by Cynthia J. Miller and A. Bowdoin Van Riper, 169–84. London: Rowman & Littlefield.

Chapter 16

'Girls Just Wanna Have Fun': Feminist Camp Gothic

Thomas Brassington

Introducing Feminist Camp/Gothic Feminism

The Gothic's relationship to women and feminist movements is undeniable. Women authors and readers have been instrumental in the genre's development since its inception in the eighteenth century; the second-wave feminist movement is interfused with Gothic motifs and feminist literary studies have been intrinsic to the development and consolidation of Gothic studies as an area of serious academic endeavour. In this respect, a seminal text that draws together queer, feminist and Gothic studies is Eve Kosofsky Sedgwick's *The Coherence of Gothic Conventions* (1986) and it is from there that I shall begin an examination of Gothic camp, its feminist potential and its relation to Comic Gothic.

Sedgwick examines how many significant Gothic works 'all point somehow toward an aesthetic based on pleasurable fear, [but] leave very different tastes in the reader's mouth and exercise very different faculties in their authors' (1986, 11). Across four different texts (*The Castle of Otranto*, *The Monk*, *The Mysteries of Udolpho* and *Melmoth the Wanderer*), Sedgwick identifies a recurrent gesture towards the affect of this aesthetic. Whereas the fear element has been thoroughly examined in feminist Gothic work, examinations of pleasure are much thinner on the ground.

The Comic Gothic provokes examinations of this pleasurable component. It is especially striking that Avril Horner and Sue Zlosnik's *Gothic and the Comic Turn* (2005) evokes the affective complexity of Gothic works when they argue that 'in mingling emotional opposites such as mirth and terror, it [the Gothic] reflects the psychic world more accurately than realist writing' (8). For Horner and Zlosnik, Comic Gothic has greater resonances with our affective realities precisely for its representation of ostensibly conflicting, but simultaneously present, emotional states. Considering this as akin to pleasurable fear, it then becomes arguable that Comic Gothic is a particularly appropriate mode for feminist examination of Gothic's more pleasurable resonances.

In this chapter, I will examine these resonances through what is perhaps the Gothic's most obviously pleasurable moments: when it is campy. Gothic's campness is something of a truism, despite there being little extended scholarly work examining those qualities, their effect and what they say about the mode (Punter 1996; Sontag 1999, 56–7; Babuscio 1999, 121; Horner and Zlosnik 2005, 17; Hughes and Smith 2009, 2–3). Even the more extended examinations of Gothic camp are situated as part of other studies on the Gothic (Benshoff 1997, 187–217; Spooner, 2004, 8–9; Fincher 2007, 87–109; Spooner 2017, 108–12; Bruin-Molé 2020, 99.)

In *Guilty Pleasures* (1996), Pamela Robertson performs an examination of camp which draws attention to its feminist potential, continuing a strain of queer scholarly work repoliticising camp in response to Susan Sontag's influential essay 'Notes on Camp'. In *Guilty Pleasures*, she argues that 'camp has an affinity with feminist discussion of gender construction, performance and enactment' offering a means to 'examine forms of camp as feminist practice' (Robertson 1996, 6). In doing so, Robertson challenges latent assumptions about camp as the exclusive practice of effeminate gay men, one that generates responses that align these men with misogyny and inversion. Likewise, the exclusion of women from articulations of camp presupposes that female audiences of camp icons like Mae West 'take their stars "straight"' (Robertson 1996, 6). Interestingly, these challenges complement Horner and Zlosnik's own observations about Comic Gothic as 'a conscious, self-reflexive engagement with the Gothic mode that sets up a different kind of contract with the reader and the text' (2005, 13). By identifying alternative positions of engagement with literary and media texts, these authors' feminist contributions on the pleasures of Comic Gothic involve a challenge to any assumption that its audience is liable to be duped. Pleasure, especially comic pleasure, is far more complex than it at first appears.

Both Helene Shugart and Catherine Waggoner's *Making Camp* (2008), and Katrin Horn's *Women, Camp and Popular Culture* (2017) provide updates to Robertson's study, and continue drawing connections between Gothic and camp with references to *Buffy the Vampire Slayer* and Lady Gaga respectively (Shugart and Waggoner 2008, 1; Horn 2017, 193–252). In providing twenty-first-century touchstones, both indicate a continued nexus between women, camp, the Gothic and feminist politics worthy of closer examination.

Feminist Gothic Camp

There are three components to feminist camp which are significant to feminist Gothic camp. These are awarishness, recycling and multidirectionality. Robertson borrows the term 'awarish' from burlesque studies, applying it to Mae West to more clearly delineate camp uses of sexuality. She argues that 'West's "awarish" and transgressive sexuality is taken at once as a pose or joke and a real source of power; and fans, especially female fans, could identify with both sides through camp practices' (Robertson 1996, 48). Awarishness is a self-reflexive and conscious articulation of the politics of objectification in which the subject manipulates the gaze. In her study on nineteenth-century *fin de siècle* burlesque and pin-ups, Maria Elena Buszcek argues that awarishness is apparent in 'the representations of the multiplicitous, shifting, even unstable womanhood of the actress', whose 'ordinarily taboo expression of the female sexual agency and self-awareness many contemporary feminists were promoting was viewed as acceptable under the rubric of burlesque theatricals' (2006, 27, 22). For Buszcek, this produces a 'subversive, expressive sexuality that period feminists would increasingly view as an essential part of woman's emancipation' (22). Awarishness, then, affords the performer agency through their expressions of sexuality, which are themselves self-conscious and comical renditions of female objectification. This sentiment carries through to contemporary burlesque performances, as Claire Nally indicates in her article on neo-burlesque where she argues that 'there is a collapse of the strict lines between performer and audiences, and therefore we must speculate how the "gaze" is a hostile, heterosexual one, or rather, whether there is a sense of celebration, internal interrogation, and identification' (2009, 638). Since there is no denying the Gothic's own campness, awarishness can be applied to Gothic studies via camp, consequently modifying examinations of how female characters 'show the girl', or engage in forms of stripping, as something comic or empowering. Awarish subjects are in on their own joke, and thus craft the space in which they perform their sexuality.

Awarishness extends Jerrold E. Hogle's notion that the Gothic is a mode which is 'quite openly faked' (2012, 496). Awarishness provides a critical mechanism for a camp understanding of how Gothic fakes sexuality as a form of self-reflexive objectification which facilitates the consolidation of agency and power in the female character. These are characters who becomes objects of the gaze, yet have a peculiarly self-fashioned component to their theatricals, for which awarishness posits a more complex examination of the relationship between gazer and gazed at, subject and object. Examples include Rosario/Matilda in *The Monk* and Angela Carter's Beast in 'The Tiger's Bride'.

Awarishness is directly linked to sexuality and its performance, forming the core of Robertson's feminist camp, since she argues that 'the figure of the gold digger is central to feminist camp, [and] prostitution is the hidden threat behind feminist camp' (1996, 84). This reference to sexual labour suggests that Gothic awarishness relies on a critical examination of moments which are both comical and eroticised, with some form of labour (performance) undergirding that representation of the comical, the erotic, the terrifying and all their permutations.

A cognate core component of feminist camp is its reliance on cultural recycling. Camp has a risqué predilection for stereotype and cliché where femininities, surface and performance are concerned. 'Camp may appropriate and expose stereotypes, but it also, in some measure, keeps them alive' (Robertson 1996, 142). However, penchant for stereotype calls forth an examination of 'the hold and power those stereotypes have over us. [Camp] is always a guilty pleasure. Thus, the stereotypes at play in camp are recoupable' (142). Camp achieves this, according to Robertson, by recycling stereotypes: 'it also displaces them by historicizing them and recoding them according to contemporary tastes and needs. Camp needs, then, to be considered as a mode of productive anachronism' (142).

Robertson builds the notion of recycling from Andrew Ross's 'Uses of Camp' (1999). Here, Ross argues that camp 'is a rediscovery of history's waste' (320). 'Uses of Camp' focuses on how campness often refers to a particular adoration of the outmoded. Notably, these are not objects of canonical or historical significance, nor can they be currently trendy.[1] Ross elaborates on how such waste is revitalised via camp, noting that campy objects are infused with a high degree of cultural capital by those groups who make it camp. He writes that 'camp, on the other hand, involves a celebration, on the part of the cognoscenti, of the alienation, distance, and incongruity reflected in the very process by which it locates hitherto unexpected value in a popular or obscure text' (Ross 1999, 316). To Ross, the camper is a kind of 'liberator, [for whom] history's waste becomes all too available as a "ragbag", but irradiated, this time around, with glamor' (1999, 320). The camp rediscovery of historical waste is characterised as a process of antiquarian love rather than ironical distancing. The former enjoys the fripperies, where the latter enjoys sneering at those fripperies.

Ross's argument here directly parallels Gothic's own temporal tendencies – what Robert Miles calls the 'Gothic cusp' (2017, 29).

Miles defines the Gothic cusp as a 'period of sensed overlap, where the medieval wanes, and the modern begins', locating Gothic's temporality as an interstitial site between past and present (29). Here, the barbarous transitions to the modern, though its incarnations desperately cling to their former power and glory, as various Gothic villains (such as Stoker's Dracula) can attest. On the Gothic cusp, then, must be myriad historical waste that is refracted through contemporary tastes by audiences and/or producers of Gothic work, provoking a camp vision of the Gothic. With Robertson's feminist arguments in mind, the detritus which feminist Gothic camp recycles must be concerned with Gothic expressions of sexualities and femininities. Feminist Gothic camp therefore considers how, for example, Gothic heroines are recycled or are themselves composed of recycled femininities, and what this cultural recycling modulates in its recoding of stereotypes and cliché. The Gothic heroine's fraught relationship with her clothes, for example, is recycled into the awarishess of burlesque theatricals.

Both awarishness and recycling indicate an unorthodox relationship with power and symbols of power. Awarishness represents 'transgressive sexuality' as 'pose', 'joke' and 'real source of power' simultaneously (Robertson 1996, 48). Likewise, camp recycling relies on the acknowledgement that an object had power, and subsequently recoding it: 'recycling also signifies transformation, change. It depends on our recognizing in a seemingly outmoded object, a throwaway, the potential for new use' (Robertson 1996, 142). In both, the power of the camp artefact is modulated. The awarish performance of sexuality might be described as a practice which choreographs desire, humour and pleasure, upending a typical association of gazer with powerful subject and gazed-at with passive object. Recycling is an overtly active process, where the kernels of power in outmoded artefacts are reorganised to new ends according to the contemporary needs and tastes of the camp subject. In both, power is modulated to feminist ends, with camp enabling a means to find power in outmoded femininities and expressions of sexualities.

Robertson extends camp's modulation of power to examine its facility for building specifically female bonds between and across celebrities and fans. Mae West's fans, for example, were able to 'identify with both sides' of her 'transgressive sexuality' as 'pose or joke' and 'as a real source of power' 'through camp practices' (Robertson 1996, 48). Robertson further argues that West's fans seem particularly 'attracted to this spectacle of personality' and engaged in playful imitations of her (1996, 51). Likewise, when analysing Ginger Rogers, Robertson remarks that camp acts as part of 'communal strategies and pleasures' and she regards 'feminist camp as a working women's practice' (1996, 58).

For Robertson, this strategy of working-class women enables them to pleasurably engage with their femininities in a fashion unpinned from misogynist figurations of femininity. The complex nature of feminist camp's modulation of stereotypical and clichéd visions of femininity uses humour to determine that modulation. She writes:

> If the female spectator is 'let in on the joke', and the joke is on the men in the film, why must we assume that she stops laughing when confronted with feminist spectacle or the resolution of a romance plot? The knowledge that the female gains about men, money, power, and economics in the primary diegesis provides her with a means to read the spectacles from a feminist camp perspective, one which enables her to recognise herself in the fetishised images but from which she is able to knowingly distance herself. (Robertson 1996, 69)

Feminist camp is therefore a comic intervention which allows the subject to engage pleasurably with a range of femininities in a manner that is for herself, rather than for a cisheterosexual masculine gaze. In Gothic contexts, this light modifies our approach to the historical prominence of female readers. Rather than the kind of cultural dupes which Jane Austen imagines in *Northanger Abbey*, a feminist camp eye on female Gothic readers and writers suggests greater complexity between female creators, consumers and characters. For example, in an early scene in *Whatever Happened to Baby Jane?* (Aldrich 1962), we see a teenage girl watching televised airings of faded star Blanche's (Joan Crawford) older films. When her mother enters the living room, the two proceed to talk about her mother's youth and gossip about the neighbours (Blanche and Jane, who is played by Bette Davies). Here, a rediscovery of historical waste facilitates intergenerational female bonding. Next door, these same televised airings act as a motivator for Jane's terrorising of Blanche. *Baby Jane* partially reignited the careers of Crawford and Davis. From this one campy classic there is evidence that pleasure, terror and economics are intimately tied together in feminist camp Gothic.

Throughout this section, I have outlined three interlinked elements of feminist camp and begun to conceptualise how they interact with the Gothic. Awarishness is indicative of the various ways in which feminist camp modulates typical comprehensions of objectifying practices in Gothic texts. Likewise, cultural recycling in feminist camp is mainly interested in how femininities and sexualities are recycled. A feminist camp eye draws attention to how Gothic femininities and sexualities are recycled and are themselves recyclings of other outmoded femininities and sexualities. Likewise, feminist camp applies pressure on how that recycling recodes stereotypes and cliché which, in turn, emancipates femininities. Finally, these camp figurations modify the flow of power surrounding these camp recastings of outmoded femininities and sexualities. Feminist camp identifies multiple instances wherein those camping something up are doing so consciously, and this consciousness invites a critical distance. Feminist camp is always making fun of its subject matter and is always in on its own joke. Ultimately, feminist camp is concerned with using humour to find pleasure in culturally unsanctioned images of sexuality and femininity. This camp is feminist because the emancipation of multiple femininities from the fetters of respectability or misogyny corresponds to an expansion of feminine expressions. Returning to Sedgwick, 'camping [. . .] is additive and accretive [. . .] it wants to assemble and confer plenitude on an object' (2003, 149). Feminist camp Gothic therefore offers an expansive examination of Gothic femininities whose method is comical and whose concerns are with pleasure and enjoyment.

The Mistress of the Dark

Cassandra Peterson's Elvira character was created in 1981 as part of KHJ-TV's attempt to revive Maila Nurmi's Vampira character, created in the 1950s. In her autobiography, Peterson recounts how 'Maila was in her sixties [in 1981] and was clearly not up to the task [of horror hostess].' The network cast for the role of 'Vampira's daughter' as the show's horror hostess instead. When the network hired Peterson over Nurmi's preferred actress (Lola Falana), she left the production team, taking the rights to Vampira with her. The network scrambled and rebranded Peterson's character as Elvira (Peterson 2021, 171–4). All this makes Vampira the first piece of historical detritus recycled in Elvira's campery.

Vampira is herself a palimpsestic recycling, intimating a lineage of historical waste being camply rediscovered through these horror hostesses. 'The idea for the Vampira character was born in 1953 when the young ingénue [Nurmi] was invited to a masquerade ball and took her inspiration for her costume from Morticia as portrayed in the *New Yorker* cartoons of Charles Addams', writes Peterson (2021, 172). Nurmi additionally characterised Vampira with reference to *Snow White and the Seven Dwarfs*' Evil Queen, actresses Theda Bara and Gloria Swanson, and the bondage fetish art of the magazine *Bizarre* (Keesey 1997, 12–17; Anderson 2015). Elvira, as a citation of Vampira, therefore represents a camp recycling of femininities which are themselves a camp recycling.

Understood as such, what becomes apparent is a lineage of discarded femininities (thus marking them as 'historical waste') being revitalised to articulate femininities as new coordinates in the present character. Notably, all the women cited in this lineage are Gothic to varying intensities: Bara is heralded as the 'first vamp' (Marshall 2017); Harriet Fletcher argues how Swanson's role in *Sunset Boulevard* 'made the ageing actress into an explicitly Gothic figure' (Fletcher 2020) and the Evil Queen's monstrous witchiness provides her with ample Gothic credentials.

In addition to this lineage, Peterson applies her own palette of femininities. In collaboration with Robert Redding (with whom she worked in the queer performance troupe *Mama's Boys*), Peterson crafted Elvira with reference to: Sharon Tate's Sarah Shagal from *The Fearless Vampire Killers*, kabuki theatre (which inspired Elvira's make-up), and Ronnie Spector of the Ronettes (from whom the beehive hairstyle takes inspiration) (Peterson 2021, 172–3). Alongside these visual referents, Peterson notes that she 'generally stand[s] in the iconic showgirl "bevel stance" – achieved when one knee is bent and pulled in toward the body's centerline and the forward toe is pointed and facing out, which apparently makes for a flattering, feminine silhouette' (Peterson 2021, 68). Overall, it is apparent that Elvira is a recycling of a range of icons of twentieth-century femininities who is characterised by a self-reflexive performance of sexualised femininities as seen through her showgirl stances. This elicits a feminist camp figure who rearticulates the various femininities she recycles into a Gothic form.

Indeed, such recycling of Gothic femininities is especially apparent in both Elvira films: *Elvira, Mistress of the Dark* (Signorelli 1988) and *Elvira's Haunted Hills* (Irvin 2001). The former is evocative of *The Wizard of Oz*, in which Elvira leaves her horror hostess job to be a Vegas showgirl, after retaliating to sexual harassment from a network executive. By way of an inheritance from a distant relative, Elvira hopes to receive funds necessary for her show. Sadly, her inheritance turns out to be a dilapidated Victorian-era mansion, a dog (Algonquin) and a recipe book (really her deceased relative's spell book). The inheritance is in effect the title (and power) of 'Mistress of the Dark', which Elvira's great-uncle Vincent Talbot (William Morgan Shepherd) schemes to usurp. In the completely unrelated *Elvira's Haunted Hills*, we find Elvira in the Carpathian Mountains of Romania in 1851. They get trapped and are spirited away to the nearby Castle Hellsubus, where Elvira discovers she bears an uncanny resemblance to the deceased wife of the current count, Vladimir Hellsubus (Richard O'Brien). These films are not connected because Peterson considers Elvira a somewhat timeless character, who can be inserted in almost any point in history (or at least a camp version of films loosely set in those periods). Arguably, Elvira's Gothic femininity is very vaguely delineated, aside from the lineage of twentieth-century femininities from which she draws. She is not quite a witch, not quite a vampire, not quite a Gothic heroine, but that very amorphousness allows her to camp up any figure she plays. In *Mistress of the Dark*, she does this to the figure of the witch and the same to the figure of the Gothic heroine in *Elvira's Haunted Hills*.

The camp perspective is especially apparent when Peterson discusses the production process for *Elvira's Haunted Hills*, during which she and her co-writer John Paragon 'hit on the idea of making a gothic-horror comedy romp with the look and feel of the early films of super-low-budget director Roger Corman – films like *the Tomb of Ligeia*, *House of Usher*, and especially *The Pit and the Pendulum*' (Peterson 2021, 254). Later she describes the production of a specific citational joke concerning Elvira's hunky love interest. In brief, they sought an actor with the physique of middle-brow romance fiction models like Fabio Lanzoni. No one met this brief apart from a Romanian actor who could not speak English. Rather than carry on their casting call or rewrite the script, Peterson and her team decided to have 'his voice dubbed, slightly out of sync, to give it that older Steve Reeves/Hercules kind of vibe' (Peterson 2021, 258). Peterson's camp eye here perfectly exhibits the feminist camp concern with carefully crafting comedy in a manner that draws together awarishness, recycling and modulations of linear comprehensions of power. Elvira excellently demonstrates how a feminist camp Gothic is often emergent from a collusion of recycled femininities and a love for 'B-grade and C-grade clunkers' (Peterson 2021, 177). In this example, Peterson recycles the femininity of middle-brow romance novels, collapses it with 'bad' cinematography and does so to appeal directly to queer and feminine audiences who share similar cultural referents and capital.

Mother Monster

Turning now from the Mistress of the Dark to Mother Monster, I shall consider how Lady Gaga crafts a feminist camp Gothic through her music videos. The character of Stefani Germanotta's is, like Elvira, a palimpsest of femininities – early in her pop career, this met with derision in magazines. Yet, if we examine Gaga and her performance art with a feminist camp eye, what becomes apparent are those awarish and recycling processes which betray greater complexity.

Throughout her oeuvre, Gaga makes numerous references to alternative figurations of femininities and gender expressions. At a cursory glance, David Bowie became an iconic figure during the *Fame* era; *Alejandro* (2010a) features numerous allusions to Madonna's work; *Thelma and Louise* and *Kill Bill* are cited in *Telephone* (2010b); *Girl Interrupted* is cited in *Marry The Night* (2011b); and the eponymous *Real Housewives of Beverly Hills* are cast as the nine Greek Muses in *G.U.Y.* (2014). Indeed, her ability to coincide all these femininities is thanks to her monstrous self-branding. In 'The Monstrous House of Gaga', Karen Macfarlane argues that from 'the moment that Gaga emerges from a swimming pool in "Poker Face", an uncanny blend of glamorous femininity and monstrous predation' occurs. This moment, for Macfarlane, is pivotal in the development of Gaga's character, for it crystallises 'the ways in which she pulls the referentiality and the corporeality of these figures together' (2012, 115). Gaga's mediation of numerous femininities is made possible through her incarnation and enactment of monstrosity, be this the femme fatales of her revenge narrative videos (*Paparazzi* (2009b), *Bad Romance* (2009a), *Telephone* (2010b), *G.U.Y.* (2014), or through chimeric embodiments (*Born this Way* (2011a), *Yoü and I* (2011c), *Applause* (2013), *G.U.Y.* (2014)). For Macfarlane, the monstrous body's ability to be 'ex-centric and disturbing of categorizations' is what facilitates Gaga's ability to inhabit numerous femininities (2012, 115). In addition to this, I argue that Gaga engages monstrosity in a feminist camp manner, thereby situating Gaga's monstrosity as an iteration of feminist camp Gothic.

Gaga's awarishness is palpable in two ways. First, she is keenly aware of her popular cultural reception. *Alejandro* is a self-reflexive homage to Madonna music videos, undoubtedly a direct reference to the regular comparison she draws with Madonna. Likewise, the beginning of 'Telephone' sees Gaga stripped by female prison guards, with one saying 'told you she didn't have a dick', another direct reference to media discussions about Gaga's gender identity. Awarishness, these examples determine, can be about sexuality to any extent (even questions about gender), but it must be in on the joke. The latter particularly draws attention to how Gaga's camp performances create an unease surrounding her gender, simply because she plays with her gender expression across her media texts. Arguably Gaga sends up this tension through her regular self-fashioning into chimeric hybrids as well. The second means of palpable awarishness is found in her deployment of monstrosity.

Laura Westengard argues that 'the figure of the monster is always outside of culture, on the margins, ugly, and horrifying in its excessive difference. Rather than working to avoid difference and ugliness, Gaga embraces it as a kind of avant-garde aesthetic' (2014, 178). Gaga is aware(ish) of her dual positionality as a centre of media attention and as cultural outsider. She is a locus for cultural understandings of pop music in the beginning of the twenty-first century, yet also uses camp distancing to become ex-centric. Rather unlike other pop stars, Gaga's career began on the neo-burlesque and drag circuits of New York City, meaning that her pop character is arguably practised in awarishness. She brings this awarishness into her performance art by maintaining a keen eye on paparazzi gossip and mocking it, as these examples demonstrate. In embracing the monster's position on the cultural fringes, Gaga performs her pop act awarishly.

Gaga's awarish referentiality is a clear strategy of cultural recycling. Conscious of the parallels she draws with Madonna, Gaga openly cites Madonna's Jean-Paul Gaultier costume from the *Blonde Ambition* tour, as well as 'Vogue' and 'Like a Prayer' in *Alejandro*. A more striking 'rediscovery of history's waste', however, can be found in *Telephone* and *Marry The Night*. Both these videos see Gaga in institutions of the cultural margins: a (women's) prison and a psychiatric hospital. Both, for want of a better phrase, house 'bad' women. That is, women whose (feminine) gender expression is clearly in excess of that sanctioned as acceptable in Western culture. Butch prisoners and guards abound, as do sex workers, white trash, cholas, Black women, and non-passing transwomen. These women form part of the video's spectacle, which articulates a feminist camp politics by showing a multiplicity of femininities. These other characters make remarks about Gaga's appearance, have lives beyond the immediate view of the video, and so the spectacle of their femininities must be read in a manner that 'speculate[s on] how the "gaze" is a hostile, heterosexual one, or rather, whether there is a sense of celebration, internal interrogation, and identification' (Nally 2009, 638). The camp eye identifies these femininities as historical detritus with special qualities, imbuing them with a certain cultural capital. The butch women crack jokes and numerous femme voices make sexualised comments about Gaga's appearance. Additionally, the women are violent and eroticised for the titillation of the other women in the prison. In all, the world Gaga creates in *Telephone* is highly resonant with Sedgwick's argument that camp 'wants to assemble and confer plenitude on an object that will then have resources to offer to an inchoate self' (2003, 149). Thanks to Gaga's monstrous persona, all these femininities stick to the world around her, and are displayed and celebrated for the possibilities offered by access to such femininities.

Marry The Night repeats the narrative of *Telephone*, but shifts the scene to a psychiatric hospital. Gaga is again surrounded by a variety of women who visually connote the periphery of respectable femininities: older women, 'mad' women, ambitious women. *Marry The Night* adds to *Telephone*'s incipient feminist camp politics a direct visual reference to camp's potential for female bonding. Upon leaving the institution, Gaga monologues that 'You may think I lost everything, but I still had my bedazzler, and I had a lot of patches, shiny ones from M&J Trimmings, so I wreaked havoc on some old denim.' Gaga then reinvents herself in the video's latter half, where she attends dance classes and 'gets back on her feet'. At the dance class, Gaga wears a bedazzled sports bra. The glittery material recalls Rebecca Coleman's arguments about glitter's literally and metaphorically sticky nature. Noting that glitter 'get(s) everywhere. It sticks to what it is and isn't intended to', the accretive qualities of glitter recall camp's own accretive qualities (2020, 1). Coleman further notes glitter's cultural associations with femininities and queerness, arguing that the sparkly stuff has an affective intensity which collapses apparent opposites (Coleman 2020, 41–4). Thus, in retaining her bedazzler, Gaga retains the capacity to accrete a multiplicity of femininities to herself and spread those qualities. Glitter's quality of being both 'celebratory *and* damaging, frivolous *and* deadly, decorative *and* violent' similarly evokes Horner and Zlosnik's argument that the Comic Gothic, in its mixture of laughter and terror, better reflects the psychic world (Coleman 2020, 44; Horner and Zlosnik 2005, 8). Arguably, Gaga's bedazzled clothing in *Marry The Night* situates the video and its recycling of disavowed femininities as a form of Comic Gothic, culminating visually when Gaga helps up a ballet dancer in the studio, allowing the two a moment of friendly, feminine bonding.

Conclusion: Feminist Camp Gothic and Comic Gothic

Throughout this chapter, I have argued that camp provides a method for examining the pleasurable elements of the Gothic which complement its terrors. In examining Gothic performers through a feminist camp lens, I have demonstrated how Gothic's pleasures are an equally fertile ground for feminist analyses of the mode. Camp's principal strategies are comic ones, and therefore a camp way of looking at the Gothic lends itself to an examination of the form's relationship with humour.

'Humour', Babuscio remarks, 'constitutes the strategy of camp: a means of dealing with a hostile environment and, in the process, of defining a positive identity' (1999, 126). For Babuscio, camp humour is a comic strategy for minimising the pain caused by queerphobia in a given culture, typified as defiant laughter. Characterised by incongruity, the comic positioning results in a laughter that simultaneously acknowledges the subject's power and oppression. Such laughter and pleasure is itself a politicised act in the contexts of queer- and femmephobic cultures. This incongruity directly aligns with Horner and Zlosnik's formulation of Comic Gothic as emergent from the 'juxtaposition of incongruous textual effects' (2005, 3). Horner and Zlosnik argue that:

> Comic Gothic turns [. . .] invite a conscious, self-reflexive engagement with the Gothic mode that sets up a different kind of contract between the reader and text, offering a measure of detachment from scenes of pain and suffering that would be disturbing in a different Gothic context. (2005, 13)

The sense of detachment noted by Sontag returns in Horner and Zlosnik's arguments on Comic Gothic as a camp aspect of Gothic humour. That sharply felt detached sentiment invites a camp sense of humour, giving Comic Gothic a high degree of potential for operating as a queer comedic gesture. In this light, Horner and Zlosnik's formulation resonates with Joseph Bristow's argument that:

> Camp is not symmetrical with the form of attack it is responding to. It is the resilience of its critical pleasures – of reflexively interrogating styles [. . .] to allow a critique of stereotyping – that can provide a starting-point for the lei[2] to consider how to enjoy the serious issue of establishing a political identity. (Bristow 1989, 71–2)

Camp therefore provides a more everyday strategy for identity formation. Comic Gothic, with its heavy camp resonances offers a pleasurable way of forming alternative queer and feminine identities, at least through the spectacular display of such ways of being. Camp provides a means for understanding moments of humour in the Gothic, one characterised by a queer form of self-reflexivity which modulates the affective responses to pleasurable fear and interrogates Comic Gothic with a fresh critical eye. The feminist possibilities of such a formulation of Comic Gothic as feminist camp Gothic are therefore a continuation of those additive and accretive qualities which characterise camp as a loving reclamation of the detritus left on the Gothic cusp.

Notes

1. This relationship to history is more clearly delineated in Caryl Flinn's 'The Deaths of Camp' (1999, 435–7).
2. Legal entity identifier.

References

Aldrich, Robert, dir. 1962. *Whatever Happened to Baby Jane?* Warner Bros.
Anderson, Kristin. 2015. *Vampira: An Appreciation of the Undersung Proto-Goth Goddess*. 29 October. https://www.vogue.com/article/vampira-maila-nurmi-fashion
Babuscio, Jack. 1999. 'The Cinema of Camp (aka Camp and the Gay Sensibility)'. In *Camp: Queer Aesthetics and the Performing Subject: A Reader*, edited by Fabio Cleto, 117–35. Edinburgh: Edinburgh University Press.
Benshoff, Harry M. 1997. *Monsters in the Closet: Homosexuality and the Horror Film*. Manchester: Manchester University Press.
Bristow, Joseph. 1989. 'Being Gay: Politics, Identity, Pleasure'. *New Formations* 9: 61–81.
Bruin-Molé, Megen de. 2020. *Gothic Remixed: Monster Mashups and Frankenfictions in 21st-Century Culture*. London and New York: Bloomsbury.
Buszcek, Maria Elena. 2006. *Pin-Up Grrrls: Feminism, Sexuality, Popular Culture*. Durham, NC: Duke University Press.
Coleman, Rebecca. 2020. *Glitterworlds: The Future Politics of a Ubiquitous Thing*. London: Goldsmiths Press.
Fincher, Max. 2007. *Queering Gothic in the Romantic Eye: The Penetrating Eye*. Basingstoke: Palgrave Macmillan.
Fletcher, Harriet. 2020. *'Gothic' TV: high-quality modern horror series providing powerful roles for Hollywood's older women*, 27 October. https://theconversation.com/gothic-tv-high-quality-modern-horror-series-providing-powerful-roles-for-hollywoods-older-women-148870
Flinn, Caryl. 1999. 'The Deaths of Camp'. In *Camp: Queer Aesthetics and the Performing Subject: A Reader*, edited by Fabio Cleto, 433–57. Edinburgh: Edinburgh University Press.
Gaga, Lady. 2008. *Lady Gaga – Poker Face* (Official Music Video). https://www.youtube.com/watch?v=bESGLojNYSo
Gaga, Lady. 2009a. *Lady Gaga – Bad Romance* (Official Music Video), 24 November. https://youtu.be/qrO4YZeyl0I
Gaga, Lady. 2009b. *Lady Gaga – Paparazzi* (Official Music Video), 26 November. https://youtu.be/d2smz_1L2_0
Gaga, Lady. 2010a. *Lady Gaga – Alejandro* (Official Music Video), 8 June. https://youtu.be/niqrrmev4mA
Gaga, Lady. 2010b. *Lady Gaga – Telephone ft. Beyoncé* (Official Music Video), 16 March. https://youtu.be/EVBsypHzF3U
Gaga, Lady. 2011a. *Lady Gaga – Born This Way* (Official Music Video), 28 February. https://youtu.be/wV1FrqwZyKw

Gaga, Lady. 2011b. *Lady Gaga – Marry The Night* (Official Music Video), 2 December. https://youtu.be/cggNqDAtJYU

Gaga, Lady. 2011c. *Lady Gaga – Yoü and I* (Official Music Video), 17 August. https://youtu.be/X9YMU0WeBwU

Gaga, Lady. 2013. *Lady Gaga – Applause* (Official Music Video), 19 August. https://youtu.be/pco91kroVgQ

Gaga, Lady. 2014. *Lady Gaga – G.U.Y* (An Artpop Film), 23 March. https://youtu.be/PNu_-deVemE

Hogle, Jerrold. 2012. 'The Gothic Ghost of the Counterfeit and the Progress of Abjection'. In *A New Companion to the Gothic*, edited by David Punter, 496–509. Malden, MA, Oxford and Chichester: WileyBlackwell.

Horn, Katrin. 2017. *Women, Camp, and Popular Culture: Serious Excess*. Basingstoke: Palgrave Macmillan.

Horner, Avril and Sue Zlosnik. 2005. *Gothic and the Comic Turn*. Basingstoke: Palgrave Macmillan.

Hughes, William and Andrew Smith. 2009. 'Introduction: Queering the Gothic'. In *Queering the Gothic*, edited by Hughes William and Andrew Smith, 1–10. Manchester: Manchester University Press.

Irvin, Sam, dir. 2001. *Elvira's Haunted Hills*. MediaPro Studios.

Keesey, Pam. 1997. *Vamps: An Illustrated History of the Femme Fatale*. Hoboken, NJ: Cleis Press.

Macfarlane, Karen E. 2012. 'The Monstrous House of Gaga'. In *The Gothic in Contemporary Literature and Popular Culture: Pop Goth*, edited by Justin Edwards and Agnieszka Soltysik Monnet, 114–34. London and New York: Routledge.

Marshall, Colin. 2017. *Meet Theda Bara, the First 'Vamp' of Cinema, Who Revealed the Erotic Power of the Movies*, 27 January. https://www.openculture.com/2017/01/meet-theda-bara-the-first-vamp-of-cinema.html

Miles, Robert. 2017. *Gothic Writing, 1750–1820*, 2nd edn. Manchester: Manchester University Press.

Nally, Claire. 2009. 'Grrrly Hurly Burly: Neo-Burlesque and the Performance of Gender'. *Textual Practice* 23, no. 4: 621–43. doi:10.1080/09502360903000554

Peterson, Cassandra. 2021. *Yours Cruelly, Elvira: Memoirs of the Mistress of the Dark*. New York: Hachette.

Punter, David. 1996. *The Literature of Terror: A History of Gothic Fictions from 1765 to the Present Day. Volume 1: The Gothic Tradition*. London and New York: Longman.

Robertson, Pamela. 1996. *Guilty Pleasures: Feminist Camp from Mae West to Madonna*. Durham, NC: Duke University Press.

Ross, Andrew. 1999. 'Uses of Camp'. In *Camp: Queer Aesthetics and the Performing Subject: A Reader*, edited by Fabio Cleto, 308–29. Edinburgh: Edinburgh University Press.

Sedgwick, Eve Kosofsky. 1986. *The Coherence of Gothic Conventions*. New York and London: Methuen.

Sedgwick, Eve Kosofsky. 2003. *Touching Feeling: Affect, Pedagogy, Performativity*. Durham, NC and London: Duke University Press.

Shugart, Helene and Catherine Waggoner. 2008. *Making Camp*. Tuscaloosa: University of Alabama Press.

Signorelli, James, dir. 1988. *Elvira: Mistress of the Dark*. New World Pictures NBC Productions.
Sontag, Susan. 1999. 'Notes on "Camp"'. In *Camp: Queer Aesthetics and the Performing Subject: A Reader*, edited by Fabio Cleto, 53–64. Edinburgh: Edinburgh University Press.
Spooner, Catherine. 2004. *Fashioning Gothic Bodies*. Manchester: Manchester University Press.
Spooner, Catherine. 2017. *Post-Millennial Gothic: Comedy, Romance and the Rise of Happy Gothic*. London and New York: Bloomsbury.
Westengard, Laura. 2014. 'Gothic Gaga: Monstrosity, Trauma, and the Strategic Artifice of Lady Gaga's Pop Stardom'. In *Star Power: The Impact of Branded Celebrity. Volume 2: The Power of Media Branding*, edited by Aaron Barlow, 175–204. Santa Barbara, CA: Praeger.

Chapter 17

Haunted TikTok: Comedy in Gothic Times
Megen de Bruin-Molé

From the page to the big screen to the small screen, at the end of this book we come to the smallest screen of all: the mobile phone. In some ways mobile media offer more of the same. The kinds of Gothic comedy discussed elsewhere in this book are certainly present on mobile media – at times literally, as media are continually reproduced, consolidated and subsumed by the smartphone. The modes of audience engagement and enticement mobile platforms invite have also been seen before, from the gags of silent film (Verstraten 2017), to the captivating 'flickering lights' of magic-lantern ads (Väliaho 2017), to the tactile pleasures of the flip-book (Horsman 2017). But there *is* something about mobile media that feels intensely Gothic, which comes in part from this derivativeness.* Today's internet, mediated through the mobile phone, is repetitive yet forgetful, is full of paranoia all along the political spectrum, and offers a potentially endless source of the taboo and barbaric. The post-millennial, post-capitalist social web is obsessed with history and archiving, performance and the repressed. It ignites the imaginations of media studies scholars with monstrous metaphors. As Wendy Hui Kyong Chun writes, new media are leaky, paradoxical and 'wonderfully creepy' (Chun 2016, 52). On the internet, suggests Melissa Gronlund, we can also find 'the Gothic tropes of the uncanny, the undead, and intrusions into the home' which 'show how notions of the individual, the family, and the domestic are in fact being newly contested' (Gronlund 2014). For Chun, social networks and online friendship offer all 'the promise and threat of networks: the promise of an intimacy that, however banal, transcends physical location and enables self-made bonds to ease the loneliness of neoliberalism', while at the same time thriving on exclusion and paranoia, 'the threat of a security based on poorly gated "neighborhoods"

---

* Content warning: This chapter contains descriptions of racism and racial slurs, and images of racist iconography.

[. . .] a monstrous, undead chimera of "friends" constructed through neighborhoods of likeness and difference' (Chun 2016, 103–4). On the Gothic internet there is intimacy but also claustrophobia. As the world opens up it grows smaller. In this chapter I will focus on one particular corner of the social internet where these Gothic modes and forms converge through practices of melodrama, irony and the absurd: a 'core aesthetic' called #HauntedTikTok (Rogers 2021, 377).

Though many of the tropes of mobile texts represent a Gothic return rather than a renewal, there is a unique intensity in the ways these texts invite a comic, Gothic rupture, as well as a particular set of functions such a rupture serves in twenty-first-century culture. Like the other texts in this book, mobile texts operate through the same 'compressed and fragmented cultural forms' that 'have long comprised the fabric of Gothic stories told and re-told, adapted, transformed, appropriated and re-appropriated across different media' (Baker 2021, 127). They simply do so in new contexts. TikTok is a Chinese-owned, internationally operated social media platform that allows users to make, share, like, comment on and remix short video content. It is an inherently fragmented medium: the videos a user will scroll through on their For You page are usually no longer than sixty seconds, and often much shorter.[1] Users are unlikely to make it to the end of most videos. If they do, the video will repeat. Sound and music are integral to TikTok; users are meant to scroll through posts with their sound on, and the app's default setting is to autoplay sound and video, though many videos are also equipped with captions. Users may come across prerecorded videos, stitch or duet videos (where one TikToker reacts to another), and videos trying out the app's various, sometimes extreme filters, as well as live streams, where TikTokers and audiences in certain regions can interact in real time. Launched in 2017, TikTok has rapidly risen to become one of the world's most popular social media platforms, with its 1.2 billion active users predominantly seeking 'funny/entertaining content' (Moran and Buckle 2022, 7).[2] Despite the continued popular assumption that TikTok is dominated by teen girls, nearly half (44 per cent) of TikTok's users identify as male, and more than half (56.7 per cent) of its users are over twenty-four years old ('TikTok Statistics and Trends' 2022).

In this chapter I am specifically interested in the multiple ways this platform is comic, Gothic and (especially) haunted. On TikTok we find an expression of the comic turn particular to short online media, in which repeated viewing provokes laughter, hysteria, confusion and unease in turn. On TikTok, horror and terror rely explicitly on a Gothic sense of duplicity and fakery, as well as an intentional equivocation between irony and sincerity. Many books could be written on Gothic TikTok, but to explore these particular assertions I will focus on four examples or fragments: two relating to TikTok as a Gothic platform, two regarding the content produced for #HauntedTikTok. The first fragment examines the Gothic othering and doubleness that arises from TikTok's status as a Chinese app. The second fragment considers TikTok's algorithm, the way this is understood as a repressed subconscious, and the Gothic ruptures this creates. Finally, I will look at two examples of viral #HauntedTikTok trends: the found footage ghost video, and the ghost photo shoot.

TikTok as Gothic Medium

In a chapter on the politics of Gothic historiography, Sean Silver describes how important, 'for good or ill [. . .] the Gothic way of telling history' has been to 'the development of the modern British nation-state' (Silver 2014, 6). The Gothic offers a mode for shoring up 'a shared way of being in the world, a shared commitment to a set of inherited values', against sinister outside forces set on tearing it apart (Silver 2014, 6). Within this tradition of imperial identity-building, Sinophobia and Orientalism unfortunately have a long history. This historical Sinophobia is mirrored in contemporary Western engagements with China, perhaps particularly in the wake of the COVID-19 pandemic (de Bruin-Molé and Polak 2021, 2–3). When Peter Kitson writes of how eighteenth- and nineteenth-century Gothic narratives 'employ exoticism to represent non-heteronormative desires and practices, safely distanced from the reality of an often-savage [. . .] social and legal repression' (Kitson 2016, 167), it is not a great stretch to imagine how this might translate to contemporary texts.

The fact that TikTok is Chinese-owned has produced a wealth of Gothic melodrama. On the one hand it appears as a threat to Western data monopolies, tech dominance, and prosperity, a dark double reductively described by US media early on as a Chinese version of the short video platform Vine ('like Vine but weirder': Langford 2019). Not only has TikTok outlived Vine, it now threatens to overtake Western-owned platforms like Facebook, Twitter and YouTube. TikTok also has a Chinese doppelgänger of its own. The version of the app available in China, Douyin (抖音), has a nearly identical interface and functionality, but as a result of China's national censorship policy the two versions of the app are hosted on different servers in different locations, and with little overlap in content. Douyin users cannot access TikTok content directly through their app, and vice versa. The relationship between Douyin and TikTok has led to additional anxieties in Western news media, as journalists speculate on whether features being pioneered on

Douyin, like video search and live shopping, will soon cross to TikTok, giving its Chinese parent company Byte Dance an even more influential edge in the international market (Chan 2022). In these discourses TikTok and Douyin are represented as both alluring and intimidating.

On the other hand, TikTok has been depicted as a 'tool of espionage' by Western politicians and political communities, spying on European and North American citizens and sending their data back to China (Woods 2022). This data, it is implied, should be controlled by Western corporations rather than Eastern ones, who would use it more altruistically. The US government considered banning TikTok in 2020 following statements by then-president Donald Trump that the app was a national security risk (though the ban was later dismissed by subsequent president Joe Biden). European countries have also expressed anxieties about the app, with the UK Parliament closing its own TikTok account after just two days following fears about data security. As Avril Horner and Sue Zlosnik suggest, citing Peter Brooks, Gothic melodrama 'polarises and hyperdramatises "forces in conflict" in order to offer what [Brooks] calls a "moral manichaeism"' or binarism (Brooks 1995, viii, 5; Horner and Zlosnik 2005, 2). The melodrama in this case serves to paint TikTok as a Gothic monster: an exoticised, desirable other and a terrifying Yellow Peril, juxtaposed against the implied normalcy, safety and wholesomeness of Western-owned media (a highly questionable realm of its own).

A second Gothic aspect of TikTok as a platform, which is less explicitly racialised, is its algorithm. Specifically, the TikTok algorithm is often seen as a kind of unconscious, dredging up repressed or subconscious aspects of a person's identity. When TikTok is cited by non-users and by the mainstream media, it is typically framed as a home for teenaged beauty vloggers, dance videos and stunt routines, often through the lens of a familiar paranoia about youth and media use. While this kind of content certainly exists on TikTok, a key driver behind the platform and a major draw for its users is its algorithm. You do not need to follow a TikToker to come across their content or even their live stream; the app's algorithm will find this for you and present it on your 'For You' page in an endless scroll. Like a virtual unconscious, the app tracks users' viewing patterns down to the second, noting which videos they like, share, rewatch or do not bother to finish. Depending on your viewing patterns and device and profile settings, your 'For You' page might prioritise #DanceTok content. Alternately, you might find yourself on #PotatoTikTok, #Fittok, #Cottagecore, #nonbinary TikTok, #BookTok, #WitchTok, or any other number of specialised genres and hashtags. Sometimes the algorithm will throw you something unexpected to see if it sticks. There is a play here between the expected and the abrupt, sometimes comical or absurd emergence of new content.

As with many commercial algorithms TikTok's code is proprietary, and though the company has made efforts to clarify to users and regulatory bodies how it operates, its algorithm is not publicly available. It is considered to be highly advanced, however, and for those who use TikTok regularly the assumption is that your For You page reflects your personal preferences and identity, rather than forcing a particular kind of content upon you. Sometimes this manifests in positive ways. There are a number of coming-out legends in circulation, for instance, where TikTok users allegedly realised or affirmed that they were gay or trans as a result of TikTok's algorithm (Joho 2022). The algorithm also has more sinister readings. As @jaronmyers writes on Twitter 'I've seen too many youth pastors be like "Be careful on TikTok, it's just girls dancing in swimsuits" and I'm like bro . . . it's an algorithm 👀' (@jaronmyers 2022). As this tweet indicates, there is a paranoia inherent in the way some users interact with the algorithm, interpreting it as an expression of the subconscious and its desires. There is also a great deal of sensationalised media reporting and public concern about what users, particularly very young ones, might be exposing themselves to on TikTok, at the same time as older users flock to the platform, drawn by the promise of the weird and taboo as well as the comforting and the repetitive (Levine 2022). In Louisa G. Rogers's words, TikTok is 'an atmosphere in which young people understand their reality primarily in relation to performing for an audience' (Rogers 2021, 379). Drawing on Chun, these performances and anxieties on TikTok can simply be read as the most recent example of how the internet 'has been perceived as an unstoppable window that threatens to overwhelm the home and existing zoning laws', and how internet users are, 'curiously inside out – they are framed as private subjects exposed in public' (Chun 2016, 12). Overall then, there are a number of ways that TikTok as a platform might offer users a Gothic glimpse into the melodrama of the modern condition. In some corners of TikTok, thrill seekers might also find content to satisfy their cravings for some scintillating terror and wondrous barbarism. It is here that we move from TikTok's Gothic form to its Gothic content, and to the core aesthetic #HauntedTikTok.

#HauntedTikTok and the Circulation of Found Horror

Rogers conceptualises TikTok's hashtags or 'core aesthetics' as 'algorithmically led micro-communities', where more obscure aesthetics 'form satellites around more popular content forms and occasionally gain virality themselves for their freakishness or downright surrealism' (Rogers 2021, 377). In this way, she suggests, core aesthetics become 'late technoculture's answer to the subculture', with all of the suggestions of liminality and rebellion that this includes (Rogers 2021, 381). Some core aesthetics dwarf others. At the time of writing, #BookTok had around 49 billion views, compared to #Fittok's 18.3 billion or #Cottagecore's 9.6 billion. The extreme and 'liminal' core aesthetics Rogers focuses on in her article, the #DarkCircles make-up trend and #Clowncore aesthetic, attract around 635 and 250 million views respectively (Rogers 2021, 377). Somewhere in the middle, between liminal and mainstream viewership at around 5.5 billion, sits the core aesthetic called #HauntedTikTok.

There is a wide variety of Gothic or horror content on TikTok, ranging from gimmicky to kooky to genuinely disconcerting. There are craftspeople who make stop-motion videos of themselves consuming dishes of (fake) eyeballs and inedibles like @frankenfood.official, comedy skits where a figure who looks like the Slenderman (a popular figure from internet folk horror) does everyday household chores (@_soggy_nugget_), special effects artists who make horror shorts (for instance @jellybo2k, or the #15secondhorrorfilmchallenge), and even a TikToker whose whole account involves covering their face in shaving cream and making disturbing faces and noises (@captain.cream). Like many other corners of the internet, TikTok has also developed its own urban legends, which are frequently shared on #HauntedTikTok. These 'haunted', found footage-style videos offer especially fruitful ground for looking at the intersections of the Gothic, the comic, and mobile horror, since it is here where the lines between fiction and reality blur, where interpretations become layered on interpretations, and where user replies range all the way from frightened to angry to amused.

The videos that go on to become #HauntedTikTok found footage often present themselves as regular TikToks on first posting, as in the following three examples from autumn 2019. In one viral video, streamer Alex Huff is in the middle of filming a make-up tutorial from her laptop when the closet door behind her slowly creaks open then suddenly slams, startling her. When she goes to check on it the lightbulb above her suddenly flickers and she jumps back in fright before the video cuts out. Huff's startled reaction seems genuine. The video caption reads 'i swear on my moms [sic] life this happened at 3am last night' (@allexhuff 2019). We can see jack-o'-lantern string lights hung in the background of the video as decoration, a clue that the video is posted around Halloween, but it is not clear from this context whether the video is purportedly genuine or meant to be a seasonal gimmick. In another viral video, a streamer with the username @Tiengerines is performing one of TikTok's staple dance routines to the song 'GRoCERIES' by Chance The Rapper, again for a stationary camera. In the middle of the routine a shadowy figure can be seen crossing the balcony above and behind her. @tiengerines does not notice this happening while she is dancing, but in the video caption she writes 'tell me im not the only one who saw that 😨😨😨😨' (@tiengerines 2019). When resharing the video on Twitter she adds: 'pls make this viral on twitter and tiktok omg im scared for my life' (tien☆ (@tienttrvn) 2019). Based on this addition, Twitter and Tiktok were divided on whether the video contained evidence of the supernatural or was just clever a bid for attention – the video made it far enough that Chance The Rapper himself commented on it just a few days later. In a third video, a person is filming their dog while getting ready for bed. Suddenly their dog notices a dark shape in the hallway. The user directs their phone camera towards it, at which point the shadowy figure jerks out of sight and the streamer likewise reels back, swearing in terror, the camera jolting wide. The caption reads 'I CANNOT believe I got that on camera. So happy to be out of that house. #ghost #haunted' (@5up3r5wa66n3al 2019). In each video, a supposedly supernatural event intrudes on an otherwise familiar TikTok trope. In the cases of Alex Huff and @5up3r5wa66n3al this intrusion is more immediate than it is for @Tiengerines, who only notices the 'ghost' when rewatching the video playback.

In each of these examples the video quality is quite poor, with low lighting and varying levels of graininess, and in the last two videos viewers might not even notice the 'apparition' at all on first viewing, relying either on the streamer's reactions, another streamer's framing, or their own repeated rewatching to experience the horror. All three videos generated debate about their authenticity, with some commenters and streamers asserting that the videos depicted real hauntings, others adamant that they were faked, and some seeming to play along with the videos, offering potentially humorous, certainly melodramatic suggestions for cleansing the house. It is at this point that we see a shift from clear-cut horror to a more Gothic ambiguity, and potentially to a comic turn. As the videos travelled further and further from their original posting, these Gothic qualities accumulated. For example, there is an element of Gothic melodrama in how the videos have been circulated and remediated on TikTok. For all three of the videos discussed above, the video has been deleted or 'purged', as often happens to old videos on the platform, but the streamers also have deleted their entire accounts, perhaps lending the spooky content an additional aura of realism, but *also* making it much more difficult to trace back to the original content and verify its authenticity. The videos continue to circulate on the platform as repostings, or in stitched or duet form, where they still receive views and comments. In Gothic fashion, then, the internet reminds us that 'to delete is not to forget, but to make possible other (less consensually hallucinatory) ways to remember' (Chun 2016, 19). The repressed always returns. Some TikTok accounts specialise in collecting and commenting on these kinds of videos. In the tradition of a long line of Gothic narrators, each of the three viral videos mentioned above is staged as a found footage fragment by streamers Sergio and Cristian Rodriguez with a knowing wink, sensationalised as 'super terrifying' examples of paranormal apparitions 'caught on TikTok' and presented for the wonderment of viewers (@therodrigueztwins 2019b; 2019c; 2019a).

A great deal has been written on the intersections of Gothic and found footage (see, for instance, Heller-Nicholas 2014; Blake and Aldana Reyes 2015; McMurdo 2023). As Xavier Aldana Reyes points out, found footage is less a genre than 'a framing technique with specific narrative and stylistic effects' – like the Gothic, the found footage can operate across many tonal ranges (Aldana Reyes 2015, 122). Writing about found footage film, Neil McRobert suggests that instead of 'merely replicating the imagery of terror/ism, these films achieve their terrifying effects by mimicking the audiences' media spectatorship of such crisis' (McRobert 2015, 137). On TikTok the audience becomes part of this effect. An often-global range of other users' comments, video responses and other engagements with a particular post are available for users to place themselves in relation to. Users can also see other accounts and comments that engage with a copy of the video at the click of a button, and if you watch one version to completion it is not unusual to see another pop up later on your For You page. These multiple copies and perspectives are framed as complementary rather than competing. When people do encounter a Haunted TikTok video, then, there are also a wide variety of responses and interpretive differences in the presentation and comments that form a part of the narrative, alternating between horror, unease, and, in quite a few cases, verging on the comic, where the shock of a jump scare shifts into a laugh of release or of derision. For instance, on the Rodriguez twins' stitch of @5up3r5wa66n3al's video, one user comments 'I'm sorry, I laughed! I LOVE the paranormal! Would love to investigate this!' (Alphin 2019). Another user commenting on another streamer's stitch shares: 'that is the first time in a long time I have been freaked. I work at a haunted hotel too' (Pick 2019).

As Avril Horner and Sue Zlosnik's work indicates, elements of humour, specifically irony and parody, have been inherent in the Gothic from its inception. The incongruity of the Gothic's hybrid nature 'opens up the possibility of a comic turn in the presence of horror or terror [and] makes possible a mixed response to the loss of transcendence that characterises the modern condition' (Horner and Zlosnik 2005, 3). Where the Gothic traditionally mourns this lost transcendence, its melodrama and the comic turn potentially offer an ironic 'position of detachment and scepticism towards such cultural nostalgia' (Horner and Zlosnik 2005, 3). This ironic position of detachment applies at least in part to TikTok, and there is certainly melodrama at work in how these viral videos circulate. I would like to suggest that there is another structure of feeling at work here also. The whole point of TikTok is to be immersed but *not* invested, to consume with all your senses but then to forget and move on to the next video. Is this position oppositional enough to be ironic? Can it be sustained enough to be transcendent? Instead, it may be yet another example of the Gothic times in which TikTok is situated, locked into a post-ironic limbo.

As with horror, humour is always subjective: what is terrifying to one person is comic to another. TikTok plays off this awareness. On TikTok users are sequestered from each other, funnelled off into their own algorithmic 'metanarratives' and core aesthetics, occasionally stumbling onto the titillating possibilities of an alternate 'For You' page. That content may arrive because a user liked similar content before, or it can arrive through the repressed 'subconscious' of the algorithm. TikTok is an app of both intimate familiarity and detached entertainment. Dutch philosophers Timotheus Vermeulen and Robin van den Akker characterise this affective indecision as 'metamodern', negotiating 'between a modern enthusiasm and a postmodern irony [...] between naïveté and knowingness, empathy and apathy'. A metamodern affect is one that is able to oscillate 'to and fro or back and forth' between these opposites, appreciating both in turns (Vermeulen and van den Akker 2010, 1). If we apply this affect to media, it is not quite the same as that present in kitsch, parody or pastiche for instance, which favour an ironic attachment to the knowledge that taste, style and what is 'good' are all subjective. It is also not a kind of engagement that is entirely serious, or allowing for boundless enthusiasm. Instead it is a little bit of both, part of the neoliberal, 'verbal-visual experiences that can be and are used in complex patterns and strategies by users who are "managing" their lives through the help of these versatile mobile devices' (Engberg and Bolter 2017, 165). Put another way, metamodern affect protects 'interior, subjective *felt experience* from the ironic distance of *postmodernism*, the scientific reductionism of *modernism*, and the pre-personal inertia of *tradition*' (Dember 2018, original italics). TikTok helps us to manage our modern anxieties by offering a kind of both/and metanarrative as a platform, responding equally to skimming and repeat viewing, engagement and apathy. There is space for all of these affective positions at the same time, in oscillation. As Joe Ondrak writes about creepypasta, another body of internet folk horror:

> The affordances of digital textuality democratise the monster-making effects of technology, while the networked social media spaces that host these stories promote a sincere engagement with the myths and monsters that they conjure. It is this mix of sincere reader engagement, ontological ambiguity and digital textuality that distinguishes the creepypasta narrative as a unique form of horror fiction, and places this new generation of paranormal encounters in part of a 'post-postmodern' cultural turn. (Ondrak 2018, 164)

The ability of viewers to both believe and not believe, to alternate between horror and wonder and laughter within the span of a single rewatch, and then to scroll on to the next video, is part of the appeal of the platform. So is the ambiguity and ephemerality of its content.

#GhostPhotoshoot and the Issues with Irony

To some extent the metamodern is an outcome of the clash between the postmodern 'end of history' and the many alternate, ongoing histories foregrounded by the process of globalisation. As Kerwin Lee Klein wrote in 1995, although metanarratives have 'become something to avoid [. . .] our global situations demand stories that can describe and explain the worldwide interaction of diverse cultures and communities' (Klein 1995, 275). The internet forms bubbles around people, but it also has the capacity to rupture those bubbles, and when global communities collide on TikTok or elsewhere, it can vividly illustrate how differently people view the world. This in itself can be terrifying, and metamodern oscillation offers one way of coping. What kinds of comic relief do Gothic TikTok texts provide to audiences from the horrors of modern life? From what kinds of horrors, and who do those horrors actually threaten? As a number of the other chapters in this book point out, not only are Gothic parody and irony political, these politics are not always progressive.

Simon Critchley argues that humour 'returns us to *locality*, to a specific and circumscribed *ethos*. It takes us back to the place we are from' (Critchley 2002, 68, original italics). In other words, humour continually retraces the boundaries of a particular community by reinforcing the ethos and identity of those in on the joke. In the context of the Gothic, it makes the unhomely homely again. This is not a politically neutral gesture. For Critchley, ironic recognition and humour represent 'a form of cultural insider-knowledge' (Critchley 2002, 67), where outsiders are excluded from the joke to the point where 'having a common sense of humour is like sharing a secret code' (Critchley 2002, 68). This system of exclusion reflects what Linda Hutcheon has referred to as 'irony's edge', which 'manages to provoke emotional responses in those who "get" it and those who don't, as well as in its targets and in what some people call its "victims"' (Hutcheon 1994, 2). Acknowledging the nostalgic element of our attachment and perceived closeness to certain texts and images can thus be as important as ironically distancing ourselves from them.

We can find one illustration of irony, its failures and its edges in the viral TikTok trend #ghostphotoshoot. In this trend, images of streamers dressed up as ghosts are displayed in a photomontage to the soundtrack of Jack Stauber's 'Oh Klahoma'. The videos are designed to be charmingly spooky, often featuring comical accessories like hats, scarves and glasses layered over bedsheets, sometimes including animals (also dressed as ghosts), and using the nostalgic lens of a faded, sepia retro filter. Many of the original videos in this trend have been deleted as part of TikTok's regular content purges, but this trend has been repeated on TikTok in subsequent years and has also been covered by a number of mainstream news outlets as part of their focus on autumn media culture. For some, #ghostphotoshoot is a charmingly spooky autumnal trend akin to trick-or-treating, pumpkin carving, or Pumpkin Spice Lattes. It represents a welcome and diverting release in an otherwise anxious time. For others, however, there was no amusement, only a Gothic sense of horror and unease. In September 2020, a few months after George Floyd's murder by Minnesota policeman Derek Chauvin, #ghostphotoshoot made waves on Twitter, and these two communities came into conversation. In a subsequently deleted tweet, *New York Times* reporter Taylor Lorenz shared a series of #ghostphotoshoot videos with her followers. For news presenter and journalist Imayen Ibanga and many others responding to this tweet, the immediate associations were not with ghosts, but with the Ku Klux Klan, a white supremacist terror organisation known for their white hoods and robes: 'When I see white people in white sheets, ghosts aren't the first thing I think of. Just looking at this makes me nervous' (Ibanga 2020). 'Especially right now!' replied columnist Kimberly Atkins Stohr (Atkins Stohr 2020). Several commenters on the original TikTok videos made similar associations. 'I saw a couple of guys doing this in the woods but their hats were way pointier' wrote one user on a video by @willywonkatiktok, in reference to the shape of the KKK hoods (Chum the Puppy Beast 2021). On a video where TikTokers used both white and red bedsheets, some users pointed out that this was 'maybe not the best combo' and 'Grand wizard hits diff😳' (@frankiesfun 2020), referring to the red versions of the robe and hood worn by senior members of the KKK.

As Leila Taylor points out in her meditation on Black history and American Gothic, the KKK uniform itself began as a ghost costume, meant to evoke the spirits of the Confederate dead and terrorise Black Americans (Taylor 2019, 71). A few pages earlier, Taylor also notes the double-edged undertones of the word 'spooky' which she ties into this discussion:

> Spooky is an ethereal unease that is difficult to place, an unformed and obscured aura of something that is not quite right. [...] The word 'spook' comes from the Dutch 'spooc', meaning 'ghost' or 'apparition'. In the 1940s spook became a word for a spy – a clandestine, sneaky person whose life is in the shadows. About the same time spook also became a derogatory word for Black people. [...] The word carries either a cartoonish innocence or bitingly racist connotations. (Taylor 2019, 64)

Taylor's etymology offers an ideal analogy for the metamodern duality that is Gothic TikTok, as illustrated in the debate over #ghostphotoshoot. The trend is whimsical and Gothic, its retro nostalgia comically charming to some, but carrying darker, repressed meanings for others. TikTok as a platform, likewise, is a powerful tool for generating both repetitive entertainment and nostalgia, and for bringing repressed anxieties and the 'edge' of irony into clear relief. In the Gothic, postcapitalist times in which we live, there is a dark secret beneath even the sunniest of stories. For TikTok this also holds true.[3]

For citizens of this Gothic landscape, as well as for Gothic scholars, it is important to remember that while the Gothic (and Gothic TikTok) can offer relief from the anxieties of modern existence, that relief is not apolitical. Likewise, the fears we project onto others are not dispersed through that projection, only displaced. For Fred Botting, in our horrific present cyberGothic functions as an alluring but false reassurance, in which Gothic images 'only serve as a disguise, a retrospective gloss on a terrifyingly prospective gaze, a blank staring ahead. They provide the camouflage, the hallucinatory and vain comfort in a history and modernity that already lies in ruins' (Botting 2008, 217). And as Wendy Hui Kyong Chun somewhat more cheerfully writes, new media are 'wonderfully creepy' (Chun 2016, 52). Haunted TikTok offers us a bit of both worlds – the nostalgic, the ironic, the wonderful and the horrific. It also

Figure 17.1 [Left] A #ghostphotoshoot TikTok video (@hanydavalos 2022). Screenshot by the author. [Right] A group of Klansmen at a christening. Triangle Studio Of Photography 1924.

suggests to us that a single perspective on these worlds is never enough, especially where comedy is concerned.

Notes

1. Before July 2021 TikTok videos were capped at 60 seconds. This gave way to a 3-minute cap, then a 10-minute cap in 2022.
2. At the time of writing, TikTok comes sixth overall in the ranking of social media giants, behind Facebook's 2.9 billion active users, YouTube's 2.5 billion, WhatsApp's 2 billion, and Instagram and WeChat, each with around 1.5 billion.
3. The way TikTok promotes familiar content, from dance routines to other viral trends, has also historically encouraged appropriation from and erasure of Black streamers (Boffone 2021).

References

@5up3r5wa66n3al. 2019. 'I CANNOT believe I got that on camera. So happy to be out of that house. #ghost #haunted'. TikTok, 21 October. https://www.tiktok.com/@5up3r5wa66n3al/video/6749370385839426821

Aldana Reyes, Xavier. 2015. 'Reel Evil: A Critical Reassessment of Found Footage Horror'. *Gothic Studies* 17, no. 2: 122–36. https://doi.org/10.7227/GS.17.2.8

@allexhuff. 2019. '#foryou i swear on my moms life this happened at 3am last night'. TikTok, 26 October. https://www.tiktok.com/@allexhuff/video/6752173901951798534

Alphin, Michelle. 2019. 'I'm sorry, I laughed! I LOVE the paranormal! Would love to investigate this!' TikTok, 24 October. https://www.tiktok.com/@therodrigueztwins/video/6762152234500377862

Atkins Stohr, Kimberly. 2020. 'Especially Right Now!' Twitter, 23 September. https://twitter.com/KimberlyEAtkins/status/1308792025802838021

Baker, Jen. 2021. 'Introduction: Gothic and the Short Form'. *Gothic Studies* 23, no. 2: 127–31. https://doi.org/10.3366/gothic.2021.0089

Blake, Linnie and Xavier Aldana Reyes, eds. 2015. *Digital Horror: Haunted Technologies, Network Panic and the Found Footage Phenomenon*. London: Bloomsbury (I. B. Taurus).

Boffone, Trevor. 2021. *Renegades: Digital Dance Cultures from Dubsmash to TikTok*. New York: Oxford University Press.

Botting, Fred. 2008. *Limits of Horror: Technology, Bodies, Gothic*. Manchester: Manchester University Press.

Brooks, Peter. 1995. *The Melodramatic Imagination: Balzac, Henry James, Melodrama and the Mode of Excess*, 2nd edn. New Haven, CT: Yale University Press.

Bruin-Molé, Megen de, and Sara Polak. 2021. 'Embodying the Fantasies and Realities of Contagion'. In *Embodying Contagion: The Viropolitics of*

Horror and Desire in Contemporary Discourse, edited by Sandra Becker, Megen de Bruin-Molé and Sara Polak, 1–12. Cardiff: University of Wales Press.

Chan, Connie. 2022. 'What China Can Teach Us About the Future of TikTok and Video Search'. Andreessen Horowitz, 21 September. https://a16z.com/2022/09/21/what-china-can-teach-us-about-the-future-of-tiktok-and-video-search/

Chum the Puppy Beast. 2021. 'I saw a couple of guys doing this in the woods but their hats were way pointier'. TikTok, 10 October. https://www.tiktok.com/@willywonkatiktok/video/6874763827938987269

Chun, Wendy Hui Kyong. 2016. *Updating to Remain the Same: Habitual New Media*. Cambridge, MA: MIT Press.

Critchley, Simon. 2002. *On Humour*. London: Routledge.

Dember, Greg. 2018. 'After Postmodernism: Eleven Metamodern Methods in the Arts'. Medium, 17 April. https://medium.com/what-is-metamodern/after-postmodernism-eleven-metamodern-methods-in-the-arts-767f7b646cae

Engberg, Maria and Jay David Bolter. 2017. 'Mobile Cinematics'. In *Compact Cinematics: The Moving Image in the Age of Bit-Sized Media*, edited by Pepita Hesselberth and Maria Poulaki, 165–73. New York: Bloomsbury Academic.

@frankiesfun. 2020. 'This was so much fun . . . w/@livelaughliam @tashatalk @jcasx #ghostphotoshoot'. TikTok, 22 September. https://www.tiktok.com/@frankiesfun/video/6875405315190344961

Gronlund, Melissa. 2014. 'Return of the Gothic: Digital Anxiety in the Domestic Sphere'. *E-Flux Journal*, no. 51 (January).

Heller-Nicholas, Alexandra. 2014. *Found Footage Horror Films: Fear and the Appearance of Reality*. Jefferson, NC: McFarland.

Horner, Avril and Sue Zlosnik. 2005. *Gothic and the Comic Turn*. Basingstoke: Palgrave MacMillan.

Horsman, Yasco. 2017. 'Of Flip Books & Funny Animals: Chris Ware's *Quimby the Mouse*'. In *Compact Cinematics: The Moving Image in the Age of Bit-Sized Media*, edited by Pepita Hesselberth and Maria Poulaki, 153–64. New York: Bloomsbury Academic.

Hutcheon, Linda. 1994. *Irony's Edge: The Theory and Politics of Irony*. London: Routledge.

Ibanga, Imaeyen. 2020. 'When I see white people in white sheets, ghosts aren't the first thing I think of. Just looking at this makes me nervous'. Twitter, 23 September. https://twitter.com/iiwrites/status/1308791474830610434

@jaronmyers. 2022. 'I've seen too many youth pastors be like "Be careful on TikTok, it's just girls dancing in swimsuits" and I'm like bro . . . it's an algorithm 👀'. Twitter, 26 January. https://twitter.com/jaronmyers/status/1486181240919183362

Joho, Jess. 2022. 'TikTok's algorithms knew I was bi before I did. I'm not the only one'. Mashable, 18 September. https://mashable.com/article/bisexuality-queer-tiktok

Kitson, Peter. 2016. 'Oriental Gothic'. In *Romantic Gothic: An Edinburgh Companion*, edited by Angela Wright, Dale Townshend and Diego Saglia, 167–84. Edinburgh: Edinburgh University Press.

Klein, Kerwin Lee. 1995. 'In Search of Narrative Mastery: Postmodernism and the People Without History'. *History and Theory* 34, no. 1: 275–98.

Langford, Sam. 2019. 'Junk Explained: What The Hell Is TikTok, And Is It The New Vine?' JUNKEE, 7 January. https://junkee.com/tiktok-app-vine-challenge/188567

Levine, Alexandra S. 2022. 'How TikTok Live Became "A Strip Club Filled With 15-Year-Olds"'. Forbes, 27 April. https://www.forbes.com/sites/alexandralevine/2022/04/27/how-tiktok-live-became-a-strip-club-filled-with-15-year-olds/

McMurdo, Shellie. 2023. *Blood on the Lens: Trauma and Anxiety in American Found Footage Horror Cinema*. Edinburgh: Edinburgh University Press.

McRobert, Neil. 2015. 'Mimesis of Media: Found Footage Cinema and the Horror of the Real'. *Gothic Studies* 17, no. 2: 137–50. https://doi.org/10.7227/GS.17.2.9

Moran, Shauna and Chase Buckle. 2022. 'Social: GWI's Flagship Report on the Latest Trends in Social Media'. *Global Web Index*. https://www.gwi.com/reports/social

Ondrak, Joe. 2018. 'Spectres Des Monstres: Post-Postmodernisms, Hauntology and Creepypasta Narratives as Digital Fiction'. *Horror Studies* 9, no. 2: 161–78. https://doi.org/10.1386/host.9.2.161_1

Pick, Jaaziel. 2019. 'that is the first time in a long time I have been freaked. I work at a haunted hotel too'. TikTok, 20 October. https://www.tiktok.com/@thekayleewalker/video/6749496711963593989

Rogers, Louisa G. 2021. 'TikTok Teens: Turbulent Identities for Turbulent Times'. *Film, Fashion & Consumption* 10, no. 2: 377–400. https://doi.org/10.1386/ffc_00031_1

Silver, Sean. 2014. 'The Politics of Gothic Historiography, 1660–1800'. In *The Gothic World*, edited by Glennis Byron and Dale Townshend, 3–14. London: Routledge.

Taylor, Leila. 2019. *Darkly: Black History and America's Gothic Soul*. London: Repeater Books, an imprint of Watkins Media Ltd.

@therodrigueztwins. 2019a. 'Ghost! Did you see it, what's your thoughts?! @tiengerines #ghost #hauntedhouse #spooky #fyp #4upage'. TikTok, 22 October. https://www.tiktok.com/@therodrigueztwins/video/6750752942623624453

@therodrigueztwins. 2019b. 'Is that a ghost?! Like and follow us for more ghost reactions @5up3r5wa66n3al #ghost #fyp #haunted #spirits #friendsgiving'. TikTok, 23 October. https://www.tiktok.com/@therodrigueztwins/video/6762152234500377862

@therodrigueztwins. 2019c. 'I think her house is haunted! What do you think?! @allexhuff like and follow us for more ghost reactions! #fyp #ghost #viral #thingsthathappened'. TikTok, 11 November. https://www.tiktok.com/@therodrigueztwins/video/6758184507762871558

tien☆ (@tienttrvn). 2019. 'pls make this viral on twitter and tiktok omg im scared for my life Pic.Twitter.Com/O4rvfDZAkI'. Twitter, 28 September. https://twitter.com/tienttrvn/status/1177966214842388480

@tiengerines. 2019. 'tell me im not the only one who saw that 👀👀👀 #fyp #foryou #SavingsShuffle #SpicySnap'. TikTok, 28 September. www.tiktok.com/@tiengerines/video/6741537465439489285

'TikTok Statistics and Trends'. 2022. Data Reportal. https://datareportal.com/essential-tiktok-stats

Väliaho, Pasi. 2017. 'Solitary Screens: On the Recurrence and Consumption of Images'. In *Compact Cinematics: The Moving Image in the Age of Bit-Sized Media*, edited by Pepita Hesselberth and Maria Poulaki, 123–31. New York: Bloomsbury Academic.

Vermeulen, Timotheus and Robin van den Akker. 2010. 'Notes on Metamodernism'. *Journal of Aesthetics & Culture* 2: 1–14.

Verstraten, Peter. 2017. 'Accelerated Gestures: Play Time in Agnès Varda's Cléo de 5 à 7'. In *Compact Cinematics: The Moving Image in the Age of Bit-Sized Media*, edited by Pepita Hesselberth and Maria Poulaki, 36–44. New York: Bloomsbury Academic.

Woods, Ben. 2022. 'TikTok Is "a Tool of Espionage and Must Be Banned in the West"'. *The Telegraph*, 7 September. https://www.telegraph.co.uk/business/2022/09/07/tiktok-tool-espionage-must-banned-west/

Notes on Contributors

Katarzyna Ancuta is a lecturer at the Faculty of Arts, Chulalongkorn University in Thailand. Her research interests oscillate around the interdisciplinary contexts of contemporary Gothic/Horror, currently with a strong Asian focus. Her recent publications include contributions to *Film Stardom in Southeast Asia* (Edinburgh University Press, 2022), *The Transmedia Vampire* (2021), *The New Urban Gothic* (2020) and *B-Movie Gothic* (Edinburgh University Press, 2018). She has also co-edited two collections – *Thai Cinema: The Complete Guide* (with Mary Ainslie, 2016) and *South Asian Gothic: Haunted Cultures, Histories and Media* (with Deimantas Valančiūnas, 2022).

Linnie Blake is founder leader of the Centre for Gothic Studies and Reader in Gothic Literature in the Department of English at Manchester Metropolitan University. Among her many publications are: *The Wounds of Nations: Horror Cinema, National Identity and Historical Trauma* (2008) and the edited collections *Neoliberal Gothic: International Gothic of the Neoliberal Age* (with Agnieszka Soltysik Monnet, 2017) and *Digital Horror: Haunted Technologies, Network Panic and the Found Footage Phenomenon* (with Xavier Aldana Reyes, 2016).

Thomas Brassington is a PhD researcher at Lancaster University. His project, *Dragging the Gothic*, examines cross-dressing in the Gothic mode through the lens of drag performance. His research interests are in contemporary Gothic, femininities, popular culture and queer Gothic more broadly.

Megen de Bruin-Molé is a Lecturer in Digital Media Practice at the University of Southampton. She specialises in 'monstrous' historical fiction, adaptation and contemporary remix culture, and is particularly interested in the digital afterlives and appropriations of historical archives and ephemera – including in GIFs and on TikTok. Her book *Gothic Remixed* (2020) examines popular remix culture through the lens of monster studies, and her co-edited collection *Embodying Contagion* (2021) explores how fantasies of outbreak narratives have infiltrated the way people view the real world. Read more about Megen's work on her blog: frankenfiction.com.

Karen Coats is Professor and Director of the Centre for Research in Children's Literature at the University of Cambridge. She has published more than fifty articles and book chapters on the intersections between youth literature and critical theory, with a special interest in psychoanalysis and affective/cognitive studies. Among other single-authored and co-edited books, she co-edited, with Anna Jackson and Roderick McGillis, *The Gothic in Children's Literature: Haunting the Borders* (2009).

Monica Germanà is Reader in Gothic and Contemporary Studies at the University of Westminster. Her most recent publications include *Scottish Gothic: An Edinburgh Companion* (2018), co-edited with Carol Davison and shortlisted for the Allan Lloyd Smith Prize, *Bond Girls: Body, Fashion, Gender* (2019), shortlisted for the Emily Toth Award, and a special issue of *Gothic Studies* on Haunted Scotlands (March 2022). She is currently working on a new project exploring Scottish/Arctic cultural links with particular reference to the 'other-wordly' and monstrous aesthetics attached to the far north and the Arctic.

Jerrold E. Hogle is Professor Emeritus of English and University Distinguished Professor at the University of Arizona. Winning Guggenheim, Mellon and other fellowships for research – and the Distinguished Scholar Award from the Keats-Shelley Association of America – he has published extensively on English Romantic literature, literary theory and the Gothic. His books include *Shelley's Process* (1989), *The Undergrounds of The Phantom of the Opera* (2002) and *The Cambridge Companion to Gothic Fiction* (2002) which has been succeeded by *The Cambridge Companion to the Modern Gothic* (2002) and by *The Gothic and Theory*, co-edited with Robert Miles (Edinburgh University Press, 2019) in the Edinburgh Companions to the Gothic series.

Michael Hollington is a retired Professor of English and Comparative Literature now living in Scotland. He has held chairs in France and Australia and taught on every continent. He was the first person appointed in Britain to teach Comparative Literature at undergraduate level – at UEA Norwich. He is best known as a Dickensian but has published numerous books and articles on many aspects of literature from Shakespeare onwards, including German literature as well as English, American and Australian.

Avril Horner is Emeritus Professor of English Literature at Kingston University, London. Her research interests include women's writing and Gothic fiction. With Sue Zlosnik she has co-authored many articles and several books, including *Daphne du Maurier: Writing, Identity and the Gothic Imagination* (1998), *Gothic and the Comic Turn* (2005) and *Women and the Gothic* (Edinburgh University Press, 2016) in the Edinburgh Companions to the Gothic series. Other works include *European Gothic: A Spirited Exchange, 1760–1960* (2002), *Edith Wharton: Sex, Satire and the Older Woman* (with Janet Beer, 2011) and *Living on Paper: Letters from Iris Murdoch, 1934–1995* (with Anne Rowe, 2015). Her biography of Barbara Comyns will be published in 2024.

Timothy Jones is a Lecturer at the University of Stirling, and an Associate Editor of *Gothic Studies*. His *The Gothic and the Carnivalesque in American Culture* (2015) was awarded the Allan Lloyd Smith prize.

Angelique Nairn is an Associate Professor in the School of Communication Studies at Auckland University of Technology, New Zealand. She teaches courses in the public relations department, specialising in digital public relations and persuasion. Angelique has been involved in a myriad of research projects that have hinged on organisational communication, identity construction, rhetoric and/or the creative industries. She is also interested in popular culture and particularly the representation of women, creative people and morality as they appear on screen. Her recent work has explored issues of racism, sexism, the Gothic and technological determinism.

Natalie Neill is an Associate Professor, Teaching Stream, at York University in Toronto. Her research interests include female authorship in the Romantic period, Gothic parody, and transmedia adaptation. She has recently edited a collection, *Gothic Mash-Ups: Hybridity, Appropriation, and Intertextuality in Gothic Storytelling* (2022). Her edition of Mary Charlton's *Rosella, or Modern Occurrences* (1799) was published in 2023.

Lorna Piatti-Farnell is Professor of Media and Cultural Studies at Auckland University of Technology, where she is also the Director of the Popular Culture Research Centre. She is President of the Gothic Association of New Zealand and Australia (GANZA), and coordinator of the Australasian Horror Studies Network (AHSN). In addition, she is a research fellow at Falmouth University (UK), and a visiting professor at Curtin University (Australia) and the University of New England (Australia). She is author and editor of many books that focus on the intersection of cultural history, popular culture and Gothic studies.

Franz J. Potter is a Professor and Director of the MA in Gothic Studies programme at National University in Southern California. His research interests include the Gothic, history of the book trade, and nineteenth-century chapbooks. He has written articles on the Gothic trade, sensationalism, chapbooks, print culture, novelist Sarah Wilkinson and is the author of *The History of Gothic Publishing, 1800–1835* (2005) and *Gothic Chapbooks, Bluebooks and Shilling Shockers, 1797–1830* (2021).

Faye Ringel, Professor Emerita of Humanities, US Coast Guard Academy, is a lifelong New Englander; her PhD in Comparative Literature is from Brown University. She has published *New England's Gothic Literature* (1995) and *The Gothic Literature and History of New England: Secrets of the Restless Dead* (2022) and articles in reference books and scholarly books and journals on such varied topics as New England vampires, Lovecraft, Tolkien, Yiddish folklore, demonic cooks, The Three Stooges, and many more. In the Before Times, she played keyboard and sang with the Klezmer band Klezmenschen of Eastern Connecticut. She was the Jewish lay leader at the Coast Guard Academy, and today she leads services via Zoom.

Neil Sammells is Emeritus Professor of English and Irish Literature at Bath Spa University, where he was formerly Deputy Vice Chancellor and Provost. He is the founding editor of *Irish Studies Review* (since 1992) and the author of *Tom Stoppard: the Artist as Critic* (1988) and *Wilde Style* (2000). He is also an experienced broadcaster, appearing most recently on Radio 4's *In Our Time*, discussing the Decadent Movement.

Cynthia Sugars is a Professor of English at the University of Ottawa, where she specialises in Canadian literature. She is the author of *Canadian Gothic: Literature, History and the Spectre of Self-Invention* (2014), and the editor of numerous collections including *Canadian Literature and Cultural Memory* (2014), *The Oxford Handbook of Canadian Literature* (2015), *Unsettled Remains: Canadian Literature* *and the Postcolonial Gothic* (2009) and *Unhomely States: Theorizing English-Canadian Postcolonialism* (2004). She is currently the editor of the scholarly journal *Studies in Canadian Literature*.

Deimantas Valančiūnas is Associate Professor of film and popular cultures of Asia at the Institute of Asian and Transcultural Studies, Vilnius University. His research interests include Indian cinema, postcolonial theory, diaspora studies, Gothic and horror cinemas in Asia. He is an editor of special journal issues and author of a number of journal articles on South Asian cinema and literature. He is also a co-editor of *South Asian Gothic: Haunted Cultures, Histories and Media* (with Katarzyna Ancuta, 2022).

Sarah Whitehead teaches English Literature at Alleyn's School, London. She has written on Edith Wharton, the Comic Gothic, J. S. Le Fanu and the magazine short story in various publications, including the *Journal of the Short Story in English*, *Short Fiction in Theory and Practice*, the *Edith Wharton Review*, the *European Journal of American Culture*, the *Times Literary Supplement* and the collection, *The New Edith Wharton Studies*. She recently brought into print three hitherto unpublished Wharton stories, 'La Famille', 'A Granted Prayer' and 'The Children's Hour'. She is currently working on a study of James Joyce's early stories in *The Smart Set* magazine.

Sue Zlosnik is Emeritus Professor of English at Manchester Metropolitan University, and former co-President of the International Gothic Association. With Avril Horner, she has published six books, including *Daphne du Maurier: Writing, Identity and the Gothic Imagination* (1998), *Gothic and the Comic Turn* (2005), *the Edinburgh Companion to Women and the Gothic* (Edinburgh University Press, 2016) as well as numerous essays and articles. Alone, she has published essays on writers as diverse as J. R. R. Tolkien and Chuck Palahniuk, and a monograph, *Patrick McGrath* (2011). She is co-editor (with Agnes Andeweg) of *Gothic Kinship* (2013).

Index

abjection, 117, 200, 219
absurd, the, 9, 65, 69, 81, 103, 138, 153, 154, 157, 158, 161, 198, 231, 235, 256
Alcock, Mary, 53
Aldana Reyes, Xavier, 262
Aldrich, Robert (dir.), *Whatever Happened to Baby Jane?*, 244
Aleichem, Sholem, 136–7
algorithm, TikTok, 257, 258–9, 263
Ammons, Elizabeth, 108, 109, 118
Amrohi, Kamal (dir.), *Mahal*, 211
Anderson, M. T., 159
Anolik, Ruth Bienstock, 139–40
Ansky, S., 140
Armon, Poj, 182
Auerbach, Nina, 23, 24
Austen, Jane, *Northanger Abbey*, 50, 51, 52, 60, 244, 103

Babuscio, Jack, 250–1
Bailey, John, 39, 40, 41, 43, 45, 46, 47
Baker, Jen, 256
Bakhtin, Mikhail, 66, 70, 71, 77, 115, 117, 119, 190
Barbauld, Anna Laetitia, 154
    'On the Origin and Process of Novel-Writing', 56–7

Barrett, Eaton Stannard, *The Heroine*, 49, 50, 59, 61 50
Beckford, William, 54–6
    Azemia, 51, 55
    Modern Novel Writing, 49, 55, 57
Bennett, Andrew and Nicholas Royle, 200–1
Benton, Jim, 159–60
Berger, Peter, 157–8
Bergson, Henri, 72, 74
Birney, Earle, 122
'bluebooks', 30
Bois, Edward du, 50
    Old Nick, 50, 55
    St Godwin, 53
Bombay Gothic, 211
Borch-Jacobsen, Mikkel, 199–200
Botting, Fred, 74, 205, 266
Bradley, Sculley, 67–8
Bradshaw, Peter, 201–2, 204
Bristow, Joseph, 251
Brontë, Emily, *Wuthering Heights*, 197
Brooks, Peter, *The Melodramatic Imagination*, 1, 186, 258
Bryant, John, 65
Bullock, Mrs, *Susanna*, 50, 51–2, 52–3, 60
Bunyan, John, 154
burlesque, 31, 231, 241, 243, 249

Burke, Edmund, *A Philosphical Enquiry into the Origins of our ideas of the Sublime and the Beautiful*, 74, 95, 99
Buszcek, Maria Elena, 241
Burton, Anthony, 43, 45
Burton, Tim (dir.), 195–210
　Alice in Wonderland, 203–5, 206
　Corpse Bride, 201–3, 204, 206
　Frankenweenie, 205–8
Byron, Glennis, 234–5
Byron, Lord George Gordon, 17, 18, 19, 20

Cameron, Allan, 227, 235
camp, 4, 9, 93–5, 97, 98, 99, 102–6, 239–54
Cannon, Mercy, 61
caricature, 29, 35, 36, 37, 42, 47, 54, 56, 69, 70, 87, 109, 117, 119, 160, 189
Carlyle, Thomas, 80, 199
carnivalesque, 4, 65–8, 70, 71, 72, 74, 119, 157, 160, 190, 196, 212, 218
Carroll, Lewis, *Alice in Wonderland*, 82, 154, 196, 199, 203–4
Carroll, Noël, 64–5, 212
cartoons, 1, 27–48, 50, 199, 245
chapbooks, 3, 27–48
Charlton, Mary, *Rosella*, 49, 52, 56, 61, 57, 58–9
Chesterton, G. K., *Robert Browning*, 117–18
chudail (female ghost), 8, 217–21
Chun, Wendy Hui Kyong, 255, 259, 262, 266
Cixous, Hélène, *The Laugh of the Medusa*, 146
Coleman, Rebecca, 250
Coleridge, Samuel Taylor, 22, 50
　'Christabel', 15–17
Condit, Jon, 183
Conrich, Ian, 226, 227, 234

Creed, Barbara, 217–18
Critchley, Simon, 264–5
Cross, Julie, 160
Cruikshank, George, 29, 42, 43, 45 47
Cruikshank, Robert, 29, 42, 45
Currie, Andrew (dir.), *Fido*, 169–71, 172, 177

Dacre, Charlotte, 54
danse macabre, 116, 202
Datta, Anik (dir.), *Bhooter Bhabishyat*, 215–17
Davies, Robertson, 5, 122–35
Dawson, Melanie, 115
Dean, Jodi, 168
Dember, Greg, 263
Dhusiya, Mithuraaj, 212
Dickens, Charles, 77–90
　Barnaby Rudge, 88–9
　Great Expectations, 77, 202
　Little Dorrit, 88
　Nicholas Nickleby, 85
　Old Curiosity Shop, 85
　Oliver Twist, 86
　Pickwick Papers, 78–88
　Sketches by Boz, 78, 85
displacement, 8, 99, 214, 227
doppelgänger, 17, 96, 101, 104, 199, 257
Douglas, Lord Alfred, 101
Dwyer, Rachel, 220
dybbuk, 138, 140–1, 142

Eagleton, Terry, 74, 99
Edgeworth, Maria, 49, 60, 154
　Angelina, 51, 58
Ellman, Richard, 100
Engberg, Maria and Jay David Bolter, 263

fakery, 2, 196, 256
Fanger, Donald, 78
feminism, 61, 143, 239–54
feminist camp, 239–54

Fisher, Benjamin, 112–13
Fleischer, Ruben (dir.)
  Zombieland, 168, 173–4, 177
  Zombieland Double Tap, 168, 173–4
Fletcher, Harriet, 246
folklore, 15, 117
  Asian, 184
  Jewish, 136, 138, 140, 141, 142, 143, 145, 146
  New Zealand, 226
Forman, Charles, 13
Frank, Frederick S., 27, 8
Freeman, Nick, 102
Freud, Sigmund, 16, 64–5, 74, 201, 203
Fry, Elizabeth, 78, 79

Galford, Ellen, 140–1
gallows humour, 80–1, 229
Gamer, Michael, 186
Gaut, Berys, 187
Girard, René, 21
Gerard, W. B., 39
#ghostphotoshoot, 265, 266
gilgul, 141–2
Godwin, William, 58
  Caleb Williams, 53
  St Leon, 53
golem, 140, 142–5
Gorey, Edmund, 154, 162
Griffin, Dustin, 98
Griswold, Jerry, 156–7
Gronlund, Melissa, 255
Groom, Nick, 96, 103
grotesque, 4, 5, 33, 65, 70, 77, 109, 115–17, 190, 234, 235
Gunning, Tom, 191

Harrington, Erin, 228, 230, 235
#HauntedTikTok, 256, 259–64
Herndl, Diana Price, 110, 118
Heller-Nicholas, Alexandra, 230, 231
Hodgson, William, 42, 43, 45, 47

Hoeveler, Diane, 2
Hoffmann, Heinrich, *Der Struwwelpeter*, 6, 154
Hogle, E. Jerrold, 125, 177, 196, 242
Hollindale, Peter, 155–6
Holm, Nicholas, 230, 231
Holocaust, 137, 141, 146
Hor Taew Tak films, 182, 188–92
Horner, Avril and Sue Zlosnik,
  Gothic and the Comic Turn, 1, 102, 103, 104, 106, 118, 122, 130, 150, 151, 177, 186–7, 192, 196, 212, 225, 233, 234, 239–40, 250, 251, 258, 262–3
  Women and the Gothic, 216, 230
Hudson, Hannah Doherty, 54
Hughes, William, 113
Hughes, William and Andrew Smith, 97, 101
humour, black, 80, 231
Hutcheon, Linda, 2, 60, 265
hybridity, 1, 7, 77, 78, 88, 183, 186, 192, 195, 199, 228, 232

Ibanga, Imayen, 265
iconography, 3, 16, 29, 30–47, 160, 206
Indian cinema, 211–24
inequality, 9, 174, 191, 220
inverse uncanny, 7, 196, 200, 201, 203, 204, 206, 208
Ircastrensis, *Love and Horror*, 50–1, 59
irony, 1, 6, 9, 16, 55, 87, 99, 110, 122, 127, 144, 159, 160, 188, 206, 231, 235, 256, 262, 263, 264, 265, 266
Irvin, Sam (dir.), *Elvira's Haunted Hills*, 246, 247

James, Henry, 77
Jameson, Fredric, 173

Jameson, Fredric (*cont.*)
  'Postmodernism, Or, The Cultural Logic of Late Capitalism', 169
  The Seeds of Time, 167–8, 169
Jentsch, Ernst, 74, 201
Johnstone, Gerard (dir.), *Housebound*, 228–31

kathoey, 189, 190
Kaushik, Amar (dir.), *Stree*, 218–21
Kawin, Bruce, 234
Kayser, Wolfgang, 77
  The Grotesque in Art and Literature, 115
Killeen, Jarlath, 96, 103
King, Jonathan (dir.), *Black Sheep*, 231–4
Kipnis, Menakhem, 145
Kitson, Peter, 257
Kiwi Gothic, 225, 226, 227, 235
Kiwi humour, 226
Kiwi splatstick, 228, 233, 234
Klein, Kerwin Lee, 264
Knights, Pamela, 110
Kristeva, Julia, *Powers of Horror*, 5, 70, 116, 200
Ku Klux Klan, 265, 266

Lady Gaga, 237–50
Lamb, Sarah, 220
Lawn, Jennifer, 227, 230, 235
Lawrence, Raghava (dir.), *Laxmii*, 221–2
Le Fanu, Sheridan, 4, 95, 96
  Carmilla, 113
Ledoux, Ellen, 230
Leotta, Alfio, 226, 227, 228, 232, 233
lesbian/lesbianism, 140, 142
Levine, Jonathan (dir.), *Warm Bodies*, 171–4, 177
Lewis, Matthew, 31, 40, 54
  The Monk, 35, 39, 41, 42, 53, 142, 239
likay, 181–2

McCarthy, Elizabeth, 29
McCormack, W. J., 95–6, 102–3
McGowan, Philip, 66–7
Macfarlane, Karen, 248
Maturin, Charles, *Melmoth the Wanderer*, 239
Marx, Karl, 172
  Das Kapital, 24
Mason, Stuart, 93, 95, 100
Massey, Vincent, 126, 130, 132
Mehta, Hardik (dir.), *Roohi*, 218, 220–1
melodrama, 1–2, 3, 7, 9, 20, 93, 102, 106, 150, 154, 169, 181–93, 211, 213, 219–22, 256–9, 261, 263
Mercer, Erin, 226, 227, 233
Miller, Cynthia J., 212–13, 231
misogyny, 5, 109, 113, 115, 117, 119, 240, 244, 245, 188, 192
monsters/monstrosity, 1–2, 6, 29, 37, 86, 109, 122, 124, 140, 143–6, 155–6, 160–2, 168, 190–2, 195, 199, 206, 207–8, 229, 247–8, 249, 255, 258, 264
monstrous-feminine, 217–22
multidirectionality, 241

Nally, Claire, 241
Nandy, Ashis, 100–1
nang phi, 181
nang sayongkhwan, 181
Natyashastra, 213
neoliberalism, 6–7, 167–72, 174–7, 255, 265
Neugroschel, Joachim, 138
New Zealand Gothic, 8–9, 226–35
Nodier, Charles, *Le Vampire*, 20

Och, Dana, 232, 233
Ondrak, Joe, 264
Other, othering, 6, 136–46, 168, 257–8
Ozick, Cynthia, 143–4

paranoia, 9, 219, 225, 255, 258–9
parody, 1–3, 5–7, 49–63, 89, 102, 105, 109, 111, 129–30, 133, 137–8, 154, 160, 174, 181–93, 198, 200, 203, 206, 208, 212–13
Patrick, F. C., *More Ghosts!*, 50
Peacock, Thomas Love, *Nightmare Abbey*, 50, 51
Pero, Allan, 94, 97, 98
Picart, Caroline Joan, 212–13
Planché, James Robinson, *The Vampire, or the Bride of the Isles*, 20–2
pleasurable fear, 239–40
Poe, Edgar Allan, 4, 65–76, 80, 88, 96
  'The Cask of Amontillado', 64, 65
  'The Fall of the House of Usher', 64, 73–4
  'Hop-Frog', 64, 65–8, 72
  'King Pest', 64, 69–71
  'The Man That Was Used Up', 65
  'The Masque of the Red Death', 64, 66–7
  'Never Bet the Devil Your Head', 65
  'The Oblong Box', 72
  'The Pit and the Pendulum', 64, 73–4
  'Tarr and Fether', 65
  'William Wilson', 68
Polidori, Dr John, *The Vampyre*, 17–22, 24
Polwhele, Richard, *Unsex'd Females*, 57

popular magazines (eighteenth century), 30–1, 39
post-apocalyptic, the, 6, 167–78
pranking, 64, 67–8, 183
Price, Vincent, 65
Pulugurtha, Nishi, 216
Punter, David, 77, 226, 228

queer, 9, 97, 99, 188, 239, 246, 247, 250–1

Radcliffe, Ann, 31, 49, 51, 52, 55, 56, 57, 78
  The Mysteries of Udolpho, 201, 239
  The Italian, 35
Reagan, Ronald, 169, 174
recycling, 241–7, 249–50
Renza, Louis A., 65, 70, 71
Riddell, Chris, 6, 154, 160
Robertson, Pamela, 94, 240, 242, 243, 244
Robinson, Mary, 57
Rogers, Louisa G., 256, 259–60
romance, 3, 14, 18, 19, 25, 50, 51, 52, 53, 56, 57, 58, 78, 138, 143–4, 151, 168, 171–3, 182, 212, 220
Ross, Andrew, 242
Russo, Mary, 116–17
Rymer, James Malcolm, *Varney the Vampire*, 23–5

Sage, Victor, 50, 177, 205
satire, 1, 4, 9, 53, 54, 56, 93, 98, 106, 168–9, 171, 191
Sedgwick, Eve Kosofsky, 239, 245
Senf, Carol, 24
sexuality, 177, 213, 222, 241–5, 248
Shelley, Mary, 83
  Frankenstein, 195, 197, 205–8
Shugart, Helene, 240
Silver, Sean, 257
Simon, David Carroll, 68

Singer, Isaac Bashevis, 139, 145
Sippapak, Yuthlert (dir.), 182–3
  Buppah Rahtree, 182–9, 191, 193
slapstick, 64, 68–9, 73, 80, 170, 182–3, 188, 212–13
Smith, Andrew, 77, 97, 101
Smith, Charlotte, 57
Smith, Jo, 227
Sontag, Susan, 93–6, 99, 105, 240
Southern Ontario Gothic, 5, 123
spectrality, 15, 21, 41, 73, 89, 115, 127–8, 130–1, 184, 199
splatstick, 228, 233–4
Spooner, Catherine, 13, 155–6, 160–2, 195–6, 204, 205, 228, 239, 231, 232
stereotype, 3, 55, 61, 117–19, 185, 189, 123, 242–5
Stoker, Bram, 65
  Dracula, 13, 137, 197–8
Stott, Andrew, 65, 68, 70
Stuart, Roxana, 22
sublime, the, 73–4, 95, 99, 199
supernatural, the, 3, 6, 7, 8, 14, 16–19, 21–2, 24, 25, 29–31, 36, 41–2, 51, 71, 88–9, 98, 102, 113–14, 123, 129, 136–9, 142, 144, 145, 150–3, 155, 158, 181, 183, 184, 189, 206, 211, 221, 225–7, 262
superstition, 5–6, 14, 20, 151, 153–4
suicide, 79, 81, 84–5, 109

taboo, 9, 115, 116, 171, 207–8, 225, 241, 255, 259
Taylor, Leila, 266
Taylor, Jonathan, 65
talok-phi-kathoey, 182
terror, 2, 4, 15, 27, 29–30, 31, 33, 35–6, 46–7, 50, 53, 57, 74, 80, 93, 95, 99, 100, 102–3, 106, 115, 118, 132, 137, 183, 186, 212–13, 218–219, 225, 229, 230, 232–3, 239, 244, 250, 256, 259, 261, 262–3, 265–6
Thai horror, 181–93
Thomson, Philip, 115
TikTok, 255–68
Townshend, Dale, 14, 150–2

uncanny, the, 6, 7, 8, 39, 65, 68, 74, 93, 96, 98–9, 104, 126, 132, 195–201, 255
unheimlich, the, 201–8, 232

Vampira, 245
vampire, 3, 5, 13–26, 112–13, 136, 144, 159, 189–90, 196, 206, 207, 227, 247
Van den Akker, Robin, 263
Van Riper, A. Bowdoin, 212–13, 231
Vermeulen, Timotheus, 263
violence, 3–4, 8, 78, 79–83, 87–8, 103–4, 154, 162, 175, 186, 191, 197, 203, 218–20

Waggoner, Catherine, 240
Walpole, Horace, *The Castle of Otranto*, 14–16, 18, 19–20, 21, 23, 25, 49, 96, 201, 137, 151
Wandering Jew, 40–1, 136, 142
Watts, Isaac, 153–4
Wecker, Helene, 144
Weinstock, Jeffrey, 195, 202, 206
West, Mae, 240–1, 243
Westengard, Laura, 248
Wevers, Lydia, 235
Wharton, Edith, 108–21
  'All Souls', 113
  'Bewitched', 108–13
  Ethan Frome, 108–11, 118
  'Miss Mary Pask', 115, 117–19
Whitehead, Charles, *Autobiography of Jack Ketch*, 81
Wilkinson, Sarah, 39–40, 42
Wilde, Oscar, 90–106, 214

The Canterville Ghost, 102, 104–5
'The Decay of Lying', 98–9
The Happy Prince and other Tales, 100
The House of Pomegranates, 100–1
The Importance of Being Earnest, 104–5
Lord Arthur Savile's Crime, 93, 102–4
The Picture of Dorian Gray, 93–101,103–5
witch, 5, 108–19, 152–3, 161, 258
Wolfreys, Julian, 99–100, 110, 116
Wollstonecraft, Mary, 53, 54, 57–8, 60

Maria, or the Wrongs of Women, 49
A Vindication of the Rights of Women, 49
Wright, Andrea, 232
Wright, Angela, 53

Yiddish, 136–40, 142, 145, 146

Zlosnik, Sue, 50, 102, 104, 106, 117, 118, 122, 130, 140, 150–1, 177, 186, 192, 196, 212, 225, 230–4, 239–40, 250–1, 258–63
zombie, 6–7, 167–78, 196, 227, 231, 233, 234
Zupančič, Alenka, 157–8